The Dark Side of
Media and Technology

This book is part of the Peter Lang Media and Communication list.
Every volume is peer reviewed and meets
the highest quality standards for content and production.

PETER LANG
New York • Bern • Berlin
Brussels • Vienna • Oxford • Warsaw

The Dark Side of Media and Technology

A 21st Century Guide to Media and Technological Literacy

Edward Downs, Editor

PETER LANG
New York • Bern • Berlin
Brussels • Vienna • Oxford • Warsaw

Library of Congress Cataloging-in-Publication Data
Names: Downs, Edward, editor.
Title: The dark side of media and technology: a 21st century guide to
media and technological literacy / edited by Edward Downs.
Description: New York: Feter Lang, 2019.
Includes bibliographical references and index.
Identifiers: LCCN 2018043706 | ISBN 978-1-4331-4901-6 (hardback: alk. paper)
ISBN 978-1-4331-4900-9 (paperback: alk. paper)
ISBN 978-1-4331-4902-3 (ebook pdf)
ISBN 978-1-4331-4903-0 (epub) | ISBN 978-1-4331-4904-7 (mobi)
Subjects: LCSH: Mass media—Social aspects. |
Information technology—Social aspects.
Classification: LCC P95.54.D37 | DDC 302.23—dc23
LC record available at https://lccn.loc.gov/2018043706
DOI 10.3726/b14959

Bibliographic information published by **Die Deutsche Nationalbibliothek.**
Die Deutsche Nationalbibliothek lists this publication in the "Deutsche
Nationalbibliografie"; detailed bibliographic data are available
on the Internet at http://dnb.d-nb.de/.

The paper in this book meets the guidelines for permanence and durability
of the Committee on Production Guidelines for Book Longevity
of the Council of Library Resources.

Printed in the United States of America

For Lindsey and Ivy
And for Dre, who believed.

Table of Contents

Figures

Preface

I used to think that writing a book was an absurd idea. Why would one spend so much time, researching, reading, and synthesizing information for an imagined audience—one who may not really care about the premise of the book anyway? Then I began teaching. As a professor, I prided myself on having read many books. I assigned books that I enjoyed to my students and passed on the knowledge of my favorite authors and scholars through their pages. Writing books in general wasn't such an absurdity, I reasoned. It would just be absurd for *me* to write one.

One day after teaching a *Dark Side of Media and Technology* class, the class from which this book draws its inspiration, a group of students working on their final project asked if there was a Dark Side textbook that they could use as a reference. I mentioned that there were a number of relevant journal articles and book chapters that would be sufficient for their needs, but, unfortunately, no dedicated Dark Side book, *per se*. Uninterested in my response, and still wishing that there were one, comprehensive resource for this topic, they suggested that I should write one.

I quickly dismissed the idea. I brought it up again later to an academic friend for a laugh. "Why don't you?" he asked. It was the first time I had really actually considered it. Sure, there were parts of other books and published manuscripts that were perfect for the class. But, there was not one single resource that brought all of the Dark Side topics that I thought were important to discuss together.

Maybe it was time to write a book. Still, I had never written one, and there was this nagging issue of consistency. How could I write a book if I still thought it an absurd idea? I wrestled with this inconsistency for some time, and then one day, completely by accident, I stumbled across the work of the French philosopher, Albert Camus. In *The Myth of Sisyphus*, Camus waxes philosophical on an idea that he calls "living the absurd life"—or briefly, the conflicting human condition where we simultaneously search for meaning, yet, rarely find it.

Without getting too deep into Camus' philosophy, two things about living the absurd life stood out to me. First, Camus recognized that the human condition was full of contradictions. As I applied this thought to society's use of media and technology, I could see that even in the 21st century, he had a point. There are many examples in our daily exercises with media and technology that would seem absurd to Camus. For example, how is it possible that something called "social media" is responsible for so many incivilities and antisocial interactions each day? Or, how is it possible that a society that is always so busy, still manages to squeeze in more screen time than sleep time each day? And of course, one of my personal favorites, why is it that people drive their cars to the gym on nice days in order to use the treadmill?

My second observation had to do with Camus' idea that in order to live the absurd life, that one could not have hope. Sisyphus, did not have hope. At the end of each laborious struggle to bring the rock to the top of the mountain, he knew he was doomed to repeat the process. For eternity. As a teacher and professor, I do have hope. I have hope that every student that enters a classroom will take away something that can make a difference. For me, writing a book on media and technology, even a Dark Side book, couldn't just be about the negative. If I were going to write a book, it had to include some symbol of hope. Not just my hope that someone would read it, or that someone might even like it, but that some person or group of people would read it and see that with some minor modifications in their daily lives, they could make a positive change. Writing a book wasn't absurd, it was an intellectual act of rebellion.

This was an *Ah-ha*! moment for me. As long as I had hope, then writing a book (more to the point, editing a volume), by definition, *couldn't* be absurd. At least, not according to Camus. Absolved of my dissonance and grateful for French philosophy, I began work on a proposal. A fortuitous meeting at a conference with some friends and colleagues, and with an acquisitions editor from Peter Lang Publishing provided me with the support, materials, and of course, paperwork, to get the ball rolling. Game on!

What follows is the culmination of a year-and-a-half's worth of work that stemmed from that proposal. This book is broken down into 25 chapters, each covering one dark side topic. The first chapter details four dark outcomes related to media and technology. Twenty-three subsequent chapters spell out how some media or technological device or idea relates to the dark side of our nature. The final chapter discusses four "points of light" that can be marshalled against these dark outcomes.

All of the chapters follow a similar format, in that they begin by framing a dark side occurrence to provide the necessary context for discussion. They then define and describe the appropriate terminology necessary for understanding the issue, as well as detailing any theories, models, or history relevant to the topic of inquiry. Relevant literature is cited and discussed throughout. In some chapters, the dark outcomes are explicitly labeled, while in others, the dark outcomes are implied. Used as part of a course or group, students or participants can discuss and debate how many of the dark outcomes are relevant to a media or technology and at which levels. The end of each chapter culminates with recommendations for how to deal with, or cope with the designated dark side issue. The chapters are short and concise by academic standards, but were designed this way purposely, to maximize information for an increasingly on-the-go readership. Readers may choose to read this book in a linear fashion from front to back, or they may choose to skip from chapter-to-chapter as their curiosity dictates.

This book is unique in that the chapter authors hail from many disciplines and subdisciplines including: communication, rhetoric, political economy, media effects, health communication, journalism, psychology, criminology, interpersonal communication, telecommunication, media law and policy, new technology, and computer science. Authors were selected because they are considered experts and each has studied and published extensively in their respective fields. The book is also unique in that it does not privilege one particular methodological approach. Chapter authors were allowed the flexibility and autonomy to present their ideas using the appropriate reporting methodologies of their fields, so the book offers a unique blend of quantitative, qualitative, critical, rhetorical, and historical methods to discuss the various dark side topics.

Understand that even though experts wrote all the chapters in this book, that the chapters by themselves should not be considered the definitive treatise for any topic. Likewise, the recommendations for insulating oneself from potential threats and harms are not comprehensive, nor are they foolproof. Different groups and different types of people will consider themselves more or less susceptible to some occurrences than others, and readers will no doubt be able to think of other recommendations and solutions that work best for them.

For those who would consider using this book in their own courses, the short, concise chapters allow for flexibility in planning across a variety of class meeting schedules. The book could be used as a standalone text for an undergraduate class, or as a primary text, supplemented with additional readings for a graduate-level seminar.

Outside of the classroom as part of a reading group, choose chapters based on need and interest. Use the chapters to help focus attention and to begin conversation. Allow group members to contribute their own experiences with the topics. Words in chapter titles can be used as keywords in search engines online to find members of the local community who can speak to the issues covered. Discuss the solutions provided to mitigate negative effects, and brainstorm what would work best in your community, your home, or your life.

Finally, for the individual reader: I encourage you to read this book with an open mind, and to read with hope. Anything less would be absurd.

Acknowledgements

There are so many people to thank when it comes to preparing a book, especially an edited text. I'd first like to thank Lindsey and Ivy, for giving me the necessary space to work on such a task, as well as for reminding me that there are more important things in this life than deadlines. To the contributing authors of this book, I owe a tremendous amount of gratitude. I cannot thank you all enough for your openness to my vision, and for sharing your expertise. I learned something new from every single one of you. I owe a special debt of gratitude to my doctoral advisor, Dr. Mary Beth Oliver, for helping to shape and mold my academic sensibilities. To my family, who have supported me over the years, I sincerely thank you. All of the late night chats around the fires, kitchens, and homes helped me to become the inquisitive person that I am today. To my academic family, thank you for the space (both literally and figuratively), course releases (Dean of the College of Liberal Arts, Susan N. Maher), and support to complete this project. To all of my friends, your encouragement, support, interest, and check-ins over the past year-and-a-half have helped to provide the necessary motivation to see this through to the end. Also, I would be remiss if I didn't include a shout-out to Kathryn Harrison, Jennifer Beszley and the editorial assistants at Peter Lang Publishing. Thank you, for your professionalism and patience. I also owe a debt of gratitude to Aaron R. Boyson for conceptualizing the front cover art, and Darren Houser for the professional, artistic rendering of that idea. Last, but certainly not least, I'd like to thank all of the students who were a part of the *Dark Side of Media & Technology* experience at UMD. I have always appreciated the conversations, insights, and perspectives that you shared. I trust that this is the book that you were looking for.

CHAPTER ONE

Dark Matters

EDWARD DOWNS & AARON R. BOYSON

I find your lack of faith disturbing.

—DARTH VADER

Forty-six authors have produced 25 chapters, 297 pages, and approximately 118,000 words, all assembled into one book which seeks to shed some light on the darker matters of our relationship with media and technology. Nevertheless, let us get something clear upfront: "media and technology can do great things." This may seem like an odd way to begin a book that plumbs the depths of our relationships with technological devices and media systems of all sorts, but it is important for the reader to recognize and understand that this book isn't simply about media bashing. Many of the contributing authors owe their livelihoods to media and technology in some manner of speaking, and all contributors have immersed themselves in some facet of media and technology professionally, academically, and socially. We get it. But at the end of the day, this *is* a Dark Side book, and exploring all the positive contributions of media and technology wouldn't make for a very interesting Dark Side chat, now would it?

Media and technology can do great things, but such an assertion, while commonsense and true, contains within it a fair amount of mischief. The word "great," for instance, is thorny. The internal combustion engine was a great invention that continues to do great things for people. It is also contributing to our reliance on fossil fuels, to traffic gridlock, and a general decrease in air quality. As another example, the production of refined sugar has been great for culinary purposes yet contributes significantly to obesity and diabetes epidemics.

"Great" comes at a cost. Indeed, Newton's third law of motion states that for every action there is an equal and opposite reaction (Kuehn, 2015). If we can extend this logic of physics and motion to media and technology, this law would imply that, at the very least, the valence of the outcomes of our interactions with technology exists somewhere on a continuum, both opposite and equal in magnitude. Do you, the reader, think of technological effects this way? Do you assume that the power of media and technology influence is (at least potentially) as harmful as it is helpful? Consider how you have eagerly folded some newly-adopted media technology into your life recently—does it suggest a lack of faith in the potential for harm?

It is more accurate to say that media and technology can do both great and horrible things for people. Such thinking usually gives rise to the "on balance" question: are media and technology better for us on balance than without? Before his passing, Stephen Hawking prodded this question during a Web Summit on technology in Lisbon, Portugal (Kharpal, 2017). In it he claimed that artificial intelligence "could be the worst event in the history of our civilization." He is not alone in his conjecture. Tesla and SpaceX founder and CEO, Elon Musk, shared this negative sentiment in a 2018 interview in Austin, Texas at the South by Southwest technology conference. He opined that the development of artificial intelligence is more dangerous than that of nuclear warheads (SXSW, 2018). How prepared are we to heed their advice, either person-by-person or culturally? Can we even take such an alarm seriously? In order to do so we must first be able to process the potential for harm more clearly.

About That

The lead author of this chapter and editor of this collection teaches a class called The Dark Side of Media & Technology, the inspiration for this book. In that class a series of questions is posed to the students on the first day. The first is this, "How many of you previously have taken a media literacy course?" Out of approximately 40 students each term, generally three or four people raise their hands, rather anxiously. The next question is, "How many of you have taken a gun safety course?" Usually, a more confident 40–60% of the hands in the classroom will rise. With these two questions in mind, we then try to figure out how much time is spent, *per day*, doing either activity. After some discussion and debate, we arrive at the conclusion that the average college student spends about six hours per day with media. Among those who use guns for sport and recreation, the average amounts to about five hours per year, or, with some quick math, less than one minute per day. The final question almost asks itself, "Why do you suppose that given the disparity in times, so many more people take gun safety courses than media and technological literacy courses?" The most common and immediate student response is, "Because guns can hurt and kill people."

Let that response sink in for a moment…

Did an estimated six million Jews not die in the Holocaust in part because of propaganda spread through technological mediums (United States Holocaust Memorial Museum, n.d.)? Do 10% (or more) of school-aged adolescents not suffer the negative effects of cyberbullying (Patchin & Hinduja, 2010)? Did almost 3,500 people not die, and were almost 900,000 not injured in 2015 on U.S. roadways because some piece of technology distracted a driver (National Highway Traffic Safety Administration [NHTSA], 2017)?

To their credit, when pressed on the issue, students quickly recognize that such a response is metaphorically picking the low hanging fruit. Of course media and technology can have a harmful impact on individuals and society, and working through that moment serves as both an awakening of their interest in the topic and a catalyst for discussion. Many acknowledge that they just never really thought about media and technology that way.

Perhaps then, it is important to spend a minute wondering about how people arrive at conclusions regarding media and technology in the first place. Our experience as media researchers and teachers tells us that there are three general orientations to thinking about media and technological effects. See where you fit as you consider them. First, there are anti-media people, often called Luddites, who are concerned about harm from technological change. They take a very austere position to adopting new technologies or simply may not adopt new technologies at all. This book *has not* been assembled to appeal to this group specifically, but these folks are, no doubt, relieved it exists. On the other side of the spectrum, are the technological enthusiasts who don't like to believe that the dark side of media and technology exists, and are aggrieved whenever people inquire about its harmful effects. This group may feel a more worthwhile book to read would be called *The Bright Side of Media & Technology*. These two groups represent the extremes (Downs, 2017). A third, much larger and very diverse group, exists somewhere in the middle. This group may know a little about the pros and cons of some types of media and technology use, or may know nothing at all. Some may be completely indifferent and some may be confused—unsure of where to stand on the issues of media and technology. Still others in this group may be curious about media and technology but are unsure where to begin the literacy process. It is with this diverse group in mind that the contents of this book have been assembled.

Becoming media and technologically literate is difficult in the 21st century for a number of reasons. First, as a culture it appears that we are inclined to adopt technologies before considering the effects. Second, the Information Age has provided us with so many new technologies all at once, that it has been near impossible to research and document all of their effects. Third, new media and technology generally require the learning of new terms and processes in order to navigate and discuss their digital spaces. Because of these difficulties, the hard truth may simply be that we are neither prepared nor well-positioned to process the perils of media and technology. We cannot readily change our previous adoption patterns, nor are we likely to slow the number of technologies available to adopt, but we can change the third part. Each of the chapters in this book will give readers the necessary terms, theories, history, and real-world examples to understand our complex relationships with media and technology.

One media scholar who spent a career using this approach to understanding our relationships with media and technology was Neil Postman. He believed that the human relationship with technological developments is a sort of "Faustian bargain," and that we should always expect that media technologies in particular, are just as likely to give as they are to take away (Postman, 1996). Media do things to us and for us, and they also *undo* things to us and for us. His book *Technopoly* (Postman, 1992) is a compelling argument that we are tilted toward the positive, biased toward what technology and media *do* rather than *undo*, and, that our lack of faith in what is undone is, quite frankly, disturbing. To that end, this book serves the purpose of providing a platform for which to discuss media and technology's dark side.

We would like to imagine that Postman would have enjoyed this book. Each chapter is an effort to carefully explore one side of that Faustian bargain. That said, however, the book is not intended to get anyone stuck on the dark side. Instead, it is offered as a (hopefully) memorable rest-stop on the rapidly evolving journey through mediated life. We suspect that on some level most people today realize media and technology *can* have a harmful impact on individuals and society and are feeling it afresh. Some data help to provide a picture of mediated life these days: A recent Nielsen survey (2017) estimates that 119.9 million out of 136.2 million homes (U.S. Census Bureau, 2017) have television, on which the average person watches more than eight hours per day. Most U.S. households, 77%, (Ryan & Lewis, 2017) have an Internet connection, and an estimated 95% of U.S. adults have a cell phone—approximately 77% of which are smart phones (Pew Research Center, 2018). From these technologies, televisions, computers, smart phones, and other mobile devices, we access and generate some portion of the following:

- *Facebook*: 350 million photos (Robertson, 2013), 4.75 billion shares (Facebook, 2013), and six billion likes daily (Domo, 2015)
- *YouTube*: Five billion hours watched daily (YouTube, 2017)
- *Snapchat*: One million "snaps" per day (Aslam, 2018a)
- *Instagram*: "like" over 4.2 billion posts and share 95 million posts per day (Mathison, 2018)
- *Twitter*: 500,000 million "tweets" per day (Aslam, 2018b)
- *Pinterest*: 14 million articles are "pinned" each day (Aslam, 2018c)
- *LinkedIn*: One billion endorsements and have currently posted three million active jobs (LinkedIn, 2013, 2018)
- *Reddit*: 853,000 subreddits, 14 billion monthly page views, 58 million daily votes (Smith, 2018)
- *Netflix*: 140 million hours of streaming video per day (Matney, 2017)
- *Mobile apps*: 487.6 million apps downloaded per day (Statistica, 2018)
- *Text messages*: Six billion sent per day in the U.S (O'Grady, 2012)
- *E-mails*: 205 billion e-mails sent per day (Radicati Group, 2015)

Consider for a moment that media and technology are just bits of information. "Way back" in 2010, even, the world produced one zettabyte of information (Potter, 2012). Just in case your "units of digital information" knowledge is a bit rusty, that is a one, followed by 21 zeros. In that year alone, we produced a quantity of information that is double the number of seconds the earth has existed. In a media milieu such as this, something as rudimentary as basic fact checking is strained. Postman knew excess would be a problem; he warned of this on numerous occasions in his writings and addresses to the public. He remarked that the problems of access to information had been solved "decisively" in the 20th century, but that in solving this problem, we had created a new one; "information glut" and "information incoherence" (Postman, 1995). In short, many of the problems we face in the 21st century are not related to issues of *access* to information, they are related to issues of *excess* information.

One modern phrase bespeaks the excess problem, *information overload*, which often comes out in the form of off-handed expressions of media or technology addictions. New technologies, together with the volume of information itself, are changing how we can and do use media. For instance, one marketing website (Cohen, 2017) published a typography of five means of contemporary media consumption. The first is *focused* consumption, concentrating all one's attention on one form of content from one device, something many people consider is harder and harder to do (for instance, see Carr, 2010). A second concept is *dual-content exposure*, more generally known as media-multitasking, such as when a group of teenage boys, for example, stack televisions two high to play video games and watch television simultaneously (Foehr, 2006). Ironically, there is a playlist of the music service *Spotify* called "Deep Focus" which purports to help someone keep calm and focus or concentrate, albeit while media multi-tasking. *Snacking* is a third type of consumption, which refers to the use of media during times that would otherwise be "wasted" doing nothing, aided dramatically by the convergence of media on, say, a smartphone so one can browse pictures on Instagram while waiting in line at the Department of Motor Vehicles. *Time-shifting* is a fourth mode of consumption—consuming media when "we're available" as opposed to "when it's on." Finally, *binging*, which may need little explanation, is the consumption of a series of episodes or portions of content in a single session, though it often refers to televisual media consumption from a digital service like *Netflix*. Though these are not scientifically validated or theoretically applied concepts, they seem to describe well some of the significant changes of modern media use.

Effects and Literacy

While understanding media effects is not the same as being media literate (more on this in the final chapter), examining our relationships with media and technology through an effects lens can contribute toward that end. We think an overview of how to think about media and technology effects will be helpful for the reader to orient to the contents of this book. Potter (2012) summarized the six main types of media effects, derived from the existing research: cognitive, affective, attitudinal, physiological, beliefs, and behavioral. These are the typical "outcomes" researchers theorize about and test and evidence of them exists across many decades. For instance, when people talk about being addicted to a technology, they may be speaking of a cognitive or physiological effect, or both. Addiction in general is considered a disease of the brain, meaning the chemistry of neurotransmission has been somehow altered and impaired. This is a *physiological* effect. But psychologists might prefer to focus on how one processes triggers in the environment, and the associations stored in memory that lead to an urge to do something. These mental associations are *cognitive* outcomes. Research investigating how seeing a news article on *Facebook* affects its credibility and therefore how favorable or unfavorable someone feels about its content deals with *attitudes*. The differential impact a news story may have on the perception of its truth whether presented on *Facebook* or the *CBS Nightly News* would be an example of an investigation of how media can affect *beliefs*. A media violence researcher who is interested in knowing if repeated first-person shooting attempts numb someone to real world violence are interested in knowing about *affective* effects. And if programming an app with variable reward mechanisms increases the number of times a person accesses it each day, this is a *behavioral* effect.

These are the "what" of traditional media effects research, simplified. But, as Sparks (2016) cautioned, thinking about them is anything but simple. Another way of thinking about media and technological influence is offered here that focuses neither on use, nor specific outcomes, but rather on how or from where the influence originates. A four-part typology including (1) content-based effects, (2) medium-based effects, (3) displacement-based effects, and (4) ecologically-based effects, illustrates this. For instance, when someone consumes sexually explicit programs on television, which then increases sexual promiscuity, as Collins et al. (2004) found in a longitudinal study, that is an effect stemming from the content of the media itself. These are referred to as "content-based effects." If attention deficit disorder results from exposure to television (see, for example, Christakis, Zimmerman, DiGiuseppe, & McCarty, 2004) because of how the pace of moving images effects the orienting-reflex in human visual attention, and not from the content itself, that can be referred to as a medium-based effect. When weight-gain results from being more sedentary while watching television than one would otherwise be, this can be referred to as a displacement-based effect, the exchange of one behavior for another technologized or mediated behavior. Finally, we can conceptualize ecologically-based effects. Routinely, it is found that homes with more media tend to have children who consume more media. This is especially true when media are allowed in a child's bedroom. Increasingly, our local and broader ecologies predispose use, like when parents use *Baby Einstein* to occupy an infant's attention, or when an elementary school incorporates a "one-to-one" program where each student gets his or her own *iPad* for school. Culture is imputing the normative nature of media and technology, which predisposes further use. In other words, technology begets more technology.

Four Dark Outcomes

Taken together, the previously mentioned frameworks inform how to think about media and technological impacts. We encourage the reader to consider these frameworks as you explore the topics in this book. The topics you are about to read were selected for their historical impact (ex. propaganda and paparazzi) current relevance in the media ecosystem (ex. drones and cyberbullying), or student interest in the topics over the years (ex. social media and internet of things). In so doing, they explore the following four dark outcomes of our relationship to media and technology:

(1) *Commodification*—more specifically to this book, *audience/user commodification,* is defined as the process of transforming *use values* or needs, into *exchange values,* or monetary terms (Mosco, 2009). Commodification of products (t-shirts, soybeans, video games, etc.) is not inherently a bad thing, but the selling of human audiences as abstract, objectified goods is problematic at best. Perhaps the darkest aspect of commodification is that decision makers become so preoccupied with assigning prices to a commodity, that they lose sight of its value.

(2) *Threats to individual rights*—this is defined as any force or pressure which intrudes upon one's individual right to privacy, health, or general well-being. Many of today's technologies are networked and are collecting and storing personal information even when we think they are not in use. Threats to individual rights are a hot topic in today's courts as new mediums and technologies are challenging existing definitions of everything from what constitutes ownership, or property, to what would be considered as admissible evidence in a court of law.

(3) *Exploitation*—is defined as using others or treating groups of people unfairly, in some cases to the point of abuse, to maximize individual power or commercial gain. In instances of exploitation, those in power seek to take advantage of a defined group because of some perceived vulnerability. Those who are targeted for exploitation may not feel as if they have any recourse in the matter and may resign themselves to compliance because they feel that there is no other way.

(4) *Threats to Democracy*—this refers to any action that undermines the right of a citizen or citizenship, to exercise their voice and power in a free system of governance. While a generally held belief is that technologies are supposed to make things easier, they also in some cases make democratic nations vulnerable to undue outside influence. Outdated, unsecured technologies (Bergal, 2018), voting scams to "text your vote" (Payton, 2016), and floods of misinformation compromise the abilities of a people to make important decisions about their governance.

The Roadmap

The chapters in this book can be loosely grouped into five categories related to media and technology. Mass media, media effects, online environments, new technologies, and technologies of the future. The following serves as a roadmap for each of the sections in greater detail.

The mass media category begins with Chapter Two, where Michael William Pfau and David Charles Gore give a brief historical account of the origins of the study of rhetoric as a persuasive technology. They then examine rhetoric's role in the 20th century and take care to distinguish between rhetoric, sophistic, propaganda, and public relations. Following this, in Chapter Three, Nicholas David Bowman and Elizabeth L. Cohen provide a timely historical account of "fake news" that harkens back to the Revolutionary War, and in Chapter Four, Anthony M. Limperos and Will R. Silberman discuss the fourth estate (the press) and the complexities that arise when automated bots and the public set the news agenda without the traditional checks and balances of gatekeepers. We then learn about media systems and the political economy of media from Matthew P. McAllister and Lars Stoltzfus-Brown in Chapter Five, and in Chapter Six, Kalen M. A. Churcher examines the Paparazzi problem, situating four privacy torts against the First Amendment and the public's right to know.

In Chapter Seven, Meghan S. Sanders and Stephanie L. Whitenack, take a media effects approach to demonstrate the processes through which media contribute to stereotypes, and in Chapter Eight, Jennifer Stevens Aubrey and Lindsay Roberts show how different types of media can influence perceptions of body dissatisfaction and the development of eating disorders. Chapter Nine continues in the effects tradition, with Mary Beth Oliver and Arienne Ferchaud, discussing media villains and immorality in the media, while in Chapter Ten, Aaron R. Boyson provides a much needed treatment of copycat murders situated against a plague of mass shootings.

Chapter Eleven begins a section that deals with our online lives. Jesse Fox, Guanjin Zhang, and Jessica Frampton explore how affordances in technological environments like social media lead to negative effects like depression, anxiety, and deception. Catalina L. Toma and Irene Sarmiento continue in this tradition examining deception and vulnerability in the world of online dating. In Chapter Thirteen, Amy Adele Hasinoff addresses issues related to sexting and the sharing of sexual images without consent. In Chapter Fourteen, Loreen N. Olson and Roy Schwartzman discuss luring communication, a theory which explains how online environments facilitate manipulative tactics used by online predators, cults, and hate-groups. Wrapping up this group of topics with Chapter Fifteen, Matthew W. Savage and Douglas M. Deiss review the literature on cyberbullying in terms of prevalence, consequences and coping strategies.

Chapter Sixteen begins a new topic, examining our relationships with new technologies. Jonathan A. Obar and Anne Oeldorf-Hirsch examine the dark consequences of ignoring the terms of service agreements and privacy policies of social media and other technologies. In Chapter Seventeen, S. Shyam Sundar, Andrew

Gambino, and Jinyoung Kim discuss the internet of things and how the gratifications provided threaten user privacy. In Chapters Eighteen and Nineteen, video games become the center of attention, with T. Franklin Waddell and James D. Ivory discussing violence, character portrayals, and toxic behaviors, followed by Rebecca J. Gilbertson and Kayla M. Walton weighing in on Internet Gaming Disorder and video game addiction. In a related Chapter Twenty, Edward Downs and Jacquelyn Harvey discuss mobile devices, distraction, and compulsive technology use.

The final broad category examines current issues with futuristic technologies. In Chapter Twenty-One, Edward Downs and Cheryl Campanella Bracken explore the immersive, dark undercurrent of augmented and virtual reality technologies as related to posttraumatic stress disorder and virtual assault. Chapter Twenty-Two from Peter A. H. Peterson and Charern Lee uses case studies to alert readers about information security, cybercrime, and the repercussions of poor cyber hygiene. Chapter Twenty-Three finds Patric R. Spence, Autumn Edwards, Chad Edwards, David Nemer and Kenneth A. Lachlan, understanding the dark side of our humanity through antisocial interactions with social robots, and in Chapter Twenty-Four, David J. Gunkel discusses agency, ethics, and responsibility in the examination of autonomous machines. In closing, Chapter Twenty-Five, by Edward Downs, balances out the dark side of media and technology and identifies four points of light, in the form of four literacies, for combatting the four dark outcomes.

That's enough to get the journey started. As you move forward, remember to consider which of the four dark outcomes is relevant to each topic and look for patterns across chapters. It is also helpful to think about how your personal experiences with media and technology or the experiences of those around you relate to the chapter topics. Pay particular attention to the terms, theories, history, and examples provided, and be sure to critically examine how the topics may intersect with your own uses of media and technology.

References

Aslam, S. (2018a). *Snapchat by the numbers: Stats, demographics & fun facts*. Retrieved from https://www.omnicoreagency.com/snapchat-statistics/

Aslam, S. (2018b). *Twitter by the numbers: Stats, demographics & fun facts*. Retrieved from https://www.omnicoreagency.com/twitter-statistics/

Aslam, S. (2018c). *Pinterest by the numbers: Stats, demographics & fun facts*. Retrieved from https://www.omnicoreagency.com/pinterest-statistics/

Bergal, J. (2018). *Bipartisan senate bill would help states beef up election cybersecurity*. Retrieved from http://www.pewtrusts.org/en/research-and-analysis/blogs/stateline/2018/01/03/bipartisan-senate-bill-would-help-states-beef-up-election-cybersecurity

Carr, N. (2010). *The shallows: What the Internet is doing to our brain.* New York, NY: Norton.

Christakis, D. A., Zimmerman, F. J., DiGiuseppe, D. L., & McCarty, C. A. (2004). Early television exposure and subsequent attentional problems. *Pediatrics, 113,* 708–713.

Cohen, H. (2017). *5 types of content consumption.* Retrieved from https://heidicohen.com/infographic-how-we-consume-content-now-what-it-means-for-your-marketing/

Collins, R. L., Elliott, M. N., Berry, S. H., Kanouse, D. E., Kunkel, D., Hunter, S. B., & Miu, A. (2004). Watching sex on television predicts adolescent initiation of sexual behavior. *Pediatrics, 114*(3), 280–289.

Domo. (2015). *Data never sleeps 3.0.* Retrieved from https://web-assets.domo.com/blog/wp-content/uploads/2015/08/15_domo_data-never-sleeps-3_final.png

Downs, E. (2017). Educational technology. In M. Allen (Ed.), *SAGE encyclopedia of communication research methods.* Thousand Oaks, CA: SAGE. doi: 10.4135/9781483381411.n152

Facebook. (2013). *Content items shared.* Retrieved from https://www.facebook.com/Facebook-Singapore/posts/did-you-know-that...-4/563468333703369/

Foehr, U. (2006). *Media multitasking among American youth: Prevalence, predictors and pairings.* The Henry J. Kaiser Family Foundation. Retrieved from https://www.kff.org/other/media-multitasking-among-american-youth-prevalence-predictors/

Kharpal, A. (2017, November 6). *Stephen Hawking says A.I. could be "worst even in the history of our civilization."* Retrieved from www.cnbc.com/2017/11/06/stephen-hawking-ai-could-be-worst-event-in-civilization.html

Kuehn, K. (2015). Newton's laws of motion. In *A student's guide through the great physics texts: Undergraduate lecture notes in physics.* New York, NY: Springer. doi:10.1007/978-1-4939-1366-4_21

LinkedIn. (2013). *1 billion endorsements given on LinkedIn.* Retrieved from https://blog.linkedin.com/2013/03/06/1-billion-endorsements-given-on-linkedin-infographic

LinkedIn. (2018). *Workforce report: March 2018.* Retrieved from https://economicgraph.linkedin.com/resources/linkedin-workforce-report-march-2018

Mathison, R. (2018). *22+ useful Instagram statistics for social media marketers.* Retrieved from https://blog.hootsuite.com/instagram-statistics/

Matney, L. (2017). *Netflix users collectively watched 1 billion hours of content per week in 2017.* Retrieved from https://techcrunch.com/2017/12/11/netflix-users-collectively-watched-1-billion-hours-of-content-per-week-in-2017/

Mosco, V. (2009). *The political economy of communication* (2nd ed.). London: SAGE Publications.

National Highway Traffic Safety Administration (NHTSA). (2017). *Traffic safety facts: Research note.* Retrieved from https://crashstats.nhtsa.dot.gov/Api/Public/ViewPublication/812381

Nielsen. (2017). *Nielsen estimates 119.6 million TV homes in the U.S. for the 2017–18 TV season.* Retrieved from http://www.nielsen.com/us/en/insights/news/2017/nielsen-estimates-119-6-million-us-tv-homes-2017-2018-tv-season.html

O'Grady, M. (2012). *SMS usage remains strong in the U.S.: 6 billion SMS messages are sent each day.* Retrieved from https://go.forrester.com/blogs/12-06-19-sms_usage_remains_strong_in_the_us_6_billion_sms_messages_are_sent_each_day/

Patchin, J. W., & Hinduja, S. (2010). Cyberbullying and self-esteem. *Journal of School Health, 80*(12), 614–621.

Payton, T. (2016). *Back to the future: Paper ballots still the best fraud prevention.* Retrieved from http://thehill.com/blogs/pundits-blog/campaign/308545-back-to-the-future-paper-ballots-still-the-best-fraud-prevention

Pew Research Center. (2018). *Mobile fact sheet.* Retrieved from http://www.pewinternet.org/fact-sheet/mobile

Postman, N. (1992). *Technopoly: The surrender of culture to technology.* New York, NY: Knopf.

Postman, N. (1995). Neil Postman on Cyberspace. *PBS' The MacNeil/Lehrer NewsHour.* Retrieved from https://www.youtube.com/watch?v=49rcVQ1vFAY

Postman, N. (1996). *The end of education: Redefining the value of school.* New York, NY: Vintage Books.

Potter, W. J. (2012). *Media effects.* Thousand Oaks, CA: Sage.

Radicati Group. (2015). *Email statistics report, 2015–2019.* Retrieved from https://www.radicati.com/wp/wp-content/uploads/2015/02/Email-Statistics-Report-2015-2019-Executive-Summary.pdf

Robertson, A. (2013). *Facebook users have uploaded a quarter-trillion photos since the site's launch.* Retrieved from https://www.theverge.com/2013/9/17/4741332/facebook-users-have-uploaded-a-quarter-trillion-photos-since-launch

Ryan, C., & Lewis, J. M. (2017). *Computer and internet use in the United States: 2015.* Retrieved from https://www.census.gov/content/dam/Census/library/publications/2017/acs/acs-37.pdf

Smith, C. (2018). *72 amazing Reddit statistics and facts.* Retrieved from https://expandedramblings.com/index.php/reddit-stats/

Sparks, G. (2016). *Media effects: A basic overview.* Boston, MA: Cengage Learning.

Statistica. (2018). *Number of mobile app downloads worldwide in 2017, 2018, and 2021 in billions.* Retrieved from https://www.statista.com/statistics/271644/worldwide-free-and-paid-mobile-app-store-downloads/

SXSW. (2018). *Elon Musk calls lack of A.I. oversight "insane," says it's more dangerous than "nukes."* Retrieved from https://globalnews.ca/video/4076983/elon-musk-calls-lack-of-a-i-oversight-insane-says-its-more-dangerous-than-nukes

United States Holocaust Memorial Museum. (n.d.). Introduction to the holocaust. *Holocaust Encyclopedia.* Retrieved from https://www.ushmm.org/wlc/en/article.php?ModuleId=10005143

U.S. Census Bureau. (2017). *Computer and Internet use in the United States: 2015.* Retrieved from https://www.omnicoreagency.com/youtube-statistics/

YouTube. (2017). *You know what's cool? A billion hours.* Retrieved from https://youtube.googleblog.com/2017/02/you-know-whats-cool-billion-hours.html

CHAPTER TWO

Propaganda's Dark Shadow in History, Rhetoric, and Media

MICHAEL WILLIAM PFAU & DAVID CHARLES GORE

Propaganda stands for a domain within the theory and practice of persuasive communication that is potentially very powerful, yet also dangerous and morally dubious. Propaganda is most commonly associated with a kind of persuasion that is almost always ethically questionable—fundamentally biased, ill intentioned, deceptive, manipulative, verging perhaps on coercive. This chapter seeks to understand propaganda in theory, history, and practice; as a technology of persuasion uniquely enabled by media technologies. During the 20th century some actors sought to harness the power of propaganda for their own purposes even as others were deeply concerned about the power of propaganda to subvert political democracy.

Propaganda marks a domain of powerful and dangerous persuasion that for most of European history was described by the term rhetoric. The term *rhetorike* was coined to describe an earlier technology of persuasion based primarily in the medium of language and the medium of orality. For most of European history, and indeed within our own time, rhetoric has also been a term of questionable distinction marking out a domain of persuasion characterized by equal parts power and danger. Parallels between the terms propaganda and rhetoric inform this chapter's analysis of how contemporary scholars within Communication Studies departments have developed a variety of rhetorical approaches to the theory and reality of propaganda. In what follows we define "propaganda," then situate it in the context of rhetoric's long historical relationship to technology and close with recommendations for developing resistance to propaganda's dark-effects.

Origins and Definitions of Propaganda

The term "propaganda" originally derived from a counter-Reformation movement within Catholicism in the late 1500s to propagate and defend the faith by means of deliberate and systematic persuasion efforts. Indeed, its original meaning refers to the production of offspring or reproduction by way of transmission. The act of extending in space and time, of transmitting to posterity is the root meaning of propagation, and thus the term is not inherently biased. "Propaganda" refers to the transmission of ideas in order to both spread them, the way a broadcaster throws seeds into an empty field, but also to develop a scheme or system in order to promote a cause or point of view.

As the theory and practice of propaganda rose to prominence with enabling mass media technologies, concerns arose about the use of manipulative or coercive techniques. In the mid-20th century, Henderson (1943) reflected this sensibility in his definition:

> *"Propaganda is any anti-rational process consisting of pressure-techniques deliberately used to induce the propagandee to commit himself, before he can think the matter over freely, to such attitudes, opinions, or acts as the propagandist desires of him"* (p. 83, italics in original).

This definition focuses on the "persuasive techniques" and processes associated with propaganda. "Techniques," a word closely related to the root Greek word *techne* mentioned earlier, is also a root word of "technology." Whatever the techniques utilized as the means of persuasion, the truest danger of propaganda was "its tendency to suppress, not stimulate, independence of thought and judgment" (White, 2006, p. 26). Propaganda "is not neutral in its effects—not mere noise or chatter—but trivializing, dehumanizing, and demeaning" because it does not treat its listeners as full-fledged humans, capable of freedom and deliberation (2006, pp. 26–27). Propaganda is often rote, canned, trivial, insincere, or, worst of all cruel and brutalizing; whereas living speech is humane, generous, sincere, and takes listeners' ethical lives and choices seriously.

This approach to defining propaganda focused upon its tendency to suppress an individual's capacity to deliberate about ideas and alternative courses of action. Henderson and Braun emphasize the capacity of propaganda to short-circuit democratic deliberations *between* citizens in the public sphere. While they emphasize that scholars define "propaganda" through manipulation, including such notions as doublespeak, logical fallacies, corporate-funded public relations, political spin, and demagoguery, the organizing framework for their volume defines propaganda as "a specific discursive practice of managed democracy—propaganda—that hinders or closes down discussion, response, inquiry, education, information, and deliberation" (Henderson & Braun, 2016, p. 3). Any set of communicative practices that "secure a political/economic system" and that "renders citizens governable rather than governing" should be regarded under the heading of propaganda (p. 3).

The general consensus is that propaganda adopts manipulative and even coercive means of persuasion, often for nefarious ends and purposes. A fuller understanding of the process by which propaganda came to be applied to a range of negatively valenced persuasive practices requires taking a rhetorical approach to see propaganda in terminological as well as historical terms and to wrestle with the ethical dimension of propagandistic techniques and practices. Rhetoric, like propaganda, has a dark side, but it also has components to its story that are noble and elevating. This next section explores the dark side of persuasion's ends and means by way of a brief history of the term rhetoric.

Rhetoric and Propaganda as Means and Ends of Persuasion

Act one of the study of communication's dark side commences in ancient Greece; as the practice of persuasion was simultaneously justified, theorized, technologized, and commercialized under the term *rhetoric*. Over two millennia later, the practice of persuasion was again justified, theorized, technologized, and commercialized, but this time under the term *propaganda*. One scholar has attempted to distinguish propaganda from persuasion by drawing upon Aristotle's distinction between rhetoric, which could be rational and ethical, and *Sophistic*, an allegedly immoral practice emphasizing irrational means of persuasion (Sproule, 1989b, p. 1). While perhaps an oversimplification of the relationship between rhetoric and sophistic in ancient Greece, this assessment is an entry point into that culture's conversation about persuasion techniques and their potential consequences.

The early history of the term rhetoric is deeply entangled in the first efforts to systematically grapple with the power and effects of language and persuasion. In most academic writings the term "media" is taken to refer primarily to technological means of conveying messages over distance—writing, printing, radio, motion pictures, television, the internet, etc. Given this conventional usage it is easy to overlook the fact that language itself was the first and prior form of "medium" between human beings. As we shall show, rhetoric was the term used to describe a potentially powerful and therefore very dangerous form of persuasion. Understanding why and how these concerns were expressed requires attention to the essential distinction between the means and ends of persuasion. The *means* of persuasion refers to the techniques and practices that bring about audience acceptance or compliance with the persuasive message or purpose. Many of the criticisms of propaganda focus on the means of persuasion. The *ends* of persuasion, on the other hand, refers to the purposes to which persuasion is applied.

While the use of persuasive speech is as old as human language itself, it was not until the 5th century B.C.E. that teachers and thinkers in ancient Greece claimed to systematically study, and teach the principles of the persuasive use of language. For the Sophists, a term used to describe an entire class of teachers and speechwriters (including prominent figures like Gorgias, Isocrates, and Protagoras), speech (or *logos*) was a powerful tool that could empower individuals and citizens. The Sophists claimed to systematically understand the means of persuasion, and to be able to impart this knowledge to their students (Conley, 1990). The ends to which the skills of persuasion would be used, of course, was up to the student. There were certainly many opportunities to practice persuasion in the dynamic city-state of Athens, where rhetorical skills allowed eloquent citizens to prevail in the democratic political institutions and the jury-centered legal institutions. However, precisely because of the power of persuasive speech, it was potentially very troubling. One could not be certain that a highly skilled persuader would pursue their goals in an ethical or public-minded fashion. And since most Sophists taught for pay, the systematic study of persuasion was generally confined to the elite classes of the Athenian citizenry, creating additional suspicion about the undue influence of elites within democratic politics. Armed with systematic knowledge, they created a lucrative profession and commercialized the emerging power of persuasive speech as a valuable commodity.

Plato invented the term Rhetoric, defining it as "an ability to persuade with words... in the law courts... the assembly" or any public forum (Plato, 1952, pp. 10, 14) and wrote about it precisely because he was so disturbed by it (Schiappa, 1992). On one hand, Plato suggested that the practitioners of rhetoric were likely to use it for improper ends. Whether they were simply ignorant as to issues of right and wrong, or deliberately willing to unscrupulously manipulate audiences for their own purposes, practitioners of rhetoric needed a philosophical and ethical education in order to understand how to properly use this power. On the other hand, Plato maintained that the teachers of rhetoric lacked a systematic understanding of their craft, and hence rhetoric is not a true technical art, or *techne* (Plato, 1952, p. 23). In other writings, however, Plato imagines rhetoric as a technical art, theorizing a "true rhetoric" informed by principles of philosophy. Only knowledge of the human soul and the nature of discourse, and the principles of right and wrong, insured that rhetoric would be effective and ethical.

Aristotle is said to have taken up Plato's challenge and, in seeking to develop a systematic understanding of rhetoric, to have "technologized" persuasive discourse under the term rhetoric (Poulakos, 1994). For Aristotle, rhetoric was an art of seeing the available means of persuasion in a given situation, and of shaping the judgment of one's audience. Aristotle theorized a variety of persuasive appeals, under the headings of *ethos* (appeals based on character or credibility), *pathos* (appeals based on emotion) and *logos* (appeals based on reason) (Aristotle, 2007, pp. 38–39). His repurposing of the Greek term *logos* (which originally referred to speech generally) to refer to rational persuasive appeals specifically is one sign that he placed greater emphasis on argumentation and rationality than previous thinkers. Such a powerful and systematic articulation of the means of persuasion was supplemented by a concern for the ends to which persuasion would be put. Aristotelean rhetoric was centrally concerned with deliberative judgment and (often) rational means of persuasion, while sophistic was concerned primarily with immoral and non-rational methods of persuasion.

We now turn to acts two and three of the story of rhetoric, persuasion, and propaganda. Next we consider the re-emergence of the term propaganda in the 20th century as a term to describe the various practices of persuasion associated with mass culture created by new and emerging forms of mass media. The final section focuses on the modalities by which contemporary rhetorical scholars of various schools conceptualized and responded to the reality of propaganda in the 20th and early 21st centuries.

Responses to Propaganda: Rise and Fall of Propaganda Analysis

Over two millennia separate the origin of rhetoric in the predominantly oral culture of ancient Greece from the origin of modern propaganda in the 20th century. Over this time societies and political communities around the world underwent innumerable changes and transformations. Most notably, perhaps from a communication perspective was the development of technologies to transmit messages across vast distance. Great political empires have always survived and thrived, according to Harold Innis's *Empire and Communications*, by way of their application and management of communication technologies. Writing technologies enabled empires in Egypt, Babylonia, Greece, and Rome; print technologies contributed to the Protestant Reformation; and mass media technologies enable empires today.

"The effective government of large areas depends to a very important extent on the efficiency of communication" (1972, pp. 7, 166). Along with communication technologies come rulers who master them to arrange power networks and social structures.

Propaganda came to prominence, and acquired its dubious reputation for describing powerful yet dangerous forms of persuasive communication, in the 20th century, as new media technologies like motion pictures, radio, and television supplemented print media as a means to reach audiences (Henderson & Braun, 2016). Despite this vast gulf in time and technology, the contemporary story of propaganda closely parallels rhetoric's story. For Sproule, propaganda was a particularly powerful theory and practice of persuasion that motivated several different characteristic social and political responses—professional, humanistic, scientific, and polemical (Sproule, 1989b). These responses, and the associated anxiety regarding the means and ends of persuasion, closely resemble ancient Greek responses to the theory and practice of persuasion under the term rhetoric.

Like the Sophists, many 20th century figures responded to the emerging power of persuasion under the term propaganda by commercializing it. The professional life as well as the writing of Edward Bernays represents such a "professional" response (Sproule, 1989b). The nephew of psychoanalyst Sigmund Freud, Bernays began his career as a medical editor, but soon transitioned to the Committee on Public Information, an agency of the U.S. Federal Government tasked with maintaining public support for the First World War. Fresh from that success, Bernays and other practitioners of persuasion shifted their attention to developing the advertising and public relations industries. To do this most effectively, Bernays needed to legitimate propaganda. His book *Propaganda* explained and justified "the structure of the mechanism which controls the public mind, and to tell how it is manipulated by the special pleader who seeks to create public acceptance for a particular idea or commodity" (Bernays, 2005, pp. 44–45). Bernays positioned himself as such a "special pleader," one favoring technical understanding of propaganda as a tool that was only harmful in the event that it knowingly distributed lies or information known to be harmful to the public.

Bernays focuses attention on the need for manipulation of opinion in a chaotic, mass mediated society, and is best known for his approach toward marketing which appealed to the emotions of the masses (*pathos*). Propaganda is, Bernays implies, what audiences want and is necessary to curb an ignorant public or to lead them where they already want to go. The need for such regimentation, Bernays claimed, is said to be a function of the fracturing of society brought on by industrialization. Bernays noted "the multitude of cleavages which exist in our society" and sought to devise forms of mass communication that could serve to overarch the divisions created by the development of special interest groups. In the process of developing these new forms of mass communication, Bernays and the field of Public Relations more broadly, conceived of propaganda as empowering "an invisible government" with the technical persuasive means "by which opinion may be regimented" (Bernays, 2005, p. 40). In his drive to monetize persuasion by serving the elite classes it may be said that Bernays was to modern print and electronic media persuasion, what the Sophists were to persuasion through language and orality.

While commercialized persuasion arose in the private sector under the term propaganda, within the 20th century University the initial response to the rise of propaganda has been called "humanistic" (Sproule, 1989b). Scholars in the social sciences and humanities such as John Dewey viewed propaganda as an obstacle to genuine democratic participation and espoused principles of "propaganda analysis" as a means to protect democratic citizens and practices (Sproule, 1989b, pp. 9–13). Such scholars were concerned with propaganda precisely because it appeared to be such a powerful means of persuasion. Propaganda analysis sought to expose deceptive practices of propaganda as a means to empower citizens and protect democratic politics, and was a central critical paradigm within the social sciences and humanities following World War I (Sproule, 1987, 1989a).

At the same time, speech teachers, the core of what would eventually become the Communication Studies discipline, were developing programs of pedagogy and research organized around creating "citizen orators," that were able simultaneously to resist propaganda messages, and utilize their own eloquence to express alternative positions and perspectives (Keith, 2008). Among these teachers, the term Rhetoric was coming to be rehabilitated as an alternative to Propaganda. Teaching rhetoric as an area of study within speech programs in the 1930s and 1940s was seen as an opportunity to counteract the powerful attraction to propaganda by governments and corporations. Like Plato and Aristotle before them, teachers and scholars within both the Propaganda Analysis paradigm and early Speech programs sought to temper and control the power of persuasion so that it could be more consistent with democratic ends.

Beginning in the 1930s and 1940s propaganda analysis increasingly came under attack by a new critical paradigm that constituted what Sproule has called the "scientific" response to propaganda (Sproule, 1989b, pp. 15–16). Advocates of social scientific research methods following World War II sought to displace the propaganda analysis paradigm on both epistemological and ideological grounds. Epistemologically, social scientists argued that the new paradigm was superior because it utilized state-of-the-art scientific techniques such as content analysis, attitude surveys, and empirical studies to measure the ascertainable effects of messages. Ideologically, social scientists shunned the overtly civic, progressive and leftist politics underlying most Propaganda Analysis, in favor of scientific neutrality and objectivity (Sproule, 1987, 1989a).

Harold Lasswell, an American political scientist, was a leader in establishing this new paradigm in propaganda research. Lasswell focused on the goal of propaganda to "manage collective attitudes by the manipulation of significant symbols" (1927, p. 627). Jacques Ellul, on the other hand, eschewed social scientific methods. Instead of statistics and quantitative methods, Ellul favored observation and logic (Kellen, 1965, p. vii). Ellul's chief insight was to illustrate how the effects of propaganda needed to be understood in structural terms. When viewed in terms of sociological structure, propaganda emerges as an involuntary phenomenon, an "inescapable influence," one produced by bureaucracies and that "pervades all aspects of public life" (Ellul, 1965, pp. xv, 119). In Ellul's view every kind of political regime must turn to propaganda because of the complexities of modern mass society.

Like Plato, these social scientists claimed to have a scientifically valid approach to systematically understanding the means of persuasion. Unlike Plato they sought to remain deliberately agnostic regarding the ends of persuasion, preferring instead a stance of scientific objectivity. Nevertheless, such scientifically informed approaches to systematically understanding the effects of persuasive messages, eventually came to be used by many. The powerful persuasive means associated with propaganda, now made even more effective by systematic scientific study, were deployed by persuasion professionals in advertising and public relations. The United States government came to rely upon such experts in persuasion and communication to conduct propaganda campaigns during World War II, and later against the Soviet Union and its allies (Simpson, 1994).

While there are striking parallels to how ancient and modern entrepreneurs and intellectuals responded to the potential powers and dangers of persuasive communication, attention to the dark side of persuasion by distinguishing means from ends reveals a notable historical transformation in propaganda's connotation. When the term was first deployed by the Catholic Church, propaganda was understood as a means of disseminating to audiences true, or otherwise valid, perspectives. Even in later secular contexts, some of the most infamous theorists and practitioners of propaganda believed that they were disseminating a form of moral and scientific truth. The Bolsheviks understood themselves to be conveying "scientifically valid" truths about revolution, and the Nazis spread dubious theories of racial superiority under the guise of "scientifically valid" claims. These examples suggest that perhaps it is the very certainty about the "ends" of propaganda that have tarnished its reputation. After all, when a regime or an individual are certain about the rightness of their goals and ends, they are sometimes willing to use any means necessary to short circuit individual thought and public deliberation.

While propaganda traditionally was associated with an epistemological certainty about the "ends" of persuasion, in the context of the 20th century persuasion industry the "ends" of persuasion have become contingent, and depend primarily upon the particular point of view of a client—be it a particular government, corporation, organization, or individual. In the case of modern propaganda what is now certain and scientifically verifiable as true is the effectiveness of the "means" of persuasion. In other words, the ends of persuasion are now governed by self-interest, preferences, or "likes," in which any one person's, government's, or corporation's view of the truth is taken as the persuasive end. At the same time, the means or ability to persuade are cast in a language of scientific certainty.

Rhetoric: An Antidote to Propaganda

Rhetoric and propaganda have been the tools of demagogues, tyrants, and oppressors for all of human history, enabling injustices ranging from wars of aggression, to witch hunts, to wanton capitalism. But the same techniques of propaganda pioneered by Bernays and others have also empowered more ordinary players like corporations and the United States government. These techniques are also deployed by benevolent entities and organizations aiming to curb teen tobacco consumption, reduce opioid overdoses, or combat climate change. Unlike Bernays or the Catholic Church, who defined propaganda largely in terms of techniques or means of persuasion, most of us tend to define propaganda in terms of its negative ends or goals. We seldom or never apply this term to our own persuasive efforts or causes with which we agree.

This paper's analysis defines propaganda primarily in terms of the means of persuasion, suggesting that the dark side of propaganda is its tendency to advocate a single point of view to the exclusion of all others, using the most powerful persuasive techniques available. Certain about the rightness of their goals and ends, and armed with powerful means of persuasion, the propagandist threatens both the freely deliberating consciousness of the individual agent, as well as free citizen deliberations. Even in its more domesticated form within the persuasion industry, in which the ends of persuasion are determined by the client, powerful propagandistic means of persuasion nevertheless threaten to shut down individual and community deliberations.

For most of history, rhetoric has been a term for a kind of persuasion that is an object of suspicion due to its powerful and dangerous persuasive potential. However, unlike propaganda, which has retained its negative connotations despite efforts of persuasion practitioners like Bernays, the term rhetoric has been rehabilitated as a means to empower citizens to resist propaganda and restore the public sphere. Rhetoric can be more than bombarding audiences with messages or the development of techniques to broker contracts or sales. Rhetoric's positive and constructive tradition, in the vein of Plato and Aristotle, is to interrogate persuasion in conversation with philosophy and ethics, emphasize the role of citizens in public life and to empower them to resist bad arguments—in sum, to counteract the one-sidedness of propaganda.

Rhetoric, at its best, aims at civic ends—ends good for the whole community, developed through a process that involves the community. Propaganda's admittedly shorter story follows a trajectory of employing messages for the greatest short-term gain by way of sophisticated methods of targeting and dissemination. "Rhetoric" describes the practice of shaping messages for desired effects, but it differs from "propaganda" because of rhetoric's central concern with *process*. Propaganda does not aim to include many perspectives, treats its audience as a means, and aims at any end whatsoever. Rhetoric, on the other hand, is a search for and discovery of common ground and is not only about making sound arguments, but also about sharing ideas and things in common to build a better world (Booth, 2004). Propaganda is generally not about these ideals, but favors instead techniques for winning arguments and shaping the world to fit the desires of the propagandist. Indeed, the dark side of propaganda has to do with its one-sided way of seeing communication, its reductionist approach to the audience, and its deliberately non-civic function. Rhetoric, on the other hand, ought to respect the power of audiences to understand and act on good reasons. Where good rhetoric examines the means and the ends of discourse in order to push both in the direction of justice, propaganda compromises on the means of persuasion, fails to imagine audiences as fully capable agents, and works toward the ends of profit and power.

This chapter calls attention to an essential ambiguity in describing the dark side of media because media, like wider processes of communication, are most often conceptualized from the point of view of their bright side. One of the important lessons from this brief study of propaganda is recognizing that the techniques of modern propaganda are all pervasive within our culture, economy, and even university. While the professional response to modern propaganda has helped to contribute to its omnipresence in our culture, politics, and society, both scientific and humanistic responses to propaganda provide us with theoretical and practical tools to better resist the one-sidedness of propaganda. These tools include those practices that see communication as a process without pre-determined or fixed ends beyond the process itself. As long as we remain open to being persuaded by good reasons and committed to those processes that promote deliberation and discussion we are building capacities and abilities that will lessen our susceptibility to propaganda. Attending to process means developing rules of discussion that serves the ends of the process itself. For example, advertisements that identify the true sponsor of the advertisement, the party who stands to benefit most from a successful "sell," empower audiences to interpret the information to which they are subjected. Moreover, promoting the importance of process requires audiences to learn how to judge bad arguments as well as how to make good ones. The dark side of media propaganda can only be resisted if audiences maintain a broad-minded outlook on life and sharpen their powers of perception so that they are undeceived by the fact that we live in a world where many wish to deceive them. Reinvigorating democratic communication practices will forever be necessary in the face of the techniques of modern propaganda. Resisting the dark side of media propaganda is only possible if communities organize to protect themselves from powerful propaganda techniques. To do this, communities need to promote individual capacities to freely reason and deliberate with fellow citizens on questions of importance about their lives and their societies. They also must organize to create spaces for effective expression—expression that promotes a wide latitude for additional voices and points of view. In short, spaces that cultivate a broad-minded, rhetorical culture.

References

Aristotle. (2007). *On rhetoric: A theory of civic discourse* (G. A. Kennedy, Trans.). Oxford: Oxford University Press.

Bernays, E. (2005). *Propaganda*. New York, NY: Ig Publishing. (Original work published 1928).

Booth, W. C. (2004). *The rhetoric of rhetoric: The quest for effective communication*. Oxford: Blackwell Publishing.

Conley, T. M. (1990). *Rhetoric in the European tradition*. Chicago: University of Chicago Press.

Ellul, J. (1965). *Propaganda: The formation of men's attitudes* (K. Kellen & J. Lerner, Trans.). New York, NY: Alfred A. Knopf.

Henderson, E. H. (1943). Toward a definition of propaganda. *Journal of Social Psychology, 18*, 71–87.

Henderson, G. L., & Braun, M. J. (2016). Introduction. In G. L. Henderson & M. J. Braun (Eds.), *Propaganda and rhetoric in democracy: History, theory, analysis*. Carbondale, IL: Southern Illinois University Press.

Innis, H. A. (1972). *Empire and communications*. Toronto: University of Toronto Press.

Keith, W. (2008). On the origins of speech as a discipline: James A. Winans and public speaking as practical democracy. *Rhetoric Society Quarterly, 38*, 239–258.

Kellen, K. (1965). Introduction. In J. Ellul (Ed.), *Propaganda: The formation of men's attitudes* (K. Kellen & J. Lerner, Trans.). New York, NY: Alfred A. Knopf.

Lasswell, H. D. (1927). The theory of political propaganda. *American Political Science Review, 21*, 627–631.

Plato. (1952). *Gorgias* (W. C. Hembold, Trans.). New York, NY: Liberal Arts Press.

Plato. (1998). *Phaedrus* (J. H. Nichols, Trans.). Ithaca, NY: Cornell University Press.

Poulakos, J. (1994). *Sophistical rhetoric in classical Greece.* Columbia, SC: University of South Carolina Press.

Schiappa, E. (1992). Rhetorike: What's in a name? Toward a revised history of early Greek rhetorical theory. *Quarterly Journal of Speech, 78*, 1–15.

Simpson, C. (1994). *Science of coercion: Communication research and psychological warfare 1945–1960.* New York, NY: Oxford University Press.

Sproule, M. J. (1987). Propaganda studies in American social science: The rise and fall of a critical paradigm. *Quarterly Journal of Speech, 73*, 60–78.

Sproule, M. J. (1989a). Progressive propaganda critics and the magic bullet myth. *Critical Studies in Mass Communication, 6*, 225–246.

Sproule, M. J. (1989b). Social responses to twentieth-century propaganda. In T. J. Smith (Ed.), *Propaganda: A pluralistic perspective.* New York, NY: Praeger.

White, J. B. (2006). *Living speech: Resisting the empire of force.* Princeton, NJ: Princeton University Press.

CHAPTER THREE

Technologies of Mass Deception?

War of the Worlds, Twitter, and a History of Fake and Misleading News in the United States

NICHOLAS DAVID BOWMAN & ELIZABETH L. COHEN

> Manipulate a little information;
> Bounce some empty rhetoric to the believers;
> And you have a fine recipe for instant violence.
> Humans are such simple creatures.
> —HIROMU ARAKAWA, *FULLMETAL ALCHEMIST*

Perhaps one of the most notable examples of a widespread "fake news" reporting would be the infamous War of the Worlds broadcast of 30 October, 1938. That evening, orator and actor Orson Welles schemed to prank his audiences on his Halloween broadcast with "a radio broadcast in such a manner that a crisis would actually seem to be happening" (Welles, as cited by Schwartz, 2015, para. 6). Welles' idea was to produce a radio adaptation of H. G. Wells' novel *The War of the Worlds* (1898). The novel is a story about an alien invasion from the planet Mars in which Martians invade the British countryside, eventually dominating humanity before succumbing to Earth-borne pathogens (a satire on British imperialism; Schwartz, 2015). Although Welles disclaimed at the start of his broadcast that it was a dramatization, many tuned in late and essentially missed the message. Research at the time suggested that as many as one million listeners were frightened by the broadcast (Cantril, Gaudet, & Herzog, 1940), and newspaper headlines from across the United States ran headlines proclaiming

"Radio listeners in panic, taking war drama as fact" (*The New York Times*), "Radio play terrifies nation" (*The Boston Daily Globe*), and "Radio fake scares nation" (*Chicago Herald and Examiner*). On reflection, these panic reactions were probably overstated (Pooley & Socolow, 2013), yet the panic story often holds in the history of mass media as an example of fake news gone amok: a broadcaster fabricating a story that is readily accepted by listening audiences, without scrutiny and with severe consequences.

In recent memory, there have been similar accounts of fake news on social media inciting real panic. For instance, in 2013 hackers gained access to the Associated Press' Twitter account (@AP) and used it to broadcast the headline, "Breaking: two explosions in the White House and Barack Obama is injured." The fake tweet incited a flash crash that resulted in nearly $136.5 billion in market value of the S&P 500 being lost, plus a loss of trust in the financial algorithms reliant on scouring social media for breaking news (Karppi & Crawford, 2016), despite containing obvious errors (ironically, the tweet contains several AP style errors). Three years later, a fake news report prompted a near-tragedy when Edgar Welch brought a semiautomatic rifle and a handgun into a Washington D.C. pizza restaurant with the intention of rescuing children from a sex trafficking ring that did not actually exist. Welch was responding to fake news claiming that then-Presidential candidate Hillary Clinton was a pedophile and sex trafficker, using the restaurant as a cover (Silverman, 2016a). This "pizzagate" conspiracy theory had begun as a Facebook post but circulated widely when it was reported by popular political sources such as the conservative-leaning Breitbart and Infowars (Robb, 2017; see also Limperos & Silberman, this volume).

These stories are but a few examples of fake news events with notable consequences that give rise to growing public concern about the circulation of misleading or fake news on social media. A 2016 Pew Research Center report found that a majority of Americans (64%) believe that fake news is causing public confusion about current issues (Barthel, Mitchell, & Holcomb, 2016). No doubt, widespread concern about the effects of fake news is healthy and justified. However, it would be a mistake to believe that fake news is a new phenomenon (cf. Love, 2007; Soll, 2016) or that the challenges of fake news are exclusively linked to social media. In the interest of contextualizing the current day concerns about fake news, this chapter presents a brief history of fake news in the United States. We also review how fears about people's ability to manage news and information have evolved with technological developments over time. Our hope is that in scrutinizing the history of fake news and the unique role emerging technologies have played in disrupting the public's relationship with information, that we can address the current challenges with misinformation.

A (Brief) History of Fake News in the United States

In the years leading up to the American Revolutionary War, colonial newspaper printers, who had traditionally published columns that represented different viewpoints on debates, found themselves taking sides and refusing balanced coverage for perspectives that they judged as being untruthful or dangerous. Eschewing the notion that there are two sides to every story, publishers became increasingly polarized, either for or against colonial resistance to the British. This opened the door for more emotionally charged partisan news. For example, "revolutionist" newspapers and pamphlets regularly published anonymously written exposés that documented instances of corruption and abuse committed by British officials and loyalists. These stories were not necessarily false, but they were often exaggerated, highly sensationalized, and carefully crafted to incite public anger and undermine Imperial authority. For example, *Journal of Occurrences* presented newspaper articles that dramatized abuses committed by the British Army in Boston. Though the authors were anonymous, it is widely believed that famous U.S. revolutionary figures such as Samuel Adams and perhaps even his cousin, future U.S. President John Adams, authored the articles. At the very least, we know that John Adams was no stranger to manipulating news to sway public perception. In 1769 Adams wrote in his diary that he had spent the night with others "Cooking up Paragraphs, Articles, Occurrences etc.—working the political Engine" (John Adams Diary, 3 September, 1769).

Paul Revere is also implicated in the creation of this so-called "patriot propaganda." Three weeks after the Boston Massacre in 1770, when the public was trying to understand who was at fault for the deaths of five Colonials (or whether or not British soldiers acted in self-defense or were the aggressors), Revere copied an engraving created by Henry Pelham which depicted a version of the event. The image, which features British soldiers firing at unarmed citizens at close range, was intended to feed colonists' resentment of British occupation. Revere leadingly titled the work "The Bloody Massacre Perpetrated in King Street," and also included notable inaccuracies in his image. For instance, Revere's version shows a British captain giving an order to a group of soldiers in an orderly line to fire into a crowd, which was contradicted by other accounts and revelations in the trials. Yet, these inaccuracies did not disqualify the engraving from being presented as evidence in trials that resulted in convictions of two British soldiers.

Arguably the boldest purveyor of fake news among the U.S. founding fathers is Benjamin Franklin. In 1782, Franklin concocted an entirely counterfeit edition of *The Independent Chronicle,* a Boston newspaper, complete with fabricated advertisements. The issue contained a fake news story containing gory details from a scalping of 700 "defenseless farmers, and women, and children" by Native Americans coordinating with the British. Like other misinformation and dramatized news that circulated during the U.S.'s formative years, it was released in the name of patriotism. Franklin intended for this lie to reinforce both American and European opposition to the British when it was picked up by other newspapers internationally. "The form may perhaps not be genuine but the substance is truth," Franklin wrote when he sent copies of his paper to others.

The presence of fake news and misinformation in the press continued into the 1800s, but not all of it was intended to sway public opinion. Prior to the 1830s, newspapers were predominantly subscribed to by upper class citizens such as politicians and businessmen. The advent of the penny press, an inexpensive paper financed by ad revenues, made news more accessible to lower and middle classes, and it also catered to working class tastes. Instead of focusing on national politics and international affairs, these papers adopted a focus on topics with mass appeal such as human-interest and crime stories. An interest in entertaining their readers sometimes opened the door for sensationalized or blatantly false stories. One paper even published a six-part series about a newly developed telescope used to discover that the moon was teaming with human-looking creatures with wings. One of the first penny press newspapers? *The New York Times.*

During the presidential election in 1864, a fake pamphlet, titled "Miscegenation: The Theory of Blending the Races, Applied to the American White Man and Negro" circulated. The booklet posited that the primary goal of the (in progress) Civil War should have been to encourage interracial marriage in order to create "the finest race on earth." Although this extremist philosophy was written by Democrats, the pamphlet was designed to look like it was penned by an Abolitionist in order to turn working class voters against President Lincoln and other Republicans. The hoax did not work, however. Lincoln won the election by a landslide.

The end of the 19th century saw the rise of "yellow journalism" in New York newspapers, a style of reporting characterized by sensationalism and misinformation. Unknown sources, pseudoscience, misleading and shocking headlines, made-up interviews, and imaginary illustrations typified the yellow press (Mott, 1941). The journalistic trend is attributed to a battle for readership between newspaper owners William Randolph Hearst and Joseph Pulitzer. At least initially, yellow journalism was a product of Hearst and Pulitzer's desire to increase their advertising revenues, but the yellow press also dabbled in deliberate manipulation of public opinion. Leading up to the Spanish-American War, their newspapers published a steady stream of sometimes real, exaggerated, and altogether fake stories about atrocities committed against the Cubans under Spanish rule (the most famous was an engraving of the USS Maine exploding in Havana Harbor, lambasting Spain's responsibility for the "cruel and cowardly destruction" of the ship). These stories served the dual purpose of both selling newspapers and drumming public support for intervention in the Cuban War of Independence, leading to the U.S. involvement in the Spanish-American War.

Sensational supermarket tabloids that have lined the shelves of American grocery store checkout lanes for decades indulging readers' taste for gossip, scandal, and conspiracy theories have their roots in both the penny press and yellow journalism. British publisher Alfred Harmsworth, creator of the *Daily Mail,* is credited with applying the term "tabloid" (a pharmaceutical word combining "tablet" and "alkaloid") to a form of newspaper that needed "to be like a small, concentrated, effective pill, containing all news needs within one handy package" (Örnebring & Jönsson, 2004, p. 287). Compared to conventional newspapers, tabloids were designed to be compact, easy to carry, quick to read, and easily digestible to a mass, working-class public. As a consequence tabloid journalism is often criticized by the media industry and other cultural elites for oversimplifying complex issues, reporting untruths, pandering to baseless and superficial tastes, and lowering the standards of public discourse. Despite these criticisms, Örnebring and Jönsson (2004) convincingly argue that tabloids serve an important function in democracy because they provide an alternative public sphere to mainstream media and politically elite groups by bringing to light Populist issues that would ordinarily be ignored, and because they stimulate political involvement by appealing to people's emotions (see also Pfau & Gore this volume).

From the patriot propaganda to tabloid journalism, all of these examples illustrate that the circulation of fake and sensational news in the United States is hardly a new phenomenon. Indeed, the persistence of exaggerations and untruths, motivated by profit and politics alike, suggests that fake news is in the country's DNA. The circulation of misinformation is neither unique to any one time period, nor any particular medium. Yet throughout history, we see a distrust of the technologies delivering the news.

Fears About Technology's Effect on Information Processing

Since the birth of printing, technology has been blamed for mishandling truth and corrupting our ability to process information. Conrad Gessner, a Swiss scientist who lived in the 16th century, believed that the invention of the printing press would overburden the human mind with information, even urging monarchs to limit the trade of printed materials so the public would not be harmed by a "confusing and harmful abundance of books."

In the mid-19th century, the telegraph made it possible for newspapers to gather and exchange news within a few minutes or hours, instead of weeks or months. One skeptic declared in the *New York Times* that the telegraph is "too fast for the truth":

> So far as the influence of the newspaper upon the mind and morals of the people is concerned, there can be no rational doubt that the telegraph has caused vast injury. Superficial, sudden, unsifted, too fast for the truth, must be all telegraphic intelligence. Does it not render the popular mind too fast for the truth? Ten days bring us the mails from Europe. What need is there for scraps of news in ten minutes? How trivial and paltry is the telegraphic column? It snowed here, it rained there, one man killed, another hanged. Even the Washington letter has deteriorated since the innovation, and I can conscientiously recommend my own epistles prior to 1844, in preference to those later years. (*So far as the influence of the newspaper*, 1858)

In fact, the early days of radio saw similar critiques about the irresponsible handling of information, such as the earlier-mentioned *War of the Worlds* broadcast. In their *Slate* article, Pooley and Socolow (2013) argue that the belief that hysteria occurred was perpetuated by the newspaper industry, which devoted heavy and sensational coverage to the event. Following the Depression, newspapers were struggling financially and competing with the new medium of radio for ad revenue. The competition between newspaper and radio was so fierce that at one point in 1932, the American Newspaper Publishers Association even denied radio broadcasters access to news wire services (Korwar, 1998). The *War of the Worlds* broadcast helped them construct a narrative that radio was neither a responsible, nor trustworthy news source, very much part of a broader press-radio war that permeated the 1930s (Lott, 1970). The irony of course, is that accounts of the panic around the fake alien invasion (many of the headlines that we gave examples of, earlier in the chapter) appear to have been fake news.

In his groundbreaking book *Amusing Ourselves to Death*, Neil Postman (1985) implicated television in the erosion of truthful reporting, arguing that in quenching America's thirst to be amused, television news was packaged as an entertainment spectacle. The image-driven medium of television he argued, leaves people with superficial emotions and impressions of candidates and issues rather than in-depth contextual information needed to form complex and informed opinions. According to Postman, television redefined what it means to be informed by confusing ignorance with knowledge. By giving people bits of entertaining but "irrelevant, fragmented or superficial information," he wrote that [television news] "creates the illusion of knowing something but which in fact leads one away from knowing" (p. 107).

We hear many similar accusations leveled against the Internet and social network sites. Just as Gessner lamented the effects of the printing press on the human mind, Nicholas Carr famously argued that "Google is making us stupid," claiming that using the Internet with all of its distractions is diminishing the ability of the human mind to concentrate and contemplate information (Carr, 2008). Much like the telegraph was accused of distorting information with its quick "scraps of news," and radio was accused of confusing the public (Lott, 1970), so too have social network sites been accused of ruining journalism by encouraging impulsive reactions from journalists instead of fairness and objectivity (Linker, 2017). Finally, like television, social media has also been accused of feeding an image-centered culture that values impressions over truth and logic (Derakhshan, 2016; McMenamin, 2017).

Technologies as (Socially) Disruptive Forces

As the above examples demonstrate, false and misleading news stories are hardly a new invention, and fears about the effects of media on people's ability to manage information are as old as media itself. This does not mean that there are no fears that we should consider in the Information Age. For example, Internet technologies give virtually anyone the power to create media content, which makes it easier for just about anyone to produce, distribute, and profit from fake news. Those same technologies have also given people access to more information, making it more time consuming and confusing to determine the quality of the information, or determining the source of the information. In this way, new media has disrupted the public's relationship with information.

Of course, this is not the first time in history that a technology has fundamentally changed how people consume information. We've been here before. Arguably the most disruptive technological innovation has been writing and printing by extension. Lists from *National Geographic* and *The Atlantic* are among those that routinely list Johannes Gutenberg's printing press as the most influential invention on humankind. For most of human history, people transmitted ideas and culture through speech and song. The prevalence of writing innovations lead to a gradual abandonment of many oral traditions in exchange for text-driven tradition, characterized by writing and reading. In Plato's *Phaedrus*, the noted philosopher recounts a (hypothetical) conversation involving his mentor Socrates, who was greatly concerned about the effects of the written word. For Socrates (emphasis added):

> ...writing is unfortunately like painting; for the creations of the painter have the attitude of life, and yet if you ask them a question they preserve a solemn silence. And the same may be said of speeches. You would imagine that they had intelligence, but

if you want to know anything and put a question to one of them, the speaker always gives one unvarying answer. *And when they have been once written down they are tumbled about anywhere among those who may or may not understand them, and know not to whom they should reply, to whom not: and, if they are maltreated or abused, they have no parent to protect them*; and they cannot protect or defend themselves. (Plato, translated by Jowett 360 B.C.E.)

Setting aside the fact that most modern philosophy owes its knowledge of Socrates to the writings of Plato, we can see that the core concern about writing is that it would separate content from its source, which he feared would make it easier for information to be misinterpreted or "spun" for ulterior motives. In an age in which knowledge was considered more discursive and rhetorical than objective and permanent, the notion of codifying information by printing it permanently was anathema to truth.

While Socrates' fears might have been overblown, at least a few of his predictions about the printed word did come to pass. Science historian George Dyson remarked that the development of the printing press marked the point in human history at which, true to Socrates' predictions, "knowledge began freely replicating and quickly assumed a life of its own" (as cited by Fallows, 2013, para. 35). Thanks to the written word, we now regularly consume information without having to directly interact with the source. Socrates also cautioned that writing would "create forgetfulness in the learners' souls, because they will not use their memories" (Plato, translated by Jowett 360 B.C.E.). In support of his contention, there is psychological research that demonstrates people are less likely to recall things if they have been recorded (Konnikova, 2012). A more limited human memory capacity may have very well been a cost of advances in writing.

But, just as there have been costs, there have also been innumerable gains from writing and printing, including widespread education and the freer, more accessible exchange of ideas. Similarly, the disruptive force of the Internet can be seen as a mixed bag of gains (such as the ability for virtually anyone to create, share, and instantly access a wealth of knowledge), and costs. The ease with which virtually any source can produce and circulate misinformation is undoubtedly one of those costs.

Moving Forward

Philosopher Philippe Verdoux (2009) explains that while concerns over technological advances will never disappear, understanding how to cope with such disruptions requires us to distinguish between two types of concerns: problems *de novo* (a novel form of an old, familiar problem) and problems *ex nihilo* (a completely new problem). The scourge of fake news is not a new phenomenon. False narratives are one of history's enduring *de novo* problems. What is new, are the media and technology used to disseminate fake news. As argued by Bakir and McStay (2017), the media ecology of the 21st century is fundamentally different than perhaps any time before it. We are in the midst of another information revolution. Just as writing and the printing press opened the door for the mass diffusion of information, the Internet has ushered in a mass of co-created information (Shirky, 2008) in which virtually anyone can be empowered to create and distribute media content. Meanwhile, social network sites and algorithms have paved the way for an era of information personalization. In our current media system, information gatekeepers are not always privileged over personal preference, and the credibility of a source and veracity of information is often in the eye of the beholder. Although these cultural shifts have been occurring over the course of the last couple of decades, they became most apparent during the 2016 U.S. Presidential election, when fake news stories routinely out-performed real news stories in terms of how often they were engaged (read and shared) via social media such as Facebook (Silverman, 2016b). The U.S. is in the midst of a "fake news epidemic" (Jazynka, 2017), the latest in a string of concerns this new information revolution, a symptom of the disruptive force of digital technology in our society.

Various solutions have been proposed to return us to the days when there were seemingly clearer distinctions between truth and fiction, and fact and opinion. Some of these suggestions approach the issue with a media literacy approach. These proposals focus on changing the habits of information consumers, for instance by encouraging them to spend more time reading news on the Internet and engaging in "lateral reading" by which a reader examines multiple sources for the same news story (Wineburg & McGrew, 2017). Others have proposed technological fixes, such as algorithms that can either detect fake news automatically (Genes, 2017) or social media designs and interventions that might hinder the sharing of fake news (Papanastasiou, 2017). Still others have begun addressing the problem through economic means, in campaigns to defund fake news purveyors by discouraging investments from advertisers (Farhi, 2017). All of these strategies have merits, and collectively they may have a very positive influence on the media system that they wish to change.

However, we would like to suggest that if the history outlined in this chapter is any indication, it would be misguided to expect any definitive cure to our fake news epidemic. Fake news has been and will continue to be an influential part of our cultural landscape. New media have and will continue to disrupt the public's relationship with information. We find ourselves in a revolution where information dissemination as we have known it for the past half millennium is being overthrown. As with any revolution, the only thing that is certain is that what happens during this change is unlikely to resemble what came before it. We will learn to adapt.

References

Bakir, V., & MsStay, A. (2017). Fake news and the economy of emotions: Problems, causes, solutions. *Digital Journalism*. Advance online publication. doi:10.1080/21670811.2017.1 345645

Barthel, M., Mitchell, A., & Holcomb, J. (2016). *Many Americans believe fake news is sowing confusion*. Washington, DC: Pew Charitable Trust. Retrieved from http://www.journalism. org/2016/12/15/many-americans-believe-fake-news-is-sowing-confusion/

Cantril, H., Gaudet, H., & Herzog, H. (1940). *The invasion from Mars: A study in the psychology of panic*. Princeton, NJ: Princeton University Press.

Carr, N. (2008, July/August). Is Google making us stupid? *The Atlantic*. Retrieved from https:// www.theatlantic.com/magazine/archive/2008/07/is-google-making-us-stupid/306868/

Derakhshan, H. (2016, November 29). Social media is killing discourse because it's too much like TV. *MIT Technology Review*. Retrieved from https://www.technologyreview. com/s/602981/social-media-is-killing-discourse-because-its-too-much-like-tv/

Fallows, J. (2013, November). The 50 greatest breakthroughs since the wheel. *The Atlantic*. Retrieved from https://www.theatlantic.com/magazine/archive/2013/11/innovations-list/309536/#printing

Farhi, P. (2017, September 22). The mysterious group that's picking apart Breitbart, one tweet at a time. *Washington Post*. Retrieved from https://www.washingtonpost.com/lifestyle/style/ the-mysterious-group-thats-picking-breitbart-apart-one-tweet-at-a-time/2017/09/22/ df1ee0c0-9d5c-11e7-9083-fbfddf6804c2_story.html?utm_term=.6de553f02c28

Genes, Y. (2017, May 23). Detecting fake news with NLP. *Medium*. Retrieved from https:// medium.com/@Genyunus/detecting-fake-news-with-nlp-c893ec31dee8

Jazynka, K. (2017, April 6). Colleges turn "fake news" epidemic into a teachable moment. *Washington Post*. Retrieved from https://www.washingtonpost.com/lifestyle/magazine/colleges-turn-fake-news-epidemic-into-a-teachable-moment/2017/04/04/04114436-fd30-11e6-99b4-9e613afeb09f_story.html?utm_term=.0fabf337cb20

Karppi, T. & Crawford, K. (2015). Social media, financial algorithms and the Hack Crash. *Theory, Culture, and Society, 33*(1), 73-92. doi:10.1177/0263276415583139

John Adams Diary. (1769, September 3, 1770, August 10–22). *Adams family papers: An electronic archive* [Electronic edition]. Massachusetts Historical Society. Retrieved from www. masshist.org/digitaladams/

Konnikova, M. (2012, April 30). On writing, memory, and forgetting: Socrates and Hemingway take on Zeigarnik. *Scientific American*. Retrieved from https://blogs.scientificamerican.com/literally-psyched/on-writing-memory-and-forgetting-socrates-and-hemingway-take-on-zeigarnik/

Korwar, A. R. (1998). Hollywood/radio controversy of 1932. In M. A. Blanchard (Ed.), *History of the mass media in the United States: An encyclopedia* (pp. 256–257). New York, NY: Routledge.

Linker, D. (2017, July 2). Twitter is destroying America. *The Week.* Retrieved from http://the-week.com/articles/702389/twitter-destroying-america

Lott, G. E. (1970). The press-radio war of the 1930s. *Journal of Broadcasting, 14*(3), 275–286. doi:10.1080/08838157009363596

Love, R. (2007). Before Jon Stewart: The truth about fake news. Believe it. *Columbia Journalism Review, 45*(6), 33–37.

McMenamin, E. (2017, May 4). Did Neil Postman predict the rise of Trump and fake news? *Paste Magazine.* Retrieved from https://www.pastemagazine.com/articles/2017/01/did-neil-postman-predict-the-rise-of-trump-and-fak.html

Mott, F. L. (1941). *American journalism: A history, 1690–1960.* New York: Macmillan.

Örnebring, H., & Jönsson, A. M. (2004). Tabloid journalism and the public sphere: A historical perspective on tabloid journalism. *Journalism Studies, 5*(3), 283–295. doi:10.1080/1461670042000246052

Papanastasiou, Y. (2017, August 31). Fake news propagation and detection: A sequential model. *Social Science Research Network (SSRN).* Retrieved from https://papers.ssrn.com/sol3/papers.cfm?abstract_id=3028354

Pooley, J., & Socolow, M. J. (2013). The myth of the War of the Worlds panic. *Slate.* Retrieved from http://www.slate.com/articles/arts/history/2013/10/orson_welles_war_of_the_worlds_panic_myth_the_infamous_radio_broadcast_did.html

Postman, N. (1985). *Amusing ourselves to death: Public discourse in the age of show business.* London: Methuen.

Robb, A. (2017, November 6). Anatomy of a fake news scandal. *Rolling Stone.* Retrieved from http://www.rollingstone.com/politics/news/pizzagate-anatomy-of-a-fake-news-scandal-w511904

Schwartz, A. B. (2015, May 6). The infamous "War of the Worlds" radio broadcast was a magnificent fluke. *Smithsonian Magazine.* Retrieved from https://www.smithsonianmag.com/history/infamous-war-worlds-radio-broadcast-was-magnificent-fluke-180955180/

Shirky, C. (2008). *Here comes everybody: The power of organizing without organizations.* New York, NY: Penguin.

Silverman, C. (2016a, November 16). This analysis shows how viral fake election news stories outperformed real news on Facebook. *BuzzFeed News.* Retrieved from https://www.buzzfeed.com/craigsilverman/viral-fake-election-news-outperformed-real-news-on-facebook?utm_term=.vyBYkBayr#.oomNY37kQ

Silverman, C. (2016b, December 5). How the bizarre conspiracy theory being "pizzagate" was spread. *BuzzFeed News.* Retrieved from https://www.buzzfeed.com/craigsilverman/fever-swamp-election?utm_term=.pm7X6QxrK#.ukPo2zVXESo far as the influence of the newspaper. (1858, August 19). *The New York Times.* Retrieved from https://timesmachine.nytimes.com/timesmachine/1858/08/19/78859815.html?pageNumber=4

Soll, J. (2016, December 18). The long and brutal history of fake news. *Politico.* Retrieved from https://www.politico.com/magazine/story/2016/12/fake-news-history-long-violent-214535

Verdoux, P. (2009). Transhumanism, progress, and the future. *Journal of Evolution & Technology,* *20*(2), 49–64. Retrieved from http://jetpress.org/v20/verdoux.htm

Wells, H. G. (1898). *The war of the worlds.* London: Chapman and Hall.

Wineburg, S., & McGrew, S. (2017). Lateral reading: Reading less and learning more when evaluating digital information. *Social Science Research Network (SSRN)* (Stanford History Education Group Working Paper No. 2017-A1). Retrieved from https://papers.ssrn.com/sol3/papers.cfm?abstract_id=3048994

CHAPTER FOUR

Agenda-Setting in the Age of Emergent Online Media and Social Networks

Exploring the Dangers of a News Agenda Influenced by Subversive and Fake Information

ANTHONY M. LIMPEROS & WILL R. SILBERMAN

The news media in the United States has a long-standing tradition of being the truth-teller of society, or more simply, a "watchdog" of political, governmental, and other public affairs. This is why it is known as the "fourth estate" (see Kovach & Rosenstiel, 2001). These estates essentially describe the gatekeepers of public discourse, in which information is created amongst the thought leaders of the first estate, the national figureheads of the second estate, and disseminated to the public—the third estate—where information is consumed and discussed. The media, or fourth estate, challenges the direction of information dissemination and acts as a verification mechanism for the information that is passed to the public. The rise of social media, blogs, and other forms of discussion have blurred the lines between the third and fourth estate and some have even referred to these new emergent online media as the fifth estate or power (Dutton, 2009). As a result of greater participation in the information process, the public seems to have become distrustful of the fourth estate because it seems as if they have become less vigilant with their verification mechanisms for important information.

Historically speaking, mainstream news organizations (e.g., ABC, CBS, NBC, New York Times, Washington Post, and others) enjoyed a place in society where audiences have trusted the reporting they provide about issues that are deemed important. Therefore, these media sources have always possessed the power to focus public attention on certain issues. Over the past 20 years, the media landscape has shifted dramatically, and emerging research has shown that the traditional function of mainstream news media might indeed be changing, due in part to the proliferation of technology, the emergence of more "news" agencies, and the softening of the traditional gatekeeping function (Boynton & Richardson, 2015). Although some have advocated that access to information means greater opportunity for dialogue, the ability of "anyone" to influence the news cycle because of reduced barriers to entry, can be problematic. Scholars have warned that the erosion of trust in traditional news media because of these blurred lines could be dangerous (Guo & Vargo, 2015; Papacharissi, 2004).

In this chapter, we will first discuss the traditional way that public opinion is shaped by the media and the issues that they choose to cover. We will then discuss how the trust in mainstream news organizations has eroded in a somewhat concurrent way with the rise in alternative and partisan sources of news. Next, we will provide some real-life examples to illustrate what can happen when the flow of information isn't brokered through traditional gatekeepers and news organizations. Finally, we will conclude by explaining how "agendas" have become more polarizing and divisive in society. In doing so, we will also provide some practical advice for how to deal with this problem, underscoring the importance of information literacy, informed news consumption, responsible journalism, and the future of the media agenda.

Traditional Agenda-Setting Research and Public Opinion

When one considers how many newsworthy things are happening at once, we have to ask ourselves exactly how and why we choose to pay attention to certain events and issues instead of others. McCombs and Shaw (1972) theorized and found empirical support for the idea that news media coverage (i.e., the news agenda) can influence the perceived importance of certain issues among the public (the public agenda). Manheim (1987) hypothesized a relationship between the agendas noted by McCombs and Shaw, arguing that a relationship exists between media discourse, public discourse, and policy implementation. To put it simply, the foundational roots of agenda setting research have shown a strong correlation between what the news media covers, what people feel is most important, and how policies are implemented as a result. Prior to this, there was a wide belief that people selectively attended to certain information that coincided with their own belief systems and that media had a relatively weak influence in day-to-day life. What started off as a simple hypothesis, blossomed into the agenda-setting theory, which states that media tells us what issues to think about, how to think about them, and sometimes how to act (McCombs & Reynolds, 2009). With the understanding that the news media can and do transfer salient aspects of issues and ways of thinking to the public, it becomes important to understand how the "news agenda" has traditionally been created and how it might be evolving.

"Gatekeepers" are essentially the key to understanding how the media agenda is typically constructed. Large media organizations have scores of journalists, reporters, producers, editors, and other administrators who cover events, filter information, and ultimately decide what issues will be reported on. While news organizations and their personnel might ultimately be responsible for determining what the public sees online, in broadcast, or in print, public relations officials, political candidates, catastrophic events, and interest groups can also help to highlight and shape issue importance (McCombs & Reynolds, 2009). So, in a traditional sense, the information that makes it into the news cycle has always been filtered by news organizations. However, with the rise of the Internet (in general) and social media (specifically), nearly anyone can have influence on the news cycle and scholars have foreshadowed that this may impact the gatekeeping function of news organizations (Delli Carpini, 2004). Instead of pushing back against this, traditional news organizations now regularly invite their audiences to participate in broadcasts through tweets and other social media platforms (Jacobson, 2013). Also, information that comes from blogs, social media, and other nontraditional sources is often co-opted and cited by traditional news organizations (Meraz, 2011). Whether or not this actually gives ordinary members of the public any influence in the agenda setting process is still up for discussion. However, research seems to suggest that this shift may be consequential.

"Intermedia agenda-setting" occurs when news organizations influence one another. Even though bigger news organizations have traditionally been more influential in this process, recent research suggests that nonmainstream sources (partisan blogs, websites, and social media) are becoming increasingly more influential in shaping the media agenda (Conway, Kenski, & Wang, 2015; Meraz, 2011). This cuts against traditional agenda-setting processes. Instead of the media agenda being constructed by the newsmakers (filtered by traditional gatekeepers), it now seems that anyone can have influence, regardless of positive and negative intent. Since journalists and gatekeepers have legitimized some of these nontraditional sources by using them in day-to-day reporting, it opens to the door to the possibility that the agenda can be constructed in heavily partisan and divisive ways. Stories which are made up, or strategically biased, can be used to drive agendas that are subversive to a healthy society and democracy.

Sources That Set the Agenda

What issues people think are important has often followed the agenda set forth by large elite media sources. While online media were initially celebrated for their ability to increase access to information and allow for greater diversity of thought, recent research suggests that many online only "news" sources contain a lot of information that is heavily partisan or factually inaccurate (Vargo, Guo, & Amazeen, 2018). The construction of false stories and partisan news has been around for quite some time, but dissemination of this information has never been as easy as it is today due to heavier participation from the public on social media. According to a recent study, two-thirds of all adults in the U.S. (67%) reported getting at least some of their news from social media (Shearer & Gottfried, 2017). This finding itself is not problematic until one considers the fact that a lot of this easily sharable information is not vetted by traditional gatekeepers and can be misleading (Fulgoni & Lipsman, 2017). In fact, in the final months of the 2016 Presidential Election, it was reported that people were engaging with and sharing more fake news than mainstream news stories on Facebook (Silverman, 2016; see Bowman & Cohen, this volume). To make matters worse, there is emerging evidence which suggests that a lot of these subversive, agenda driven articles are actually being generated and shared in a relatively automatic fashion using computerized bots (Clifton, 2017). Because the public is now actively helping to construct the media agenda through social networks, the potential for misleading information to be accepted is very real, underscoring the need for traditional media outlets to continue to filter and scrutinize information that is deemed important.

It would be easy to characterize the sharing of enticing and sensationalized news or polarized public opinion as a media literacy problem, or a problem that is tied to the rise of social media. Sharing a news article which criticizes a disliked world leader is as easy as pressing a single button on Facebook. However, emerging evidence suggests that mainstream news sources like the Washington Post, New York Times, Fox News, and others have been influenced by partisan political blogs and other sources as well (Meraz, 2011; Vargo & Guo, 2017). The relationship between mainstream news and partisan news is becoming intensely intertwined and hard to decipher. While partisan news itself is not wholly responsible for setting the entire agenda, there is evidence that it is highly influential, especially when it comes to potentially influencing the agenda put forth by the traditional elite media (Vargo et al., 2018). Thus, considering the role of the media in the present day, as well as the availability of social media, it is worth discussing how the mainstream agenda have become negatively influenced by overly sensationalist and partisan discourse as well. The myriad of influences on the mainstream agenda, shifting of the gatekeeping function of journalists, and the steady rise in alternative "news" sources could lead to an information crisis and mistrust of the very institutions that are the checks and balances of democracy.

The Dangers of an Agenda That Isn't Constructed by the "Mainstream"

The consequences of false or biased information, which is either mainstreamed unintentionally by gatekeepers or passed off as news by emerging news sources that fall outside of the mainstream, can have real-life consequences which range from divided public opinion to physical and psychological harassment. To illustrate this, we present the facts and fallout from some recent high-profile events involving online media, fake and biased information, and the news agenda.

The 2016 U.S. Presidential Election was one of the most divisive and polarizing elections of all time. One of the more outrageous stories that emerged from a single tweet and made the rounds through traditional media was known as *Pizzagate*. When James Comey, the FBI Director, told Congress that Hillary Clinton's investigation was being reopened by the FBI, a Twitter user with the handle of @DavidGoldbergNY (a since deleted white supremacy account) tweeted rumors from the NYPD linking some of the Clinton emails to an international pedophilic sex trafficking ring (Fisher, Cox, & Hermann, 2016). Shortly thereafter, the tweet was posted to anonymous discussion platforms (e.g., 4chan, Reddit), where individuals began to question the potential reality of this seemingly obscure and isolated tweet. As the mainstream news media began to increasingly discuss the reopened Clinton emails probe, Internet denizens started to advance conspiracy theories related to Clinton's emails (Sorkin, 2016). In the minds of these armchair theorists, *pizza* was a codeword for *pedophilia*, and Clinton campaign officials were planning sex parties with children using the codename *meeting for pizza*. A subforum on Reddit (aka: subreddit) was created to discuss the feasibility and plausibility of these emails among pro-Trump users while others were tweeting about these emails using the Twitter hashtag #Pizza-gate, spurring automated Twitter accounts to retweet these messages (as well as other pro-Trump media).

#Pizzagate quickly became a trending hashtag on Twitter, as well as some conservative media. *InfoWars*, a conservative talk show hosted by Alex Jones, started to produce content which suggested that Clinton was involved in this child sex ring (Fisher et al., 2016). Furthermore, *InfoWars'* Youtube account posted a video titled "Haiti PIZZAGATE: Death of Child Trafficking Investigator," in which the video attempted to link the death of Monica Peterson, an activist, to the Clinton Foundation and sex traffickers (Kessler, 2016). Jones later admitted that this video's content was false and unrelated to Clinton, but the damage was done long before his apology.

Even though most mainstream news organizations regularly dismissed this story and theory as false, the conspiracy was shared on other subversive websites. Given the tenseness of the election and the charges against the Democratic candidate Hillary Clinton, there were individuals who felt compelled to go out into the world and conduct their own investigations to prove that Pizzagate was real. Anonymous users began to bombard Washington D.C. pizza parlors with threatening phone calls and negative Yelp reviews, and it culminated when Edgar Maddison Welch stormed into Comet Ping Pong, a D.C. pizza parlor, with an assault rifle, firing multiple shots, and attempting to rescue the sexually-enslaved children believed to be hiding in the parlor's nonexistent basement (Fisher et al., 2016). While no one was harmed in this incident, the negative press generated by this intrusion, as well as the cyber-harassment, has damaged the reputation of pizza parlors in the Washington D.C. area, as well as brought into question the legitimacy of news we consume daily.

It is difficult to assess where to place blame in this incident. We could blame the media at large for letting what we now know is a conspiracy theory (put more bluntly, *fake news*) into the mainstream discourse. However, given that Pizzagate discourse seemed to legitimize among a certain subset of the population, it could simply be that this story was *perceived as real* by individuals who *clearly* were not as frequently exposed to actual news on a consistent basis (Balmas, 2014). Does social media deserve the blame? Should social media owners assume that their role involves one of potential censorship and verification of legitimate news? This is a question that seems to come up time and time again, even though we believe that many social media companies could and should be doing a lot more in this realm (Chafkin, 2017). Regardless of where blame lies, this example illustrates how a story (which has no business being part of mainstream discourse) can become influential and consequential. What is apparent from this example is that even the smallest and most obscure tweet can set off a firestorm. Although *Pizzagate* can be considered a relatively straightforward example of how a media agenda can be consequential, *Gamergate* represents a slightly more nuanced yet equally important example of the dangers of information that isn't brokered by traditional media sources.

Gamergate started in August of 2014 after Zoë Quinn and Eron Gjoni, both employees in the video game industry, ended their relationship. Shortly after the breakup, in a WordPress blog titled, "TheZoePost," Gjoni accused Quinn of cheating on him with various members of the video game industry, one of whom was an editor of Kotaku, Nathan Grayson. Gjoni's defiant manifesto begged questions of ethics in gaming journalism, justifications for his own behaviors post-breakup, as well commentary on what it means to be a *gamer*. The blog was linked to 4chan, an anonymous discussion board, spurring a wealth of users to become enraged at Quinn. Users started banding together in the 4chan thread on TheZoePost, planning to inflict physical harm upon Quinn should she show up at video game developer conferences. These plans started to show up in other places, such as Youtube, Reddit, IRC channels, and on Twitter (tagged with #GamerGate). The attacks didn't stop there. Seeing as those involved in this movement were targeting a single woman in the videogame industry, they felt compelled to reorganize their "mission" to focus on ethics in videogame journalism (Grant, 2014), attacking individuals who had allegedly slept with Quinn and wrote highly of her, as well as other female developers who felt that they were underrepresented in the gaming community. The GamerGate argument was simple—how could journalists be objective of a game if they had literally been in bed with the game's developer? These individuals *assumed* that Quinn had engaged in sexual conduct with individuals that were professionally reviewing her work in the video game industry.

The *Gamergate* controversy expanded when Gamasutra, a videogame developer website published an editorial by Leigh Alexander titled, "Gamers' don't have to be your audience. 'Gamers' are over" (Read, 2014). Alexander's post enraged some groups within the gaming community, as it insinuated that the modern gaming identity had evolved to the point of it including other demographics, including women, as well as how developers need not explicitly cater to the needs of "lonely basement kids" (Alexander, 2014, para. 12). In short, the original "gamer" identity, in the words of Alexander, was no more. In response, Gamergaters organized a harassment campaign called "Operation Disrespectful Nod," in which members were to target *anyone* critical of the gaming culture and female representation/sexism in videogames (Wingfield, 2014). Participants were also told to complain to advertisers of companies publishing critical articles. Intel, one of the main advertisers on Gamasutra, received hundreds of complaints, prompting them to pull all their advertisements from the website. Many other prominent women in the game industry were also targeted. If an entity felt that women needed to have stronger roles in video games, they were inundated with disturbing content.

If you are wondering how this example fits with the argument at the beginning of the paper, it is rather simple: There are *still* individuals who ardently believe that Quinn has no credibility in the game industry because she was sleeping with everyone. This, in spite of the fact, that many of those she was accused of sleeping with have gone on the record to debunk it (Totilo, 2014). These individuals use this example as a hallmark example of ethical violations in videogame journalism and are still on an ardent crusade to legitimize and maintain their "gamer" identity, the same identity created from exclusion by the mainstream and forced into the darker portions of society into rooms lit by television screens, high-end monitors, and videogame consoles. The present GamerGate discourse involves questioning the qualifications of individuals reviewing games that typically would be outside of their comfort zones, and if those reviews still carry meaning (Turton, 2017). Meanwhile, the mainstream media struggles just as much as the movement itself to discuss and define the movement, as the two competing interpretations of this movement are either Gamergate being a hate-fueled group of misogynists, or a group waging a culture war to defend ethics in gaming journalism. To the point where a debunked story is driving hordes of individuals to construct agendas, some of which qualify as treading into the territory of conspiracy, we consider this to be problematic on many levels.

Coping with Eroding Trust in the Media Agenda

Though Pizzagate and Gamergate are somewhat niche examples of how conspiracy laden discourse transcended into the mainstream with real life consequences, these two stories only scratch the surface when it comes to potential problems of questionable information, the media agenda, and public opinion. Even though fact-checking is something that has become easier in recent years, many don't seem to care when stories contain inaccurate information or when politicians get caught lying, but instead shift blame to the media (Kurtzleben, 2016). The fourth estate and the practice of journalism itself is under assault due to emergence of the so-called fifth estate, which unfortunately contains a lot of one-sided information that seeks to politically and ideologically divide the masses.

Even though the analysis of information that we present here paints a relatively dark picture of what might happen if we no longer trust and believe what the mainstream elite media tells us is important, there is still a silver lining.

According to Vargo et al. (2018), conspiracies still have relatively little impact on the media's agenda overall, but, heavily partisan emergent media sources do appear to be influencing the issues that elite media sources cover (and how they cover them). As a society, we have long relied on journalists to filter information and inform us, and there is evidence that trust in large media organizations is eroding. In a recent op-ed about the state of professional journalism, Cohen (2017) implores us to remember that professional journalism follows a code of ethics and that the profession itself is one that is a fact-driven enterprise. As such, journalists serve an important function in a healthy democracy. Historically speaking, rises in authoritarian leadership and the tearing down of longstanding institutions has often started with undermining a free press (Cohen, 2017). Why? Because without an honest and independent media, society would no longer have a fact-checker, which could be very dangerous.

News programs in the U.S. are subsidized just like entertainment programing. Stations rely on advertising revenue and market share tied to the number and type of people in a particular viewing demographic. This means that the news stories that are chosen to air are often ones that producers feel will resonate with their target audience (see McAllister & Stoltzfus-Brown this volume). Does that mean news programming isn't trustworthy? No. But, it does mean that the responsibility of the media literate consumer is to distinguish between *facts* and *opinion* when tuning in to a news broadcast. When watching news programming, it is also important to recognize that news sources contain biased perspectives. With so many channels to choose from, it is very easy to find a news source that is consistent with one's pre-existing attitudes and beliefs, but this comes at a cost. The resulting echo chamber, while comfortable and familiar, has a tendency to insulate us from news stories and perspectives that we may not otherwise be familiar with. Attending to news programming that consistently promotes one perspective is not beneficial for a balanced, diverse, global perspective.

Agenda setting researchers have often taken a value neutral position when it comes to agenda setting research. Is it good or bad that the media has the ability to focus our attention on certain issues that they deem important? It really depends on whether we believe that media institutions have our best interests in mind or if they simply exist to protect monetary interests of few and project relatively narrow ideals. Edelman's *Trust Barometer* (2017), reveals that trust in media is at an all-time low. Even though this report doesn't detail exactly why trust in the media is so low, evidence suggests a connection to the emergence of the fifth estate, which despite much promise, frequently contains questionable and distorted "news" content. It could also be occurring because politicians and other newsmakers regularly call the validity of news media into question. The absence of a healthy functioning "fourth estate" could ultimately lead to less shared ideology, more divisiveness, and potentially the downfall of our functioning democracy as we know it.

References

Alexander, L. (2014, August 28). "Gamers" don't have to be your audience. "Gamers" are over. *Gamasutra*. Retrieved from https://www.gamasutra.com/view/news/224400/Gamers_dont_have_to_be_your_audience_Gamers_are_over.php

Balmas, M. (2014). When fake news becomes real: Combined exposure to multiple news sources and political attitudes of inefficacy, alienation, and cynicism. *Communication Research, 41*(3), 430–454. doi:10.1177/0093650212453600

Boynton, G. R., & Richardson, G. W. (2015). Agenda setting in the twenty-first century. *New Media & Society, 18*, 1916–1934.

Chafkin, M. (2017, October 31). Facebook is still in denial about fake news. *Bloomberg*. Retrieved from https://www.bloomberg.com/news/articles/2017-10-31/facebook-is-still-in-denial-about-fake-news

Clifton, D. (2017, October 12). Twitter bots distorted the 2016 election—Including many from Russia. *Mother Jones*. Retrieved from www.motherjones.com/politics/2017/10/twitter-bots-distorted-the-2016-election-including-many-controlled-by-russia/#

Cohen, E. (2017, November). The dog whistle of "fake news" requires more conversation about journalism. *Minnesota Post*. Retrieved from https://www.minnpost.com/community-voices/2017/11/dog-whistle-fake-news-requires-more-conversation-about-professional-journal-nal

Conway, B. A., Kenski, K., & Wang, D. (2015). The rise of Twitter in the political campaign: Searching for intermedia agenda-setting effects in the presidential primary. *Journal of Computer-Mediated Communication, 20*, 363–380.

Delli Carpini, M. X. (2004). Monica and Bill all the time everywhere. *American Behavioral Scientist, 47*, 1208–1230. doi:10.1177/0002764203262344

Dutton, W. H. (2009). The fifth estate emerging through the network of networks. *Prometheus, 27*, 1–15.

Edelman, R. (2017, January). 2017 Edelman trust barometer reveals global implosion of trust. *Edelman*. Retrieved from https://www.edelman.com/news/2017-edelman-trust-barometer-reveals-global-implosion/

Fisher, M., Cox, J. W., & Hermann, P. (2016, December 6). Pizzagate: From rumor, to hashtag, to gunfire in D.C. *The Washington Post*. Retrieved from https://www.washingtonpost.com/local/pizzagate-from-rumor-to-hashtag-to-gunfire-in-dc/2016/12/06/4c7def50-bbd4-11e6-94ac-3d324840106c_story.html

Fulgoni, G. M., & Lipsman, A. (2017). The downside of digital word of mouth and the pursuit of media quality: How social sharing is disrupting digital advertising models and metrics. *Journal of Advertising Research, 57*, 127–131. doi:10.2501/Jar-2017-020

Grant, C. (2014, October 17). On GamerGate: A letter from the editor. *Polygon*. Retrieved from https://www.polygon.com/2014/10/17/6996601/on-gamergate-a-letter-from-the-editor

Guo, L., & Vargo, C. (2015). The power of message networks: A big-data analysis of the network agenda setting model and issue ownership. *Mass Communication and Society, 18*, 557–576. doi:10.1080/15205436.2015.1045300

Jacobson, S. (2013). Does audience participation on Facebook influence the news agenda? A case study of the Rachel Maddow Show. *Journal of Broadcasting & Electronic Media, 57*, 338–355.

Kessler, G. (2016, December 6). "Pizzagate" rumors falsely link death of sex-worker advocate to nonexistent Clinton probe. *The Washington Post*. Retrieved from https://www.washingtonpost.com/news/fact-checker/wp/2016/12/06/another-false-pizzagate-tale-the-death-of-a-sex-worker-activist-in-haiti/

Kovach, B., & Rosenstiel, T. (2001). *The elements of journalism: What news people should know and the public should expect*. New York, NY: Random House.

Kurtzleben, D. (2016, Sepetember 27). Do fact checks matter? *NPR*. Retrieved from https://www.npr.org/2016/09/27/495233627/do-fact-checks-matter

Manheim, J. B. (1987). A model of agenda dynamics. *Annals of the International Communication Association, 10*(1), 499–516.

McCombs, M., & Reynolds, A. (2009). How the news shapes our civic agenda. In J. Bryant & M. B. Oliver (Eds.), *Media effects: Advances in theory and research* (pp. 1–16). New York, NY: Routledge.

McCombs, M. E., & Shaw, D. L. (1972). The agenda-setting function of mass media. *Public Opinion Quarterly, 36*, 176–187.

Meraz, S. (2011). Using time series analysis to measure intermedia agenda-setting influence in traditional media and political blog networks. *Journalism & Mass Communication Quarterly, 88*, 176–194.

Papacharissi, Z. (2004). Democracy online: Civility, politeness, and the democratic potential of online political discussion groups. *New Media and Society, 6*, 259–283. doi:10.1177/1461444804041444

Read, M. (2014, October 22). How we got rolled by the dishonest fascists of gamergate. *Gawker*. Retrieved from http://gawker.com/how-we-got-rolled-by-the-dishonest-fascists-of-gamergat-1649496579

Shearer, E., & Gottfried, J. (2017, September 7). News use across social media platforms 2017. *Pew Research Center*. Retrieved from www.journalism.org/2017/09/07/news-use-across-social-media-platforms-2017

Silverman, C. (2016, November 16). This analysis shows how viral fake election news stories outperformed real news on Facebook. *Buzzfeed*. Retrieved from https://www.buzzfeed.com/craigsilverman/viral-fake-election-news-outperformed-real-news-on-facebook?utm_term=.gyk3RZBlx#.slyZYmXbv

Sorkin, A. D. (2016, December 5). The age of Donald Trump and Pizzagate. *The New Yorker*. Retrieved from https://www.newyorker.com/news/amy-davidson/the-age-of-donald-trump-and-pizzagate

Totilo, S. (2014, September 20). In recent days I've been asked several times.... *Kotaku*. Retrieved from http://kotaku.com/in-recent-days-ive-been-asked-several-times-about-a-pos-1624707346

Turton, W. (2017, September 7). Gamergate is never going away. *The Outline*. Retrieved from https://theoutline.com/post/2218/gamergate-will-never-die-alt-right-trump

Vargo, C. J., & Guo, L. (2017). Networks, big data, and intermedia agenda-setting: An analysis of traditional, partisan, and emerging online U.S. news. *Journalism & Mass Communication Quarterly, 94*, 1031–1055. doi:10.1177/1077699016679976

Vargo, C. J., Guo, L., & Amazeen, M. A. (2018). The agenda-setting power of fake news. A big data analysis of the online media landscape from 2014 to 2016. *New Media & Society, 20*, 2028–2049. doi:10.1177/1461444817712086

Wingfield, N. (2014, October 2). Intel pulls ads from site after "Gamergate" boycott. *The New York Times*. Retrieved from https://bits.blogs.nytimes.com/2014/10/02/intel-pulls-ads-from-site-after-gamergate-boycott

CHAPTER FIVE

Understanding Corrosive Elements in the Political Economy of Media

MATTHEW P. McALLISTER & LARS STOLTZFUS-BROWN

In modern societies, media systems are vital to our democratic and aesthetic lives. We look to our media for basic information, analysis, creativity, and entertainment that maintain and enhance our democracy, our culture, and our personal and social lives. Most of us know that sometimes media do not do these things very well, and may even behave in ways that run counter to these goals. One important reason for less-than-optimal media trends is the economic incentives and structures under which many media organizations operate. Sometimes the way media make money counteracts what we as a society need from media.

Critical political economic perspectives of media offer analyses of this relationship between media's economic nature in capitalism and their democratic/ aesthetic contributions. As Hardy (2014a) notes, a central assumption of this perspective is that "different ways of organizing and financing communications have implications for the range and nature of media content, and the ways in which these are consumed and used" (p. 190) (see also Hardy, 2014b; Mosco, 2009). Such work can certainly be optimistic, including when focusing on the potential of alternatively funded media, media activism or progressive policies designed to limit media monopolies and enhance diversity (McChesney, 2014; Schejter & Stein, 2009).

A strength of this research tradition, however, is to document and critique how media economics and industrial factors can be corrosive to democracy and creativity. Critical political economy of media is inherently concerned with the dark side of how concentrated power, wealth, and information intersect in ways detrimental to a populace. How can the way media are organized and financed, then, contribute to negative tendencies? Taking a political-economic perspective, this chapter will highlight two broad arenas of US media structures: media organization ownership and the role of advertising as a funding system for media, illustrating how these two industrial/economic factors may undermine democratic goals in a variety of ways.

The Dark Side of Media Ownership

The Sinclair Broadcast Group is one of the largest owners of US broadcast television stations, with over 190 local stations. Although an attempt to purchase Tribune Media, which would have added another 40+ stations, failed in 2018, Sinclair broadcasting outlets are still prominent in nearly 90 US markets and provides affiliates for the major broadcasting networks ABC, CBS, FOX and NBC (Wilen, 2018).

On just its size and scope alone, the case of Sinclair is a troubling instance of the dark side of media ownership, specifically raising issues of the economic power and political influence wielded by the largest owners in a media industry, the lack of content diversity that may result, and the hesitation, or failure, of policy to constrain such powers. But the specifics of Sinclair are especially problematic for our democracy, including this company's history of eroding the autonomy of local stations, its strict enforcement of its centrally produced content, and its overt political slant and reach. Sinclair's partisan news coverage "is a systemic problem—one that stems from the commercial pressures and profit imperatives that privilege particular types of news" (Pickard, 2016, p. 2). In Sinclair's case, conservative ideology and a close relationship with Donald Trump benefited the conglomerate politically and economically. For example, Sinclair's chief political analyst Boris Epshteyn consistently provides positive commentary on President Trump's actions and criticizes liberal and conservative news outlets for "their insufficiently admiring coverage of Trump" (Gillette, 2017, para. 4). Epshteyn's severely partisan commentary reached a large audience when Sinclair mandated its stations run his commentary multiple times a week. Another example of Sinclair's problematic ethics can be found in a solicitation letter asking news directors and executives to donate to the Sinclair Political Action Committee and financially support lobbying efforts on behalf of deregulation (Farhi, 2018). Not only do these examples blur the line between journalistic autonomy and impartiality, it also marks a grey area between persuasion and coercion of one's workforce.

However, from a global point of view, Sinclair is small potatoes. Media corporations created in the analog/legacy media days (Time Warner, Disney, Viacom), in digital environments (Facebook, Google), and those solidly in both worlds (Comcast), extend their media brands and reach well outside of the US, and are major players in multiple media industries. Critical political economic scholars have long written about the allure and dangers of the concentration of media ownership as a way for large players to guarantee industry control and revenue streams, but at the cost of media diversity. Early work about news owners includes Bagdikian (1983), while Meehan (1991) wrote about the coordinating strategies of large Hollywood conglomerates (for an overview of media ownership concerns, see McAllister & Proffitt, 2008).

A major danger of large-scale media ownership is the standardization of content, a concern about industrialized media raised by the Frankfurt School scholars back in the 1940s. There are two basic versions of how standardization occurs. One version is simply economies of scale and the cost efficiencies of using the same content as widely as possible. When a media owner controls many different outlets, the same content can appear in many different media subsidiaries which reduces the cost of developing new content. With owners of news outlets like Sinclair, this would mean moving the same syndicated story through outlets. This cuts down on journalistic labor costs as well as offering a consistent brand image for the different subsidiaries (for a discussion of this and examples, see Hardy, 2010).

Large-scale entertainment media similarly use a kind of "self-promotional standardization," where a branded license owned by a large corporation can be placed and promoted throughout various subsidiary outlets. Meehan (1991, 2005) wrote about this strategy in the 1990s and early 2000s as typically manifesting itself through repetition. When a Batman movie was released during this era, the various subsidiaries owned by Time Warner would promote the movie or offer adaptations: the same plot/version of the movie Batman appears in a book novelization (when Time Warner-owned Warner Books), a tie-in comic book (DC Comics), a sound track (Warner Records), television promotion (such as on The Cartoon Network), and a theme-park ride (Six Flags), all complementing and promoting the Warner Brothers-distributed film. This was old fashioned media "synergy," where the licensing whole was greater than the sum of its subsidiary parts (Meehan, 1991).

We certainly still see plenty of examples of media promoting their owned properties in straightforward ways, such as the broadcast networks plugging their television shows and other owned content on late-night talk and morning-news programs. Digital media and complex media-ownership structures have made such synergy more complex. Take Amazon Prime, the streaming video service in which the viewing context is of course Amazon, the giant on-line shopping site. Its consumption-based nature greatly expands the notion of promotional synergy. *The Tick*, a superhero parody co-produced by Amazon Studies and available on Amazon Prime, aired a 2017 episode in which a supervillain, The Terror, asks his Amazon Alexa-controlled Echo to "play ominous music" when he torments a character. Alexa also made a prominent appearance in a 2018 episode. In addition, a promotional spot for the Echo used The Tick as an example, and one may download "The Tick's Housework Hero" app to have the Tick's soundtrack and sayings accompany household tasks (Ask Alexa: The tick, 2017). Such tie-ins seem trivial, but they point to an industrial incentive for media corporations to use their subsidiaries to promote other subsidiaries. In such cases, it may be unclear when such decisions are audience-centered aesthetic decisions or self-serving promotional decisions (Baker, 2007).

Companies like Disney can leverage their owned properties—both branded licenses and media outlets—to create interconnecting, multi-media narratives. Although such narratives may expand creative possibilities and fan pleasures though "trans-media storytelling" (Jenkins, 2006), they also greatly increase the flow and presence of a limited number of large-scale properties, pushing out other ideas, and pressuring fans to engage in "narratively necessary purchases" (Proffitt, Tchoi, & McAllister, 2007). In the case of Disney, their ownership of Marvel Entertainment, Disney film distribution and cable channels, and the ABC broadcasting network means that they can move not just characters, but expanded storylines through various owned media outlets and artifacts (see Yockey, 2017). Disney-distributed film franchises such as Captain America, The Avengers, Thor, Spider-Man and Guardians of the Galaxy can be interconnected with the ABC-distributed programs *Marvel Agents of S.H.I.E.L.D.* and *Inhumans*; with Marvel-produced programs on Netflix such as Daredevil and The Defenders; and with Marvel comics such as *Agents of S.H.I.E.L.D.* the comic book. Ownership ties will become even stronger as major media conglomerates such as Disney add exclusive streaming services to their subsidiaries.

Social media also incentivize different kinds of ownership patterns. As will be discussed, advertising-based social media look to collect data about users that can then be used to create and place targeted advertising. This may affect ownership decisions, as exemplified by Alphabet, the holding company that owns Google. Alphabet's basic business model is to collect data on audiences to facilitate targeted advertising, and its ownership of digital services are designed to entice users to offer up information in multiple ways to create a complete data profile of desirable consumers. Google's ownership of outlets and services that allow keyword searches (Google), email (Gmail), blogs (Blogger), photos (Picasa), online meetings (Google Hangouts), research (Google Scholar) and videos (YouTube), among others, are fun and useful, but also gather our digital information as we use these services that their internal advertising-placing and pricing services (AdSense, Double-Click) implement into strategically placed and timed ads.

The Dark Side of Advertising-based Funding

In February 2018, ESPN.com published a post with the headline, "How avoiding Wendy's helped Preston Brown become the NFL's leading tackler." The story involved Brown, a linebacker at the time for the Buffalo Bills, switching from eating regularly at Wendy's, the fast-food restaurant, to a healthier diet, losing 10 pounds and playing better as a result. The story was supported by posts on Facebook and Twitter. However, Wendy's is an advertising partner for ESPN, and purportedly complained about the story and the headline. The original Twitter and Facebook posts were deleted, and the story's headline was changed to "How a diet helped turn Preston Brown into NFL's leading tackler" (Redford, 2018).[1] What is especially striking about this example is not that it happened—advertising routinely influences media content in a variety of subtle and blatant ways—but that it became news. Often criticism of advertisers is swept away from media before it comes close to reaching the level of public awareness.

When people reflect about advertising, normally and logically what they tend to think about first are the ads themselves. Ads are, after all, designed to be noticed, and therefore they are a large part of our cultural and symbolic environment. But a major way that advertising functions in our media lives—in fact, maybe *the* major way—is that it also funds our media systems. Other ways of funding media content include direct funding from media users (such as in the book industry)—and from the government (what is known as public or state-funded media). However, much of our media generate revenue through advertising and even those that do not—such as Netflix and HBO—carry programming that was created by advertisement-funded media, or are owned by media corporations that generate revenue through advertising in other subsidiaries.

Advertising is not a neutral way to fund our media. Advertising financing creates incentives and disincentives, and there are social costs when our media make money through that system. These costs affect the kind of media content we have access to, what audiences are targeted for this content (and what audiences aren't), and the amount of information media collect about us. The rest of this chapter will explore three elements of media advertising as a funding system for media: effects on the availability of some content over others, perpetuation of commercialism, and implications for audience privacy and manipulation.

A starting point for understanding how media are affected by advertising funding is the concept of the "audience-commodity," a concept developed by the political economist Dallas Smythe (1977). Advertising complicates the product-market conceptualizations of media economics. Normally when we think of how media generate revenue, we may believe that the content is the product they sell, and the audience is the market to which they sell that product. This, though, is not the case with advertising funding. When media such as newspapers, broadcast television, and social-media websites use advertising as a main funding system, the product they sell is not content, but rather advertising-friendly audiences. The market/customers are the advertisers that purchase ads on those media. Because of this, the logic of the audience-commodity encourages media to keep advertisers happy, to create content that attracts sizable but also particular audiences, to cultivate a consumerist mindset in those audiences, and to generate information about those audiences to create more targeted and effective advertising placement and appeals.

This has implications for the kind of content produced, the audiences who have access to content, and even the kind of media that thrive. For example, content that attracts advertising-friendly demographics and that cultivate advertising-friendly symbolic environments are privileged in this system. A comparison of two US broadcast TV programs illustrates this. The venerable primetime CBS news program *60 Minutes* ranked #11 out of all programs in its size of audience, averaging 12.6 million total viewers, for the 2016–17 season. This compares favorably with the ABC scripted program *Scandal*, which averaged 8.6 million total viewers, ranking #38 (Schneider, 2017). Therefore *60 Minutes* should be the more lucrative program for their respective network in terms of advertising revenue, right? It is not even close. For the 2017–18 season, *60 Minutes* costs advertisers $124K for a 30-second ad, but *Scandal* costs $194K, or $70K more, despite the smaller total audience (Poggi, 2017). This difference in ad price is largely because *Scandal* generated a younger demographic in its audience, an attractive market for advertisers. In the 2016–17 season, *Scandal* ranked #15 out of all programs for the specific 18–49 demographic, while *60 Minutes* ranked #50. The audiences are worth more for one program than the other. This is why, Meehan argues (2005), when television (and other ad-supported media) claim they are "democratic" because we vote for content by watching it, it is not true: some audience-commodities—ones that advertisers seek—are literally more valuable than others.

Some audiences, in other words, have a more important "vote" in the ad-media system.

But another reason, besides audience demographics, for the difference in price is also the mindset cultivated by different content. *60 Minutes* is a journalistic program that often explores corporate malfeasance, a theme that does not flow well with messages of the good life offered by the consumption of brands that are communicated by ads. *Scandal* featured good-looking upper-class professionals—often with themes of the government rather than corporations behaving badly—and *Scandal*'s characters wore nice clothes, drove nice cars, and ate at fancy restaurants. Commercial messages flow very well with such displays of material privilege.

The economic incentives created by advertising also have significant implications for content availability; this is especially salient for our journalistic media. So, although *60 Minutes* has hung on over the years on Sunday evenings, other news-oriented broadcast TV programs have been altered or moved in the advertising-infused media landscape. Some have tried to attract younger viewers by focusing more on sensationalistic "true crime" stories (*Dateline NBC*; CBS's *48 Hours*), or, failing this, have been exiled to crappy nights and timeslots (ABC's *20/20* as well as *Dateline* and *48 Hours*, typically airing on Friday or Saturday nights). Similarly, the dire crisis experienced by the newspaper industry—a staple for journalistic activity in the United States—was largely triggered by advertisers' abandonment of the medium for the more consumption-oriented, and younger-user Internet.

In fact, digital media have sparked some of the worst excesses of commercial financing, including deceptive practices, targeted manipulation, and a lack of privacy. One important characteristic for media literacy is the ability of media users to distinguish advertising and other commercial content—content that is designed explicitly to persuade, and originates from self-service sources such as brand marketers—from non-commercial media content. The latter includes a larger number of genres (news, documentaries, comedy, drama) that are not explicitly persuasive, but rather are available because content providers believe the audience will benefit from or enjoy the content (this is the theory, anyway). When an ad comes on, our critical radar engages, since we know that ads are trying to persuade us to do something we may not want to do (spend money, for example). Media often blur the lines between the commercial and the non-commercial: product placement in movies and sponsored college football bowl games where the brand logo appears throughout the stadium and on-screen graphics are examples. Sinclair-owned television stations, mentioned earlier, have a reputation for blurring the lines between their news and commercial interests, hyping tourist destinations and health centers on their programs without revealing financial ties to those marketers (Macek, 2017).

Digital and social media, however, erode these distinctions even more aggressively. As scholars such as Mara Einstein (2016) note, commercial forms like "native advertising" and "content marketing" are designed to make commercial forms seem to be ordinary media content. BuzzFeed and other sites integrate web-based native ads into the site architecture, sponsoring various features so that it is difficult to determine where site content ends and an ad begins (Berberick & McAllister, 2016). Similarly, branded video game sites such as Mattel's BarbieGirls and Disney's Club Penguin—both also known as "advergames"—are examples of content marketing where the whole point of the site or media artifact is to promote a brand (Grimes, 2015). Digitally distributed commercial videos, many of which are longer than found on television and emphasize humor or touching moments, are designed to trigger widespread liking and sharing by users on social media, taking advantage of the implied endorsement from the ordinary user to enhance the video's credibility. In such cases, the commercial source of messages and their persuasive intent are downplayed or masked, undermining the ability to evaluate the degree to which we can trust such content.

Scholars have updated and expanded Smythe's concept of the commodified media audience in the digital and social-media era (McGuigan & Manzerolle, 2014), including highlighting the idea of a "big data commodity audience" (McAllister & Orme, 2017). As with the earlier example of Google, advertising-supported digital outlets gather information about their main commodity—the online user. Data is collected as these users visit sites (leaving a digital footprint via cookies), interact with sites via sharing, liking, and commenting, and use smart devices with GPS-enabled location information. Such data can then be correlated with other user data sets (such as shopper and media-subscription lists) and create targeted advertising to reach users in various places and at various times to maximize the effectiveness of the persuasive messages of the ads.

These user-data practices have clear privacy implications. Legally, companies must disclose how they may use such data, but language can be vague and confusing, and the dense language of such data disclosure agreements often means users do not read them carefully (Obar & Oeldorf-Hirsch, 2016; see also Obar & Oeldorf-Hirsch, this volume). Even if websites and other services were strictly ethical in their use of data about users, the collection of such large data sets still may leave such information vulnerable to government requests/orders for access or from illegal hacking.

In addition, the data-driven audience-commodity also raises issues about the power difference between media persuaders and the persuadable. As advertisers and media sites gather more information about us, they may refine their media-placement and persuasive analytics in such a way that moves the bar from being persuaders to being manipulators. Anxieties, impulses, and prejudices can be exploited when ads reach us at specific times, in specific places, and with specific appeals. The stakes may be low when we're talking about pizza ads that are sent to us when we're hungry or near a pizza chain. They increase when products are associated with health, gambling, alcohol or other branded commodities that are emotionally loaded or even associated with compulsion or addiction. As other chapters in this volume discuss, when such metrics become involved with our political lives, the targeting of political advertising to manipulate our emotions about key social issues in partisan and extreme ways, for example, the stakes are arguably at their highest.

Conclusions and Solutions

This chapter explored two trends in modern media's political economy that are often highlighted by critics as encouraging media's dark side: ownership and advertising. Ownership can lead to concentrated control by media organizations, a lack of diversity in content, and coordinated promotion of media brands. Advertising as a funding system privileges some audiences and content over others, promotes consumption orientations, and can trigger significant concerns about media literacy, privacy and manipulation.

Fortunately, as noted earlier in this chapter, other elements addressed by critical political economists—assertive media policy, alternatively funded media, organized citizen activism—can help counter or at least critique these trends. McChesney (2014) and Miéville (2004) point to breaking up monopolistic internet corporations, protecting network neutrality, and creating community-led broadband services from municipalities as examples of policy and praxis combining to make media more democratic. Realistically, however, such assertive media policies cannot happen until legal systems contend with less-than-democratic favoring of the already very wealthy and powerful. Other democratic interventions include non-hierarchical media organizations funded by donations or subsidization, open access to media content, and/or teaching media literacy and criticism. These tie in to larger questions of citizen activism as well (Fuchs, 2010). Springer (2016) argues we should embrace values that are anathema to capitalism to counter trends such as concentration of ownership and disingenuous corporate practices.

These values include creating true "commons" that eschew private ownership and fostering an ethics of care for all (p. 287). In an era of superheroes dominating the film industry, camouflaged commercials, advertising pressure, impoverished journalism, and anxieties about manipulative political advertising and polarization, such strategies can offer hope for our media future.

Note

1. Thanks to Ph.D. student Michael Krieger, at Pennsylvania State University for suggesting the ESPN/Wendy's incident as an example of advertising intrusiveness.

References

Ask Alexa: The tick. (2017, September 17). YouTube video. 23 sec. Retrieved October 22, 2017, from https://www.youtube.com/watch?v=whxm4nJ7kiQ

Bagdikian, B. H. (1983). *The media monopoly*. Boston, MA: Beacon Press.

Baker, C. E. (2007). *Media concentration and democracy: Why ownership matters*. New York, NY: Cambridge University Press.

Berberick, S. N., & McAllister, M. P. (2016). Online quizzes as viral, consumption-based identities. *International Journal of Communication, 10*, 3423–3441.

Einstein, M. (2016). *Black ops advertising: Native ads, content marketing, and the covert world of the digital sell*. New York, NY: O/R.

Farhi, P. (2018, February 10). Sinclair Broadcast Group solicits its news directors for its political fundraising efforts. *The Washington Post*. Retrieved March 5, 2018, from https://www.washingtonpost.com/lifestyle/style/sinclair-broadcast-group-solicits-its-news-directors-for-its-political-fundraising-efforts/2018/02/10/0e3d8a08-0c54-11e8-8b0d-891602206fb7_story.html?utm_term=.a84d9829257e

Fuchs, C. (2010). Alternative media as critical media. *European Journal of Social Theory, 13*(2), 173–192.

Gillette, F. (2017, July 20). The Sinclair revolution will be televised. It'll just have low production values. *Bloomsburg Businessweek*. Retrieved August 17, 2017, from https://www.bloomberg.com/news/features/2017-07-20/the-sinclair-revolution-will-be-televised-it-ll-just-have-low-production-values

Grimes, S. M. (2015). Playing by the market rules: Promotional priorities and commercialization in children's virtual worlds. *Journal of Consumer Culture, 15*, 110–134.

Hardy, J. (2010). *Cross-media promotion* (pp. xi–xiii). New York, NY: Peter Lang.

Hardy, J. (2014a). Critical political economy of communications: A mid-term review. *International Journal of Media & Politics, 10*(2), 189–202.

Hardy, J. (2014b). *Critical political economy of the media: An introduction.* New York, NY: Routledge.

Jenkins, H. (2006). *Convergence culture: Where old and new media collide.* New York, NY: New York University Press.

Macek, S. (2017, September 21). A bigger Sinclair is bad for TV and bad for democracy. *Illinois Times.* Retrieved October 22, 2017, from http://illinoistimes.com/article-19150-a-bigger-sinclair-is-bad-for-tv-and-bad-for-democracy.html

McAllister, M. P., & Orme, S. (2017). The impact of digital media on advertising: Five cultural dilemmas. In P. Messaris & L. Humphreys (Eds.), *Digital media: Transformations in human communication* (2nd ed., pp. 71–78). New York, NY: Peter Lang.

McAllister, M. P., & Proffitt, J. M. (2008). Media ownership in a corporate age. In L. Wilkins & C. G. Christians (Eds.), *Handbook of mass media ethics* (pp. 328–339). Mahwah, NJ: Lawrence Erlbaum.

McChesney, R. W. (2014). Be realistic, demand the impossible: Three radically democratic Internet policies. *Critical Studies in Media Communication, 31*(2), 92–99.

McGuigan, L., & Manzerolle, V. (Eds.). (2014). *The audience commodity in a digital age: Revising a critical theory of commercial media.* New York, NY: Peter Lang.

Meehan, E. R. (1991). "Holy commodity fetish, Batman!": The political economy of a commercial intertext. In R. E. Pearson & W. Uricchio (Eds.), *The many lives of the Batman: Critical approaches to a superhero and his media* (pp. 47–65). New York, NY: Routledge.

Meehan, E. R. (2005). *Why TV is not our fault: Television programming, viewers, and who's really in charge.* Lanham, MD: Rowman & Littlefield.

Miéville, C. (2004). *Between equal rights: A Marxist theory of international law.* Boston, MA: Brill.

Mosco, V. (2009). *The political economy of communication* (2nd ed.). Thousand Oaks, CA: Sage.

Obar, J. A. & Oeldorf-Hirsch, A. (2016, August). The biggest lie on the Internet: Ignoring the privacy policies and terms of service policies of social networking services. Presented at TPRC 44: The 44th research conference on communication, information and Internet policy 2016. Retrieved October 15, 2017, from https://ssrn.com/abstract=2757465

Pickard, V. (2016). Media and politics in the age of Trump. *Origins: Current Events in Historical Perspective, 10*(2). Retrieved August 17, 2017, from http://origins.osu.edu/article/media-and-politics-age-trump

Poggi, J. (2017, October 2). TV's most expensive ads: Brands pay for football and tears. *Advertising Age.* Retrieved October 15, 2017, from http://adage.com/article/news/tv-ad-pricing-chart/310429/

Proffitt, J. M., Tchoi, D. Y., & McAllister, M. P. (2007). Plugging back into *The Matrix*: The intertextual flow of corporate media commodities. *Journal of Communication Inquiry, 31*(3), 239–254.

Redford, P. (2018, February 16). Source: ESPN.com altered a headline and buried stories to placate advertisers. *Deadspin.* Retrieved March 4, 2018, from https://deadspin.com/source-espn-com-altered-a-headline-and-buried-stories-1823014722

Schejter, A., & Stein, L. (2009). Guest editor introduction: Media reform and public policy. *Journal of Communication Inquiry, 33*(4), 307–309.

Schneider, M. (2017, May 26). These are the 100 most-watched TV shows of the 2016–17 season: Winners and losers. *IndieWire*. Retrieved October 15, 2017, from http://www.in-diewire.com/2017/05/most-watched-tv-show-2016-2017-season-the-walking-dead-this-is-us-football-1201832878/

Smythe, D. (1977). Communications: Blindspot of Western Marxism. *Canadian Journal of Political and Social Theory, 1*, 1–27.

Springer, S. (2016). Fuck neoliberalism. *ACME: An International Journal for Critical Geographies, 15*(2), 285–292.

Wilen, S. (2018, August 29). Sinclair fires back at Tribune with countersuit over failed acquisition. *Baltimore Business Journal*. Retrieved September 17, 2018, from https://www.bizjournals.com/baltimore/news/2018/08/29/sinclair-fires-back-at-tribune-with-counter-suit.html

Yockey, M. (2017). *Make ours marvel: Media convergence and a comics universe.* Austin, TX: University of Texas Press.

CHAPTER SIX

Paparazzi, Drones, and Privacy

KALEN M. A. CHURCHER

In 2010, Leon Gast was a Sundance Film Festival winner with the documentary film, *Smash His Camera* (2010). The story chronicles paparazzo Ron Galella, whose cache of millions of photos includes such celebrities as Angelina Jolie, Elizabeth Taylor, Marlon Brando, and perhaps his most famous subject, Jacqueline Kennedy Onassis. In addition to the glimpse into Galella's life, the film explores the oft-contentious relationship between the First Amendment—specifically freedom of the press—and privacy, the latter of which was originally labeled a tort within the U.S. legal system and given an unclear definition at best. In fact, it wasn't until 1960, more than 150 years after the constitution guaranteed free speech that the Dean of the College of Law at UC Berkley, William Prosser, broke down the tort of privacy into four digestible subsections that were more palatable for public understanding.

Fast forward to 2017. The year marked the 20th anniversary of the death of Diana, Princess of Wales. The "People's Princess" died in 1997 after the car she was riding in crashed on the Pont de I'Alma in Paris. News reports published she was "chased by photographers on motorcycles," and with her death, came a firestorm of criticism that stretched across the pond and ignited a debate surrounding the validity of paparazzi. Were the photographers simply doing their jobs? Or was the driver, who was found to have been drinking, more culpable for the crash? Nearly as fast as the debate began, it ended, at least from news headlines and popular public debate. Behind the scenes, however, in courtrooms throughout the United States, the effects of Princess Diana's death were felt in the form of legislation that limited the media's ability to "take the kind of voyeuristic photographs and videotape that are the fodder of both the print and television tabloids," (Calvert, 2004, p. 191).

The debate between a free press, the public's right to know, and an individual's privacy have long been a discussion. Mix in the spectacle and curiosity of celebrity lifestyles and the discussion becomes more cumbersome as sides argue whether public persons, such as celebrities, truly deserve less privacy than private individuals. The argument is not as clear-cut when one considers that a favorite American pastime—voyeurism—must be curtailed in order to achieve this goal. Indeed, although fame has been a constant, the concept of celebrity culture and the behavior that surrounds it are relatively new (Harmon, 2004). As voyeurs, individuals seek pleasure in viewing others, no matter what their social status. Though often associated with taboo (read; sexual) behavior, the actual meaning is much more inclusive and may include much more mundane activities. Similarly, voyeurism need not include public or celebrity figures to exist, allowing the average (private) person to be the object of a voyeur's delight.

History of Paparazzi

The term paparazzi is an eponym, referring to the person for whom something is named. In the case of paparazzi, we turn to Paparazzo, the photographer in Federico Fellini's 1960 film, *La Dolce Vida*. Paparazzo was modeled after Tazio Secchiaroli who, in the late-1950s, was known to have hopped a Vespa in order to capture shots of unsuspecting celebrities (Boxer, 1998). These photos fetched a solid price from magazine editors who found them more interesting than planned shots (Boxer, 1998). It is a 1962 photo of Warren Beatty and Natalie Wood at the Palais des Festivals at Cannes that is considered what has become to be known as paparazzi photography (Schwartz, 2010). Now, the art of such photography is "part illusion, part circus act, as much as performance" (Wood, 2006).

Princess Diana's death forced the public to consider the worthiness of such tabloid infotainment. While the opposition pointed to the death as isolated, proponents of access to information argued that any limits placed on the collection and distribution of information would seriously stymie the watchdog function of the press (see Limperos & Silberman, this volume). This argument was a leap to some who questioned whether paparazzi and tabloid journalism should enjoy the same privileges as traditional journalism, which was founded on a basis of checks, balances, and objectivity. Tabloid journalism had a reputation of eschewing all of those things in favor of a more sensational, biased approach that some might say bordered on the verge of fiction. Although Princess Diana's death brought about debate over these journalistic forms, it did not bring about an end to the paparazzi or even a clear-cut way to extinguish or curtail its behaviors. Instead, arguments with roots in the First Amendment forced some to consider if trampling the rights of some were necessary in order to serve and protect the rights of many (the essence of which formed the foundation of the United States). Or, as Calvert posed, whether "the voyeur's gaze—must be sacrificed to privilege the rights of another person—the voyeur" (Calvert, 2004, p. 135).

Privacy Law

Historically, one of the problems with privacy law has been the ambiguity surrounding it. William Prosser's deconstruction and categorizing of the subject matter into four more manageable privacy torts has been heralded by many as the landmark analysis for those dabbling with privacy law. To be sure, Prosser did not create privacy law, nor was he even the first to write about it. That title goes to Samuel Warren and Louis Brandeis, who in 1890 "popularized privacy in American law" with *The Right to Privacy* (Richards & Solove, 2010, p. 1888). In actuality, Richards and Solove (2010) question if Prosser's study actually inhibits the development of privacy laws, particularly as electronic and online issues become more relevant. At its most basic level, privacy laws explore if and how an individual's personal solitude is being challenged by an outside or online entity. Prosser (1960), breaks privacy law down into four categories: *appropriation*, *false light*, *publication of a private fact*, and *intrusion into seclusion*.

Of the four privacy torts outlined by Prosser, appropriation is addressed less frequently in the context of paparazzi, yet remains most applicable. Appropriation (also referred to as misappropriation) refers to the use of a person's name or likeness to receive financial gain. Consider if you will, simply taking a pre-existing photograph of a favorite celebrity and then using that photograph—without expressed permission—to promote a particular business or cause.[1] If no agreement with said celebrity has been reached, not only has a right to privacy been violated, but a right to publicity as well. The celebrity, as does anyone, has a right to be left alone as well as a right to reap financial gain from his or her fame. This does not mean that celebrity images cannot be integrated into a project, etc; however, they must be transformed into a new entity that is purchased not because of the authenticity of the celebrity, but for the new product/message that has been created.

Appropriation serves as a one-two punch for celebrities and public people, however. The first hit occurs when the photograph or video is taken and the celebrity's privacy is violated. It should be noted that this is not addressing photography surrounding a newsworthy event. Instead, it is referring to those photos taken for the voyeur, in the case of the paparazzi, those taken for monetary gain. The second hit occurs when money exchanges hands and it is the paparazzo, not the "model" that benefits from the exchange. In the former, it is the individual's right to privacy that is violated; in the latter, it is the person's right to publicity.

The remaining three torts speak directly to not only the paparazzo, but to the celebrity being targeted. If we divorce ourselves from the idea that such "assault photography" is a form of journalism, and is instead sensationalism at best, we are able to break from the idea that the paparazzo equates to a photojournalist. Once this is accomplished, we can walk away from the idea that the paparazzo is capturing and documenting the world around us. A 2009 editorial by the *California Sun Dial* argued that paparazzi celebrity photos are not photojournalism because the producers are driven by cash and work under the guise of "exploiting the lives of the rich and famous" (Staff Editorial, 2009, n.p.). This then creates the clash between what is legal and what is ethical. This clash is commonly debated but not always decided upon. In the case of Princess Diana, one must ask if the throng of reporters that followed her car that fateful August night was on a journalistic mission, or if the reporters, instead, sought to catch the princess and her suspected lover.

Should the latter be the case, it would be entirely logical to examine the second privacy tort: false light. When coupled with cleverly written headlines, a celebrity photo or video is often purchased because of what it *could* convey and not what it actually *does* convey. The privacy tort of false light is illegal if: the light in which the person is placed would be highly offensive to a reasonable person and if the publisher of said material was at fault when the publication was made plays directly into the ethicality of paparazzi and "scandal sheet" newspapers. This tort aligns itself closely with defamation, yet is distinct in its own right. With defamation, the plaintiff must prove damage to his or her reputation. In contrast, with false light, the plaintiff need only show that the material would be considered highly offensive to a reasonable person.

It has long been established that truth remains the best defense for many things, including libel, which involves the intentional publication or broadcast of material that lowers an individual's reputation by holding them up to contempt, ridicule or scorn. However, while truth may be the argument when defending one's actions, it is not foolproof. Similar to libel, within the realm of privacy, even the publication of a truth can be problematic. Hence Prosser's privacy tort of publication of a private fact. Publication of a private fact is largely self explanatory: An entity must communicate to the public at large information that was meant to be private, actively maintained to *not* be public, and not newsworthy. What does this mean for celebrities and the paparazzi? As public people, celebrities already are afforded less protection than the average citizen. However, even for a celebrity, a private fact may be entitled to be kept private. For the paparazzi, how said facts were obtained may play a critical role should they come under attack.

What about telephoto lenses, tenacious videographers waiting outside private clubs or photographers following celebrities on their morning runs through their grounds? Intrusion into seclusion marks the fourth and final privacy tort, as categorized by Prosser. It also stands to be the tort that most people are talking about when they say that someone or something has *invaded their privacy.* With intrusion into seclusion, Prosser (1960) refers to some entity invading the physical or mental solitude and space of someone. It should be noted that the space invaded must be a private one such as the home or property of someone, a private club, a hospital room or other space where there is a presumed expectation of privacy. Because there is more "action" involved with this particular tort, it tends to be discussed more frequently. However, it also brings with it a high degree of subjectivity. Items like the aforementioned camera lenses or hidden cameras are not only the tools of the paparazzi. Traditional journalists may utilize similar tools depending on the circumstances, but frequently not until extensive conversations with editorial boards occur.

The Clash

Consider it too much of a good thing, or perhaps consider it a double standard. The relationship between the paparazzi and celebrities is a strong one. The two have a mutualistic relationship with each needing the other to survive. A celebrity is nothing without publicity. Likewise, considering society's fascination with the celebrity spectacle, media would be nothing without celebrity news fodder. From a news perspective, be it entertainment news or more serious, traditional news, there is also a clash between the public's right to know and an individual's right to privacy. However, this is the site of yet another disconnect. Although the courts have recognized that individuals have a right to privacy, it is not a specifically guaranteed right outlined in the Constitution (see: *Griswold v. Connecticut,* 381 U.S. 479, 484 (1965) and *Galella v. Onasis,* 353 F. Supp. 196, 231 (SDNY 1972)). Celebrities are, however, privy to the same general rights as non-celebrities. Their burden of proof remains higher because of their status as public and not private individuals. (Nordhaus, 1999). The argument, as it is for most, is that as a public person who makes their living from being in the public eye, one has indirectly consented to a lesser degree of privacy than the average private person. However, there are often other (familial) parties involved who, although not public individuals, give up their privacy because of their association with the organization.

When one side has taken too much, we see verbal, physical and emotional clashes occur, fueling the cyclical nature of celebrity news. In this instance, the paparazzi become a part of the actual news story. Take the following examples from more recent incidents.

- In 2017, One Direction member, Louis Tomlinson, was arrested following an altercation with a paparazzo who had also placed Tomlinson under a citizen's arrest.
- In fall 2014, Justin Bieber allegedly threw a punch at paparazzi as he tried to have dinner at a Parisian hotel.
- In 2013, Alec Baldwin reportedly grabbed a photographer on a New York City street and threw him up again a car during an altercation.
- In 2013, presumably tired of the constant surveillance, NBA star, Lamar Odom attacked paparazzi and their equipment.
- In 2010, Adam Lambert attacked a paparazzo while the photographer captured Lambert and friends on a Miami beach.

The aforementioned attacks represent a small sampling of those incidents that made headlines, with media questioning in some cases the celebrities' sanity while not taking into consideration the stressors experienced by the celebrities.

Changing the Law

The anti-paparazzi/celebrity-privacy movement following the death of Princess Diana was strong, both in England and in the United States (largely due to the high number of U.S. celebrities). The United Kingdom's independent press association seemed most effective in drawing up agreements with its publishers and photographers, as well as the paparazzi, though the regulations specifically addressed "journalists". To avoid similar incidents. the U.K.'s Press Complaints Commission released the following:

i) Journalists must not engage in intimidation, harassment, or persistent pursuit.
ii) They must not persist in questioning, telephoning, pursuing, or photographing individuals once asked to desist; nor remain on their property when asked to leave and must not follow them. If requested, they must identify themselves and whom they represent. (Pajer, 2017, n.p.)

Already, there have been sanctions taken against media who have violated this agreement. Interestingly, prior to Princess Diana's death, the Protection from Harassment Act was passed, though, according to *Time* magazine, the section of the act that could have helped her was not instituted until just a few months before her death. The act has since become the U.K.'s weapon of choice for dealing with the media (Samuelson, 2017). In addition, following Princess Diana's death, The Press Complaints Commission created a stricter set of guidelines to limit the press.

In the United States, though plenty of discussion took place immediately following Princess Diana's death, few regulations actually came to fruition. California, due to its high concentration of celebrities, also tried its hand in regulating aggressive reporting techniques. The state primarily attached hefty fines to photographers who trespassed (a crime that was already not legal). It also passed a regulation punishing individuals who interfered with drivers by acting recklessly or making it difficult for drivers to drive. Paul Reif was the first person charged under this law in 2012 when he recklessly pursued Justin Bieber on an LA highway (Pajer, 2017). A Los Angeles Superior Court judged ruled the law unconstitutional, but had his ruling overturned when a District Court judge ruled the law not overbroad or at odds with the First Amendment. In 2013, California Gov. Jerry Brown signed into law a bill that made it illegal to harass children because of their parents' job. Though Halle Berry and Jennifer Garner testified on behalf of Senate Bill 606, the passing of the law was met with some mixed reactions and opposed by the California Newspapers Association on the grounds that it would make their jobs more challenging (Reuters, 2013).

Nordhaus (1999) doesn't argue that celebrities be given *more* protection or additional laws than those afforded to non-celebrities. However, it must be acknowledged that there is a societal fascination with celebrities, making them more likely targets for such intrusion. That being said, it makes sense to address paparazzi and the implications of them. Indeed, the public may become outraged upon learning of a death like Princess Diana's. They may rally to change laws. Yet they do all of this while reading their tabloid magazines and watching their tabloid entertainment programming.

Droning on the Issue

The potential for encroaching upon individuals' privacy increases almost monthly, as technology companies fight to stay ahead of one another. With such being the case, where do electronic devices like drones fit into the newsgathering spectrum? Should paparazzi be lumped in with more traditional journalists for deciding these types of questions? If not, how should they be classified? Although drones entered public awareness as part of the military, they quickly became mainstream. With more than two million recreational drones sold in 2016 (Platt, 2017) and the interest in commercial drones growing (Farber, 2017), the popularity of drones has become apparent. "In particular, tabloids and news reporting agencies have capitalized on drone technology to take and publish otherwise difficult-to-obtain photos and film of celebrities and their children without consent" (Tate, 2015, p. 74).

The FAA Modernization and Reform Act, passed in 2012, required that drones be included and recognized by the national airspace system (Platt, 2017; FAA Modernization and Reform Act of 2012). This prompted federal and state legislation regulating drones; however, much of this regulation has dealt with operation and space and *not* with issues of privacy. When privacy issues surrounding drones *have* come up, it has largely been to address governmental intrusion and violations of the Fourth Amendment, though applicability to paparazzi seems obvious. The civil tort of intrusion into seclusion—invading someone's privacy—again is the most easily identifiable of the privacy torts, in this situation. That the torts are predominantly civil (verses criminal) in nature, however, creates a burden on the potential victim in that they are responsible for any court action. The current legal lag in dealing with drones and paparazzi specifically is not entirely surprising. One needs only to look at the slow and unsteady history of laws regarding internet content to see that lawmakers often are anything but quick to respond immediately to changes in technology. A similar situation also existed with camera phones. The solution being a combination of existing privacy laws and new legislation (Larson & Roberts, 2017). Indeed, several federal guidelines exist regarding drones and their operation, while states have largely been left to identify what they see as most pertinent to regulate (Platt, 2017).

Nonetheless, some states have taken action to secure the privacy of their citizens. Since 1998, California legislation has "focused on banning the use of drones and other advanced photo and video technology in order to safeguard against invasion of the privacy of celebrities" (Azriel, 2014, p. 2). For example, California's legislature passed an "anti-paparazzi statute prohibiting individuals from using a drone to capture an image or recording a person engaging in a private, personal, or familial activity without permission," (Platt, 2017, p. 36). What was problematic in this instance was that the law went against established federal law. The Air Commerce Act, and eventually the Civil Aeronautics Act of 1938 redefined the airspace over a property that could be considered owned by an individual (Platt, 2017). Basic drone technology is such that drones could effectively fly in a safe space and still record photography of a high degree of quality. While some may view the state-focus as an opportunity for more citizen input on issues of particular relevance to them, it also leaves a sometimes confusing bricolage of legislation that changes at states' borders. Rhode Island surely does not have the celebrity population of California, but that does not mean that it disregards the privacy rights of its private citizens (Remillard, 2018). Similarly, Kansas, Louisiana, and Texas are among states that have also taken steps to regulate drones, some connecting privacy concerns to existing stalking laws (Remillard, 2018).

In addition to the obvious technological limits to existing, more-established laws, Richards and Solove (2010) contend that Prosser's taxonomy of privacy does not allow for technological advancements to be considered within its structure and could possibly explain the challenges in dealing with legalities surrounding drones. This creates a potential chilling effect that forces users into a technological quandary. If they utilize said technology, they risk being reprimanded for inappropriate use. To avoid the risk, they may choose to use none. Some may inquire why this is problematic, particularly when dealing with something as questionable as a paparazzo. If journalists are afforded the authority to utilize drones for photo and video gathering, a slippery slope is created if paparazzi are not. Rosenfeld (2010) supports the notion that paparazzi are journalists—"rogue journalists"—but journalists nevertheless (p. 485). To isolate them because of what news they cover would be dangerous. "While the value of paparazzi-driven journalism is low, regulations limiting paparazzi tactics could be a detriment to society. Since paparazzi are journalists, all rules applying to them will apply (to) the rest of the journalism profession" (Rosenfeld, 2010, p. 486). To equate the two professions is not an easy task for some, but needs to occur in order to establish consistency.

Distinguishing between public and private individuals has long been a key marker in creating laws pertaining to (but not limited to) libel and privacy. Historically, public individuals, those people who put themselves out into the public for purposeful celeb-status or to effectuate change must meet a higher burden of proof when establishing a case against someone. Conversely, private individuals— the average citizen—need to meet a much lower threshold. One might expect that drone regulations would follow a similar suit, thereby increasing the preexisting inconsistencies.

Final Thoughts

In the case of privacy verses the right to know or free speech, one must consider how much privacy one is willing to give up in order to maintain a lifestyle of voyeurism, where a gaze is turned on an Other to further note differences. While current legislation is based off a tiered approach to privacy rights and expectations that affords the average (private person) much more control over their own exposure to items like the paparazzi than it does to a celebrity (public person), as technology becomes more pervasive and invasive, consumers must expect that the difficulty in maintaining control over exposure will become more challenging. As that happens, one might wonder if a realization might occur that causes private individuals to question the overall fascination with celebrities and the spectacle surrounding them. Once the elusiveness of celebrity lifestyles is broken, what would be next? Would private citizens be content to simply watch one another, and would they change their routines if they knew they were the ones being watched? Is the watching even an issue? If it was an issue to someone, what is the proper way to handle an instance where privacy has been invaded? There is not yet a standard way to handle these types of situations. Conventional wisdom suggests that one not take the law into their own hands. Following protocol by notifying law enforcement is the best way to proceed as laws concerning protection of privacy differ from state-to-state.

Younger generations that have grown up with their lives posted to Facebook and Instagram and announced through Twitter really have never experienced a time when voyeurism *wasn't* a positive. As such, questioning the paparazzi as to the appropriateness of how much access they are granted may be a moot point. Individuals have never been so intertwined as both consumers and producers of media. Likewise, the ease and speed at which content can be posted to the internet leaves little cooling off time for producers to consider appropriateness and repercussions of content. Where does that leave society? Technological advancements that are years ahead of legislators require content producers and consumers to be more media literate and proactive in being aware of their environments—media and actual. Privacy, as older generations have known it to exist is not necessarily the expected norm, leaving the opportunity to exist for the whole world to be watching.

Note

1. To be sure, appropriation deals not only with the photographic visual. Someone's voice, likeness, etc. may also be misappropriated; however, it is photography that is most applicable in the current situation.

References

Azriel, J. (2014). Reining in the California paparazzi: An analysis of the California legislature's attempts to safeguard celebrity privacy. *California Journal of Politics and Policy, 8*(4), 1–11.

Boxer, S. (1998, July 25). Tazio Secchiaroli, the model for "Paparazzo," dies at 73. *The New York Times.* Retrieved November 3, 2017, from http://www.nytimes.com/1998/07/25/world/tazio-secchiaroli-the-model-for-paparazzo-dies-at-73.html

Calvert, C. (2004). *Voyeur Nation: Media, Privacy and Peering in Modern Culture,* Westview Press: Boulder, Col.

FAA Modernization and Reform Act of 2012, Pub. L. No 112–95, §§ 331–336, 126 Stat. 11 (2012).

Farber, H. B. (2017). Keep out: The efficacy of trespass, nuisance and privacy torts as applied to drones. *Georgia State University Law Review, 33*(2), 359–409.

Galella v. Onasis, 353 F. Supp. 196, 231 (SDNY 1972).

Griswold v. Connecticut, 381 U.S. 479, 484 (1965).

Harmon, K. (2005). Celebrity culture: Bibliographic Review. *The Hedgehog Review,* 98–106.

Larson, D., & Roberts, P. S. (2017). How two traditions of privacy defenses in image capture technology inform the debate over drones. *I/S: A Journal of Law and Policy for the Information Society, 13*(2), 465–495.

Nordhaus, J. E. (1999). Celebrities' rights to privacy: How far should the paparazzi be allowed to go? *The Review of Litigation, 18*(2), 286–315.

Pajer, N. (2017). How paparazzi laws have changed since Princess Diana's death. *Yahoo! Entertainment.* Retrieved from https://www.yahoo.com/entertainment/paparazzi-laws-changed-since-princess-dianas-death-001001650.html

Platt, T. (2017). The drone wars: The need for federal protection of individual privacy. *Washington Journal of Law, Technology & Arts, 13*(1), 27–48.

Prosser, W. L. (1960). Privacy. *California Law Review, 48*(3), 383–423.

Remillard, D. M. (2017). Highway to the danger drone: Reconciling First Amendment rights of drone owners and privacy rights of individuals in creating a comprehensive statutory scheme in Rhode Island. *Roger Williams University Law Review, 22*(3), 640–669.

Reuters. (2013). California bill protecting children of celebrities from paparazzi signed into law. *New York Daily News.* Retrieved from http://www.nydailynews.com/news/national/halle-berry-jennifer-garner-supported-california-bill-protecting-children-paparazzi-signed-law-article-1.1467192

Richards, N., & Solove, D. (2010). Prosser's Privacy Law: A Mixed Legacy. *California Law Review, 98*(6), 1887–1924. Retrieved from http://www.jstor.org/stable/25799958

Rosenfeld, S. (2010). Lights, camera, sanction? Whether a proposed anti-paparazzi ordinance would limit investigative journalism in the news business. *Hastings Business Law Journal, 6*(2), 483–500.

Samuelson, K. (2017). The Princess and the Paparazz: How Diana's Death Changed the British Media. *Time.* Retrieved from http://time.com/4914324/princess-diana-anniversary-paparazzi-tabloid-media/

Schwartz, V. R. (2010). Wide angle at the beach: The origins of the paparazzi and the Cannes Film Festival, Études Photographiques, 26. Retrieved from https://journals.openedition.org/etudesphotographiques/3455?lang=en

Staff editorial: Paparazzi is not photojournalism. (2009). *The Sundial.* Retrieved from http://sundial.csun.edu/2009/10/staff-editorial-paparazzi-is-not-photojournalism/

Tate, A. (2015). Miley Cyrus and the attack of the drones: The right of publicity and tabloid use of unmanned aircraft systems. *Texas Review of Entertainment and Sports Law, 17*(1), 73–99.

Warren, S. D., & Brandeis, L. D. (1890). The right to privacy. *Harvard Law Review, 4*(5), 193–220.

Wood, G. (2006). Camera, movie star, Vespa … it all began on the Via Veneto. *The Observer.* Retrieved from https://www.theguardian.com/media/2006/sep/24/pressandpublishing1

CHAPTER SEVEN

The Role of Media in Perpetuating Stereotypes

MEGHAN S. SANDERS & STEPHANIE L. WHITENACK

In late 2017, the beauty/skincare line Dove faced national criticism when the company released a video of women changing out of t-shirts. The criticism wasn't because of nudity, provocative attire or poses. It was because of the shade of the women's skin compared to the colors of the t-shirts. The video began with a woman of color changing out of a darker t-shirt. As the video progressed, the women's complexions became lighter as did the colors of the t-shirts. The video went viral with the fiercest of criticisms calling it racist because it seemed to imply that women of color are dirtier than White women. In early 2018, the clothing brand H&M faced similar criticism when they released an ad featuring an African American boy wearing a t-shirt featuring a monkey and the words, "Coolest Monkey in the Jungle." Critics argued the image perpetuated associations of Africans and African Americans with animals, and savage, animalistic behavior. Regardless of whether you agree with the criticisms, at the heart of them is the fear of negative stereotypes serving as unfair judgments of entire groups in society.

Many historical and contemporary stereotypes exist. Italians as mobsters or members of the mafia. The drunk Irish. Asian men as asexual. Latinos as hypersexual. Women as emotional by nature. African American men as violent, criminals. And, not all stereotypes are intrinsically negative. Some consist of positive characteristics, generalized to entire groups in ways that produce harm and encourage prejudices. One could think of stereotypes as existing along a continuum of benign to severely harmful. At their best, stereotypes lead to unfair judgments about subgroups within a society and divisiveness. At their worst, they can lead to prejudices, discrimination, and even hate.

Media are very powerful institutions with the ability to influence individuals' social perceptions, attitudes, beliefs, behaviors, and self-perceptions. News, television, film, and other forms of media play a significant socializing role (Bandura, 2009), often providing experiences and interactions that exist beyond the purview of daily interpersonal experiences. Scholars in mass communication, psychology, sociology, and women's studies (just to name a few) have explored and attempted to explain these influences. When media messages consist of stereotypes, they become problematic in perpetuating harmful attitudes, especially when contact outside of media depictions is minimal (Fujioka, 1999; Ramasubramanian & Oliver, 2007). The present chapter provides a broad overview of what stereotypes are, why we use them, and the role media play in perpetuating inaccuracies about ethnic, racial, and other social groups. The chapter will also touch upon strategies that content creators and audiences can use to counteract the application of media stereotypes in our everyday lives.

What Are Stereotypes?

Stereotypes are generalizations of individuals or groups that are based on characterizations of group memberships rather than individual characteristics of people belonging to those groups. While the process of thinking in terms of categories is a basic form of human cognitive processing, the process of stereotyping reduces the complexity of individuals through categorization that is often inappropriate, inaccurate, and distorted (Fiske & Taylor, 1991; Lippmann, 1922/1949). Despite the inaccuracies, stereotypes are not entirely fictional; rather they are based in some semblance of social reality. Because of this, they are culturally bound and can change over time. For example, early film representations of Latinos depicted men as hypersexual and hyper masculine, in addition to slovenly and lazy. In the 1990s the bandito stereotype morphed into the gang member (Merskin, 2017). While there may be individuals who fit these molds, it is when these characteristics are generalized as being representative of the entire Latino experience that problems arise. Quite often, when asked about their beliefs and use of stereotypes, many individuals will deny endorsing and using them. This denial is sometimes attributed to a need to protect one's reputation and self-esteem, but other times it is a result of lack of insight into one's own vulnerabilities and unconscious biases. Regardless of the reason, it's a commonly held belief that stereotypes have a generally negative impact.

Why do we use stereotypes, then, if we consciously know them to be bad and unfair? Their use relates to how individuals process information from the environment around them. We live in stimulus-rich environments that would overload the human brain if attempts were made to process all incoming information. Instead, we use shortcuts or engage in cognitive processing strategies that allow us to make sense of incoming stimuli in manageable ways. These shortcuts, collectively referred to as heuristic processing, may make use of schemas.

A schema is a cognitive structure that represents what is known about the attributes of a concept and the relationships between those attributes (Fiske & Taylor, 1991). To that end, schema theory focuses on how information is stored, retrieved, and used to process new information. Within a schema, there are three components: (1) a central concept, (2) associated concepts and (3) relationships among those concepts. Together these components provide meaning or knowledge (Fiske & Taylor, 1991). Central concepts are primary ideas. These ideas can be constructs or categories. For example, "news" may be considered a construct or category of media. Associated concepts are lower-order but related ideas and characteristics that have connections with central concepts and sometimes with one another. Associated concepts with "news" may include "newscaster," "journalist," "crime," "community," "experts," and "story." The actual relationships between central and associated concepts vary in distance and strength, but they come together to create one schema that visually resembles a social network. The relationships between core and associated concepts can differ between individuals and cultures as they are influenced by one's environment, experiences, and even media.

Putting it all together, schemas focus on generic knowledge that holds across many particular instances rather than the details of the individual experience. Concepts are linked in memory based on observations, such that when one central concept is activated, associated concepts are also activated. Thus, stereotypes are a specific type of schema that represent social, ethnic, racial, or other groupings of people and the characteristics we associate with those groups. For example, in the case of Native Americans common stereotypes include that of savage, wise elder, squaw, or princess (Merskin, 2017). When the concept of Native American or "tomahawk" is activated, so too might the concepts savagery and violence. According to media scholars and psychologists, schemas allow individuals to be miserly in allocating attentional resources so that we spend more time processing the details of information that are considered most relevant to our functioning and survival, while spending less time on information that is less immediate. However, their use does not exclude more detailed processing of incoming information or the ability for schemas to change or grow.

Mental models are similar to schemas in regard to their role. Whereas schemas provide connections between concepts to provide meaning, mental models provide knowledge about *how* conceptions or processes function. Event models, a specific form of mental model, are most applicable to stereotypes as these models represent specific episodes and experiences. Vicarious experiences, such as ones presented through media where the audience envisions themselves as part of the experience, explain how individuals understand information unfolding within a story or event. Characters or character models are part of this process as they refer to how viewers and readers learn about the traits, goals, and motivations of individuals within a story. Such models are based on information provided in the narrative but also on the information individuals bring to the experience about similar people. This may or may not include stereotyped information. For example, if a story begins with a group of surgeons standing in a hospital hallway, a viewer's stereotypes about doctors (e.g. workaholics with a God complex, etc.) will likely be activated. But if the story focuses on one particular doctor, say Meredith Grey (from the television program *Grey's Anatomy*), viewers learn more about her personality, how her mother influenced her to become a surgeon, the challenges she has in her romantic life, and her feelings of parental abandonment. Thus, a viewer could utilize stereotyped information as well as specific information to develop a character model of doctors.

Both schemas and mental models serve to guide one's attention when receiving new information. Both mechanisms provide assistance in organizing and storing information for later use, filling in missing information, and helping us interpret new situations. When it comes to people, schemas and mental models provide guidance based on previously encountered interpersonal and mediated situations.

Media play a role in telling us how others look and how they ought to be; especially when we don't have our own reference points to work from. This is why media can serve as such a strong socializing force—both positively and negatively. While schemas can vary from person to person, the more universal the experiences, the more likely it is that individuals' schemas may resemble one another, especially within the same culture. Repeated exposure to stereotyped portrayals in news, entertainment and other forms of media make stereotypes more frequently and easily accessible, even though we may not always use them to make decisions (Banaji, Hardin, & Rothman, 1993). In other words, when a person frequently encounters stereotypes or encounters many of them within a short period of time, they are more easily activated. Thus, when a person is in an unfamiliar or new situation similar to the one in which a stereotype was encountered the stereotypes are likely to be activated and used in interpreting that environment if cues discouraging their application are either absent from the environment, not strong enough, or not noticed. With each new activation, the beliefs are reinforced, sometimes to such a degree that they become automatic. When a specific schema or mental model is activated by a news story, social media video, or film, individuals anticipate that the incoming information will follow the activated or expected structure.

Theories Related to Stereotyping

There are many theories and models commonly associated with the examination and understanding of stereotypes. Some of them explain their effects while others focus on how, when, and why we may use them. This chapter will focus on five of them: *framing, cultivation, social identity theory, self-categorization theory*, and the *stereotype content model*.

Framing is a process often-used in constructing media messages, including news. Framing has been described as a strong influencer of public perception because it explains how media content organizes and provides perspective on information. Like a picture frame or the frame of a building, media framing provides a structure through which content can be interpreted. Often, framing strategies may include certain pieces of information about government policies, controversial topics and even groups of individuals, to the exclusion of other relevant information. For example in news, Latinos are often presented as both legal and illegal immigrants without the context of the circumstances that led to immigration into the U.S. (Dixon & Williams, 2015). There are practical considerations for the use of frames—all information can't be presented in a brief story about a given issue or situation. But, the frames themselves are also powerful mechanisms because they teach media consumers how to perceive situations, that then become a part of their general perceptions. Frames, essentially, can help create the aforementioned schemas. Thus, when frames are repeatedly presented, they have the potential to perpetuate stereotypes about social, racial, and ethnic groups.

Consider media coverage of individuals with mental illnesses. Specifically in news and crime dramas, these individuals, regardless of the illness, are presented as lacking control over their actions, representing a threat to society. Common mental health issues like depression and anxiety get lumped in with the types of mental illnesses that are associated with violence in a way that makes viewers concerned that everyone with a mental health issue is violent. While some mental illnesses are associated with aggression, not all are. According to Paterson (2006) there has been a concern that this "excessive" focus by the news media on violence in association with mental illness reinforces pre-existing stereotypes and stigmas about mental health.

Cultivation analysis focuses on the contributions media make to individuals' conceptions of reality. The core hypothesis is that those who spend more time consuming media are more likely to see the real world as being similar to that of the mediated one. This is the case because they are influenced by common, recurrent messages. Those who consume less media have a different conception of social reality. In the case of stereotyping, cultivation analysis suggests that absent personal contact with various groups, individuals are likely to see members of social groups in reality as being similar to the portrayals presented by the media. For example, examination of news portrayals of Blacks and Hispanics have found that they are more often presented as perpetrators of crimes, as nameless, threatening, and more likely to be accompanied with prejudicial information (Dixon, 2000; see Mastro, 2009). Repeated exposure to these presentations across multiple news platforms, over time will lead viewers to believe that Blacks and Hispanics are less educated, have lower income levels, commit more crimes, are likely to be violent, and are less likely to be officers enforcing the law. One study found that when news stories are presented without a photo or reference to ethnicity, people are more likely to assume the perpetrator is Black (Dixon, 2000). In the realm of sports, Black athletes are often noted for their physical prowess as opposed to intellectual, strategic strengths when compared to White counterparts. This perpetuates the belief they are unable to provide team leadership. In the case of Black, female athletes, woman-ness is stripped altogether as these athletes are described as more masculine in appearance when at the peak of their game (Serena Williams being the most notable example).

In another example, the media's fascinations with disability, both physical and intellectual, creates a paradigm where individuals are not necessarily seen as an average person, but as a hero because they are overcoming great odds to live with their disability. However, most of what the media shows is not an accurate representation of what persons with disabilities go through on a day-to-day basis. While most would think that referencing people with disabilities as heroes would create perceptions of them as fully capable, "average" human beings, it creates a false façade of what really happens in their daily lives.

Social identity theory (SIT) and *self-categorization theory* are two related frameworks that address why stereotyped content, may be attractive to individuals. These theories consider at their core, the importance of how one identifies themselves. According to SIT, individuals categorize themselves as belonging to various groups. The group could be based on gender, ethnicity/race, profession, religious affiliation, or even a fan base. Depending on the situation, certain social group memberships may be more relevant than others. Given that the social group is considered an important part of the person's self-identity, using some relevant aspect of the group to which they belong, (referred to as an *in-group*) they compare themselves to another similar and proximate group(s) to which they don't belong in an effort to establish their worth. Individuals protect their self-identity and bolster self-esteem by comparing favorable in-group characteristics to unfavorable out-group ones (Fiske & Taylor, 1991), and maximizing the differences between groups. When the evaluation doesn't work in favor of the in-group, competition or other cognitive strategies such as comparing the groups on some other dimension or comparing the in-group to another less threatening out-group, are used in order to establish a more positive in-group perception. The social identity model of media effects (see Trepte & Loy, 2017) suggests that media can nurture the need for positive social identity and increase self-esteem through media use. Stereotypes often provide the best unfavorable comparisons, but at the expense of understanding others.

Self-categorization theory (SCT) is an extension of SIT in that it examines levels of self-categorization, more specifically personal and social identity as guides for behavior and cognition. While social identity depends on a person's group membership, personal identity is independent and more closely connected with personal attributes. With this in mind, the theory suggests that one's behavior is influenced by either or both types of identity depending on the relative salience of situation for each identity. Media content can trigger emotionally relevant and accessible categories for a consumer. When a particular identity becomes salient, a person may overly accentuate their similarity with other members of that group and define themselves according to the needs of that group which may include holding a competitive edge over others.

The stereotype content model (SCM) looks at various conceptions of identities, those self-prescribed or those assigned to us by others. The SCM (Fiske, Cuddy, Glick, & Xu, 2002) argues that groups and individuals are evaluated and differentiated along two primary dimensions: warmth and competence. How groups fall along these dimensions results in distinct forms of prejudice, some of which incorporate positive characteristics into their makeup. So, whereas elderly individuals may be thought of as highly warm, they may also be thought of as inept or unable to perform basic functions, therefore, being pitiable and recipients of paternalistic prejudice related to feelings of sympathy and an air of superiority over this group. Stereotypes can be positive in their characteristics but their application can have detrimental effects. For example, Asians and Asian Americans are commonly extolled for intellectual aptitudes and accomplishments, specifically in fields such as math, science, and technology. Many examples are apparent in entertainment such as the television shows *Heroes, Community,* and *Lost.* However, they are simultaneously presented as having rigid family and personal values. While still admired, the stereotypic trait of coldness makes the admiration a grudging feeling as they are perceived as depriving others of control, as being too ambitious, unsociable, and competitive to the point of harming others. The end result is envious prejudice. There is support of these assumptions as they apply to media entertainment (Sanders & Ramasubramanian, 2012) as media not only present the content of stereotypes but also opportunities to engage in the comparison process.

Not only can stereotypes affect how one perceives others, they can also influence how one conceives of the self. For example, African American children and adolescents' self-concepts are affected by not only the media presentations but also the absence of their social group. Continued exposure to stereotypes about one's own group can also negatively influence one's self-esteem and how powerful and influential they feel their group to be (see Sanders & Banjo, 2013). In some instances, individuals will avoid stereotyped media fare, while in others the content can be internalized.

Solutions for Stereotyping

There is no escaping the fact that stereotypes exist, and that as humans we will continue to use categories to make sense of our environments. But, just because stereotypes may be activated does not mean that we're at their mercy. Audiences can play a role in the frequency of their use, but content creators must also share in this job from rethinking the stories they choose to tell and considering the depth of information provided about the context.

News outlets can make use of the unlimited capacity of online venues, telling more in-depth stories and creating supplementary programs that cover in more detail the complexities of an issue. Entertainment creators have used multiple strategies to counter the effects of stereotypes. Diverse, ensemble casts in television shows such as *Grey's Anatomy*, *S.W.A.T.* and *This is Us* attempt to show positive cross-racial and gender interactions while also delivering storylines that transcend social boundaries. Entertainment also attempts to show more of a culture's experience to counter cultural stereotypes (Squires, 2009). While seeing diverse characters is important, it's also important to present individuals in as accurate and complete a light as the medium allows. Disney's *Moana* was extolled for attempting to show various aspects of Polynesian cultures including family, beliefs about the afterlife, and the beauty of the islands, but also elicited an amount of trepidation for how the culture was presented—from the full-body tattoos of Maui, to the treatment of Polynesian cultures as only one culture. Pixar's 2017 venture, *CoCo* opened to more positive acclaim for its presentation of Mexican culture particularly in regard to family, death, respecting heritage, and the legacy left behind for family members. Likewise, Marvel's *Black Panther* was celebrated for showing more nuanced reflections of African culture, language, and people within the context of a superhero film. The film also tapped into historical and political themes and contexts strongly connected to African American and African communities, while also capturing the conversation of many of its diverse audience members. These efforts are important for processing information about individuals and groups as they present the opportunity for audiences to see counter-stereotypes (stereotype disconfirming information) which in some cases trigger more detailed processing of information about individuals and decrease specific types of prejudice (Ramasubramanian & Oliver, 2007). They can have the opposite effect, however, either strengthening stereotyped attitudes or individuals are subtyped- meaning they are treated as the exception. The presence of counter-stereotypes, other cues within the content, more availability of cognitive attention, individuals motives (e.g. the need to avoid guilt, feel or display egalitarian values, etc.), all have the potential to suppress the *use* of stereotypes, albeit not necessarily their activation.

Professional journalism organizations have made repeated calls for more diverse newsrooms, arguing it would lead to less stereotyped storytelling. In 2018, Frances McDormand referenced "inclusion riders" during her Academy Awards acceptance speech for best actress. Since then, various production companies have committed to using them in future film productions. Inclusion riders, first proposed in 2014 by University of Southern California professor Stacy Smith, are contractual clauses that A-list actors and directors can require that stipulate the make-up of a film's cast and crew reflect the population in regard to ethnicity, gender, LGBTQ, and a variety of other categories. In this way, cast and crew would reflect the world in which we live and create a stronger pipeline for more diverse storytelling on-screen. The stories would naturally reflect the diverse lived experiences of the individuals as they relate to the acting, directing, costume design, set design, scores, and even special effects.

From an audience perspective, media consumers can take an active approach in minimizing the use of stereotypes by recognizing and taking advantage of the full range of content the media provide. By diversifying media consumption, people can experience the lives of and understand individuals from a variety of ethnic, marginalized, and stigmatized groups. While not a substitute for first-hand contact, news and entertainment can serve as a positive socializing force and reduce prejudice by providing people the opportunity to see and learn prosocial behaviors, attitudes, and about others' lived experiences through media and others' interpersonal interactions. For example, Ritterfeld and Jin (2006) found that viewing an accurate and empathetic movie portrayal increased knowledge about schizophrenia and influenced stigma reduction. Through social media, individuals should be aware of echo chambers that feed algorithms can create, limiting the amount of exposure to information that is counter to or generally dissimilar from one's own views. Even though it takes effort, individuals should seek out these voices to better understand multiple perspectives and engage in more meaningful dialogue with others.

Some media forms actually encourage us to engage in the aforementioned strategies. Meaningful and sad films, and some romances and dramas, are entertainment that often explore human values and issues related to the purpose of life. Individuals experience appreciation and deep gratification that in turn elicits feelings of meaningfulness, elevation, and of wanting to be better people and do good things for others (Oliver, Hartmann, & Woolley, 2012). Media also provide many opportunities for cross-cultural experiences and openness toward others through vicarious experiences. Recent studies have found that online videos, such as those that go viral through social media platforms or that may be shared on websites such as *Upworthy* and *Little Things*, may encourage individuals to be more open to outgroup members through not only the feelings of meaningfulness but also inspiration.

Lastly, content creators will arguably create what audiences seem to want. While awareness is key, action is paramount. Audiences do have the ability to engage in changing the media landscape. For example, in 2017 Hollywood not only faced the conversation of lack of diversity through #OscarsSoWhite but in many other forms, driven by the audiences. The *white-washing* of Asian roles in film has long been a regular occurrence, the most recent examples including Scarlett Johansson as Motoko Kusanagi in *Ghost in the Shell* (a film based on Japanese manga and anime) and Tilda Swinton's casting as the Ancient One (a Tibetan sorceress) in *Marvel's Doctor Strange*. Studio heads claim these decisions stem from the lack of available Asian movie stars who can draw audiences to theaters. #StarringJohnCho became a widespread response to these claims. The online social movement shared images of blockbuster movie posters featuring Asian-American actor John Cho as the male lead to show what films would look like with more diverse casting. For example, images depicted Cho as Captain America in *Avengers: Age of Ultron*, Ethan Hunt in *Mission Impossible: Rogue Nation*, and as James Bond in *Spectre*. The project is one attempt to draw attention to the lack of diversity in the actors cast in big-budget films even in stories that call for diverse casts. It also served as an opportunity to change the archetype of what is considered a Hollywood "leading man."

There are multiple strategies to combatting the detrimental effects of stereotypes. Conscientiousness in selection, interpretation, and application outside of the media world can all lead to a better understanding of individuals regardless of race, ethnicity, gender, sexuality, ability, and any other categorization. While heuristic processing may be a necessary component of human cognition, stereotyping is not a necessary component of perception.

References

Banaji, M. R., Hardin, C. D., & Rothman, A. (1993). Implicit stereotyping in person judgment. *Journal of Personality and Social Psychology, 65*, 272–281.

Bandura, A. (2009). Social cognitive theory of mass communication. In J. A. Bryant & M. B. Oliver (Eds.), *Media effects: Advances in theory and research* (pp. 94–124). New York, NY: Routledge.

Dixon, T. L. (2000). A social cognitive approach to studying racial stereotyping in the mass media. *African American Research Perspectives, 6*(1), 60–68.

Dixon, T. L., & Williams, C. L. (2015). The changing misrepresentation of race and crime on network and cable news. *Journal of Communication, 57*(2), 229–253. doi: 10.1111/j.1460-2466.2007.00341.x

Fiske, S., & Taylor, S. (1991). *Social cognition* (2nd ed.). New York, NY: McGraw-Hill.

Fiske, S. T., Cuddy, A. J. C., Glick, P., & Xu, J. (2002). A model of (often mixed) stereotype content: Competence and warmth respectively follow from perceived status and competition. *Journal of Personality and Social Psychology, 82*, 878–902.

Fujioka, Y. (1999). Television portrayals and African American stereotypes: Examination of television effects when direct contact is lacking. *Journalism & Mass Communication Quarterly, 76*, 52–75.

Lippmann, W. (1922/1949). *Public opinion.* New York, NY: Macmillan.

Mastro, D. (2009). Effects of racial and ethnic stereotyping. In J. A. Bryant & M. B. Oliver (Eds.), *Media effects: Advances in theory and research* (pp. 325–341). New York, NY: Routledge.

Merskin, D. (2017). Media representation: Minorities. In P. Rössler, C. A., Hoffner, & L. van Zoonen (Eds.), *International encyclopedia of media effects* (pp. 1–10). New York, NY: Wiley.

Oliver, M. B., Hartmann, T., & Woolley, J. K. (2012). Elevation in response to entertainment portrayals of moral virtue. *Human Communication Research, 38*, 360–378.

Paterson, B. (2006). Newspaper representations of mental illness and the impact of the reporting of "events" on social policy: The "framing" of Isabel Schwarz and Jonathan Zito. *Journal of Psychiatric and Mental Health Nursing, 13*(3), 294–300.

Ramasubramanian, S., & Oliver, M. B. (2007). Activating and surprising hostile and benevolent racism: Evidence for comparative media stereotyping. *Media Psychology, 9*, 623–646. doi: 10.1080/15213260701283244

Ritterfeld, U., & Jin, S. A. (2006). Addressing media stigma for people experiencing mental illness using an entertainment-education strategy. *Journal of Health Psychology, 11*(2), 247–267.

Sanders, M. S., & Banjo, O. (2013). Mass media and African American identities: Examining Black self-concept and intersectionality. In D. Lasorsa & A. Rodirigue (Eds.), *New agendas: Social identity and communication* (pp. 126–148). New York, NY: Routledge.

Sanders, M. S., & Ramasubramanian, S. (2012). Stereotype content and the African American viewer: An examination of African Americans' stereotyped perceptions of fictional media characters. *Howard Journal of Communication, 23*, 17–39.

Squires, C. (2009). *African Americans and the media.* New York, NY: Polity.

Trepte, S., & Loy, L. S. (2017). Social identity theory and self-categorization theory. In P. Rössler, C. A., Hoffner, & L. van Zoonen, L. (Eds.), *International encyclopedia of media effects* (pp. 1–13). New York, NY: Wiley.

CHAPTER EIGHT

The Dark-Side Gateway of Self-Objectification

Examining the Media's Role in the Development of Body Dissatisfaction and Eating Disorders

JENNIFER STEVENS AUBREY & LINDSAY ROBERTS

The Kardashian sisters (Kim, Khloe, Kourtney, Kylie Jenner, and Kendall Jenner) are among the most popular social media "influencers" today ("Top 10 Highest Paid Celebrities on Instagram," 2017). With their ubiquitous presence on Instagram, Facebook, Snapchat, and Twitter, combined with their E! television empire, *Keeping Up with the Kardashians*, their impact on fashion, bodies, and beauty in the 21st century is undeniable. In the Kardashian world, an obsessive focus on one's appearance, and importantly, an obsessive focus on how one *looks to other people*, are normalized in their everyday lived experience. Some critics argue that this promotion of seemingly relentless self-scrutiny—heaps "pressure on young women and girls to maintain a picture-perfect, Instagram-worthy image around the clock" (McGrath, 2016, para 7). It is likely that young people who idolize and attempt to emulate the Kardashian lifestyle are prone to internalizing a view of the self in which priority is given to how they look to others over all other things (accomplishments, character, values). This tendency, called self-objectification, has been shown to lead to a host of detrimental outcomes, such as anxiety, shame, depression, sexual dysfunction, and eating disorders (see Moradi & Huang, 2008, for review).

This chapter will review evidence of the media's influence on bodies and appearance. Guided by objectification theory (Fredrickson & Roberts, 1997), we will first review evidence on the media's influence on young women and men's tendency to treat their bodies as objects or "sights" for others' consumption (i.e., self-objectification). We argue that self-objectification is a "dark-side gateway" to other problematic body-related outcomes, including affective (appearance anxiety, body shame, body dissatisfaction) and behavioral (eating disorders) consequences. Given the importance of appearance and body image for identity formation in adolescence and young adulthood, our review will focus mainly on research on adolescents and emerging adults.

The Dark-Side Gateway: Self-Objectification

Many individuals learn to perceive themselves based on how they think their bodies appear to others (Fredrickson & Roberts, 1997). Self-objectification can be a chronic, trait-like tendency or a temporary state-like condition. Habitual exposure to sexually objectifying media is associated with a trait level of self-objectification among emerging adults (Aubrey, 2006) and adolescents (Vandenbosch & Eggermont, 2012). Additionally, by making one's appearance particularly salient in the moment, certain situations or sexually objectifying stimuli can make one self-objectify temporarily (Harrison & Fredrickson, 2003) but then quickly dissipate as the mind moves on to other thoughts and stimuli. Conceptually similar to self-objectification is body surveillance, which is a tendency to habitually monitor one's appearance in anticipation of others' evaluations.

The extant literature has demonstrated that diverse types of media exposure is positively associated with self-objectification, including television (Aubrey, 2006), magazines (Aubrey, 2010; Slater & Tiggemann, 2014), sports media (Harrison & Fredrickson, 2003), social media (Slater & Tiggemann, 2014), and a general sexually objectifying media exposure composite (Vandenbosch & Eggermont, 2012). Three main theoretical explanations for this link dominate the literature. First, media, such as advertising, movies, and social networking sites, all feature role models who are concerned about their own bodies and appearance (e.g., Kardashian sisters). Thus, by observational learning, individuals, especially girls and women, might learn to relentlessly submit their bodies to self-surveillance because that is precisely what their role models do.

Second, sexually objectifying media are effective in setting one's appearance standards (e.g., Vandenbosch & Eggermont, 2012); thus, the effect of media exposure on self-objectification might occur when an individual considers the societal norms of size and appearance to be appropriate standards for his or her own size and appearance (Thompson & Stice, 2001). These standards, in turn, could determine which appearance attributes and body parts are important for positive appearance evaluation, thus leading to a more objectified self-view and more frequent monitoring of appearance (Vandenbosch & Eggermont, 2012).

Third, the media frequently reinforce an objectified view of bodies, especially women's bodies, in the way they visually present people. For example, women's bodies are often shown as a collection of body parts, even disconnected from their heads, while the presentation of men is more visually focused on their faces (Archer, Iritani, Kimes, & Barrios, 1983). Additionally, an implicit gaze on women's bodies is also demonstrated through close-ups on their body parts, and an explicit gaze is demonstrated by characters visually checking out women's bodies in a variety of media platforms. It stands to reason that individuals who continuously see others' bodies being objectified in the media learn the importance of the body to their overall self-worth. If one internalizes this belief, body surveillance and self-objectification are likely to follow.

Further, Fredrickson and Roberts (1997) argue that self-objectification is a rather dehumanizing view of the self that can lead to profound and wide-ranging consequences, both proximal (i.e., anxiety, shame, disruption of "flow", and lowered interoceptive awareness) and distal (i.e., depression, sexual dysfunction, and eating disorders). In this chapter, we focus on negative body emotions (appearance anxiety and body shame) and eating disorders in particular.

Individuals who self-objectify likely anticipate others' evaluations of their bodies, thus making them anxious about their bodies. Indeed, there is consistent empirical evidence that self-objectification is linked with appearance anxiety (see Moradi & Huang, 2008). Additionally, body shame is experienced when individuals evaluate themselves in light of a cultural ideal of how bodies should look, and they surmise that they fall short of this standard (Fredrickson & Roberts, 1997). Chronically monitoring the body, such as the case when one self-objectifies, is associated with body shame (Moradi & Huang, 2008). Appearance anxiety and body shame can manifest into a generalized negative affective orientation toward the body, i.e., body dissatisfaction.

Focusing on eating disorders, it is important to acknowledge that the development of eating disorders is a primarily female experience. Current estimates suggest that 90% of those who are diagnosed with eating disorders are women between the ages of 12 and 25 (Substance Abuse and Mental Health Services Administration, 2017). This is not surprising given that the cultural body ideal is based on thinness for women, particularly young women. One of the ways that women attempt to meet the thin ideal, and at the same time alleviate shame and anxiety, is by restrained eating and dieting. In some rare cases, these behaviors may develop into more drastic means of manipulating the body, such as starvation and purging. Indeed, chronic self-objectification is conducive to eating disorders. Treating the self as an object necessarily detracts from the subjective experience of "being in one's body." For example, because self-objectifying individuals are less aware of their body states, it is easy for them to ignore hunger pains (Fredrickson & Roberts, 1997).

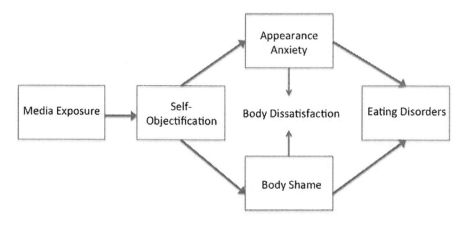

Figure 8.1. Model of Media Exposure and Self-Objectification.
Self-objectification as a dark-side gateway between media exposure and negative body affect and eating disorders.

While objectification theory (Fredrickson & Roberts, 1997) was initially conceived to explain the lived experiences of women and girls, a pervasive question in this literature concerns whether its premise applies to boys and men. Media pressures regarding men's bodies have increased dramatically in recent years as have "equal opportunity" instances for sexual objectification of both women's and men's bodies in the media (Hatton & Trautner, 2011). For men, the primary issue is not conforming to the thin ideal, but rather, a lean and muscular ideal. Advertisements for diet supplements, fitness programs, and grooming products reinforce the idea that bodies and appearance are important to men's self-worth. Although self-objectification levels are generally higher for girls and women than for boys and men, certain types of media exposure, such as pornography (Vandenbosch & Eggermont, 2013), sexualizing television (Vandenbosch & Eggermont, 2013), and sexually objectifying magazines (Aubrey, 2006), are predictive of self-objectification for boys and men. The findings are more divided on whether self-objectification leads to the detrimental consequences for boys and men that it does for girls and women. For example, in a classic study, Fredrickson, Roberts, Noll, Quinn, and Twenge (1998) found that it was possible to evoke self-objectification in young-adult men in an experimental context (by having them try on swimsuits), but they did not subsequently experience cognitive deficits and enact eating restraint as did the young-adult women in the study.

Media and Negative Body Emotions and Body Dissatisfaction

As a gateway to the dark side of body image, we can posit a two-step flow from media exposure to body dissatisfaction, i.e., media exposure → self-objectification → negative feelings about the body. In support of this model, Myers and Crowther (2007) found that college women's internalization of media ideals of attractiveness positively predicted self-objectification, which further predicted body dissatisfaction. Similarly, in a study on early adolescent girls (mean age = 11.6 years), both magazine and Internet exposure predicted self-objectification, which, in turn, predicted body shame (Tiggemann & Slater, 2015).

The findings for media exposure on negative feelings about the body through self-objectification is more mixed for young men. For example, Daniel and Bridges (2010) found that the internalization of male-typed media ideals of attractiveness positively predicted men's body surveillance, which is a person's habitual body monitoring, but not self-objectification. In turn, body surveillance further predicted men's body shame. However, in an experimental study, Michaels, Parent, and Moradi (2013) did not find an effect of exposure to muscularity-idealizing media images on college men's body surveillance, appearance anxiety, body shame, or body dissatisfaction.

Given a plethora of research on the direct link of media exposure and body dissatisfaction, we next review research on particular types of media (i.e., fitness/health magazines, pornography) that are particularly demonstrative of this process.

The case of fitness/health media. Fitness/health media regularly conflate health and fitness goals with appearance goals. For example, women's health and fitness magazines are just as likely to advise women to do healthy things in order to look good as they to advise women to do healthy things in order to feel good (Aubrey, 2010). In addition, the current body ideal for women has been described as thin, but also as lean and toned, evidenced by the immense popularity of "fitspiration" content and imagery on social media (Holland & Tiggemann, 2017). The repeated representation of only one body type (lean and toned) and the promotion of appearance-related rather than health benefits of diet and exercise raise concerns about what "fitspiration" media are inspiring young people to do (Tiggemann & Ziccardo, 2015).

Instead of health/fitness media encouraging young people to take a competence-focused, instrumental view on the body (by examining the question "What can I do?"), research suggests that these media actually do the opposite, by increasing self-objectification (by examining the question, "How do I look?"). Health and fitness magazine reading was a significant predictor of body dissatisfaction and eating disturbances amongst all adolescents, but especially among young women (e.g., Botta, 2003). Aubrey (2010) also found that young-adult women who were exposed to health articles with an appearance frame reported more body shame than women who read health articles with a health frame.

Likewise, reading fitness magazines also enhances body dissatisfaction among young men and boys. Adolescent boys who read fitness magazines were more likely to take supplements and were more committed to gaining muscle (Botta, 2003). A meta-analysis of experimental studies showed that exposure to muscular media stimuli resulted in male participants having lower body satisfaction (Barlett, Vowels, & Saucier, 2008).

The case of pornography. Pornography is replete with sexual objectification of women, more so than of men (Fritz & Paul, 2017), so it is somewhat surprising that pornography consumption seems to affect adolescent boys and men's feelings about their bodies. One explanation is based on cultural scripts in which women are valued for being sexually attractive, but men are valued for their sexual prowess (Vandenbosch & Eggermont, 2013). Thus, seeing men perform sexually in pornography might make male viewers more attuned to their bodies, especially their sexual body parts. Indeed, Vandenbosch and Eggermont found that online pornography not only directly increased adolescent boys' self-objectification, but it also affected their self-objectification indirectly through the internalization of media ideals. Similarly, among college men, Tylka (2015) showed that men's frequency of pornography use was positively linked to body dissatisfaction indirectly through internalization of the muscular body ideal.

Interestingly, pornography use is also positively associated with romantic relationship anxiety and romantic attachment avoidance (Tylka, 2015), highlighting the relational dimensions of these effects for college men. Aubrey and Taylor (2009) argued that exposure to sexual objectification of women's bodies, even without the presence of male sexual partners, could generate negative feelings about the body for young-adult men. In that study, college men who were exposed to sexually objectifying imagery of women (i.e., centerfolds) in male lifestyle magazines (e.g., *Maxim*) reported more anxiety about how others evaluate their appearance than those who were exposed to other parts of the magazine (e.g., sports, technology, fashion). The authors concluded that male lifestyle magazines might lead young men to believe that they must abide by muscular body standards or else they will not be physically attractive to the types of women who are sexually objectified and idealized in these magazines.

Media and Eating Disorder Symptomatology

Although research has demonstrated that exposure to the thin ideal in the media is directly related to eating disorder symptomatology (Harrison, 2001; Harrison &

Cantor, 1997), nearly two decades of research on objectification theory has yielded sufficient evidence to conclude that self-objectification is a mediator in this link (Tiggemann, 2013). For example, in a multi-stage model, Mitchell and Mazzeo (2009) found that self-objectification predicted the internalization of the thin ideal from the media, which predicted body dissatisfaction and subsequently eating disorder symptomatology.

Self-objectification provides a compelling explanation for media's influence on eating disorders (Tiggemann, 2013). In most media (with perhaps the sole exception of pro-anorexia websites that encourage Anorexia Nervosa as a "lifestyle choice" and not an eating disorder), eating pathology is not necessarily modeled and celebrated by role models. Thus, the effect of media exposure on disordered eating requires reading between the lines (Harrison, 2001). One must first recognize implicit values (e.g., "thin is good") in the media and then see them as functional or important in achieving success (e.g., "I will gain social approval by being thin"). In contrast, as we have already argued, the obsession with one's appearance is abundantly modeled. Thus, through observational learning, exposure to and identification with appearance-obsessed role models can directly encourage individuals to also develop an observer's perspective on the self. Extreme eating restraint, over-exercise, and purging can thus be seen as functional ways of garnering positive evaluations of one's appearance.

To explain, let us revisit the appearance-obsessed Kardashian sisters. To be sure, their body types do not strictly conform to the typical thin ideal, and together, their bodies might be aptly described as "curvaceously thin" (Harrison, 2003). However, the Kardashian sisters' media appearances, television show, and social media posts make it clear that they are overly concerned with how other people view their appearance and bodies, especially in a sexualized way. With self-objectification, the emphasis is on how much one is preoccupied with how he or she looks. Prioritizing how one looks over other qualities is associated with negative outcomes, especially for women. In the current case, sharing the Kardashian obsession with appearance, even though it is curvaceous, still likely motivates individuals to find ways to make their bodies fit with their cultural ideals of attractiveness.

In terms of the types of media that are related to eating disorder symptomatology, most of the research has focused on magazines and television, though some recent research has focused on social media, too. Women's lifestyle magazines, including fashion and beauty magazines, are argued to be thinness depicting and promoting; thus, exposure to magazines has been shown to be correlated with eating disorder symptomatology (Harrison & Cantor, 1997). Television seems to promote two corresponding ideals: being thin is good, and being fat is stigmatizing and subject to ridicule (Harrison, 2001). Both of these themes work to promote disordered eating (Harrison, 2000). Finally, popular social media applications (e.g., Instagram, Facebook, Snapchat) are highly visual and image-driven, which leads to ample opportunities for social comparison (Santarossa & Woodruff, 2017). Moreover, the content on social media is circulated by people the viewer actually knows (e.g., friends) or admires (e.g., celebrities), and posting one's own content is subject to the evaluation of others. In light of these features, recent research has shown that social media use is positively associated with body surveillance (Tiggemann & Slater, 2013) and disordered eating among young adults and adolescents (Mabe, Forney, & Keel, 2014; Santarossa & Woodruff, 2017).

Recommendations for Mitigating Risk

Our emphasis on self-objectification implies that individuals who seek to mitigate their risk of developing negative body emotions or disordered eating should focus first on self-objectification. That is, one's personal "emphasis on appearance needs to be decreased and the observer's perspective on the self relinquished" (Tiggemann, 2013, p. 40). The emphasis would be on how the media reinforce the belief that one's appearance is the most important aspect of their self-worth. Being practiced at mindfulness and disrupting ruminations about how he or she looks to other people would be potentially useful here. Minimizing exposure to potentially sexually objectifying contexts and situations would also be protective.

More broadly, media literacy interventions that critique and deconstruct the cultural rules and norms about sexualization would helpfully mitigate risk. In these efforts, it is imperative to recognize sexualization as a cultural process. This approach takes the focus away from individuals and individual behaviors and directs thoughts toward cultural-level processes that create pressures for appearance, body shape, and weight for both boys and girls.

On the other side of the picture, young people, especially girls and women, need encouragement to view their bodies in terms of their instrumentality and body competence, rather than in terms of their external appearance (Tiggemann, 2013). Participation in sports in which achievement is based on performance (e.g., soccer) rather than appearance (e.g., cheerleading) is one way to encourage body instrumentality.

To learn more about eating disorders, including symptoms and treatments, the National Eating Disorder Association is an excellent resource (https://www.nationaleatingdisorders.org).

Conclusion

Our purpose in this chapter was to provide an explanation of why exposure to the sexualized and thin media ideal predicts body dissatisfaction and disordered eating among young people. Our argument is that self-objectification, an insidious and inherently dehumanizing view of the self, opens the gateway to other dark-side body outcomes. However, we do see avenues for media to have an impact on the "bright side" of body image. For example, body appreciation has been shown to be a protective factor in the effects of appearance-based media exposure on body image concerns (e.g., Andrew, Tiggemann, & Clark, 2015). Social media seem especially conducive to encouraging body appreciation, perhaps an antidote to self-objectification. "Love Your Body Day," started by the National Organization for Women in 2014, and the Dove Campaign for Real Beauty are examples of social media campaigns that target body appreciation. Further research to discover how the media can facilitate positive body image outcomes is sorely needed.

References

Andrew, R., Tiggemann, M., & Clark, L. (2015). The protective role of body appreciation against media-induced body dissatisfaction. *Body Image, 15*, 98–104. doi:10.1016/j.bodyim. 2015.07.005

Archer, D., Iritani, B., Kimes, D. D., & Barrios, M. (1983). Face-ism: Five studies of sex differences in facial prominence. *Journal of Personality and Social Psychology, 45*, 725–735. doi:10.1037/0022-3514.45.4.725

Aubrey, J. S. (2006). Effects of sexually objectifying media on self-objectification and body surveillance in undergraduates: Results of two-year panel study. *Journal of Communication, 56*, 366–386. doi:10.1111/j.1460-2466.2006.00024.x

Aubrey, J. S. (2010). Looking good versus feeling good: An investigation of media frames of health advice and their effects on women's body-related self-perceptions. *Sex Roles, 63*, 50–63. doi:10.1007/s11199-010-9768-4

Aubrey, J. S., & Taylor, L. D. (2009). The role of lad magazines in priming men's chronic and temporary appearance-related schemata: An investigation of longitudinal and experimental findings. *Human Communication Research, 35*, 28–58. doi:10.1111/j.1468-2958.2008.01337.x

Barlett, C. P., Vowels, C. L., & Saucier, D. A. (2008). Meta-analyses of the effects of media images on men's body-image concerns. *Journal of Social and Clinical Psychology, 27*, 279–310. doi:10.1521/jscp.2008.27.3.279

Botta, R. A. (2003). For your health? The relationship between magazine reading and adolescents' body image and eating disturbances. *Sex Roles, 48*, 389–399. doi:0360-0025/03/0500-0389/0

Daniel, S., & Bridges, S. K. (2010). The drive for muscularity in men: Media influences and objectification theory. *Body Image, 7*, 32–38. doi:10.1016/j.bodyim.2009.08.003

Fredrickson, B. L., & Roberts, T. A. (1997). Objectification theory: Toward an understanding of women's lived experiences and mental health risks. *Psychology of Women Quarterly, 21*, 173–206. doi:10.1111/j.1471-6402.1997.tb00108.x

Fredrickson, B. L., Roberts, T., Noll, S. M., Quinn, D. M., & Twenge, J. M. (1998). That swimsuit becomes you: Sex differences in self-objectification, restrained eating, and math performance. *Journal of Personality and Social Psychology, 75*(1), 269–284. doi:10.1037/0022-3514.75.1.269

Fritz, N., & Paul, B. (2017). From orgasms to spanking: A content analysis of the agentic and objectifying sexual scripts in feminist, for women, and mainstream pornography. *Sex Roles, 77*, 639–652. doi:10.1007/s11199-017-0759-6

Harrison, K. (2000). The body electric: Thin-ideal media and eating disorders in adolescents. *Journal of Communication, 50*(3), 119–143. doi:10.1093/joc/50.3.119

Harrison, K. (2001). Ourselves, our bodies: Thin-ideal media, self-discrepancies, and eating disorder symptomatology in adolescents. *Journal of Social and Clinical Psychology, 20*, 289–323. doi:10.1521/jscp.20.3.289.22303

Harrison, K. (2003). Television viewers' ideal body proportions: The case of the curvaceously thin woman. *Sex Roles, 48*, 255–264. doi:10.1023/A:1022825421647

Harrison, K., & Cantor, J. (1997). The relationship between media consumption and eating disorders. *Journal of Communication, 47*, 40–67. doi:10.1111/j.1460-2466.1997.tb02692.x

Harrison, K., & Fredrickson, B. (2003). Women's sports media, self-objectification, and mental health in Black and White adolescent females. *Journal of Communication, 53*, 216–232. doi:10.1093/joc/53.2.216

Hatton, E., & Trautner, M. N. (2011). Equal opportunity objectification? The sexualization of men and women on the cover of *Rolling Stone*. *Sexuality & Culture, 15*(3), 256–278. doi:10.1007/s12119-011-9093-2

Holland, G., & Tiggemann, M. (2017). "Strong beats skinny every time": Disordered eating and compulsive exercise in women who post fitspiration on Instagram. *International Journal of Eating Disorders, 50*(1), 76–79. doi:10.1002/eat.22559

Mabe, A. G., Forney, K. J., & Keel, P. K. (2014). Do you "like" my photo? Facebook use maintains eating disorder risk. *International Journal of Eating Disorders, 47*, 516–523. doi:10.1002/eat.22254

McGrath, M. (2016, November 13). Selfie society: Are the Kardashians ruining womanhood? *The Independent*. Retrieved from https://www.independent.ie/style/voices/selfie-s ociety-are-the-kardashians-ruining-womanhood-35201655.html

Michaels, M. S., Parent, M. C., & Moradi, B. (2013). Does exposure to muscularity-idealizing images have self-objectification consequences for heterosexual and sexual minority men? *Psychology of Men & Masculinity, 14*(2), 175–183. doi:10.1037/a0027259

Mitchell, K. S., & Mazzeo, S. E. (2009). Evaluation of a structural model of objectification theory and eating disorder symptomatology among European American and African American undergraduate women. *Psychology of Women Quarterly, 33*, 384–395. doi:10.1111/j.1471-6402.2009.01516.x

Moradi, B., & Huang, Y. (2008). Objectification theory and psychology of women: A decade of advances and future directions. *Psychology of Women Quarterly, 32,* 377–398. doi:10.1111/j.1471-6402.2008.00452.x

Myers, T. A., & Crowther, J. H. (2007). Sociocultural pressures, thin-ideal internalization, self-objectification, and body dissatisfaction: Could feminist beliefs be a moderating factor? *Body Image, 4,* 296–308. doi:10.1016/j.bodyim.2007.04.001

Santarossa, S., & Woodruff, S. J. (2017). #SocialMedia: Exploring the relationships of social networking sites on body image, self-esteem, and eating disorders. *Social Media + Society, 3*(2), 1–10. doi:10.1177/2056305117704407

Slater, A., & Tiggemann, M. (2014). Media exposure, extracurricular activities, and appearance-related comments as predictors of female adolescents' self-objectification. *Psychology of Women Quarterly, 39*(3), 375–389. doi:10.1177/0361684314554606

Substance Abuse and Mental Health Services Administration. (2017, May). *Eating disorders.* Retrieved from https://www.samhsa.gov/treatment/mental-disorders/eating-disorders

Thompson, J., & Stice, E. (2001). Thin-ideal internalization: Mounting evidence for a new risk factor for body-image disturbance and eating pathology. *Current Directions in Psychological Sciences, 10,* 181–183. doi:10.1111/1467-8721.00144

Tiggemann, M. (2013). Objectification theory: Of relevance for eating disorder researchers and clinicians? *Clinical Psychologist, 17*(2), 35–45. doi:10.1111/cp.12010

Tiggemann, M., & Slater A. (2013). NetGirls: The Internet, Facebook, and body image concern in adolescent girls. *International Journal of Eating Disorders, 46,* 630–633. doi:10.1002/eat.22141

Tiggemann, M., & Slater, A. (2015). The role of self-objectification in the mental health of early adolescent girls: Predictors and consequences. *Journal of Pediatric Psychology, 40,* 704–711.

Tiggemann, M., & Ziccardo, M. (2015). "Exercise to be fit, not skinny": The effect of fitspiration imagery on women's body image. *Body Image, 15,* 61–67. doi:10.1016/j.bodyim.2015.06.003

Top 10 highest paid celebrities on Instagram. (2017). *Mediakix.* Retrieved from http://mediakix.com/2017/04/highest-paid-celebrities-endorsement-rates-on-instagram/

Tylka, T. L. (2015). No harm in looking, right? Men's pornography consumption, body image, and well-being. *Psychology of Men & Masculinity, 16,* 97–107. doi:10.1037/a0035774

Vandenbosch, L., & Eggermont, S. (2012). Understanding sexual objectification: A comprehensive approach toward media exposure and girls' internalization of beauty ideals, self-objectification, and body surveillance. *Journal of Communication, 62,* 869–887. doi:10.1111/j.1460-2466.2012.01667.x

Vandenbosch, L., & Eggermont, S. (2013). Sexualization of adolescent boys: Media exposure and boys' internalization of appearance ideals, self-objectification, and body surveillance. *Men and Masculinities, 16*(3), 283–306. doi:10.1177/1097184X13477866

CHAPTER NINE

The Bad Guys

Evil and Immorality in Media Entertainment

MARY BETH OLIVER & ARIENNE FERCHAUD

From ancient Greek writings to Shakespearean dramas to comic books to motion pictures—heroes and protagonists have formed the basis of entertainment throughout history, with audiences experiencing deep admiration and inspiration in response to portrayals of their beloved characters. But just as we relish cheering on our heroes, we also seem to take delight in believable and formidable villains who strike terror into the hearts of fictional characters and audiences alike. Freddy Kruger, the Wicked Witch of the West, Slender Man, and Darth Vader not only represent some of our deepest fears, but they also seem to elicit a fascination that keeps us returning to their evil clutches again and again. In short, the study of media entertainment would not be complete without a recognition of the importance of both "good guys" *and* "bad guys." This chapter focuses on evil and immoral characters in media entertainment. We first consider prototypical traits associated with media villains, and then turn our attention to how they function in audience enjoyment of narrative. We then turn our attention to accounts of individuals' attraction to media villains, including both individual differences that may be consequential, as well as media portrayals and contexts that may heighten audiences' attraction to the "dark side" of media characters. Finally, we end our chapter by considering possible effects of media villains on viewers' behaviors and attitudes, and looking at future directions, including ways to overcome potentially negative effects of villains on viewers, as well as implications of newer technologies.

Characteristics of Media Villains

Before jumping into an exploration of villainy, we first point out a distinction between a villain and an antagonist. While these character roles often overlap, a villain is marked by alignment with evil, willingness to commit immoral acts, and a general opposition to goodness. The morality of an antagonist, in contrast, need not necessarily be evil; the only key to an antagonist is that they are set up in opposition to a protagonist. In fact, many beloved villains may not function as antagonists, such as Hannibal Lecter in *Silence of the Lambs*, because they are not directly opposing the protagonist in the narrative. Thus, the terms villain and antagonist, while often used interchangeably, are not synonyms, and understanding this distinction is important to any exploration of villainy.

If villains and antagonists are not synonymous, then what best describes what is meant by a "villain"? As mentioned previously, perhaps the most central characteristic of media villains is their lack of morality. But as some scholars have noted, individuals often use different standards by which to judge morality (Haidt & Joseph, 2008). In particular, Haidt (2001) pointed out that five basic standards typically account for how individuals judge a person or behavior as good or bad: care/harm, loyalty, obedience to authority, fairness, and purity.

Among these five standards, villainous characters seem to most closely embody violations of care, as they often create feelings of dread, fear, and psychological and physical harm to their hapless victims (Eden, Oliver, Tamborini, Limperos, & Woolley, 2014). Indeed, Sanders (2005) employed the term "duplicity" to refer to the villainous character traits associated with danger, violence, and aggression. Such frightening villains are easy to envision, including the horrific clown, Pennywise, in Stephen King's *It*, the Penguin in the Batman series, and even the shark in *Jaws*.

In addition to being perceived as violating standards of care, Eden et al. (2014) reported that audiences also perceive villains as likely to violate standards of fairness. Perhaps such perceptions reflect strong correlations between hurting another person and treating them unfairly. However, some characters seem to be particularly known from their lack of fairness, including even characters from well-known Disney movies such as the evil stepsisters in *Cinderella*.

Although Eden et al. (2014) did not find that perceptions of impurity were particularly salient compared to other violations of morality, other research suggests that villainous characters are frequently "marked" in terms of some physical deformity. Indeed, Cantor (2008) argued that the distortion of "natural forms" (often in terms of physical characteristics) is one type of stimuli that appears to naturally elicit fright reactions, even among very young children. Consistent with this argument, Croley, Reese, and Wagner (2017) recently reported that among the top 10 villains and heroes identified by the American Film Institute, 60% of villains (compared to only

10% of heroes) were depicted as having some sort of dermatology condition, including patches of hair loss (alopecia), warts, facial scars, and discoloration of the skin (e.g., the Wicked Witch of the West). Grizzard, Huang, Fitzgerald, Ahn, and Chu's (2017) recent experimental research also highlights the importance of character appearance on the depiction of villains. In their study, participants rated their perceptions of a character based on visual appearance alone. The character depicted as frowning, having darker hair and clothes, and having a facial scar was rated as more villainous and immoral in comparison to an analogous character depicted identically except for a neutral expression, lighter hair and clothes, and having flawless skin. Importantly, these perceptions of the characters were based on appearance alone—not on any behavior that the character was depicted as enacting.

Finally, we note that although immoral and villainous characters are frequently depicted in overwhelmingly negative ways, many of these characters also seem to have a least one or more redeemable traits. For example, although Hannibal Lecter may be a cannibal, he also embodies an air of sophistication. Although Tony Soprano may be a mobster, he also loves his family and is a powerful leader. Although Dexter is a serial killer, he targets his violence toward other serial killers who are depicted as being particularly calloused. These three examples are among many that illustrate the ambiguity involved in many depictions of evil characters. Namely, in many instances, rather than referring to immoral characters as villains, many scholars have noted that a host of characters who do "bad" things may be more appropriately identified as "morally ambiguous characters" (MACs; Krakowiak & Oliver, 2012). In general, MACs refer to characters who may be motived by both moral and immoral concerns—some things they do are good and upstanding, whereas other things they do may be cruel or calloused.

To summarize, media villains are largely characterized in terms of their immoral behaviors. Further, many villains "look the part" in terms of some physical abnormality or visual aberration. At the same time, however, we would be remiss in suggesting that villains or "bad" characters are entirely bad. Rather, many villains seem to harbor some admirable traits such as power, intelligence, or even some semblance of moral standards, as twisted as they may be. With these complex traits in mind, we now turn our attention to how villains function in narratives, how they serve to heighten audience enjoyment, and how they may even be the object of admiration or liking.

Villains, Narratives, and Audience Enjoyment and Liking

To fully understand the ways in which villains often function in enjoyment and appreciation, it first becomes necessary to understand how they frequently function within narratives themselves. Villains are often characters we do not like or want to succeed. Yet their prevalence in stories that are highly regarded are voluminous and salient. If villains are disliked characters in narratives that are otherwise loved by audiences, how do they function in the story world? Ultimately, we believe that villains are frequently included, in part, because they provide obstacles for the heroes to overcome. In their representation of evil or injustice, they create a sense of uncertainty—will the heroes triumph over evil or will justice be restored? It is this uncertainty that frequently creates a sense of suspense that propels the reader or viewer through the story (Zillmann, 1980).

Disposition theory, moral disengagement, and media enjoyment. Although there are numerous accounts of audience enjoyment of entertainment (see, for example, Zillmann & Vorderer, 2000), dispositional accounts of audience enjoyment seem particularly relevant to questions regarding the role of media villains. In particular, affective disposition theory suggests that we, as viewers, enjoy narratives when good, moral characters succeed and/or when immoral characters fail (Bryant & Miron, 2002; Zillmann & Cantor, 1977). For example, few viewers of *Game of Thrones* would deny feeling pleasure when psychopathic man-child King Joffrey finally meets his end. Disposition theory suggests that when a character is truly bad, we take particular delight when they come to an unhappy ending.

Although the demise of bad or immoral characters is a frequent portrayal, it is also easy to come up with examples of "bad" or "immoral" characters who play the protagonist. Walter White in *Breaking Bad* is but one such example—a character who cooks and sells methamphetamine, who lies to his family, and who kills numerous people. But rather than hope for his demise, audiences generally cheer for Walter White, and particularly when he enjoys some success or he overcomes some obstacle. What might cause us to hope for good outcomes for characters who do immoral things? Why don't we harbor strong distaste for such characters and hope that they fail in their evil pursuits?

One approach to understanding these seemingly paradoxical audience responses is in terms of moral disengagement (Bandura, 1999). In brief, moral disengagement refers to the justification of immoral actions. For example, a person may hit or punch another person, but such aggression is understood if the hit or punched person was attempting an armed robbery. With this in mind, a number of scholars have provided arguments and evidence for the idea that audiences often engage in moral disengagement when protagonists are depicted as doing immoral things. For example, Raney (2004) proposed a revised and expanded model of disposition theory that recognizes that audiences often begin a narrative with some idea of who is the "good person" and who is the "bad person." For example, a person who decides to view *The Sopranos* likely knows in advance that Tony Soprano is the protagonist—the person the audience is supposed to like (or at least not intensely dislike). With these perceptions of the character already in place, the viewer then may see the character engage in immoral acts. However, rather than altering their perceptions of Tony Soprano, viewers may experience moral disengagement, providing a greater latitude of acceptance or justifying Tony Soprano's behaviors as somehow warranted or understandable (e.g.,. the other mobster was threatening Tony's family).

Additional models of anti-heroes stress how perceptions of the morality of characters and our judgements of them can shift and change throughout a narrative. For example, Sanders' (2010) character impression formation model (CIF) suggests that when first seeing a media character, viewers initially categorize the character based on existing schema (e.g., this person is a hero). If that categorization is confirmed, judgements will reflect category-based impressions. If disconfirmed, the viewer will seek additional information about the character's attributes to try to reconcile the discrepancy. In the case of anti-heroes, for example, such reconciliation may involve moral disengagement (see also Lee & Shapiro, 2014).

Identification with immoral characters. As we hope our previous discussion makes clear, characters who do bad things may not always be disliked. Sometimes we forgive them for their misdeeds or overlook their flaws. At other times, though, individuals may like immoral characters not because their anti-social behaviors are perceived as justifiable, but rather because their immorality is disregarded or because their immorality actually serves to heighten viewer affinities.

One such approach to understanding liking of immoral characters is via the notion of identification. In general, identification with media characters refers to the experience of seeing the (narrative) world *through the perspective* of the characters. Although research on media identification has generally examined media characters who harbor favorable traits, we believe that identification may also occur with villains or immoral characters. First, we believe that narrative engagement or transportation into a story world that often involves identification is enjoyable in and of itself. As Green, Brock, and Kaufman (2004) explained, the transportation experience does not depend upon whether or not the narrative elicits emotions of joy, sadness, or suspense. Rather, the experience of transportation (and identification) is one that, in itself, is gratifying. In other words, identifying with a character, be they good or evil, may be an experience that viewers find gratifying.

Relatedly, we also believe that the process of identification allows the viewer to "try on" different identities—including immoral ones—without having to actually engage in immoral acts or to suffer the ramifications for performing anti-social activities. In other words, we can virtually experience what it is like to be a thief, a thug, or a psychopath via identification. Why might such identification be gratifying for some viewers? On the one hand, we believe that seeing the world through the eyes of a "bad guy" may be simply a fun type of role-playing that allows us to take on a persona that we would otherwise dislike. On the other hand, as Klimmt, Hefner, and Vorderer (2009) explained in their discussion of video games, sometimes identifying with aggressive or violent characters may allow us to experience those aspects of the self that we believe need bolstering (e.g., hyper-masculinity predicts identification with violent game characters; see also Johnson, Slater, Silver, & Ewoldsen, 2016).

Still yet, some viewers may identify with villains and evil characters because the villains enact behaviors that viewers themselves admire or share. For example, Williams, McAndrew, Learn, Harms, and Paulhus (2001) examined entertainment preferences with elements of the "dark triad" personality traits. In brief, the dark triad refers to three traits—Machiavellianism, psychopathy, and narcissism, that are considered to be aversive and predictive of anti-social behavior (Furnham, Richards, & Paulhus, 2013). Williams and colleagues found that psychopathy in particular was associated with greater liking of violent sports, violent movies, and violent games, and lesser liking of non-violent sports and pro-social films. These results are consistent with Hoffner and Levine's (2005) meta-analysis showing that the enjoyment of violent and frightening entertainment was associated with lower levels of empathy and with higher levels of aggressiveness and sensation-seeking. Of course, enjoyment of violent content is not necessarily synonymous with liking of the villains that frequently populate such genres. Nevertheless, it stands to reason that that the association of anti-social traits with liking of violent genres likely reflects, at least to some degree, a liking of the characters who share such dispositions.

Effects of Media Portrayals of Villains

Our discussion of media villains thus far has primarily focused on the entertainment experience itself—how villains function in narratives and how audiences respond to immoral characters. However, we think it also important to consider the impact of these portrayals after the consumption has ended. In other words, how do media portrayals of villains effect viewers? Although this approach has been studied much less frequently than questions pertaining to audience enjoyment, here we consider three possible outcomes: increased aggression, increased tolerance of immorality, and increased stereotyping.

One of the prototypical characteristics of media villains is the threat they pose to other characters in the narrative. Often this threat takes the form of physical or psychological violence, and hence presents potential models for viewers engaging in observational learning or developing scripts regarding appropriate behaviors. In general, scholarship on the effects of violent content on viewers' aggressiveness generally stresses that viewers are unlikely to enact violence themselves unless the portrayal suggests that violence is appropriate and/or justified (Anderson & Bushman, 2002; Bandura, 2002).

Given this background and the notion that villainous behaviors, by definition, are ones that are immoral, one possible implication is that the portrayal of violent villains should not increase aggression and could possibly even *reduce* aggression. However, as mentioned previously, media villains, while anti-social, frequently harbor other favorable traits such as power, "coolness," or intelligence. Indeed, Kunkel et al.'s (1996) wide-scale content analysis of television portrayals of aggression showed that aggressive characters are frequently successful, rarely punished for their behaviors, and are often depicted as attractive both in terms of appearance and in terms of personality. Consequently, it stands to reason that favorable depictions of characters who commit violent acts may run the risk of increasing aggression, regardless of the role of hero or villain.

Related to the concern regarding aggression, an additional concern is that the consumption of content featuring immoral media characters may shift the viewer's moral compass. For example, in arguing that viewers sometimes engage in moral disengagement when viewing anti-heroes, Raney (2004) also expressed concerns that such engagement may transfer to perceptions of real-life moral violations:

> Does readily justifying the actions and motivations of characters in the fictional world enable or encourage us to do the same more often in reality? If we can and are willing to quickly stretch our real-world moral code for the sake of enjoyment, it seems reasonable to think that we can become conditioned to do so in real-world situations as well. Does the practice of moral disengagement that we participate in regularly with media fare serve as a training ground of sorts for moral disengagement in the real world? If so, our lack of moral reasoning in some fictional situations possibly prepares us to morally disengage in reality. (p. 364)

Finally, we believe it important to consider the possibility that the portrayal of media villains may lead to viewer stereotyping—particularly when villains are depicted as homogenous or as typically associated with certain social groups or with typical physical characteristics (see Sanders, this volume). Unfortunately, film and television has a history of portraying people of color as dangerous, villainous characters. For example, TV shows such as *The Godfather* and *The Sopranos* clearly associate organized crime with Italians. Likewise, numerous movies show a strong tendency for Arabs to be portrayed as terrorists. In these instances, and particularly when these villains are *not* given extensive characterization and exist merely as nameless obstacles for the heroes to face, viewers may begin to form associations between that group of people and the negative portrayal.

Summary and Future Directions

Throughout our chapter we have attempted to provide a broad overview of the "dark side" of media characters—villains that scare us, that we often despise, but that we sometimes admire and like. In addition to considering how these portrayals may enhance our enjoyment of media narratives, we have also pointed out some possible unintended consequences on audiences' aggression, moral judgments, and stereotyping.

As social scientific research on media villains continues to draw the attention of scholars, we believe that there are numerous potential avenues that may be particularly important to pursue. First, because we believe that the depictions of villains run some risk of negative outcomes, we think it important that scholars consider ways of cultivating greater media literacy that could inhibit or reduce negative effects. For example, recent research on media violence has shown that some forms of violent portrayals may be particularly meaningful to viewers in heightening their sensitivities and in making them more aware of human suffering (Bartsch & Mares, 2014). Consequently, we think that arming viewers with an awareness of the implications of immorality may represent a potentially profitable avenue by which to address concerns of the effects of villainous portrayals on viewer aggression and/or callousness.

Second, we think that further research on the active role of parents or co-viewers mitigating potentially deleterious effects is needed. For example, a host of studies have examined children's fright reactions to media portrayals, including portrayals of characters who may be portrayed as hideous in appearance (as many villains are portrayed; for an overview, see Cantor, 2008). In general, these studies suggest that for older children (approximately 7 years and older), stressing the unreality of the portrayals or the improbability of it happening in real life may be an effective strategy in reducing fear. In contrast, younger children (approximately 6 years and younger) may respond better to avoidance of the portrayal altogether, or at least distraction from it (e.g., Wilson, 1987). In terms of evil characters increasing aggression on viewers, scholarship has revealed mixed results. For example, Cantor and Wilson's (2003) overview of scholarship in this area found that whereas many interventions such as media-literacy curricula or prosocial programming reported that their approaches were effective in reducing aggression, boomerang effects were not uncommon. However, more recent longitudinal scholarship among adolescents reported that media-consumption patterns coupled with parental approaches may converge to be effective strategies (Fikkers, Piotrowski, & Valkenburg, 2017). Specifically, this research found that a combination of both parental restriction of overly violent content coupled with communication that recognized the child's autonomy and that explained the viewing options served to mitigate aggressive behaviors. Together, these studies point to the complexity of reducing harmful effects and the importance of considering a host of factors, including the age of the viewer, the communication with the child, and parental styles. Third, we believe it is imperative that scholars turn their attention to the implications of emerging technologies on audiences' responses to immoral characters. Throughout our chapter, we have explored the role of villains in what might be called "passive media" (e.g., film, television). However, there are numerous additional implications for villains in more contemporary, interactive entertainment such as games. For example, how does playing a villain and taking on their role affect viewers' senses of moral judgement? Does "performing" immoral actions heighten aggression because the user is provided the opportunity to practice and is encouraged to identify with the villainous character (Lin, 2013)? Or does being hoisted into the role of performing unjustified violence result in feelings of shame or guilt, instead (Hartmann, Toz, & Brandon, 2010)?

Finally, as technologies continue to evolve, we think it worth considering how media villains may not only be fictional. For example, the portrayal of "real life" violence for purposes of entertainment on streaming sites such as YouTube may constitute immoral "characters" that actually walk the streets (Mann, 2008). Likewise, contemporary villains may not only take the form of evil clowns and murderous mobsters, but may also populate our media content in the form of cyberbullies or trolls (see Savage & Deiss, this volume). As such, just as our technologies continue to grow and change, so do our theories of how villains function in our media diets.

In sum, villains have always been among us, as they form the basis of many beloved narratives. There seems to be no "good" without evil, no virtue without vice, and no decency without corruption. They capture our imaginations and haunt our dreams. But ultimately, villains—for (lack of) good or for evil—are likely with us to stay, and we, as the audience, are likely to continue to fear them and to sometimes secretly love and admire their devious cruelties.

References

Anderson, C. A., & Bushman, B. J. (2002). Human aggression. *Annual Review of Psychology, 53*, 27–51. doi:10.1146/annurev.psych.53.100901.135231

Bandura, A. (1999). Moral disengagement in the perpetration of inhumanities. *Personality and Social Psychology Review, 3*(3), 193–209. doi:10.1207/s15327957pspr0303_3

Bandura, A. (2002). Social cognitive theory of mass communication. In J. Bryant & D. Zillmann (Eds.), *Media effects: Advances in theory and research* (2nd ed., pp. 121–153). Mahwah, NJ: Lawrence Erlbaum Associates.

Bartsch, A., & Mares, M. L. (2014). Making sense of violence: Perceived meaningfulness as a predictor of audience interest in violent media content. *Journal of Communication, 64*(5), 956–976. doi:10.1111/jcom.12112

Bryant, J., & Miron, D. (2002). Entertainment as media effect. In J. Bryant & D. Zillmann (Eds.), *Media effects: Advances in theory and research* (2nd ed., pp. 549–582). Mahwah, NJ: Lawrence Erlbaum Associates.

Cantor, J. (2008). Fright reactions to mass medi. In J. Bryant & M. B. Oliver (Eds.), *Media effects: Advances in theory and research* (3rd ed., pp. 287–303). New York, NY: Routledge.

Cantor, J., & Wilson, B. J. (2003). Media and violence: Intervention strategies for reducing aggression. *Media Psychology, 5*(4), 363–403. doi:10.1207/s1532785xmep0504_03

Croley, J. A., Reese, V., & Wagner, R. F., Jr. (2017). Dermatologic features of classic movie villains: The face of evil. *JAMA Dermatology, 153*(6), 559–564. doi:10.1001/jamadermatol.2016.5979

Eden, A., Oliver, M. B., Tamborini, R., Limperos, A., & Woolley, J. (2014). Perceptions of moral violations and personality traits among heroes and villains. *Mass Communication and Society, 18*(2), 186–208. doi:10.1080/15205436.2014.923462

Fikkers, K. M., Piotrowski, J. T., & Valkenburg, P. M. (2017). A matter of style? Exploring the effects of parental mediation styles on early adolescents' media violence exposure and aggression. *Computers in Human Behavior, 70*, 407–415. doi:10.1016/j.chb.2017.01.029

Furnham, A., Richards, S. C., & Paulhus, D. L. (2013). The Dark Triad of personality: A 10 year review. *Social and Personality Psychology Compass, 7*(3), 199–216. doi:10.1111/spc3.12018

Green, M. C., Brock, T. C., & Kaufman, G. E. (2004). Understanding media enjoyment: The role of transportation into narrative worlds. *Communication Theory, 14*, 311–327. doi:10.1093/ct/14.4.311

Grizzard, M., Huang, J., Fitzgerald, K., Ahn, C., & Chu, H. (2017). Sensing heroes and villians: Character schema and the disposition-formation process. *Communication Research*. Advance online publication. doi:10.1177/0093650217699934

Haidt, J. (2001). The emotional dog and its rational tail: A social intuitionist approach to moral judgment. *Psychological Review, 108*(4), 814–834. doi:10.1037//0033-295x.108.4.814

Haidt, J., & Joseph, C. (2008). The moral mind: How five sets of innate intuitions guide the development of many culture-specific virtues, and perhaps even modules. In P. Carruthers, S. Laurence, & S. Stich (Eds.), *The innate mind. Foundations and the future* (Vol. 3, pp. 367–392). New York, NY: Oxford University Press.

Hartmann, T., Toz, E., & Brandon, M. (2010). Just a game? Unjustified virtual violence produces guilt in empathetic players. *Media Psychology, 13*(4), 339–363. doi:10.1080/152132 69.2010.524912

Hoffner, C. A., & Levine, K. J. (2005). Enjoyment of mediated fright and violence: A meta-analysis. *Media Psychology, 7*(2), 207–237. doi:10.1207/S1532785XMEP0702_5

Johnson, B. K., Slater, M. D., Silver, N. A., & Ewoldsen, D. R. (2016). Entertainment and expanding boundaries of the self: Relief from the constraints of the everyday. *Journal of Communication, 66*(3), 386–408. doi:10.1111/jcom.12228

Klimmt, C., Hefner, D., & Vorderer, P. (2009). The video game experience as "True" identification: A theory of enjoyable alterations of players' self-perception. *Communication Theory, 19*, 351–373. doi:10.1111/j.1468-2885.2009.01347.x

Krakowiak, K. M., & Oliver, M. B. (2012). When good characters do bad things: Examining the effect of moral ambiguity on enjoyment. *Journal of Communication, 62*(1), 117–135. doi:10.1111/j.1460-2466.2011.01618.x

Kunkel, D. D., Wilson, B. J., Linz, D., Potter, J., Donnerstein, E., Smith, S. L., ... Gray, T. (1996). Violence in television programming overall: University of California, Santa Barbara Study. In *National Television Violence Study: Scientific papers, 1994–1995* (pp. I1– I172). Studio City, CA: Mediascope.

Lee, T. K., & Shapiro, M. A. (2014). The interaction of affective dispositions, moral judgments, and intentionality in assessing narrative characters: Rationalist and intuitionist sequences. *Communication Theory, 24*(2), 146–164. doi:10.1111/comt.12031

Lin, J. H. (2013). Identification matters: A moderated mediation model of media interactivity, character identification, and video game violence on aggression. *Journal of Communication, 63*(4), 682–702. doi:10.1111/jcom.12044

Mann, B. L. (2008). Social networking websites: A concatenation of impersonation, denigration, sexual aggressive solicitation, cyber-bullying or happy slapping videos. *International Journal of Law and Information Technology, 17*(3), 252–267. doi:10.1093/ijlit/ean008

Raney, A. A. (2004). Expanding disposition theory: Reconsidering character liking, moral evaluations, and enjoyment. *Communication Theory, 14*, 348–369. doi:10.1093/ct/14.4.348

Sanders, M. (2005, May). *Evil is as evil does?: An examination of the impression content of media villains.* Paper presented at the annual meeting of the International Communication Association, New York.

Sanders, M. S. (2010). Making a good (bad) impression: Examining the cognitive processes of disposition theory to form a synthesized model of media character impression formation. *Communication Theory, 20*(2), 147–168. doi:10.1111/j.1468-2885.2010.01358.x

Williams, K., McAndrew, A., Learn, T., Harms, P., & Paulhus, D. L. (2001). *The Dark Triad returns: Entertainment preferences and antisocial behavior among narcissists, Machiavellians, and psychopaths.* Poster presented at the 109th Annual Convention of the American Psychological Association, San Francisco, CA.

Wilson, B. J. (1987). Reducing childrens emotional-reactions to mass-media through rehearsed explanation and exposure to a replica of a fear object. *Human Communication Research, 14*(1), 3–26. doi:10.1111/j.1468-2958.1987.tb00119.x

Zillmann, D. (1980). Anatomy of suspense. In P. Tannenbaum (Ed.), *The entertainment functions of television* (pp. 133–163). Hillsdale, NJ: Lawrence Erlbaum Associates.

Zillmann, D., & Cantor, J. R. (1977). Affective responses to the emotions of a protagonist. *Journal of Experimental Social Psychology, 13*, 155–165. doi:10.1037/0022-3514.35.8.587

Zillmann, D., & Vorderer, P. (Eds.). (2000). *Media entertainment: The psychology of its appeal.* Mahwah, NJ: Lawrence Erlbaum Associates.

CHAPTER TEN

Copycat Murder

Specious Mimesis or Natural Nemesis?

AARON R. BOYSON

After 50 years and over 1,000 studies (a conservative estimate), there is, I submit, not a single research study which is even remotely predictive of the Columbine massacre or similar high school shootings in the last few years.

—STUART FISCHOFF, ADDRESSING THE AMERICAN
PSYCHOLOGICAL ASSOCIATION (1999)

More people have died from ordinary homicide in the United States since 1950 than in all the wars in which the United States has ever fought, combined (Beeghley, 2003). Konrad Lorenz told us that the human species is uniquely good at killing each other (Lorenz, 1966), and criminologists tell us that we are uniquely good at killing each other in this country (Beeghley, 2003). The majority of homicides in the U.S. feature two young men, who get into an argument where a handgun is present, which is then used to take another's life (DOJ, 2011). All other modes of homicide are less common. Mass murders (where more than three people are killed at one time) are far less common, less than 1% of the total (DOJ, 2011). The same goes for school shootings, typically, although there is evidence they are increasing, as will be discussed later. What feels like the correct next sentence to write is that copycat crimes are also rare, and then go on to explain how they are important to study anyway.

Actually, it is not at all clear from the empirical literature that they are either rare or important to study. Surette (2014) reviewed the existing literature where criminal offenders were asked about the role of media in the perpetration of their crimes. Across 10 studies from 1971 to 2011, roughly 25% reported engaging in a copycat crime. In a multi-year investigation of news reports about copycat crime in the United States by the author, 86 credible copycat cases were located, with a total of 1,283 victims. The first report occurred in 1952. Movies were the most frequent copycat source mentioned ($n = 49$; news $n = 12$). More than one-third of the reports contain a specific imitative aspect, and in just more than half of the reports a movie's general influence was mentioned (For a copy of the comprehensive list of copycat news reports, contact author; see also Coleman, 2004; Helfgott, 2015). The single greatest inspirational media appears to be *Natural Born Killers* (*NBK*).

So, are they rare? Complicating that answer is that it is not yet clear what constitutes a copycat crime. Copycat researcher, Ray Surette, says a copycat crime must (1) be a pair of crimes linked through the media, (2) where the perpetrator must have been exposed to the media content, and (3) must have incorporated major elements of that crime into his or her crime (Surette, 2015). Much of the existing literature does not employ this definition. Surette (2015) acknowledges the definition makes them hard to locate.

Emulated news events would be harder to ascertain, like say, school shootings, compared to the copycat of a character in a movie, but increasingly school shootings are discussed as copycat acts. In fact, a Harvard School of Public Health report, published in 2014 (Cohen, Azrael, & Miller, 2014), had found that the rate of school shootings tripled since 2011. Prior to 2011, dating back to 1982, a school shooting happened roughly once every 200 days—but between 2011 and 2014, a school shooting occurred every 64 days, on average (Cohen, Azrael, & Miller, 2014). In the two year time period between the Sandy Hook Elementary School shooting in December, 2012 and the publication of Follman's report (December, 2014) there were 21 more deadly shootings in 16 states, featuring 32 victims, and 11 injured. Five shooters were killed, four of whom committed suicide (Follman, 2014).

Follman (2014) reported that there have been 74 copycat cases since the Columbine school shooting; 53 of which were thwarted by law enforcement, 14 of which were planned for the anniversary of the Columbine event, 13 of which involved plotters who hoped to surpass the amount of killings committed at Columbine, and 10 of which cited the Columbine shooters as heroes, idols, martyrs, or Gods. Indeed, school shootings seem to be on the rise, but that tragic event seems now to be a kind of anchor for other school shootings.

And yet, school shootings may overshadow an uncomfortable, larger trend. A recent analysis of a large sample of mass shootings (defined as four or more deaths) and school shootings from a *USA Today* dataset gathered between 2006 and 2013 suggests that there is one mass shooting every 12.5 days, while there is a school shooting on average every 31.6 days. There is evidence of a "cluster" effect lasting roughly 13 days, inciting .30 new incidents for mass shootings. Isolating school shootings, the effect lasts for the same amount of time, but incites .22 new incidents (Towers, Gomez-Lievano, Khan, Mubayi, & Castillo-Chavez, 2015). Simon (2007) analyzed press coverage before and after school shootings to find that there is also a predictable increase in bomb threats, which corresponded to news coverage of the event, accounting not just for actual copycat attempts but also threats.

At this point, the reader might be surprised to learn that many mass communication scholars doubt that the mass media can have a relationship to serious violence at all. Take, for instance, this excerpt from Stuart Fischoff's address to the American Psychology Association:

> But, as for making the explicit connection between on-screen mayhem by the bodies of Stallone and Schwarzenegger, the minds of Oliver Stone and Wes Craven, and real-life singular, serial, or mass murder, scientific psychology, albeit noble and earnest in its tireless efforts, has simply not delivered the goods. (Fischoff, 1999)

Fischoff is certainly not the only prominent voice to question the media violence aggression link (see, for example, "Scholars' Open Statement to the APA Task Force on Violent Media"; APA, 2013). In the main, this substantial cohort of scholars doubts the general aggression from media exposure link, not just its potential effect on serious violence or homicide.

Researchers and entertainment industry people alike have doubted the causal link for decades, though for different reasons. But if one pans out beyond aggression to consider if and how powerful the media can be, skepticism is harder to muster. For instance, the people at Smith and Wesson are likely not skeptical of the power of the mass media. Their 1955 Model 29 was a horrible selling handgun, about to be removed from production when it appeared in the hands of Clint Eastwood in *Dirty Harry*, after which the company could hardly produce enough of them. According to a *20th Century Fox* survey of movie buffs (Anthony, 2008), the Model 29, known colloquially as the .44 Magnum, is the second favorite film weapon of all time.

Or, consider the controversial disrobing 14 years ago that earned Janet Jackson a place in the *Guinness Book of World Records* for generating the most internet searches for any person in history. Of course, Justin Timberlake perpetrated the "wardrobe malfunction" in question, during the Super Bowl halftime show. Jawed Karim cited the malfunction as the main motive for his creation of *YouTube*, after being frustrated that the video could not be located easily online. *Merriam-Webster* subsequently entered "wardrobe malfunction" into its dictionary. But, perhaps the least well-known effect of that event is that, according to a *USA Today* report (Susman, 2004), nipple piercings increased, as did requests for the "sun shield" nipple ring that adorned Jackson's exposed breast. Consider again the power of media in light of this event: This one moment (1) affected attitudes toward piercing, and, with what to adorn that part of the body, (2) significantly altered our media technology, and (3) changed our language.

These examples, though anecdotal, reveal to us how powerful the mass media *can* be for *some*. Connecting media to serious violence and homicide is much harder, in part, because one cannot study homicide itself in the laboratory. But copycat researchers are confronted with yet a different problem: Scholars who study media violence often do not consider these instances to be anything more than idiosyncratic oddities. Gentile and Sesma (2003, p. 19) voiced this concern:

> These and countless other tragedies are the types of incidents that often come to mind when one mentions the effects of media violence on people. While such stories suggest an immediate, direct effect of media on perpetrators, these highly publicized "media effects" stories may actually demonstrate more about how not to think about media effects, because they oversimplify complex situations.

Their position is supported by direction from arguably the most influential of media violence theorists today, Albert Bandura. Known widely for the "Bobo-Doll" studies of imitative learning (see, for example, Bandura, Ross, & Ross, 1961), showing that, after a brief exposure to a mediated model engaging in violent actions, both imitated and abstracted violent responding increased. But the latter caught Bandura's fancy more. In his book detailing the foundations of social learning he claimed, "The conceptualization of modeling as simply response mimicry has left a legacy that minimizes the power of modeling and has limited the scope of research for many years" (Bandura, 1986). Twenty years after his initial imitation study, the index entry for "imitation" communicates the necessary point. It says, "see, abstract modeling." There is no index entry for copycat.

Ironically, Fischoff invoked Gordon Allport's call to the field from around the same time of Bandura's initial work in his address referenced earlier:

> Allport believed that psychology did not have the proper frame of reference to be able to predict, understand, and control human behavior. ... In order to predict critical behaviors, one must actually deal with those behaviors, not with analogues or overly simplified imitations that bear little resemblance to the real thing.

The extant literature suggests that media violence researchers heeded Bandura rather than Allport. So if copycat homicide is (overall) a rare form of murder, and leading scholars in the field have cautioned that focusing on them contributes to misunderstandings in media influence and stunts the growth of theory, why is this chapter being written at all?

For one thing, some research does connect media violence to homicide. Centerwall's (1989) epidemiological study accurately predicted both the amount and when homicides would increase after South Africa introduced TV, based on homicide increases following its introduction in Canada and the United States. He concluded that 10,000 homicides each year in the U.S. are attributable to the influence of television. For another, research on individual events points to a short-term influence on homicide. Phillips (1983) found that when heavyweight prize fights were televised broadly, increases in homicide followed roughly three to four days later, leading him to conclude that such events elevate homicide by about 10%—new ones too, not just inevitable ones moved ahead on some time-line of murder. More recently, Peterson-Manz (2002) analyzed 9,442 homicide reports from 1990 to 1994 and found that front-page homicides significantly increased subsequent homicides in the two-weeks following the reports. These studies provide some basis for connecting media violence to homicide, although they say far less about copycat murder.

The Copycat Notion

Increasingly, copycat criminality is a subject of interest. At least, *Google's* NGram of the word copycat shows a precipitous increase in the word's appearance in print since 1980. The term is an evolution of an idea by a much older name. Mimesis is the Aristotelian term referring to the situation when art imitates life. Oscar Wilde preferred the opposing view, when in 1889 he said, "Life imitates art far more than art imitates life" (Wilde, 2010). As a general philosophy, his notion is called anti-mimesis. Perhaps the first documented case of anti-mimesis dates back to the 18th century, stemming from Goethe's (1774) novel *The Sorrows of Young Werther*. That book inspired what came to be known as "Werther Fever," or the tendency to dress in yellow pants and blue coats and host parties as the characters had done. Noting also that there were documented cases of imitative suicides from *Werther*, sociologist David Phillips (1978) would later coin the term "The Werther Effect," to describe the modern phenomenon whereby news coverage of suicides, especially by celebrities, begets more suicide.

A century after Goethe's novel, the "Jack the Ripper" murders would provide another widely mediated event with copycat connections. Between 1888 and 1891, four copycat murders were believed to have occurred in the Whitechapel district of London, which, incidentally, is around the same time the word "copycat" first appears in print (Seigelberg, 2011). No doubt the Whitechapel murders influenced Gabriel Tarde, perhaps the first criminologist to theorize about imitative crimes, referring to them as "criminal fashions." He coined the term *suggesto-imitative assaults,* and the phrase "epidemics of crime follow the line of the telegraph" (Tarde, 1912). He composed three laws of imitation, summarized well by Wilson (1954, p. 6):

> Tarde's explanation of crime was simply the application of the general laws governing social relations, as he conceived them, to the phenomena of crime. All science, in his view, rested upon the recognition of certain similarities in the world of phenomena or of repetitions of movement or being. Periodic movement is the form of repetition in the physical world, and heredity is that shown by life in the world. Correlative and equivalent to these is imitation in the world of social relations. Crime, like any other social phenomenon, starts as a fashion and becomes a custom. Its intensity varies directly in proportion to the contacts of persons. Its spread is in the direction of the superior to the inferior. Every imitation or imitative ray, in the language of Tarde, tends to spread and enlarge itself indefinitely, whence arise interferences between these rays of imitation, thus producing contradictions or oppositions. When two mutually exclusive fashions come together, one tends to be substituted for the other. When two fashions which are not mutually exclusive come together, the distinct rays of imitation combine or complement each other and so by adaptation organize themselves into a larger scheme.

Interestingly, both Tarde and Wilde believed in the inevitability of imitation, that there is an impulse toward it, which is in some sense unavoidable. Simplified, Tarde's three laws are (1) men (sic, although it generally is) imitate others in proximal clusters, (2) inferiors repeat superiors, and (3) new methods of killing will displace one another.

A noticeable gap in the literature exists between Tarde and research today. This gap may be explained in part, by Bandura's redirection of the field away from imitation. Most work on copycat acts is recent and comes from outside mass communication or psychology. For example, Meloy and Mohandie (2001) relied on forensic research to detail media connections in seven copycat homicides. To summarize one example they found, in 1992 a man dressed up as Arnold Schwarzennegger's character from *Terminator Two: Judgment Day,* walked into his old high school in Yuba County, California and shot and killed three students and one teacher, taking 86 others hostage. His appearance and his weaponry were designed to match the film, and police found the soundtrack from the movie loaded into his home stereo set to play very loudly. In a second case, the perpetrator was known to have a close connection to violent films, including *Demolition Man* which he viewed twice, within an hour of a killing. During the subsequent murder, he enucleated (or, gouged out eyes with a knife) his victim by stabbing him 74 times and then breaking off the tip of the knife in the skull, as was done in the film. In the court case, it was the forensic psychologist's opinion that *Demolition Man* played a copycat role for three reasons: (1) temporal proximity of the film viewing and the murder, (2) scene specificity of the stabbing, and (3) the rarity of killing another person in this manner among all homicides.

Analyses of five other cases like these lead Meloy and Mohandie (2001) to posit five key concepts relevant to understanding copycat homicide in their view: (1) *aggression immersion* (i.e., heightened intensity of exposure, usually co-morbid with repetitive viewing, but also including the substitution of fantasy for mundane life, and the use of stimuli for mood management and character identification); (2) *theme consistency* (i.e., a pattern of thought, feeling or behavior in the perpetrator which closely parallels the violent actor and his performance in the stimulus); (3) *scene specificity* (i.e, displaying imitation of certain words, gestures, dress, or exact behavior of the actor before or during the commission of the crime); (4) *repetitive viewing*; and (5) *self-editing* (i.e., selective exposure and/ or re-exposure to portions of a stimulus).

Meloy and Mohandie's (2001) concepts have not been developed into a scale for measuring copycat behavior, although attempts to do so would be warranted. Surette developed a copycat score, generated from five questions about copycat acts, which has been administered to incarcerated criminals. One question, "Can you ever recall having to commit the same crime that you have seen, read, or heard about in the media?" In a survey of 68 juvenile offenders (Surette, 2002), 18 answered yes (26.5%). The other four questions are suggestive (i.e., "about trying the same crime," or, "have you ever watched a movie and afterwards gone out looking for a fight?"). Interestingly, only 41.2% of the sample answered no to all five copycat questions (also, only 7% answered all five yes). In this particular study the copycat score was correlated positively with those who were incarcerated for a gun-related offense and with having already attempted a copycat crime.

More recently, Chadee, Surette, Chadee, & Brewster (2017) sampled 373 per-sons from detention centers at high- and low-risk high schools to examine a larger copycat model which included variables similar to those developed by Meloy and Mohandie (2001), including narrative persuasion (akin to aggression immersion), and character identification. Both variables had significant, positive relationships with a pre-existing motivation to commit a copycat crime, which in turn signifi-cantly predicted the self-reported likelihood to commit a future crime (asked un-der the guise, "If you knew you wouldn't get caught, would you …"). Surprisingly, convicted criminals and non-criminal juveniles alike admitted to media influence and copycat motivation (importantly, Surette is measuring all forms of copycat crime in this study, not just homicide).

Helfgott (2015), together with Meloy and Mohandie (2001) and Surette (2015) each have offered theoretical mechanisms or models to explain copycat crime or murder. Helfgott (2015) provides an analysis of some unique cinematic features of *NBK*, noting that the whole film is based on an actual couple who went on a murder spree in the late 50s. Helfgott defines *NBK* as a loop, a kind of replay, within the film itself. Director Oliver Stone's cinematography often looped violent actions in slow motion, from different camera angles. The Columbine tragedy might have been looped in a slightly different way. It became such a big story, the news itself became a subject of discussion, a phenomenon called "what-a-story" (Berkowitz, 2000; Frank, 2003) when the coverage of a story becomes the story itself, its own sort of loop. These aspects probably deserve serious attention by researchers, as both *NBK* and Columbine seem to have a stronger than usual potential for stimulating copycat homicides.

Surette's individual model (2015) relies heavily on traditional media effects theories, such as social information processing theory notions (Huesmann & Taylor, 2006), social cognitive theory (Bandura, 1986), and priming theory (Berkowitz, 1984) and the general aggression model (Anderson & Bushman, 2002). Surette's model, like other media effects theories, shows the importance of how someone orients to the media. Similarly, Helfgott (2015) cites 13 distinct reasons having to do with how the individual is oriented to media in the first place, many of which are standard-brand media effects constructs, including: (1) trust/realism in media, (2) extent of media interaction, (3) identification with perpetrators, and (4) cognitive script-building.

Conclusion

There now seems to be enough empirical research to call into question the certitude in the quote that began this chapter. Like it or not, anti-mimesis, or life imitating art, seems to be an increasingly tragic social problem for society to solve, and an increasingly urgent problem for scholars to explain. While the purpose of this chapter was to review the research and fit it into some historical context perhaps a little theorizing is permissible here at the close. Three explanatory ideas are posited next.

First, consider a recent shooting at the time of this writing (in 2018) at Santa Fe High School. In the early reporting about the shooter's motives—who allegedly spared some victims so his "story" could be told—there is evidence of copycat behavior, especially linking to the Columbine incident. One article on hand shows the perpetrator's face, talks about his demeanor both prior to and during the attack, and explains that he was bullied by some, including perhaps his football coaches. A three-part model could be surmised, wherein the news media presents the perpetrator as a victim, connects him or her to a sub-culture of violence, and which is then used to morally justify the injurious behavior. Three theories support each part of this model. A) The news media, which often is encouraged to report on events contextually, as opposed to episodically (see, Iyengar, 1994), may well do so. But this may have an unintended effect of victimizing the perpetrators. B) By connecting personality or behaviors to others known to be violent, they may reinforce the legitimacy of a subculture of violence, which is a general theory of violence in criminology. C) In telling the perpetrator's "story," the news media can tacitly suggest that the violence was in some sense justified morally, as in the case of the Santa Fe shooter who allegedly was bullied. This aspect is supported by a host of research following from Bandura's social cognitive theory known as moral disengagement. There are aspects of all three of these tendencies in the news media's coverage of the Santa Fe shooting thus far.

Second, the Columbine shooters produced their own video for a school project called *Hitmen for Hire*, in which they acted out killing students in the school. Using both Meloy and Mohandie (2001) and Helfgott (2015) as guides, "texts" such as this that are available should be compared not just for similarities in matching behavior or style, but also in cinematic features. Perhaps it is not the *what* but *how* media violence is presented that primarily stimulates copycat murders.

Third, and finally, when it comes to attention paid to mass or school shootings. The story is about the news, which is, at bottom, a signal of *what* and *how* much a culture or community thinks about an event. Maguire, Weatherby, and Mathers (2002) conducted a content analysis of school shootings on nightly newscasts and found that two main trends emerged: the most violent school shootings receive the most coverage, and that these cases reflect a "herd-mentality" nature of the media itself (i.e., encouraging "what-a-story"). Tufekci (2012) has made a call to action about how not to cover them. Newsmakers voluntarily adopted their own standards when it comes to suicide reporting, guided by the Centers for Disease Control and the National Institutes of Mental Health.

Perhaps as a result, Tufekci (2012) uses that precedence to stress that the media avoid four things when covering copycat or copycat-potential stories. First, law enforcement should not release the methods or the manner of the killings. Second, law enforcement should work to shut down any social media profiles the perpetrators may have. Third, the name of the killer(s) should not be revealed immediately. Finally, survivors and loved ones should not be interviewed in their most vulnerable moments.

Recall the first paragraph of this chapter; the United States has a murder problem which deserves an all-hands-on-deck approach to solving it. Perhaps while the research continues to make gains in understanding copycat criminality, it would be prudent and humane to err on the side of reducing future deaths by heeding Tufekci's call (2012). After all, both Tarde and Wilde believe we are dealing with natural born imitators. If they are right, it would be tragic if the media environment encouraged natural born imitators to become natural born killers. Perhaps that is why Wilde also said, "Be yourself; everyone else is already taken."

References

Anderson, C. A., & Bushman, B. J. (2002). Human aggression. *Annual Review of Psychology, 53,* 27–51.

Anthony, J. (2008, January 21). What are your top 10 movie weapons? *The Guardian.* Retrieved from https://www.theguardian.com/film/filmblog/2008/jan/21/top10movieweapons

Bandura, A. (1986). *Social foundations of thought & action: A social cognitive theory.* Englewood Cliffs, NJ: Prentice-Hall.

Bandura, A., Ross, D., & Ross, S. H. (1961). Transmission of aggression through imitation of aggressive models. *Journal of Abnormal and Social Psychology, 63*(3), 575–582.

Berkowitz, D. (2000). Doing double duty: Paradigm repair and the Princess Diana what-a-story. *Journalism, 1*(2), 125–143.

Berkowitz, L. (1984). Some effects of thoughts on anti- and prosocial influences of media events: A cognitive-neoassociation analysis. *Psychological Bulletin, 95*(3), 410–427.

Centerwall, B. S. (1992). Television and violence: The scale of the problem and where to go from here. *Journal of the American Medical Association, 267,* 3059–3063.

Chadee, D., Surette, R., Chadee, M., & Brewster, D. (2017). Copycat crime dynamics: The interplay of empathy, narrative persuasion, and risk with likelihood to commit future criminality. *Psychology of Popular Media Culture, 6*(2), 142–158.

Cohen, A. P., Azrael, D., & Miller, M. (2014, October 15). Rate of mass shootings has tripled since 2011, Harvard research shows. *Mother Jones.* Retrieved from https://www.mother-jones.com/politics/2014/10/mass-shootings-increasing-harvard-research/

Coleman, L. (2004). *The copycat effect: How the media and popular culture trigger the Mayhem in tomorrow's headlines.* New York, NY: Paraview Pocket Books.

Dressler, D. (1961, December 10). Case of the copycat criminal. *New York Times,* pp. 42 and 47.

Fischoff, S. (1999, August 21). *Psychology's Quixotic quest for the media violence connection.* Invited address at the Annual Convention of the American Psychological Association. Boston, MA. Retrieved from http://www.apadivisions.org/division-46/about/fischoff-media-psy-chology.pdf

Follman, M. (2014, December 9). America's many fatal shootings since Newtown. *Mother Jones.* Retrieved from https://www.motherjones.com/politics/2014/12/fatal-school-shootings-data-since-sandy-hook-newtown/

Frank, R. (2003). These crowded circumstances: When pack journalists bash pack journalism. *Journalism, 4*(4), 441–458.

Gentile, D. A., & Sesma, A., Jr. (2003). Developmental approaches to understanding media effects on individuals. In D. A. Gentile (Ed.), *Media violence & children: A complete guide for children* (pp. 19–37). Westport, CT: Praeger.

Helfgott, J. B. (2015). Criminal behavior and the copycat effect: Literature review and theoretical framework for empirical investigation. *Aggression and Violent Behavior, 22*, 46–64.

Huesmann, L. R., & Taylor, L. D. (2006). The role of media violence in violence behavior. *Annual Review of Public Health, 27*, 393–415.

Iyengar, S. (1994). *Is anyone responsible? How television frames political issues.* Chicago, IL: University of Chicago Press.

Maguire, B., Mathers, R. A., & Weatherby, G. A. (2002). Network news coverage of school shootings. *The Social Science Journal, 39*, 465–470.

Meloy, J. R., & Mohandie, K. (2001). Investigation the role of screen violence in specific homicide cases. *Journal of Forensic Science, 46*(5), 1113–1118.

Peterson-Manz, J. (2002). *Copycats: Homicide and the press.* Dissertation Abstracts International (Unpublished doctoral dissertation). Claremont Graduate University.

Phillips, D. P. (1974). The influence of suggestion on suicide: Substantive and theoretical implications of the Werther effect. *American Sociological Review, 39*(3), 340–354.

Phillips, D. P. (1982). The impact of fictional television stories on U.S. adult fatalities: New evidence on the effect of the mass media on violence. *American Journal of Sociology, 87*, 1340–1359.

Phillips, D. P. (1983). The impact of mass media violence on U.S. homicides. *American Sociological Review, 48*, 560–568.

Siegelberg, B. (2011, August 12). What a copycat: Why do we call imitators "cats"? Why not monkeys? *Slate.* Retrieved from http://www.slate.com/articles/news_and_politics/explainer/2011/08/what_a_copycat.html

Simon, A. (2007). Application of fad theory to copycat crimes: Quantitative data following the Columbine massacre. *Psychological Reports, 100*, 1233–1244.

Surette, R. (2002). Self-reported copycat crime among a population of serious and violence juvenile offenders. *Crime & Delinquency, 48*(1), 46–69.

Surette, R. (2015). *Media, crime, and criminal justice.* Stamford, CT: Cengage Learning.

Susman, G. (2004, February 3). Janet Jackson apologizes for Super Bowl stunt. *Entertainment Weekly.* Retrieved from ew.com/article/2004/02/03/janet-jackson-apologizes-super-bowl-stunt/

Tarde, G. (1912). *Penal philosophy.* Boston, MA: Little, Brown.

Towers, S., Gomez-Lievano, A., Khan, M., Mubayi, A., & Castillo-Chavez, C. (2015). Contagion in mass killings and school shootings. *PLoS One, 10*(7). doi:10.1371/journal.pone.0117259

Tufekci, Z. (2012, December 19). The media needs to stop inspiring copycat murders. Here's how. *The Atlantic.* Retrieved from https://www.theatlantic.com/national/archive/2012/12/the-media-needs-to-stop-inspiring-copycat-murders-heres-how/266439/

Wilde, O. (2010). *The decay of lying and other essays.* London: Penguin Books.

Wilson, M. S. (1954). Pioneers in criminology I—Gabriel Tarde. *Journal of Criminal Law and Criminology, 45*(1), 3–11.

CHAPTER ELEVEN

The Dark Side of Social Networking Sites

JESSE FOX, GUANJIN ZHANG, & JESSICA FRAMPTON

Social networking sites (SNSs) have become popular because they provide quick and easy access to social connections, entertainment, and news. Research has identified a number of benefits associated with SNS use, including friendship maintenance, social capital generation, and identity development (see reviews by Wilson, Gosling, & Graham, 2012, and Zhang & Leung, 2015). Users and researchers alike, however, tend to overlook the dark side of SNSs. Users can present themselves in a way that is more idealized than the true self or be completely deceptive. These idealized disclosures can lead to negative effects for the audience, including negative social comparisons, envy, loneliness, and depression. Posters may also have negative experiences as their content can result in negative feedback posted by other users, conflict, or even terminated relationships. These negative outcomes may be far-reaching given the audience on an SNS can include diverse groups of friends, family, co-workers, and even the general public.

This chapter will explain why SNSs are different from offline contexts and other online environments. It will then discuss existing research about negative psychological and social experiences tied to SNSs and clarify how the features of SNSs may exacerbate these issues. Finally, it will provide some insight on how users can mitigate or avoid some of these dark side phenomena while still capitalizing on the social benefits of SNSs.

What's Different about Social Networking Sites?

Social networking sites are defined by three properties. Users must be able to (1) create a personal profile that (2) they can link to other profiles, and (3) they must be able to identify others' connections within the broader network (boyd & Ellison, 2008). Additionally, SNSs feature distinct affordances compared to face-to-face interaction or other computer-mediated channels (Fox & McEwan, 2017; Treem & Leonardi, 2013). *Affordances* are the properties of an object that enable specific actions (Gibson, 1979), and how people perceive these affordances influences their behaviors. Affordances determine how social information is conveyed and transmitted throughout the network, which influences how users receive, interpret, and are affected by this information.

The affordances of SNSs make them optimal for social interaction and information sharing. *Association* enables network members, no matter how disparate or geographically distant, to recognize each other's presence and typically view each other's content through a common node or "friend." *Visibility* or *privacy* means that information that was not easily accessible or publicized previously is now shared among the network. SNSs are designed to afford various methods of *social feedback* such as comments, "likes," or emojis. Because of the prevalence of mobile devices, SNSs are high on *accessibility*: anyone can create and maintain an account, and information can be obtained at any time in any place with internet access. Finally, SNSs facilitate *scalability*. Through easy sharing, retweeting, and reblogging, posted content can be widely disseminated. Throughout this chapter, we will also discuss other relevant affordances of computer-mediated communication, including *asynchronicity, editability, anonymity, persistence,* and *bandwidth* (Fox & McEwan, 2017; Treem & Leonardi, 2013).

Thus, it is important to consider that the same affordances that allow us to share experiences and memories amongst friends also have the potential to challenge, complicate, or damage relationships. As the following sections will demonstrate, many studies have shown that SNSs can initiate, promote, and exacerbate the dark side.

Impression Management, Context Collapse, and Social Feedback

One of the most popular areas of research on social media is self-presentation and impression management. As social beings, humans are faced with a constant pressure to maintain a positive image among others to achieve social goals (Goffman, 1959).

The *asynchronous* nature of computer-mediated communication enables *editability*: people can modify their self-presentation because they have time to think about and revise messages before sharing with an audience. According to the hyperpersonal model, these affordances enable *selective self-presentation*, in which a more idealized version of the self is presented online compared to face-to-face interaction (Walther, 1996).

Although asynchronicity and editability make it easier to maintain a desirable self-presentation, another affordance complicates the process. On SNSs, the association of many different audiences—which may include close friends, acquaintances, family, co-workers, people from the past, or unknown second-degree network ties—creates *context collapse* (Vitak, 2012). Across these groups, we have different roles and may maintain different versions of the self. For example, Sarah is a party animal among her friends, but a stern boss at work. Offline, we would not expect these groups to converge, but on an SNS, everyone is connected. Versions of the self that may normally only be visible to a certain segment of one's social network are now made visible to everyone.

Having to manage various impressions across diverse groups can create tension and stress for SNS users. Given there are inevitable variations in self-presentation to different groups, users may be seen as inconsistent or inauthentic in their interactions with different people. Additionally, association enables individuals from different groups to identify each other and interact on the SNS, which may create tension or provide opportunities for relational interference. For example, Romeo may be upset to find that his family members expressed their disapproval of his relationship through comments on his girlfriend Juliet's posts. It is unlikely this social feedback would have been visible to Juliet's friends or co-workers in another context.

Social feedback is an essential element of the selective self-presentation process (Ellison, Heino, & Gibbs, 2006). Unlike most face-to-face exchanges, feedback on an SNS is visible to one's entire social network and may persist online indefinitely. Positive feedback (e.g., "likes," compliments, supportive comments) is socially rewarding, boosts self-esteem, and encourages further posting of similar content, whereas undesirable feedback (e.g., criticism, mockery, indifference) typically evokes negative affect (Valkenburg, Peter, & Schouten, 2006). Over time, individuals may learn to hide aspects of their identity or stay silent rather than face social disapproval or rejection (Fox & Warber, 2015). For example, LGBTQ adolescents may avoid expressing their identity on SNSs because they fear getting teased, condemned, or ostracized by hostile peers, relatives, or other network members. In extreme cases, often bolstered by the ability for users to maintain *anonymity*, negative feedback can manifest as harassment, trolling, or cyberbullying, all of which have been associated with diminished well-being (see Savage & Deiss, this volume).

Psychological Well-Being

SNSs have raised concerns about their impact on psychological well-being, which includes subjective happiness and feelings of meaningfulness in life (Ryan & Deci, 2001). Diminished psychological well-being may manifest as anxiety, loneliness, or depression. Intuitively, it seems that platforms designed to help people connect with each other and engage in more social interaction would mitigate distressful, lonely, or depressed feelings. Several studies have indicated, however, that SNSs do not necessarily function as stress buffers (e.g., Choi & Toma, 2014; Kross et al., 2013; Verduyn et al., 2015). Here, we consider three explanations. First, SNSs themselves can divert time and attention, potentially yielding negative effects. Second, SNSs give the illusion of being a positive and supportive environment but do not necessarily function that way in practice. Finally, posted content may evoke negative feelings further magnified by the affordances of SNSs.

Tethered to SNSs

Even if users do not encounter negative content, SNSs can evoke stress because of their demands on our time and attention. Because of the accessibility of SNSs, users may feel anxious and pressured to keep up with the near constant stream of social information. In part, this anxiety may be tied to a fear of missing out (FoMO) on others' rewarding experiences, which is associated with greater SNS use. Stress resulting from FoMO and the need to constantly check SNSs can ultimately lead to burnout, depression, and anxiety (Przybylski, Murayama, DeHaan, & Gladwell, 2013; Reinecke et al., 2017).

Although SNSs may seem like a fun and leisurely activity, devoting too much time and attention to SNSs necessarily detracts from other obligations. Spending more time on SNSs has been associated with a variety of negative outcomes, including lower work productivity, lower academic performance, lower life satisfaction, and higher levels of anxiety and depressive symptoms (Rosen, Cheever, & Carrier, 2015; Woods & Scott, 2016). SNS use can also have an impact on physical health. For example, using social media at night can interfere with a good night's sleep (Woods & Scott, 2016).

In extreme cases, being unable to resist the urge to post can have deadly consequences. For example, a woman was taking selfies and posting to Facebook while driving on a U.S. interstate. Immediately after posting about the song she was listening to—"The happy song makes me so HAPPY"—she crossed the divider, killing herself and injuring another driver (Withnall, 2014).

Disclosure and Support Seeking

Another issue is that although SNSs are often seen as a way to communicate with "friends," their affordances do not necessarily make this an optimal platform for sharing negative experiences or seeking social support. Expressing emotions is a common way for people to cope, but doing so on SNSs may backfire. First, disclosing negative experiences on SNSs increases, rather than diminishes, negative affect (Bevan, Gomez, & Sparks, 2014; Choi & Toma, 2014). Second, SNSs encourage forming and maintaining weak ties (Ellison, Steinfield, & Lampe, 2007). Although users usually have a substantial number of "friends" or "followers," many of these relationships are superficial (i.e., weak ties) rather than close (i.e., strong ties, such as family and good friends). Thus, the majority of network members may not feel compelled to offer social support. Over time, they may block, mute, defriend, or unfollow individuals who frequently post negative self-disclosures or seek help (Fox & Moreland, 2015). Third, even if network members wish to offer genuine consolation, there is limited *bandwidth* for providing support. Posts on many SNSs are limited in terms of length, so thoughtful messages may be difficult to convey. On an SNS, there is no physical shoulder to cry on or comforting hugs. The type of interactions that are normative on SNSs (brief comments, "likes," emojis) are typically not suited for offering meaningful social support.

A final issue is that posting about loneliness or depression may elicit negative evaluations from other network members. Given loneliness and depression are often socially stigmatized, sharing those feelings on an SNS can be seen as inappropriate, desperate, and unprofessional (Choi & Toma, 2014). Posting negative feelings can evoke negative feedback from network members (Forest & Wood, 2012), which may be counterproductive and make the poster feel worse. A lack of reaction from one's network could also be damaging, as the individual may feel ignored and more isolated. Another consideration is that posting negative feelings could have a broader and more long-lasting impact on the individual. Due to the affordances of association, persistence, and scalability, such posts could jeopardize the person's current or future efforts to make friends, initiate a romantic relationship, or find a job.

Negative Experiences with SNS Content

Social Comparison. Social comparison on SNSs is another cause of decreased psychological well-being (e.g., Chou & Edge, 2012; Lee, 2014). Upward comparisons involve evaluating oneself in relation to others who are better off, whereas downward comparisons involve judging against those who are worse off (Festinger, 1954; Wills, 1981). SNSs enable people to make both upward and downward social comparisons in a variety of domains given the accessibility and visibility of social information. For example, people can go to another user's profile to compare the number of friends they have, their physical attractiveness, and their careers (Fox & Moreland, 2015; Haferkamp & Krämer, 2011). Social comparisons are not always part of the dark side of social media, as downward social comparisons can be used to improve one's mood (Johnson & Knobloch-Westerwick, 2014). However, research shows that social comparisons to others on SNSs tend to be negative and can lead to lower self-esteem, lower life satisfaction, body dissatisfaction, lower perceived social competence, anxiety, and depression (de Vries & Kühne, 2015; Fox & Vendemia, 2016; Frison & Eggermont, 2016; Lee, 2014). Moreover, the need to impress or look better than others on social media can be a dangerous motivation. Several people have died trying to capture the "ultimate selfie" to share on social media. For example, a teenage girl in Romania was electrocuted trying to snap a selfie on top of a train; in another case, two Russian soldiers were killed as they tried to snap a selfie while holding a live grenade (Lovitt, 2016).

Envy. Envy is a negative emotion that is related to upward social comparisons made via SNSs. Envy is an unpleasant feeling of inferiority and resentment in response to coveting an attribute possessed by another person (Smith & Kim, 2007). Envy is especially likely to be evoked when social information indicates that a peer is superior in a domain that is relevant to the self. Given the nature of selective self-presentation on SNSs, SNS users are likely exposed to idealized images of peers and may experience envy as a result (Krasnova, Widjaja, Buxmann, Wenninger, & Benbasat, 2015). Unfortunately, envy stemming from SNS use has been linked to depression and decreased affective well-being (Tandoc, Ferrucci, & Duffy, 2015; Verduyn et al., 2015).

Jealousy. Jealousy is the feelings, thoughts, and actions that occur in response to a perceived threat to a valued relationship, and several studies have shown that SNS content can be perceived as a threat and evoke jealousy (see Bevan, 2013, for a review). For example, due to the visibility and association afforded by SNSs, someone may see a rival's flirty message posted on their romantic partner's profile and become jealous.

SNSs also provide opportunities for individuals to make social comparisons to a romantic partner's exes because they afford persistence. These social comparisons have the potential to evoke jealousy about the past (i.e., *retroactive jealousy*). Many people monitor their romantic partners on SNSs in an attempt to alleviate jealousy, but partner monitoring may backfire and increase jealousy instead (Muise, Christofides, & Desmarais, 2009).

SNS-related jealousy can have serious and even fatal consequences. There is no shortage of instances in which romantic partners or rivals have been assaulted or murdered because of content or interactions on SNSs. Three such cases occurred in the United Kingdom. In one instance, a woman stabbed and killed her boyfriend during a fight about the time he spent on Facebook connecting with other women (Sims, 2016). In another instance, a man got into a fight with his friend for "poking" his girlfriend on Facebook. The jealous boyfriend punched his friend multiple times, who then died when he fell and his head struck the pavement. In yet another case (BBC, 2009), a man stabbed his estranged wife to death after she changed her relationship status on Facebook from "married" to "single." As these examples show, the affordances of visibility and association may provoke jealous individuals by aggravating their insecurities or existing tensions in the relationship.

Other Negative Experiences. Studies have identified a variety of other negative responses to content posted on SNSs. Repetitive or trivial posts, such as sports scores or food pictures, can annoy users (Fox & Moreland, 2015). Additionally, users experience embarrassment, frustration, and anger when their privacy is violated by what others post about them, such as scandalous pictures from a party (Debatin, Lovejoy, Horn, & Hughes, 2009).

External life events can also make SNSs dangerous territory. For example, seeing information about romantic ex-partners can exacerbate feelings of distress and regret (Fox & Tokunaga, 2015; Marshall, 2012). People can also have negative emotional experiences from reading news people share on SNSs as well as its accompanying social commentary. Natural disasters, human tragedies, or political events may evoke feelings such as sadness, anger, and anxiety (e.g., Hasell & Weeks, 2016).

Offensive or hurtful SNS content can have a notable impact on users. One study found that racist posts lead minority group members to experience anger and shame, and in turn report a greater likelihood to consume alcohol (Lee-Won, Lee, Song, & Borghetti, 2017). Repetitive or extreme hurtful content, such as cyberbullying or revenge porn, has even lead to users' suicides (see Hasinoff, this volume). In summary, the frequency, timing, nature, and extremity of SNS posts can trigger a variety of negative experiences for users.

Conclusion

Although there is a dark component to SNSs, research suggests several ways that individuals can mitigate negative effects. First, users should engage with SNSs mindfully and avoid spending too much time online. Removing SNS apps from your phone can limit easy and mindless access, and several browser apps are available to limit your time on certain sites (see Downs & Harvey, this volume). Mindfulness should be engaged when posting your own content as well. If you are unsure if you should post something, save it in a different document and revisit it the next day.

Taking a break from SNSs is also beneficial. Tromholt (2016) found that people who took a week off of Facebook experienced more positive emotions and increased life satisfaction. Sabbaticals may also help during stressful life events. Staying away from SNSs in the wake of a breakup can facilitate a faster recovery because you can avoid ruminating over old photos and stalking your ex's profile to see whom they date next. If an infuriating political debate is dominating your newsfeed, avoiding social media until it dies down may help lower your blood pressure.

Users should also determine the network members or specific content triggering negative emotional experiences. If you are feeling envious, keep in mind that SNS presentations are not completely authentic; most people do not live the perfect life reflected in their profiles. If a particular person's posts are causing distress, you have several options. A racist relative, for example, may not know how hurtful their hostile posts are. With a strong tie, a private conversation may be a good first step. If it is a weak tie, the person can be defriended or unfollowed. In some cases, a network member's posts may be temporarily undesirable, such as a co-worker whose posts become unbearably inane during football season. Muting or blocking them for a while will allow you to maintain the connection without having to suffer trivial or annoying posts.

Unfortunately, using mainstream SNSs may offer limited benefits to people who are already experiencing negative emotions such as anxiety, loneliness, or depression. Users should seek more private channels and disclose feelings to closer ties or professional counselors rather than broadcasting their feelings to their entire social network. Alternatively, research has shown benefits to disclosing in more anonymous environments such as online support groups.

Finally, users should reflect on the overall role of SNSs in their lives. If the costs of a particular SNS are exceeding the benefits, remember: you don't have to stay tied to your ties.

References

BBC. (2009, January 23). *Wife murdered for Facebook status.* Retrieved February 15, 2018, from http://news.bbc.co.uk/2/hi/uk_news/england/staffordshire/7845946.stm

Bevan, J. L. (2013). *The communication of jealousy.* New York, NY: Peter Lang.

Bevan, J. L., Gomez, R., & Sparks, L. (2014). Disclosures about important life events on Facebook: Relationships with stress and quality of life. *Computers in Human Behavior, 39*, 246–253. doi:10.1016/j.chb.2014.07.021

boyd, D. M., & Ellison, N. B. (2008). Social network sites: Definition, history, and scholarship. *Journal of Computer-Mediated Communication, 13*, 210–230. doi:10.1111/j/1083-6101.2007.00393.x

Choi, M., & Toma, C. L. (2014). Social sharing through interpersonal media: Patterns and effects on emotional well-being. *Computers in Human Behavior, 36*, 530–541. doi:10.1016/j.chb.2014.04.026

Chou, H. G., & Edge, N. (2012). "They are happier and having better lives than I am": The impact of using Facebook on perceptions of others' lives. *Cyberpsychology, Behavior, and Social Networking, 15*, 117–121. doi:10.1089/cyber.2011.0324

Debatin, B., Lovejoy, J. P., Horn, A. K., & Hughes, B. N. (2009). Facebook and online privacy: Attitudes, behaviors, and unintended consequences. *Journal of Computer-Mediated Communication, 15*, 83–108. doi:10.1111/j.1083-6101.2009.01494.x

de Vries, D. A., & Kühne, R. (2015). Facebook and self-perception: Individual susceptibility to negative social comparison on Facebook. *Personality and Individual Differences, 86*, 217–221. doi:10.1016/j.paid.2015.05.029

Ellison, N., Heino, R., & Gibbs, J. (2006). Managing impressions online: Self-presentation processes in the online dating environment. *Journal of Computer-Mediated Communication, 11*, 415–441. doi:10.1111/j.1083-6101.2006.00020.x

Ellison, N. B., Steinfield, C., & Lampe, C. (2007). The benefits of Facebook "friends": Social capital and college students' use of online social network sites. *Journal of Computer-Mediated Communication, 12*, 1143–1168. doi:10.1111/j.1083-6101.2007.00367.x

Festinger, L. (1954). A theory of social comparison processes. *Human Relations, 7*, 117–140. doi:10.1177/001872675400700202

Forest, A. L., & Wood, J. V. (2012). When social networking is not working: Individuals with low self-esteem recognize but do not reap the benefits of self-disclosure on Facebook. *Psychological Science, 23*, 295–302. doi:10.1177/0956797611429709

Fox, J., & McEwan, B. (2017). Distinguishing technologies for social interaction: The perceived social affordances of communication channels scale. *Communication Monographs, 84*, 298–318. doi:10.1080/03637751.2017.1332418

Fox, J., & Moreland, J. J. (2015). The dark side of social networking sites: An exploration of the relational and psychological stressors associated with Facebook use and affordances. *Computers in Human Behavior, 45*, 168–176. doi:10.1016/j.chb.2014.11.083

Fox, J., & Tokunaga, R. S. (2015). Romantic partner monitoring after breakups: Attachment, dependence, distress, and post-dissolution surveillance on social networking sites. *Cyberpsychology, Behavior, and Social Networking, 18*, 491–498. doi:10.1089/cyber.2015.0123

Fox, J., & Vendemia, M. A. (2016). Selective self-presentation and social comparison through photographs on social networking sites. *Cyberpsychology, Behavior, and Social Networking, 19*, 593–600. doi:10.1089/cyber.2016.0248

Fox, J., & Warber, K. M. (2015). Queer identity management and political self-expression on social networking sites: A co-cultural approach to the spiral of silence. *Journal of Communication, 65*, 79–100. doi:10.1111/jcom.12137

Frison, E., & Eggermont, S. (2016). "Harder, better, faster, stronger": Negative comparison on Facebook and adolescents' life satisfaction are reciprocally related. *Cyberpsychology, Behavior, and Social Networking, 19*, 158–164. doi:10.1089/cyber.2015.0296

Gibson, J. J. (1979). *The ecological approach to visual perception.* Boston, MA: Houghlin Mifflin.

Goffman, E. (1959). *Presentation of self in everyday life.* Garden City, NY: Anchor Books.

Haferkamp, N., & Krämer, N. C. (2011). Social comparison 2.0: Examining the effects of online profiles on social-networking sites. *Cyberpsychology, Behavior, and Social Networking, 14*, 309–314. doi:10.1089/cyber.2010.0120

Hasell, A., & Weeks, B. E. (2016). Partisan provocation: The role of partisan news use and emotional responses in political information sharing in social media. *Human Communication Research, 42*, 641–661. doi:10.1111/hcre.12092

Johnson, B. K., & Knobloch-Westerwick, S. (2014). Glancing up or down: Mood management and selective social comparisons on social networking sites. *Computers in Human Behavior, 41*, 33–39. doi:10.1016/j.chb.2014.09.009

Krasnova, H., Widjaja, T., Buxmann, P., Wenninger, H., & Benbasat, I. (2015). Why following friends can hurt you: An exploratory investigation of the effects of envy on social networking sites among college-age users. *Information Systems Research, 26*, 585–605. doi:10.1287/isre.2015.0588

Kross, E., Verduyn, P., Demiralp, E., Park, J., Lee, D. S., Lin, N., … Ybarra, O. (2013). Facebook use predicts declines in subjective well-being in young adults. *PloS One, 8*(8), e69841. doi:10.1371/journal.pone.0069841

Lee, S. Y. (2014). How do people compare themselves with others on social network sites? The case of Facebook. *Computers in Human Behavior, 32*, 253–260. doi:10.1016/j.chb.2013.12.009

Lee-Won, R. J., Lee, J. Y., Song, H., & Borghetti, L. (2017). "To the bottle I go … to drain my strain": Effects of microblogged racist messages on target group members' intention to drink alcohol. *Communication Research, 44*, 388–415. doi:10.1177/0093650215607595

Lovitt, B. (2016, July 16). Death by selfie: 11 disturbing stories of social media pics gone wrong. Retrieved February 15, 2018, from https://www.rollingstone.com/culture/pictures/death-by-selfie-10-disturbing-stories-of-social-media-pics-gone-wrong-20160714/accidental-explosion-20160714

Marshall, T. C. (2012). Facebook surveillance of former romantic partners: Associations with postbreakup recovery and personal growth. *Cyberpsychology, Behavior, and Social Networking, 15*, 521–526. doi:10.1089/cyber.2012.0125

Muise, A., Christofides, E., & Desmarais, S. (2009). More information than you ever wanted: Does Facebook bring out the green-eyed monster of jealousy? *CyberPsychology & Behavior, 12*, 441–444. doi:10.1089/cpb.2008.0263

Przybylski, A. K., Murayama, K., DeHaan, C. R., & Gladwell, V. (2013). Motivational, emotional, and behavioral correlates of fear of missing out. *Computers in Human Behavior, 29*, 1841–1848. doi:10.1016/j.chb.2013.02.014

Reinecke, L., Aufenanger, S., Beutel, M. E., Dreier, M., Quiring, O., Stark, B., ... Müller, K. W. (2017). Digital stress over the life span: The effects of communication load and internet multitasking on perceived stress and psychological health impairments in a German probability sample. *Media Psychology, 20*, 90–115. doi:10.1080/15213269.2015.1121832

Rosen, L. D., Cheever, N. A., & Carrier, L. M. (2015). *The Wiley handbook of psychology, technology, and society*. West Sussex: Wiley Blackwell.

Ryan, R. M., & Deci, E. L. (2001). On happiness and human potentials: A review of research on hedonic and eudaimonic well-being. *Annual Review of Psychology, 52*, 141–166. doi:10.1146/annurev.psych.52.1.141

Sims, A. (2016, February 22). Woman stabs boyfriend to death after claiming he's spent too much time on Facebook. Retrieved February 15, 2018, from https://www.independent. co.uk/news/uk/crime/woman-stabs-boyfriend-to-death-after-claiming-he-spent-too-much-time-on-facebook-a6890131.html

Smith, R. H., & Kim, S. H. (2007). Comprehending envy. *Psychological Bulletin, 133*, 46–64. doi:10.1037/0033-2909.133.1.46

Tandoc, E. C., Ferrucci, P., & Duffy, M. (2015). Facebook use, envy, and depression among college students: Is Facebook depressing? *Computers in Human Behavior, 43*, 139–146. doi:10.1016/j.chb.2014.10.053

Treem, J., & Leonardi, P. (2013). Social media use in organizations: Exploring the affordances of visibility, editability, persistence, and association. In C. T. Salmon (Ed.), *Communication yearbook* (Vol. 36, pp. 143–189). New York, NY: Routledge.

Tromholt, M. (2016). The Facebook experiment: Quitting Facebook leads to higher levels of well-being. *Cyberpsychology, Behavior, and Social Networking, 19*, 661–666. doi:10.1089/cyber.2016.0259

Valkenburg, P. M., Peter, J., & Schouten, A. P. (2006). Friend networking sites and their relationship to adolescents' well-being and social self-esteem. *CyberPsychology & Behavior, 9*, 584–590. doi:10.1089/cpb.2006.9.584

Verduyn, P., Lee, D. S., Park, J., Shablack, H., Orvell, A., Bayer, J., ... Kross, E. (2015). Passive Facebook usage undermines affective well-being: Experimental and longitudinal evidence. *Journal of Experimental Psychology: General, 144*, 480–488. doi:10.1037/xge0000057

Vitak, J. (2012). The impact of context collapse and privacy on social network site disclosures. *Journal of Broadcasting & Electronic Media, 56*, 451–470. doi:10.1080/08838151.2012.732140

Walther, J. B. (1996). Computer-mediated communication: Impersonal, interpersonal, and hyperpersonal interaction. *Communication Research, 23*, 3–43. doi:10.1177/009365096023001001

Wills, T. A. (1981). Downward comparison principles in social psychology. *Psychological Bulletin, 90*, 245–271. doi:10.1037/0033-2909.90.2.245

Wilson, R. E., Gosling, S. D., & Graham, L. T. (2012). A review of Facebook research in the social sciences. *Perspectives on Psychological Science, 7*, 203–220. doi:10.1177/1745691612442904

Withnall, A. (2014, April 27). Selfie crash death: Woman dies in head-on collision seconds after uploading pictures of herself and "HAPPY" status to Facebook. Retrieved February 15, 2018, from http://www.independent.co.uk/news/world/americas/selfie-crash-death-woman-dies-in-head-on-collision-seconds-after-uploading-pictures-of-herself-and-9293694.html

Woods, H. C., & Scott, H. (2016). #Sleepyteens: Social media use in adolescence is associated with poor sleep quality, anxiety, depression and low self-esteem. *Journal of Adolescence, 51*, 41–49. doi:10.1016/j.adolescence.2016.05.008

Zhang, Y., & Leung, L. (2015). A review of social networking service (SNS) research in communication journals from 2006 to 2011. *New Media & Society, 17*, 1007–1024. doi:10.1177/1461444813520477

CHAPTER TWELVE

Love and Lies

Deception in Online Dating

CATALINA L. TOMA & IRENE G. SARMIENTO

Online dating refers to the practice of using websites (e.g., Match.com, OKCupid) and mobile applications (e.g., Tinder, Coffee Meets Bagel) to meet potential romantic partners for both committed and casual liaisons. On these platforms, users typically describe themselves through textual descriptions and photographs, and then either search for partners themselves, or allow compatibility algorithms to connect them with potential partners. Dating websites tend to include longer profiles where users can describe themselves in detail, whereas mobile applications present more streamlined information, focusing on photographs and brief self-descriptions.

Both types of platforms have attracted a remarkable following. No longer a niche activity undertaken by geeks or by those taking desperate measures to find love, online dating is now the second most popular venue for meeting romantic partners (Rosenfeld & Thomas, 2012). Fifteen percent of American adults have tried an online dating site or mobile app and 5% of Americans who are currently married or in a long-term committed relationship reported that they met their partner online (Smith & Anderson, 2016). Among marriages and committed relationships that began between 2006 and 2012, a full third had met online (Cacioppo, Cacioppo, Gonzaga, Ogburn, & VanderWeele, 2013).

Not only is online dating popular, but it also appears successful in producing healthy relationships. In a nationally representative study, couples who had met online reported higher satisfaction with their relationships and even had a slightly lower rate of divorce than couples who had met offline (Cacioppo et al., 2013). There are certainly many advantages to online dating. First, it greatly simplifies the process of identifying potential romantic partners. Many websites have large databases of users—for instance, Match.com currently has over twelve million, so it is highly likely that users will find someone who piques their interest. Meanwhile, in traditional dating, getting just one date can be a challenging and time-consuming process, especially for people who are not embedded in social networks comprising many singles. Second, online dating broadens the pool of potential partners from whom to choose. Prior to online dating, people became romantically involved with those who were literally around them—in school, at work, or in their neighborhoods. Online dating casts a much wider net, permitting users to establish relationships with people with whom they would never have crossed paths in everyday life.

Nonetheless, online dating has problematic aspects. Chief among them appears to be deception (Brym & Lenton, 2001; Couch, Liamputtong, & Pitts, 2012; Madden & Lenhart, 2006). People are worried that online daters lie about important matters such as their physical appearance, financial situation, and even relationship status, and that these lies would result in dashed hopes and heartbreak. In the best case scenario, online dating lies could lead to a bad first date, where online daters quickly catch on to their match's lies about observable characteristics (e.g., age, physical attractiveness) and promptly terminate the date. While everybody has bad dates occasionally, this scenario could become especially disheartening if repeated numerous times—which many people fear is the case with online dating. In the worst-case scenario, online dating lies can produce enormous heartbreak, when online daters find out that their partner is not single or has become involved with them for the sole purpose of defrauding them. How likely are these scenarios to play out? Are the popular fears surrounding online dating deception well-founded? The purpose of this chapter is to summarize the existing research on the prevalence of online dating deception.

Catfishing or Small Lies?

The popular television series *Catfish* presents the stories of people who were deceived by romantic prospects they had met online. Often these romantic prospects lied substantially about their age, with the old pretending to be young and vice versa; gender-switched; or posted photographs of other people who look nothing like them. These lies are so egregious that they have captured the public's imagination, leading to the coining of the term "catfishing" to denote the telling of big online lies, especially in a romantic context. One particularly notorious episode of cat-fishing involved Notre Dame football player Manti Te'o. Te'o publicly and repeat-edly claimed to be in love with a woman who was sick with leukemia. Upon this girlfriend's alleged death, it emerged that she had never existed and that she was fabricated by Te'o's best friend, who was secretly in love with him. Te'o maintained his innocence, claiming that he had conducted this years-long romance exclusively via mediated interactions (e.g., phone, Twitter, texting), without ever meeting his girlfriend in person. He allegedly did not realize that he was interacting with his best friend, masquerading as a woman. In short, he claimed to have been catfished.

The much-publicized Manti Te'o affair, as well as the eponymous television show, have intensified the public's fears about the prevalence and magnitude of online dating deception. But the root of these fears likely runs deeper. Catfishing, as described above, would never have been possible in face-to-face dating, where claims about gender, age, and physical appearance can be verified visually. If Manti Te'o had even one face-to-face encounter with his alleged girlfriend, the whole house of cards would have come crashing down. Conversely, the online environ-ment makes possible the dissemination of lies that could never be sustained face-to-face. From a scholarly perspective, the online dating environment offers certain features (or affordances) that make lying easier than in face-to-face environments:

- *A reduction in nonverbal cues* means that online daters can craft profiles and interact with matches without having to manage their nonverbal behaviors (e.g., eye contact, facial expressions, gestures, posture, and tone of voice). People believe that nonverbal cues betray deception, with liars avoiding eye contact, and increasing their fidgeting and stuttering (Global Deception Research Team, 2006). Thus, the absence of these cues should be perceived as beneficial for liars, who no longer have to monitor and worry about their nonverbal signals. At a more basic level, the absence of nonverbal cues in online dating means that users can impersonate someone else altogether, since they don't have to technically show themselves.

- *Unlimited composition time* means that creators of online dating profiles can take time to ponder their lies and then can take the time to compose them in a believable manner. By contrast, face-to-face liars have to say their piece on the spot, and oftentimes also have to field questions, which makes it harder for them to produce believable lies.

- *Editability* means that online liars can revise and polish their statements until they are satisfied with them. Meanwhile, face-to-face communica-tors cannot take back their lies and improve upon them once these lies are spoken out loud.

- *Anonymity* means that online daters do not have to reveal their real names or post photographs of themselves (although, in practice, the majority of them do). This lack of identifiable information should make lies more difficult to verify.

These technological features of the online dating environment can be construed as *deception enablers*, because they facilitate the telling and inhibit the detection of lies. We suspect that people believe lying is rampant in online dating because they focus on deception enablers. Since lying online takes little effort, surely people will do it! But the notion that people lie simply because it is easy to do so is a myth. Deception is a motivated act, with the majority of people (save for pathological liars) lying for specific reasons and trying hard to avoid being detected. In other words, people do not lie simply because they can, but they lie because they believe it is a good strategy for them.

In the same vein, it is important to recognize that the online dating environment *also* contains features that make lying harder or equally hard as it is face-to-face:

- *Recordability* means that online dating profiles can be saved and archived. Thus, an undeniable record of the lie can be preserved. Conversely, face-to-face is an evanescent environment, meaning that utterances literally disappear into the thin air, unless they are recorded through some technological device (which they typically are not). Face-to-face liars can then pretend that the lie was a misunderstanding, or that they had never uttered the lie in the first place. Such justifications are unavailable to online daters if their partner had preserved a copy of their profile.
- *The anticipation of future interaction* means that online dating is not meant to stay online, but rather to progress to face-to-face encounters. Thus, lies that can be detected face-to-face are not a viable option for online daters, or at least are as viable as they are for traditional, face-to-face daters. It bears noting that, when it comes to romantic relationships, lying is typically perceived as a deal-breaker. People are very judgmental of liars, as trust is essential within close relationships. Therefore, the anticipation of forming romantic relationships should significantly deter lying.

The previous technological features can be construed as *deception constraints*, as they inhibit the telling of lies in online dating. We suspect that people disregard these deception constraints when forming opinions that online dating is rife with deception. One study provides evidence that, when people estimate how much deception takes place online, they tend to focus on deception enablers much more so than on deception constraints. In this study, people reported that the difference between their peers' deceptiveness and their own deceptiveness was greater in email and instant messenger than it was face-to-face, arguably because they thought peers were more influenced by deception enablers than they themselves were (Toma, Jiang, & Hancock, in press).

Let us now return to our original question: How much deception is there in online dating profiles, given that these profiles contain both deception enablers and constraints? Researchers, including the lead author of this chapter, tackled this question. We hypothesized that online daters would not lie simply because they can, but rather that they would lie strategically in order to accomplish their relational goals. These goals should be to come across as (1) attractive, to appeal to potential mates; but also (2) to be perceived as honest, because lying is generally frowned-upon. Thus, online daters should take advantage of deception enablers (e.g., unlimited composition time, editability) to increase their attractiveness, but should simultaneously be mindful of deception constraints, especially the anticipation of future interaction. Lies were expected to be small and strategically-placed, just enough to give daters an attractiveness boost in areas where such a boost was needed, but not big enough to raise red flags.

To test these predictions, a sample of heterosexual online daters was recruited from the New York City metropolitan area. Participants were invited to a university lab, where they were presented with a printout of their online dating profile and asked to rate the accuracy of each of their profile statements, on a scale from 1—not at all to 5—completely accurate. This methodology—self-report, presents some challenges for deception research because, paradoxically, it requires researchers to rely on liars to tell them the truth about their own lies. To counteract this limitation, researchers also utilized a ground-truth procedure, which involved objectively verifying some of the claims online daters had made in their profiles. Unfortunately, not all claims are verifiable—for instance, it is difficult for researchers to ascertain what daters' hobbies or interests are, or the last book they read. But some claims are, in fact, verifiable. Daters' weights were measured on a scale, after they removed shoes and outer clothing. Their heights were measured using a standard measuring tape. Their ages were recorded from their drivers' licenses, and their photographs were taken in the lab.

As predicted, researchers observed a pattern of frequent, but small and strategic deceptions. Self-report measurements indicated that daters considered their statements to be fairly accurate—all were rated above 4 on the 1–5 scale used. Ground-truth measurements revealed a more complex picture. Over 80% of participants lied at least about height, weight, or age, suggesting that online daters did take advantage of deception enablers to craft a more attractive persona. But the magnitude of the lies was small and gendered. On average, men added close to an inch to their height, whereas women presented their height honestly; women subtracted about eight pounds from their weight, whereas men presented their weight fairly honestly; and age was honestly presented across the board, with only a few outliers, mostly women, presenting themselves as younger. The fact that age was presented more honestly than height or weight reveals just how strategic online daters were. Deceptions about height or weight can be justified through ignorance ("I haven't weighed myself in a long time!"; "My height was never properly measured by a doctor"), but this does not apply to age. Height and weight are also more malleable characteristics—people can lose weight or wear heels to match profile claims, but such artifices do not apply to age deceptions (Toma, Hancock, & Ellison, 2008).

To ascertain the accuracy of photographs, daters were asked to report how long ago the photograph was taken; then, their lab photograph was shown side-by-side with their main profile photograph to a group of unacquainted judges. The judges were instructed to rate the accuracy of the profile photograph by comparing it to the lab photograph. Results show that, on average, women presented themselves as younger than men, with women's photographs taken about 17 months prior to their lab appointment and men's only six months prior. Judges rated women's photographs as significantly more deceptive than men's, finding that women were more likely to look younger and have better skin and hairstyles in their profile photo than in the lab photo. Across the board, the photograph was judged to be the least honest element of the profile—a fact which, again, highlights how strategic online daters were. The photograph is often the first profile element seen by potential mates performing database searches, and it is used heavily for deciding whose profile to even click on. Having an attractive photograph is therefore essential for online dating success. Additionally, photography is a subjective medium—because it is two-dimensional and static, it cannot render an embodied, dynamic human being in the same way that face-to-face interaction does. This subjectivity provided leeway for deception (Hancock & Toma, 2009).

The gendered nature of lies (i.e., women lied more about their weight, physical attractiveness, and age—as depicted in photographs; men lied more about their height) is also strong evidence of the strategic nature of online dating deception. Specifically, men and women in this heterosexual context appear to have lied to suit the preferences of the opposite sex, and thus to increase their chances of attracting potential partners. These preferences are well-documented (e.g., Gangestad & Scheyd, 2005) and explained by evolutionary theory (Buss & Schmitt, 1993). According to this theory, men and women have come to value different characteristics in romantic partners, based on the different sets of challenges they experienced in the environment in which humans evolved, several millennia ago. The characteristics men and women gravitated towards increased their likelihood of passing on their genes to the next generation, ensuring the survival of the species. Men developed a preference for young and physically attractive women, because youthfulness is a signal of women's fertility (much more so than it is for men), and physical attractiveness is a signal of healthy genes. Women developed a preference for men who could provide and protect, because women's ability to fend for themselves was decreased during pregnancy and childrearing, and they needed partners to take care of them and their offspring. In the environment in which humans evolved, height was a reliable signal of a man's strength and ability to provide and protect. In the current environment, markers of high status (income, education, job prospects) serve the same function. It is notable that even though Toma et al. (2008) did not find gender differences in lies about social status indicators, these differences emerged in a follow-up study. A survey of over 5,000 online daters revealed that men were more likely to misrepresent their personal assets, and also replicated the finding that women were more likely to lie about their weight (Hall, Park, Song, & Cody, 2010).

A final piece of evidence about the limited and strategic nature of online dating deception comes from a study on the relationship between daters' physical attractiveness and their tendency to lie in their profiles (Toma & Hancock, 2010). Results show that less attractive daters lied more about their physical descriptors (height, weight, age) and about their photographs; however, physical attractiveness was unrelated to lies about other profile elements. In other words, daters only lied to remedy their shortcomings, but not to embellish aspects of self that did not need embellishment.

In sum, the scholarly evidence shows that a majority of online dating lies are not of the catfishing variety, but rather that they are small and strategically-placed, despite being frequent. Further support for this conclusion comes from data gathered by the online dating site, OkCupid. Researchers compared the claims made by OkCupid users about their height and income with the average distribution of these characteristics in the American population. They found that, on average, users present themselves as two inches taller and as 20% wealthier than they should be based on national averages. The researchers also looked at the metadata from posted photographs and found that the more attractive these photographs were, the more likely they were to be out-of-date (Rudder, 2010). Even though these findings were not published in a scientific journal, they are compelling because of their large sample of participants—over 1.5 million OkCupid users.

To conclude, catfishing does not appear to be the norm in online dating. This should be unsurprising given online dating's vast popularity and success in generating romantic relationships. Surely people would stop using these sites if they were full of liars. People's concerns about online dating deception might subside the more exposure and experience they have with these sites—a likely scenario given the growing popularity of the medium.

Online Dating Romance Scams

While the majority of online dating lies tend to be small and fairly innocuous, some lies are, in fact, instances of catfishing. We will focus here on monetary scams, which are typically perpetrated by international criminal groups and produce substantial financial and psychological damages to victims. In these scams, criminals create fake profiles using stolen photographs and made-up identities, then contact or wait to be contacted by potential victims. After identifying a suitable victim, usually someone lonely and socially isolated, the criminals go through the stages of relationship formation: They shower the victim with attention, engage in intimate self-disclosure, declare their love, and gain the victim's trust. During this grooming stage, communication tends to be frequent and intense, and is usually conducted through instant messenger or texting applications. Grooming can take place for weeks, months, or even years. The victim slowly becomes emotionally reliant on the criminal and ends up falling in love with them. At this stage, the criminal tests the waters by asking for small gifts, such as perfume or a mobile phone. If the victim acquiesces, the demands escalate to more and more money (for more about luring communication, see Olson & Schwartzman, this volume). Often the criminal invents stories of personal emergencies, meant to tug at the victims' heartstrings, such as needing money for medical expenses. Another common practice is asking money for plane tickets and visas to visit the victim. The scam ends once the victim ceases to provide the money, either because they don't have it or they have realized they are being scammed (Whitty & Buchanan, 2016).

There are no reliable statistics about the prevalence of online dating scams, although there is some indication that they are the most common type of internet fraud (see Rege, 2009). In the United Kingdom, one study found that at least 230,000 individuals had been the victims of these sweetheart swindles (Whitty & Buchanan, 2012). Even so, it is likely that online dating scams are underreported, because many victims suffer from embarrassment or may not even realize they had been scammed. As for the effects of these scams on victims, they are severe. In addition to the financial loss, victims tend to suffer mental health problems akin to post-traumatic stress. They are ashamed and embarrassed, feel a loss of trust in others, and miss the romantic connection they thought they had. Compounding these problems is a lack of social support, as many victims are reluctant to tell their stories to friends and family for fear of judgment (Whitty & Buchanan, 2016).

What can be done to combat these scams? Most online dating companies put the onus of safety and security on the daters themselves, offering them only tips for how to manage their romantic connections. Some companies have attempted background checks for their members, but these tend to be costly and ineffective, because scammers often use stolen credit cards and fake identities. A more effective strategy has been screening out members who send mass emails on a daily basis, and members whose IP addresses are known to be associated with criminal groups. However, it is unclear to what extent online dating companies engage in these practices. Online daters victimized in these scams also have little support from law enforcement agencies, because jurisdiction tends to be vague, with scammers often residing in other states or countries (Rege, 2009). By way of combating these scams, this research suggests that online daters should be highly suspicious of any requests for money from potential partners and that they should insist on face-to-face meetings early in the relationship, before they become emotionally attached.

Summary and Practical Implications

This chapter has taken a critical view of deception as one of the dark sides of online dating. The scholarly literature shows that, despite online dating's popularity and success, people are still concerned about deception, rating it as the biggest disadvantage of online dating. We have argued that such beliefs likely stem from highly popularized examples of deception in the mass media, such as the show *Catfish*, and from people's excessive focus on technological features that appear to make online deception easy, such as anonymity, editability, and the reduction of nonverbal cues. Contrary to these beliefs, research shows that most online dating lies tend to be small and strategic, with people lying just enough to give themselves an advantage in the dating arena, but not so much as to jeopardize future relationship prospects. This pattern of deception is attributable to technological features that make deception difficult, such as the anticipation of future interaction, where many lies can be caught, and the recordability of profiles. In addition to these small and fairly trivial lies, online dating is a space where consequential lies can also be observed, although these are much rarer. We have also reviewed the handful of studies available on online dating romance scams, where criminals swindle victims for money by pretending to be in love with them and in need of financial help. These scams register as a "double-whammy" for victims, who lose not only money, but a romantic relationship in which they had become invested.

While online daters' likelihood of encountering big lies and of being scammed is relatively small, it is still useful to consider the steps they can take to protect themselves against these possibilities. For this, dating sites offer much advice. First and most evidently, any request for money should be treated as highly suspect, especially when there has been no face-to-face contact with one's partner. Second, it is useful to obtain identifiable information about the partner, such as their full name and location. This information can be used to look them up on online search engines, social network sites, and publicly available sex offender and criminal records registries. Oftentimes these searches return reassuring information. Potential partners have difficult-to-fake online identities, such as profiles on company webpages, social media accounts with plentiful information accumulated through years of use, and reviews, comments, and likes from friends. The absence of this reassuring information is not a red flag *per se*, as many people lack an online presence and keep their social media accounts private. However, it should prompt users to try to find out more about their partner through other means. Third, users should proceed to face-to-face meetings relatively quickly. These meetings can reveal visually identifiable deceptions, such as those about physical appearance and age, enabling daters to walk away from liars before having made a significant investment of time and emotional energy. Protracted online interactions pose the danger that an emotional bond will develop, and any deceptions found out afterwards might be overlooked by a dater who is already attached. This is one reason behind the proliferation of online romance scams. Online daters might be suspicious of monetary requests, but they are already emotionally involved and don't feel they can easily extricate themselves from the relationship. This being said, face-to-face meetings are not a panacea for deception detection. Certain significant deceptions, such as those about relationship status, are not immediately obvious and might only be revealed by third parties. For this reason, daters are advised to seek introductions to a potential partner's social circle (friends, family) once they become serious about the relationship. Finally, parents are advised to be aware of the potential for deception on dating apps geared towards teens, such as Yubo (formerly known as Yellow). These apps do not screen for age and may be used by sexual predators to groom victims. To combat against teens becoming victimized on these sites, parents and caregivers should foster an open and safe environment for communication with their teenagers about safe online dating practices.

To conclude; deception is not unique to online dating sites and will likely never disappear. However, there are ways to manage it, such that users can reap the many advantages for relationship initiation offered by online dating.

References

Brym, R. J., & Lenton, R. L. (2001). Love online: A report on digital dating in Canada. Retrieved from http://www.nelson.com/nelson/harcourt/sociology/newsociety3e/loveonline. pdf

Buss, D. M., & Schmitt, D. P. (1993). Sexual strategies theory: An evolutionary perspective on human mating. *Psychological Review, 100*(2), 204.

Cacioppo, J. T., Cacioppo, S., Gonzaga, G. C., Ogburn, E. L., & VanderWeele, T. J. (2013). Marital satisfaction and break-ups differ across on-line and off-line meeting venues. *Proceedings of the National Academy of Sciences, 110*(25), 10135–10140. doi:10.1073/ pnas.1222447110

Couch, D., Liamputtong, P., & Pitts, M. (2012). What are the real and perceived risks and dangers of online dating? Perspectives from online daters: Health risks in the media. *Health, Risk & Society, 14*(7–8), 697–714. doi:10.1080/13698575.2012.720964

Gangestad, S. W., & Scheyd, G. J. (2005). The evolution of human physical attractiveness. *Annual Review Anthropology, 34*, 523–548.

Global Deception Research Team. (2006). A world of lies. *Journal of Cross-Cultural Psychology, 37*(1), 60–74.

Hall, J. A., Park, N., Song, H., & Cody, M. J. (2010). Strategic misrepresentation in online dating: The effects of gender, self-monitoring, and personality traits. *Journal of Social and Personal Relationships, 27*(1), 117–135. doi:10.1177/0265407509349633

Hancock, J. T., & Toma, C. L. (2009). Putting your best face forward: The accuracy of online dating photographs. *Journal of Communication, 59*(2), 367–386. doi:10.1111/j.1460-2466.2009.01420.x

Madden, M., & Lenhart, A. (2006). Online dating. Retrieved from http://www.pewinternet. org/files/old-media/Files/Reports/2006/PIP_Online_Dating.pdf.pdf

Rege, A. (2009). What's love got to do with it? Exploring online dating scams and identity fraud. *International Journal of Cyber Criminology, 3*(2), 494.

Rosenfeld, M. J., & Thomas, R. J. (2012). Searching for a mate: The rise of the Internet as a social intermediary. *American Sociological Review, 77*(4), 523–547. doi:10.1177/ 0003122412448050

Rudder, C. (2010, July 6). The big lies people tell in online dating [Blog post]. Retrieved from https://theblog.okcupid.com/the-big-lies-people-tell-in-online-dating-a9e3990d6ae2

Smith, A., & Anderson, M. (2016, February 29). *5 facts about online dating*. Retrieved from http://www.pewresearch.org/fact-tank/2016/02/29/5-facts-about-online-dating/#

Toma, C. L., & Hancock, J. T. (2010). Looks and lies: The role of physical attractiveness in online dating self-presentation and deception. *Communication Research, 37*, 335–351. doi:10.1177/0093650209356437

Toma, C. L., Hancock, J. T., & Ellison, N. B. (2008). Separating fact from fiction: An examination of deceptive self-presentation in online dating profiles. *Personality and Social Psychology Bulletin, 34*, 1023–1036.

Toma, C. L., Jiang, L. C., & Hancock, J. T. (in press). Lies in the eye of the beholder: Asymmetric beliefs about one's own and others' deceptiveness in mediated and face-to-face communication. *Communication Research*.

Whitty, M. T., & Buchanan, T. (2012). The online romance scam: A serious cybercrime. *CyberPsychology, Behavior, and Social Networking, 15*(3), 181–183. doi:10.1089/cyber.2011.0352

Whitty, M. T., & Buchanan, T. (2016). The online dating romance scam: The psychological impact on victims—both financial and non-financial. *Criminology & Criminal Justice, 16*(2), 176–194. doi:10.1177/1748895815603773

CHAPTER THIRTEEN

Image-Based Sexual Abuse

It's Not *Revenge* and It's Not *Porn*

AMY ADELE HASINOFF

Many people choose to share personal sexual images with partners via mobile phone or other technologies. This practice is called *sexting*, and research suggests that around one-third of older teens and well over half of young adults sext (Klettke, Hallford, & Mellor, 2014). Around 90% of sexters report that their recipients have never distributed their images.[1] But when people choose to share or post another person's private sexual images without permission, this is a form of sexual violence widely known as *revenge porn*.

Victims of revenge porn report negative effects on their careers and ongoing stalking, harassment, threats, and blackmail; as a result, they often have intense feelings of fear, anxiety, emotional distress, depression, and shame (Citron & Franks, 2014; Lenhart, Ybarra, & Price-Feeney, 2016; Wolak & Finkelhor, 2016). Research has found that around 2%–8% of all adults report that someone shared their private sexual images without permission and a further 5%–6% have experienced threats to distribute images (Eaton, Jacobs, & Ruvalcaba, 2017; Lenhart et al., 2016). Rates of victimization are up to five times higher for women than for men (Wolak & Finkelhor, 2016). While networked digital media make this form of harm easier to commit and amplify the potential for damage, this phenomenon is not entirely new—for example, *Hustler* was successfully sued in 1984 for publishing reader-submitted nude photos of women without their consent ("Wood v. Hustler magazine," 1984).

What's known as *revenge porn* is better understood as sexual assault and intimate partner abuse in a new digital format: the victims are disproportionately women and girls and the perpetrators are often current or former male intimate partners who engage in a pattern of humiliating and dominating victims in order to control them. In general, sexual violence is a problem that emerges out of engrained cultural norms of masculinity that celebrate—or at least tolerate—sexual pursuit and aggression and the control and domination of women (e.g. Jensen, 2007; Smith, Richie, & Sudbury, 2006). While some men reject these messages about masculinity, dominant gender norms teach men that they are entitled to sexual access to women's bodies and that sexual intimacy is a prize to pursue and win—or even steal. This same sense of entitlement allows people to share sexual images of women without their permission.

This system of gender and sexual norms is so powerful and engrained that people routinely disbelieve and blame victims of many forms of sexual violence. Women in particular who are victims of sexual assault are seen as "asking for it" and are blamed for being out late, wearing certain clothing, or flirting with the perpetrator. In the same way, when a perpetrator distributes a woman's sexual image without her permission, many people blame her for creating the image in the first place. This response ignores the fact that the perpetrator deliberately chose to commit an act of harm and implies that he was entitled to sexually humiliate and control his victim. This chapter explains why what's known as *revenge porn* is actually sexual abuse, examines the inconsistent and inadequate laws that exist in the US, and concludes by suggesting some legal, technological, and personal solutions that might help address this issue.

It's Not Porn, It's Sexual Abuse

Like pornography, image-based sexual abuse[2] involves sexual images and might be used for sexual gratification, but what distinguishes the two is consent. While criticisms of pornography since the 1980s have questioned performers' capacity for genuine consent[3] and view pornography as violence against women (e.g. Dworkin, 1981), it is vital to distinguish legal pornography from revenge porn. Producers of legal commercial pornography must maintain documentation of performers' consent to the production and distribution of images that depict them (Stoya, 2015). Though some producers exploit and manipulate performers, others are committed to fair labor practices (Taormino, Shimizu, Penley, & Miller-Young, 2013). So, using the term *porn* to mean *exploitation* is inaccurate because many porn performers do not see themselves as victims. At the same time, the term *porn* in *revenge porn* also diminishes the harm and minimizes perpetrators' actions by associating them with a commercially produced entertainment product.

A sexual privacy violation is better understood as a form of sexual and gendered violence that can be motivated by a desire for power, control, and degradation. While some legal pornography offers fictional scenarios of sexual violation and humiliation (Jensen, 2007), there is a lot of variety in commercial pornography: some offers feminist, anti-racist, and queer representations of sexuality that model consent and safer-sex practices (Taormino et al., 2013). Sexual privacy violations, in contrast, are often motivated by an urge to harm and control victims. For example, thirty thousand members of the Marine Corps were members of a secret Facebook group for sharing access to sexual images of female Marines. Some of the images were shared without permission and others were also—even more egregiously—produced without the knowledge of those depicted. If these Marines' goal was merely sexual gratification, the men could have shared widely available legal pornography. Instead, they chose to share images of people they worked with. As Cauterucci explains, "By violating their co-workers' privacy and reducing them to sex objects, members of [this Facebook group] asserted power over the women in their ranks" (2017). In sharing—and even creating—sexual images of women without permission, these men seemed to take a disturbing pleasure in violating the sexual agency and autonomy of their female co-workers.

For some viewers, the violation, humiliation, and assertion of power over women is precisely what's appealing about non-consensually distributed images. Emma Holten, a victim of nonconsensual image distribution, concluded that men found her sexual violation erotic, leading them to prey on her further by sending her threatening and harassing emails. She explains:

> The realisation that my humiliation turned them on felt like a noose around my neck. The absence of consent was erotic, they relished my suffering. … My body was not the appealing factor. … I saw that my loss of control legitimised the harassment. I was a fallen woman, anyone's game. What was I aside from a whore who had got what she deserved? (Holten, 2014)

The now-defunct website IsAnyoneUp.com (2010) is another example of the appeal of sexual violation. This website posted nonconsensual images collected from ex-partners and hacking, and displayed them alongside personal information about the victims to facilitate their harassment and humiliation.

The circulation and demand for nonconsensual images can only exist in a context of slut-shaming and the sexual double standard. The sexual double standard describes the way that men are praised as *studs* while women are condemned as *sluts* for engaging in exactly the same kinds of sexual behaviors. This practice of stigmatizing and criticizing women who are perceived as sexually active or expressive is known as *slut-shaming*. Men typically cannot be slut-shamed, but anyone can be stigmatized for being perceived as gay or transgressing gender norms. Slut-shaming is particularly relevant for white women while women of color also contend with racist assumptions about their sexual passivity or aggressiveness. Langlois and Slane find that on websites that host revenge porn images, the victims are "framed as disgusting active female sexual agents, accused of being dirty, diseased, indiscriminate in choosing their sexual partners" (2017, p. 125). Indeed, the reason nonconsensual images are appealing to some people is because they satisfy a desire to sexually degrade and humiliate others. Nonconsensual images can only satisfy that desire if sexual expression and victimization is seen as shameful for the victim.

Perpetrators who distribute sexual images also depend on a culture of slut-shaming to harm their victims. They can expect that their victims will probably be blamed and slut-shamed by friends, family, and employers and harassed by strangers on the internet. Indeed, the bystanders to a sexual privacy violation contribute to the harm when they fail to respond compassionately to sexuality-based bullying in schools, when they fire victims from teaching positions, when they post nasty comments online, or even when they shrug and say, "Well, what did she expect?" In a few high-profile cases, teen girls have died by suicide after being photographed during sexual assaults at house parties, ostracized by peers, and let down by the adults in schools and justice departments who should have supported them. Audrie Pott was 15 when she took her own life (Mendoza, 2013) and Rehtaeh Parsons was 17 years old (Visser, 2013). Gender norms mean that people can condemn women as *sluts* for exercising sexual agency and, even more tragically, shame and blame them for being victims of sexual assault. If bystanders didn't engage in this slut-shaming, the distribution of private sexual images would probably have far less power to harm.

It's Not Revenge, It's Sexual Abuse

In many cases, *revenge porn* is not about revenge but is instead a form of intimate partner abuse. Wolak and Finkelhor explain: "Many perpetrators appeared to be malicious current, former or would-be romantic or sexual partners who were determined to use their victims' sexuality to humiliate, harass and control them" (2016, p. 53). In their study, 55% of victims who knew the perpetrator face-to-face said that the motive for threatening to expose images was to try to make the victim stay in a relationship (Wolak & Finkelhor, 2016). One 18-year-old victim explained:

> I was in a controlling, emotionally abusive relationship and when I finally had the strength to break away I was still trapped by his threats to [distribute] my nude pictures. (Wolak & Finkelhor, 2016, p. 8)

In many cases, instances of privacy violations occur within relationships that are abusive in other ways as well: 78% of victims reported threats, stalking, and/or harassment for a number of weeks or months and 43% of victims were physically and/or sexually assaulted by the same perpetrator (Wolak & Finkelhor, 2016). Citron and Franks (2014) argue that the lack of legal attention to the issue of image-based sexual abuse echoes a history of trivializing all forms of gendered and sexual violence.

The term *revenge* frames the harm as the victims' fault by implying that they did something wrong. As Jeong (2015) notes, the term implies that this kind of violation is a rational response to a personal slight or dispute and reflects an implicit assumption that the victim deserved the privacy violation, especially if they initially sent images to the perpetrator. As discussed above, it is a serious problem that perpetrators and bystanders alike view any evidence of women's sexual agency—for example, choosing to create and share a sexual image—as a justification for sexual violation. One 19-year-old female victim of sexual abuse reported: "[My parents] told me I was a whore for doing anything like that online in the first place" (Wolak & Finkelhor, 2016, p. 41). Another 15-year-old female victim explained: "There was a lot of slut shaming. I had my phone taken away from me and was punished for sending the image. I was made to feel ashamed of my sexuality and it made me sort of give up on myself" (Wolak & Finkelhor, 2016, p. 41). Research has found that both media representations of sexual privacy violations and people answering survey questions often blame the person who created the image in the first place rather than the perpetrators who chose to commit a privacy violation (Hasinoff, 2015; Henry & Powell, 2015).

While the majority of victims report that they knew the perpetrator in-person, in one study, 40% of victims said their only relationship to the perpetrator was online (Wolak & Finkelhor, 2016). In one case, a man tricked over 200 victims into downloading malware that gave him control of the victims' computers, including all their files as well as their webcams, and then harassed and manipulated them to send more sexually explicit images and videos (Wittes et al., 2016). Indeed, when victims were targeted by a perpetrator they knew only online, the perpetrator's main objective was to get more images (Wittes et al., 2016; Wolak & Finkelhor, 2016). Though the internet gives perpetrators new ways to sexually exploit and victimize people, their motivations are likely similar to perpetrators of serial in-person sexual exploitation. In some cases, images are produced without consent, stolen, or coerced, including "recordings of a sexual assault, or upskirt images, or from voyeurs" (McGlynn & Rackley, 2016). In one study, 45% of all victims reported that perpetrators obtained images without their consent, including from webcam recordings, stealing images from their phones, and hacking (Wolak & Finkelhor, 2016).

For a small number of perpetrators, the motive is not revenge, sexual gratification, or power, but is instead profit: 9% of victims in one study reported that the perpetrator threatened to expose photos in order to blackmail them for money (Wolak & Finkelhor, 2016). Financial incentives are also a key motive for the distribution of private images. So-called *revenge porn* websites capitalize on sexual exploitation, profiting both from hosting the images for viewers and extorting victims for money to remove those images. One 17-year-old female victim explained: "I was able to click on my posts [on myex.com] and found a 'remove my name' link ... the website said I had to pay thousands of dollars to remove my name" (Wolak & Finkelhor, 2016, p. 47). Langlois and Slane (2017) explain that revenge porn websites use trackers, pop-up ads, and links to paid pornography sites to generate profit from viewers. The reputation management industry also benefits from these violations because victims sometimes use their services to try to manage the fallout of a violation (Langlois & Slane, 2017).

Perpetrators sometimes share private images thoughtlessly—without consideration for the effect on the victim but also without intentional malice or a goal of revenge. In one study, 79% of perpetrators said they only shared the image with friends and did not intend to hurt the victim (Eaton et al., 2017). Only 12% of perpetrators said that they shared images "because they were upset with the victim and/or wanted to harm them" (Eaton et al., 2017, p. 19). In this study, many perpetrators regretted their actions: two-thirds reported that they would not have done it if they had taken more time to think about it or if they knew how much it would hurt the victim (Eaton et al., 2017). The fact that many perpetrators say they did not see their behavior as intentionally malicious suggests they may have felt entitled to violate their victims' sexual privacy without initially considering the potential for serious harm.

Legal Challenges

While there are new laws in some places to address image-based sexual abuse, they are inconsistent and often inadequate. For example, in some US states, some laws only cover someone publicly posting a private image rather than sending it to a third party; others only apply if the perpetrator knowingly intended to cause emotional distress. There is also no US federal law that exactly captures the specific crime of threatening to expose images in order to blackmail a victim to produce more images or engage in some other sexual activity (known as *sextortion*), and unless the victim is a child, prosecution is erratic and typically minimal (Wittes et al., 2016). In addition to criminal charges, victims of any age can pursue privacy and emotional distress lawsuits to try to collect damages. Some victims have successfully sued the perpetrators of image-based sexual abuse, but lawsuits are expensive, they can be futile if perpetrators are unable to pay damages, and they typically require victims to use their real names, risking further publicity.

Minors who experience image-based sexual abuse are in a particularly precarious legal position because sexual images of a person under 18 years old could count as child pornography. On one hand, the harshness and inflexibility of child pornography laws means that underage victims who report that their sexual images have been shared or published can expect a response—police will often take the incident seriously and most US websites will quickly take down images. On the other hand, these same child pornography laws can also be used against victims. This is because it is illegal to create, send, or possess any sexually explicit images of anyone under 18—including images of oneself. Some states have made teen sexting a misdemeanor or other lesser charge, but it generally remains illegal (Hinduja & Patchin, 2015). Current child pornography and sexting laws are so broad that a teenage victim of a privacy violation and the person who harmed them can both be charged with the same crime.

Even when reasonable laws exist, prosecutors sometimes blame the victims of sexual abuse rather than supporting them. In a survey of victims of privacy violations, some reported that when they approached the police for help, they were told that they'd committed a crime too. One 17-year-old girl wrote: "I feel really intensely angry that you can get in legal trouble for sending naked pictures of YOURSELF when under 18. You literally can be charged as a sex offender for it, which is so incredibly wrong because I was the victim. All that law does is protect abusers" (Wolak & Finkelhor, 2016, p. 52). While adult victims who created images of themselves cannot usually be charged with any crime, some victims describe being mocked and blamed when they reported the abuse to police. A 22-year-old female victim explained: "Police told me that it was my fault and to not do things like video chat in the future to avoid this happening again," and a 20-year-old male victim had a similar experience: "The officer just said that there was nothing that could be done, kind of laughed at me, and told me to be more careful" (Wolak & Finkelhor, 2016, p. 51).

In general, the application of all criminal laws against sexual violence has been problematic: people of color are disproportionally charged with crimes and ignored when reporting victimization (Alexander, 2010), conviction rates are low overall, and the justice system rarely serves sexual assault victims' interests (Daly, 2014).

Responding to Image-Based Sexual Abuse

If someone you know is victimized by a sexual privacy violation, respond with compassion and support rather than blame and sexual shaming. Like any sexual activity, sexting is risky, but that doesn't make it wrong, deviant, or shameful. If you can, collaborate with your peers to develop strategies to resist slut-shaming and/ or homophobic reactions to the victim. Help the victim understand that they did not deserve to be a victim of a sexual privacy violation no matter what they shared consensually with whom. Help everyone understand that receiving private content does not give anyone the right—ethically and in some cases legally—to share that content with anyone else. If victims are being stalked, harassed, blackmailed, or otherwise harmed by the perpetrator, they can talk to a lawyer and report the incident to the police, but be aware that they still may not be offered adequate support or justice.

Victims of nonconsensual image distribution can also request that websites remove their private images. Starting in 2015, a number of social media websites and search engines, including Reddit, Twitter, Facebook, and Google, began adopting policies to remove unauthorized nude or sexual images upon request. These new policies are a significant improvement, but it begs the question: why should any website allow nude images to be posted and circulated in the first place without the depicted person's explicit and affirmative consent?[4] As Stoya points out: "I think executives at these companies can do a little better than just allowing users to report violations of their updated terms of service: They should require proof of consent before a nude image is posted, period" (Stoya, 2015). After all, the legal pornography industry is held to much higher standards: producers must have documentation verifying that performers are at least 18 years old and are consenting to the production and distribution of their sexual images. Better laws could also hold websites responsible if they knowingly host content that violates privacy (Nunziato, 2012).

People can also advocate for policies that require companies to build better privacy protections into mobile phones and other devices (Cavoukian, 2009), such as having better default options for user-controlled digital locks on the content they produce. Currently, the laws and digital rights management systems protecting companies' profit on the copyrighted media they produce are much stronger and more effective than the protections for the private images individuals produce—even when safety is at stake. While any digital lock is hackable, making these tools more widely available to users might at least help deter some of the more impulsive and thoughtless privacy violators.

Some victims of nonconsensual image distribution have fought back by going public about their abuse and raising awareness about this issue. Three years after an ex-partner distributed Holly Jacobs' private images, she created the End Revenge Porn campaign to advocate for criminalizing this act of harm. Jacobs now runs the Cyber Civil Rights Initiative, which provides victims with information, support, and referrals to *pro bono* legal assistance. Emma Holten, discussed earlier, responded to her victimization by creating new nude images of herself on her own terms, and published one accompanied by an essay on consent. She explains that taking the new photos was "an attempt at making [myself] a sexual subject instead of an object. I am not ashamed of my body, but it is mine. Consent is key. Just as rape and sex have nothing to do with each other, pictures shared with and without consent are completely different things" (Holten, 2014). While most victims choose not to risk further publicity, those that step forward can help people recognize the serious harms of this form of sexual abuse.

Social and legal changes could also help reduce the negative effects of the distribution of sexual images. As Jeong explains: "When a woman has her Google results bombed with nude photos and fake sex ads, she won't pass a screening when she tries to get a job—because she'll be mistaken for a sex worker. The solution … [is] to remove what bars a sex worker from getting that job" (Jeong, 2015). Those barriers include unfair shame and stigmatization for women who appear to exercise sexual agency—which includes both sex workers and those who choose to sext. Anti-discrimination laws protecting sexual expression could help prevent people from being fired for their sexual behaviors—or instances of sexual victimization, which are obviously unrelated to job performance. For example, a basketball coach was fired (and later reinstated after filling a grievance) when school administrators discovered a photo she had posted on her own Facebook page of herself in a bikini with her fiancé's hand on her breast (Jauregui, 2013). The larger social problem to combat is the sexual double-standard; if women were not slut-shamed, the tactic of distributing private sexual images to cause harm would be far less effective.

One of the simplest and easiest things everyone can do is promote respect for digital privacy by always asking for permission[5] before posting or sharing any photo of another person—especially if it's a potentially private photo. Just ask: "Can I post this photo of you?" and respect the answer. Parents might also want to consider the messages they send about digital privacy if they routinely post photos of their children on social media without getting their permission, if they use surveillance cameras in their kids' rooms, or if they install tracking apps on their kids' phones. Protecting one's digital information and respecting others' digital privacy are important new life skills everyone needs to develop. If we all commit to asking others for consent before distributing images that depict them—an easy act of human decency—we'll be helping to build a culture of consent and respect for privacy online.

Resources

- Without My Consent: withoutmyconsent.org
- Cyber Civil Rights Initiative: cybercivilrights.org
- "What to do if your privacy has been violated:" amyhasinoff.wordpress.com/privacy-violations

Notes

1. In one study (Englander, 2012), 92% of un-coerced 18-year-old sexters reported that sexting caused them no problems, including from unauthorized distribution.
2. In this chapter, the phrase *image-based sexual abuse* (McGlynn & Rackley, 2016) refers to a broad range of harms including privacy violations, harassment, coercion, and threats that involve sexual images while *sexual privacy violations* refers specifically to the distribution of private images without permission.
3. Others stress performers' agency within cultural and economic systems they do not control (Taormino et al., 2013).
4. In the US, federal communications policy usually prevents platforms from being held legally responsible for the content their users post unless they have been notified that it violates copyright or child pornography laws.
5. Meaningful consent is contextual and may be invalidated by abuse of power, intoxication, badgering, or coercion.

References

Alexander, M. (2010). *The new Jim Crow: Mass incarceration in the age of colorblindness*. New York, NY: The New Press.

Cauterucci, C. (2017). Marines' secret trove of nonconsensual nude photos is about power, not sex. *Slate*. Retrieved from http://www.slate.com/blogs/xx_factor/2017/03/06/the_marines_secret_trove_of_nonconsensual_nude_photos_is_about_power_not.html

Cavoukian, A. (2009). Privacy by design ... take the challenge. Retrieved from http://www.privacybydesign.ca/content/uploads/2010/03/PrivacybyDesignBook.pdf

Citron, D. K., & Franks, M. A. (2014). Criminalizing revenge porn. *Wake Forest Law Review*, *49*, 345–391.

Daly, K. (2014). Reconceptualizing sexual victimization and justice. In I. Vanfraechem, A. Pemberton, & F. M. Ndahinda (Eds.), *Justice for victims: Perspectives on rights, transition and reconciliation* (pp. 378–396). London: Routledge.

Dworkin, A. (1981). *Pornography: Men possessing women.* London: The Women's Press.

Eaton, A. A., Jacobs, H., & Ruvalcaba, Y. (2017). 2017 nationwide online study of nonconsensual porn victimization and perpetration. *Cyber Civil Rights Initiative.* Retrieved from https://www.cybercivilrights.org/wp-content/uploads/2017/06/CCRI-2017-Research-Report.pdf

Englander, E. (2012). *Low risk associated with most teenage sexting: A study of 617 18-year-olds.* Bridgewater, MA: Massachusetts Aggression Reduction Center.

Hasinoff, A. A. (2015). *Sexting panic: Rethinking criminalization, privacy, and consent.* Champaign, IL: University of Illinois Press.

Henry, N., & Powell, A. (2015). Beyond the "sext": Technology-facilitated sexual violence and harassment against adult women. *Australian & New Zealand Journal of Criminology, 48*(1), 104–118.

Hinduja, S., & Patchin, J. W. (2015). State sexting laws: A brief review of state sexting and revenge porn laws and policies. *Cyberbullying Research Center.* Retrieved from http://cyberbullying.org/state-sexting-laws.pdf

Holten, E. (2014). Consent: An objection. *Hysteria.* Retrieved from https://web.archive.org/web/20151229061134/http://www.hystericalfeminisms.com/consent/

Jauregui, A. (2013, November 12). Laraine cook, high school coach, fired over facebook photo that shows fiance holding her breast. *Huffington Post.* Retrieved from http://www.huffingtonpost.com/2013/11/07/laraine-cook-fired-facebook-photo-breast_n_4234128.html

Jensen, R. (2007). *Getting off: Pornography and the end of masculinity.* Cambridge, MA: South End Press.

Jeong, S. (2015). In between revenge porn and sex work. *Bitch.* Retrieved from https://www.bitchmedia.org/article/snap-judgment-revenge-porn

Klettke, B., Hallford, D. J., & Mellor, D. J. (2014). Sexting prevalence and correlates: A systematic literature review. *Clinical Psychology Review, 34*(1), 44–53.

Langlois, G., & Slane, A. (2017). Economies of reputation: The case of revenge porn. *Communication and Critical/Cultural Studies, 14*(2), 120–138.

Lenhart, A., Ybarra, M., & Price-Feeney, M. (2016). *Nonconsensual image sharing: One in 25 Americans has been a victim of "revenge porn".* New York, NY: Data & Society Research Institute.

McGlynn, C., & Rackley, E. (2016, February 15). Not "revenge porn", but abuse: Let's call it image-based sexual abuse. *Inherently Human: Critical Perspectives on Law, Gender & Sexuality.* Retrieved from https://inherentlyhuman.wordpress.com/2016/02/15/not-revenge-porn-but-abuse-lets-call-it-image-based-sexual-abuse/

Mendoza, M. (2013, April 12). 3 teens arrested for assault after girl's suicide. *Associated Press.* Retrieved from http://news.yahoo.com/3-teens-arrested-assault-girls-suicide-024221519.html

Nunziato, D. C. (2012). Romeo and juliet online and in trouble: Criminalizing depictions of teen sexuality (c u l8r: G2g 2 jail). *Northwestern Journal of Technology and Intellectual Property, 10*, 57–91.

Smith, A., Richie, B. E., & Sudbury, J. U. (Eds.). (2006). *Color of violence: The incite! Anthology.* Cambridge, MA: South End Press.

Stoya. (2015, March 13). The porn industry I work in most certainly requires consent. *Splinter.* Retrieved from http://splinternews.com/the-porn-industry-i-work-in-most-certainly-requires-co-1793846389

Taormino, T., Shimizu, C. P., Penley, C., & Miller-Young, M. (Eds.). (2013). *The feminist porn book: The politics of producing pleasure.* New York, NY: Feminist Press at the City University of New York.

Visser, J. (2013, April 9). "The justice system failed her": Nova scotia teenager commits suicide after being raped, bullied: Mother. *National Post.* Retrieved from http://news.nationalpost.com/2013/04/09/the-justice-system-failed-her-nova-scotia-teenager-commits-suicide-after-being-raped-bullied-mother/

Wittes, B., Poplin, C., Jurecic, Q., & Spera, C. (2016). *Sextortion: Cybersecurity, teenagers, and remote sexual assault.* Washington, DC: Center for Technology Innovation at Brookings.

Wolak, J., & Finkelhor, D. (2016). *Sextortion: Findings from a survey of 1,631 victims.* New Hampshire: Crimes Against Children Research Center & Thorn.

Wood v. Hustler magazine, 736 F.2d 1084 (5th Cir. 1984).

CHAPTER FOURTEEN

Child Sexual Predators' Luring Communication Goes Online

Reflections and Future Directions

LOREEN N. OLSON & ROY SCHWARTZMAN

Sadly, far too many children around the world are subjected to sexual abuse. Approximately 10% of U.S. children and one in seven girls will be sexually abused before their 18th birthday (Darkness, n.d.). Contrary to public perception that these crimes are committed by strangers, 90% of abused children know the perpetrator. Research shows that in 30% of the cases involving abused children, a family member committed the act. This number jumps to 60% when accounting for those abused by trusted family friends (Darkness, n.d.).

To help explain how perpetrators entrap children into ongoing sexual relationships, Olson, Daggs, Ellevold, and Rogers (2007) advanced the Luring Communication Theory (LCT) to articulate the dark communicative processes involved. The purpose of this chapter is to review LCT, situate it within relevant dark mediated communication processes, and articulate suggestions for how students, researchers, and advocates can further examine this social and mediated ill.

Luring Communication Theory and Child Sexual Assault

According to Olson and colleagues (2007), the first step of the luring communication process used by child sexual predators is to *gain access* to a potential child victim. At this stage the predator begins to scout his[1] victims. As stated above, most child sexual predators are family members or acquaintances. For example, coaches, scout leaders, camp counselors, members of the clergy, and teachers have been able to initiate untoward relationships with child victims because they are respected members of the community, trusted by the family, and, importantly, have opportunities to be alone with the child.

Moreover, family structure is considered the greatest risk factor in child sexual abuse (Darkness, n.d.). The risk of being sexually abused is lowest for children who live with both biological parents and rises substantially for those living with single parents or in a step-family. Children living without both biological parents are ten times more likely to be sexually abused than those living with both parents (Sedlak et al., 2010). Children at most risk are those who live in homes where one parent has a live-in partner. Sedlak et al. (2010) note that these children are twenty times more likely to be sexually abused than children living with both parents.

Clearly the family structure itself does not "cause" the violence or even allow it to happen. Instead, the stress and strain of single-parenting, for instance, can create a situation where a parent is emotionally and financially overwhelmed and needs assistance. According to Olson's team (2007), child predators exploit these types of situations, looking for single or neglectful parents who "need" help caring for their children. In this role, they become the friendly neighbor next door or the "uncle" who is willing to help watch the child at any time, giving the parent a much-needed break or the child some refuge from an unhealthy home life. Olson and colleagues note that "by creating situations that put themselves in contact with children and especially in positions of authority, child sexual predators are continuing to lay the groundwork to achieve their ultimate goal—sexual activity with minors" (p. 240).

Once the adult has gained access, he begins to build a relationship with the child. This *Cycle of Entrapment* is central to LCT. It is instructive to think of this cycle as a radial circle, with a central hub and three interdependent constructs that work in concert with each other while simultaneously supporting the core (see Figure 14.1). *Deceptive trust development* is the core phenomenon of LCT and the central hub of the Cycle of Entrapment. Olson et al. (2007) define this as "a perpetrator's ability to cultivate relationships with potential victims and possibly their families that are intended to benefit the perpetrator's own sexual interests" (p. 240).

The three interdependent constructs surrounding deceptive trust development in the radial circle are *grooming, isolation,* and *approach.* As the perpetrator gains access to the child, he begins to sow the seeds of trust with the child and possibly his/her parents. It is important to remember that this trustworthiness is a façade which hides the perpetrator's dark ulterior motives. This trust building, communicative process is called grooming, which is "defined as the subtle

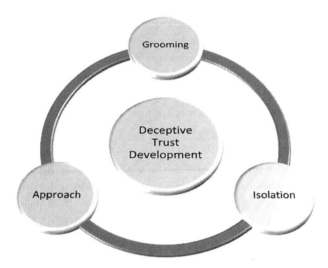

Figure 14.1. Luring Communication Theory's Cycle of Entrapment.

communication strategies that child sexual abusers use to prepare their potential victims to accept the sexual contact" (Olson et al., 2007, p. 241). Desensitizing the child to sexual contact is one form of grooming. These acts may include behaviors such as watching the child undress, "accidentally" touching the child's private parts, rubbing the child's neck, back, or thigh, or showing the child pornographic pictures. Abusers often communicatively manipulate children into reframing sexual acts between adults and children, convincing them that such acts are normal and helpful later in life. During the desensitization process, the abuser begins by rather innocently touching the child at first and then, slowly over time, begins to touch in more sexually explicit ways—all the while gauging how the child responds.

As the grooming intensifies, the perpetrator also works to *isolate* the child mentally and physically. Regarding mental isolation, "perpetrators aim to create or enlarge the mental space between the targeted victim and the victim's support network so that the perpetrator can then step into that space" (Olson et al., 2007, p. 243). Perpetrators may capitalize on already strained parent-child relationships, giving the child a "safe" place to vent about problems at home, to engage in illegal behavior such as drinking or doing drugs, or to escape an abusive home environment. The child may suffer similar mental isolation from peers. Because of the fun, safe environment the perpetrator manufactures, the youth becomes interested in spending more time with the adult, thereby isolating the child further. As the child becomes further separated from his/her support network, the perpetrator grooms more intensely, testing the waters for actual sexual contact.

Approach, the final concept in the Cycle of Entrapment, is defined as "the initial physical contact or verbal lead-ins that occur prior to the actual sex act" (p. 243). Here perpetrators use verbal seduction and physical touch in seductive ways in hopes of such behaviors paving the way to sexual contact. Known tactics include back-rubs, "accidental" touches in private parts, wrestling, bathing, or undressing with, or in front of, the child. Testing LCT, Adamson, Albert, Campbell, and Olson (2013) found that Penn State assistant football coach Jerry Sandusky, convicted of child sexual assault, used many such tactics, including touching/massaging the boys he was victimizing on the top of their thighs while getting uncomfortably close to their groins, accidentally touching their privates while wrestling or horsing around with them, lying in bed next to them, massaging their backs while they lay on top of him, and playing games with them while showering. All such acts of approach were ways of desensitizing the boys to additional benign types of physical contact that were sexual in nature but could still be "misinterpreted" as non-sexual.

The more recent case of U.S.A. Gymnastics and Michigan State University physician, Larry Nassar, also reveals how this trusted doctor was able to entrap and sexually assault more than 150 women and girls over the past few decades. The victims' testimonies reveal a pattern of grooming, isolation, and approach used by Nassar as he sowed his deceptive trust and carried out his violent assaults. The horrific reality of what happened to these young girls is best reflected in their own words (see Read Rachel, 2018 for victim testimony). Thankfully, the survivors of Nassar's abuse will never have to fear him again as he was sentenced to 40–175 years in prison and will spend the rest of his days incarcerated (Levenson, 2018).

One additional factor that emerged very clearly from the Nassar case is how the organizations and institutions (U.S.A. Gymnastics and Michigan State University) let the women down by downplaying the seriousness of the allegations when they reported the maltreatment. This notion of "organizational betrayal" served to further victimize the women and, like the institutional structures involved in the Sandusky case, merits further scrutiny as the LCT continues to evolve and account for the ways in which individuals, systems, and structures work together to create a knot of complicit actions that allow sexual predation to occur in the first place and to continue even after reported.

In sum, through the cycle of entrapment, the perpetrator cultivates trust with the child and possibly his/her parents. While doing so, he is grooming his child victim, exacerbating the child's sense of emotional and physical isolation from others, and slowly approaching the child in sexual ways. The child's trust of the perpetrator increases as these interconnected processes are successfully orchestrated. According to Olson et al. (2007), "all of these interwoven constructs work together to tighten the bond with the perpetrator, forming the entrapment cycle and making sex with that child more likely" (p. 244).

LCT Goes Online: Child Sexual Predation in Digital Realms

The number of children at risk for online sexual predation cannot be ignored. Studies have found that 20% of youth had been solicited for sex online (for a summary, see Black, Wollis, Woodworth, & Hancock, 2015). With so many young people online and at risk for sexual solicitation, we assert that LCT provides a mechanism for understanding the process used by predators. As noted earlier, however, LCT was originally created to explain face-to-face sexual predation. While there may be overlap between the luring communication practices used by child sexual predators in offline and online environments, unique features of the mediated world merit consideration when seeking to understand how children are entrapped in virtual worlds by sexual predators. Although the online environment does not inherently foster sexually predatory behavior, six affordances, or key features can prove accommodating.

First, the sheer size of audience reachable through mass emails or social media drastically increases the potential victim catchment rate. In the context of LCT, online messages expand the reach of initial approach exponentially. Some online predators use a "shotgun" approach to send mass messages, then follow up with whoever responds. Predators typically monitor multiple online chat rooms and other interactive platforms, grooming several potential victims simultaneously (Briggs, Simon, & Simonsen, 2011). For predators seeking sexual contact with strangers, online solicitation can prove far more efficient than personally scouting nearby locales.

Second, in addition to broadcasting a message, online communication can efficiently microtarget potential victims. Predators can focus on thematically oriented discussion boards, chat rooms, and other interactive forums to identify targets who might be receptive to the kind of luring the predator prefers (Winters, Kaylor, & Jeglic, 2017). For example, a predator could troll sites where teens gather to discuss sexual inhibitions or experimentation and purport to offer wise counsel—thereby deceptively cultivating trust.

Third, the perceived privacy of some forms of online communication can intensify the grooming process by enabling predator and target to engage more frequently in synchronous and asynchronous one-to-one communication (Kloess, Beech, & Harkins, 2014). Texts, personal messaging through social media, and similar tools allow predators to ping their targets more often, offering micro-reinforcements of interest. Furthermore, the targeted child can conveniently acknowledge a predator's messages, providing fuel for the predator to escalate intimacy. Online messaging facilitates rapid responses that can provide instant gratification and lead to deeper personal probing. This hyperpersonal aspect not only helps to isolate the targeted youth from communication that might mitigate the grooming, but also accelerates the perception of a close bond between the youth and the groomer (Lorenzo-Dus, Izura, & Pérez-Tattam, 2016).

Fourth, the anonymity of some digital communication can accommodate child sexual predation, allowing ample opportunity to create an idealized persona more likely to attract interest. This image construction can range from relatively banal distortions and exaggerations to fantasies that the predator can use to satisfy the child's emotional needs. Since "Internet users have the ability to manage what demographics are observed" and the capacity to tailor images or videos to suit their objectives, predators can selectively and deceptively portray their attributes (Hertlein & Stevenson, 2010, p. 2).

Fifth, the mediated realities of online communication provide fertile ground for sexualized or suggestive interactions without the risks and inhibitions attendant to direct physical contact. Webcams, videoconferencing apps, and similar technologies can desensitize children to watching or performing acts that they may feel reluctant to do publicly. Rapid exchange of personal information and images accelerates the online grooming process. Some research finds that personal data and contact information often get disclosed within the first day of interaction (Winters et al., 2017).

Sixth, predators can use multiple channels—voice messages, video, still images, emails, texts, etc.—to flood the child with messages that make the predator seem omnipresent. These multiple channels combined with both synchronous and asynchronous communication can deepen immersion in the predator's apparent affection. Multimodal online communication also enables multiple means of potential arousal that segue from grooming toward sexual contact. Interviews with apprehended online sexual predators reveal that ready access to sexually suggestive or explicit content could facilitate moving from a platonic to a physical relationship (Quayle, Allegro, Hutton, Sheath, & Lööf, 2014).

These aspects of digital worlds provide an important backdrop for understanding predators' strategic mediated communication. Yet, as we discuss next, much more knowledge about how online predators successfully lure their victims is needed.

LCT and the Digital World: Rhetorical Aspects of Online Grooming

Thus far, the strategies and tactics that induce the child to comply with online luring remain relatively opaque (Lorenzo-Dus et al., 2016). Recent research about online sexual predation of children concedes "there is still much to be understood in terms of the characteristics of the offenders and their conversations with potential victims" (Winters et al., 2017, p. 62). Since online grooming progresses from initial communication toward a sexual encounter, it requires persuading the intended victim to trust and to comply with the predator. Although this form of communication deviance (Olson et al., 2007) relies on deception and often coercion, it systematically influences the targeted child and thus qualifies as persuasion. Given the persuasive nature of luring communication—particularly the grooming stage wherein the predator steers the child toward compliance—its examination through a more rhetorical lens could yield useful insights.

Sequential Requests

Grooming typically proceeds as a series of escalating requests and actions, incrementally moving toward riskier and more sexually intrusive behaviors (Villacampa & Gómez, 2017). In this incremental approach, observable among online predators who sustain their interactions over extended time periods, messages become progressively more sexually explicit (Black et al., 2015). This technique embodies the *foot-in-the-door* (FITD) strategy, which begins with one or more small requests that—upon acceptance—enable easier compliance with a larger request. The ease of repeated, rapid contact makes online sequential requests far more feasible than in person. FITD can desensitize children to increasingly suggestive sexual messages by progressively expanding the scope of content deemed "normal." As Eisenberg, Cialdini, McCreath, and Shell (1987) observe, children as young as seven years of age demonstrate susceptibility to FITD. If a child refuses to move to more intimate communication, the predator can appeal to consistency: "But you've already come this far in our relationship, so you must think it's OK." FITD uses the child's previous instances of compliance as rationales for moving toward closer contact.

The reverse strategy, *door-in-the-face* (DITF), initiates a request that the recipient refuses, then offers a lesser request that stands a greater chance of acceptance because it seems reasonable by comparison. Black et al. (2015) note that some online predators prefer to introduce sexual content rapidly in an attempt to get the target to reciprocate. If the child refuses, then a subsequent, more moderate request demonstrates an apparent concession and thereby can generate compliance. DITF can prove particularly potent in grooming because it relies on reciprocal concessions (after refusal, the child now "owes" the groomer) or the child's sense of responsibility to avoid repeatedly disappointing someone the child trusts. Reciprocity and social responsibility are two well-established *modus operandi* for DITF (Turner, Tamborini, Limon, & Zuckerman-Hyman, 2007).

Cult-ivation of Deceptive Relationships

In their overview of propaganda techniques, Pratkanis and Aronson (2000) offer an inventory of the methods cults use to recruit, indoctrinate, and build loyalty among members. Four of these tactics also can apply to online sexual predators: isolation to breed dependency, a charismatic authority figure, escalating commitments, and inoculation.

While cults traditionally physically isolate recruits to separate them from information unauthorized by the cult leader, LCT suggests that predators can saturate the child's online networks to magnify the predator's apparent power. Although some predators use supplication to induce pity (Campbell, 2009), children's testimonies show that predators also use surveillance and threats to acquire the stature of "superheroes who can see and do anything" (Katz, 2013, p. 1539). Various digital tools can cultivate this perception of power prized by cult leaders, especially locating technologies (e.g., the child "checking in" at physical locations), monitoring social media contacts and activity, or controlling access to resources within an online gaming environment (e.g., withholding or bestowing rewards to encourage contact outside that virtual world).

Digitally induced isolation elevates the predator's perceived stature as an authority figure. Relinquishing contacts with people who might disapprove, the child unwittingly may build greater reliance on the predator as a powerful and trustworthy figure to obey. Children who are ignored, abused, or outcast succumb more easily to a predator (Olson et al., 2007, p. 238) cast as a savior from misery. Disaffected youths can find a haven with someone who appears to offer acceptance (the predator liking them "just the way they are") and guidance (portrayed as the path toward fulfillment of "natural" desires or "normal" maturation). The predator's online image can conform to the target's emotional needs and vulnerabilities, proving a seemingly perfect (utopian) companion without the disappointing flaws of customary everyday (quotidian) relational partners.

Research extensively documents the tendency of predators to bestow praise or gifts on their targets (e.g., Lorenzo-Dus et al., 2016). Similarly, cults induce progressively deeper devotion by lavishing recruits with attention and affection, generating an obligation to respond with greater involvement. In both cases, greater investment in the relationship (e.g., sharing more personal information or returning sexually suggestive compliments) constitutes proof of loyalty and devotion.

In cult-like fashion, predators also build loyalty by preventing apostasy, defined as abandoning religious faith or here as seeming to abandon the groomer. To silence possible objections, predators reframe their advances as harmless play or platonic friendship (Olson et al., 2007). Outsiders who might not condone the relationship get cast as killjoys or malicious intruders. These unbelievers become antagonists in the predatory reframing, with the predator emerging as the lone hope for happiness. The relational exclusivity and insularity of cults recall the apologetics employed by early Christian evangelicals who defended the faith against infidels and apostates (Golden, Berquist, Coleman, & Sproule, 2011). Inoculation against objections intensifies in online environments, as demonstrated with online political extremism.

Exclusion and Intensification Practices

To maintain loyalty and intensify commitment, cults and online hate groups inoculate against alternative views. Cults instruct members on how to refute the claims of non-believers. Online hate groups encourage insularity among adherents by categorically indicting all conflicting information as illegitimate (McNamee, Peterson, & Pena, 2010). By globally discrediting all unauthorized sources, hate groups fuel exclusive dependency on sources aligned with the group's ideology. Sexual predators can leverage an array of online methods to render themselves exclusive authorities, especially under the guise of a special friend who shares secrets only with the targeted child (Katz, 2013).

Sunstein (2017) points to how personalization of online content creates echo chambers that reinforce existing beliefs and preferences while restricting exposure to different viewpoints. Ongoing intensification of attitudes and beliefs energizes a cycle of confirmation bias, cultivating an appetite for more information that supports the same views. As a result, attitudes become more polarized and extreme as dissident views are disqualified and rejected (Del Vicario, Scala, Caldarelli, Stanley, & Quattrociocch, 2017). Blanket dismissal of all dissenting views (e.g., as "fake news") allows the reinforced perspectives to intensify unchecked.

Poisoning the well also serves the interests of online sexual predators, elevating their stature as authoritative and trustworthy. Aside from confirming the child's limited nascent beliefs (about their own sexual maturity or eligibility for deep intimacy), predators also activate desirability bias, defined as preference for messages that the recipient prefers to be true even if counterfactual (Tappin, van der Leer, & McKay, 2017). Thus, a child may treasure flattering messages from a sexual predator because they confirm a desirable self-image. When delivered online, flattery accomplishes more than ingratiation. By reinforcing the child's status as important and desirable, these messages provide welcome respite for children who otherwise feel outcast or degraded. The child therefore increases and intensifies exposure to the predator's praise and ego-boosting while blocking or ignoring messages that challenge the predator.

By understanding the specific techniques used by child sexual predators, quicker interventions can occur thereby decreasing the success of predatory attempts. We end this chapter with a discussion of specific intervention possibilities for the online environment.

Implications for Prevention and Remediation

Thwarting child sexual predation online requires exploring ways to counteract the persuasive appeals that drive the cycle of luring communication. As the most familiar measure, automated content restrictions such as filters and site blocking offer blunt and questionably effective remedies. Countermeasures against online sexual predation should avoid stigmatizing legitimate online interaction as dangerous (Holmes, 2009). Blanket restrictions could unintentionally curb productive online activities such as virtual support networks and explorations of personal identity (e.g., learning about different sexual orientations).

Whatever psychosocial disorders may afflict online sexual predators, they nevertheless display high skill in their agile employment of compliance-seeking techniques (Lorenzo-Dus & Izura, 2017). This perverse, dark communication competence (Olson, 2016) calls for measures that can identify the broadest possible range of luring tactics. Preventive and corrective measures also should address online communication from both the predator and the targeted child (Kloess, Beech, & Harkins, 2014). We recommend a three-pronged approach combining automated monitoring with human intervention.

Automated tools can scan message content and monitor online behaviors. Several content analysis programs show promise in identifying patterns used by online sexual predators in chat rooms (e.g., McGhee et al., 2011). The characteristics of rhetorical techniques such as sequential requests, cult-like recruitment and retention practices, and silencing or discounting voices of dissent—combined with content and thematic scanning for sexually suggestive material (Rahman Miah, Yearwood, & Kulkarni, 2011), could flag potentially problematic material. The accounts or sites in question then could qualify for further examination and referral for intervention.

Direct observation of online behaviors can trigger timely thwarting of inappropriately escalating relationships. Responsible adults can note potentially problematic usage patterns and investigate further by engaging directly with the child. Concrete signs of increased isolation include reductions in numbers of friends or people followed on social media, abandonment of long-time teammates or party members in online multiplayer games, or significant alterations in texting habits. Many such behaviors are publicly observable, enabling others to notice uncharacteristic shifts toward isolation. Choo (2009) also recommends establishing online reporting hotlines that could activate interventions from counselors or law enforcement.

Finally, preventive education could offer the most effective deterrent. Educating youths in judicious online communication may prove more effective than focusing on criminal penalties (Villacampa & Gómez, 2017). Teaching more general, transferable life skills such as privacy management, emotional control, willingness to seek advice, and critically assessing online claims can equip youths to resist or terminate interactions with online sexual predators (Kloess, Hamilton-Giachritsis, & Beech, 2017). Any combination of countermeasures to the rhetorical tactics discussed above can cultivate healthier online interactions built on mutual respect, forging bonds built through care rather than the bondage of manipulative control.

Note

1. While we recognize that females also commit sexual assault against children, the vast majority of child sexual predators are male. Therefore, we use the pronoun "he" throughout this chapter. This practice also follows the precedent set by Olson et al. (2007).

References

Adamson, N. A., Albert, C. S., Campbell, E. C., & Olson, L. N. (2013, October). *Face-to-face sexual abuse and Luring Communication Theory: A case study of Jerry Sandusky.* Paper presented at the Carolinas Communication Association conference, Charlotte, NC.

Black, P. J., Wollis, M., Woodworth, M., & Hancock, J. T. (2015). A linguistic analysis of grooming strategies of online child sex offenders: Implications for our understanding of predatory sexual behavior in an increasingly computer-mediated world. *Child Abuse and Neglect, 44,* 140–149.

Briggs, P., Simon, W. T., & Simonsen, S. (2011). An exploratory study of internet-initiated sexual offenses and the chat room sex offender: Has the Internet enabled a new typology of sex offender? *Sexual Abuse: A Journal of Research and Treatment, 23*(1), 72–91.

Campbell, A. M. (2009). False faces and broken lives: An exploratory study of the interaction behaviors used by male sex offenders in relating to victims. *Journal of Language and Social Psychology, 28*(4), 428–440.

Choo, K. R. (2009). Responding to online child sexual grooming: An industry perspective. *Trends and Issues in Crime and Criminal Justice, 379,* 1–6.

Darkness to Light: End Child Sexual Abuse (n.d.). *Child sexual abuse statistics.* Retrieved from https://www.d2l.org/wp-content/uploads/2017/01/all_statistics_20150619.pdf

Del Vicario, M., Scala, A., Caldarelli, G., Stanley, H. E., & Quattrociocch, W. (2017). Modeling confirmation bias and polarization. *Scientific Reports, 7*(40391), 1–9.

Eisenberg, N., Cialdini, R. B., McCreath, H., & Shell, R. (1987). Consistency-based compliance: When and why do children become vulnerable? *Journal of Personality and Social Psychology, 52*(6), 1174–1181.

Golden, J. L., Berquist, G. F., Coleman, W. E., & Sproule, J. M. (2011). *The rhetoric of Western thought* (10th ed.). Dubuque, IA: Kendall/Hunt.

Hertlein, K. M., & Stevenson, A. (2010). The seven "As" contributing to internet-related intimacy problems: A literature review. *Cyberpsychology, 4*(1), 1–8.

Holmes, J. (2009). Myths and missed opportunities. *Information, Communication and Society, 12*(8), 1174–1196.

Katz, C. (2013). Internet-related child sexual abuse: What children tell us in their testimonies. *Children and Youth Services Review, 35*(9), 1536–1542.

Kloess, J. A., Beech, A. R., & Harkins, L. (2014). Online child sexual exploitation: Prevalence, process, and offender characteristics. *Trauma, Violence and Abuse, 15*(2), 126–139.

Kloess, J. A., Hamilton-Giachritsis, C. E., & Beech, A. R. (2017). A descriptive account of victims' behaviour and responses in sexually exploitative interactions with offenders. *Psychology, Crime and Law, 23*(7), 621–632.

Levenson, E. (2018, January 24). Larry Nassar sentenced to up to 175 years in prison for decades of sexual abuse. *CNN.* Retrieved from https://www.cnn.com/2018/01/24/us/larry-nassar-sentencing/index.html

Lorenzo-Dus, N., & Izura, C. (2017). "cause ur special": Understanding trust and complimenting behaviour in online grooming discourse. *Journal of Pragmatics, 112*, 68–82.

Lorenzo-Dus, N., Izura, C., & Pérez-Tattam, R. (2016). Understanding grooming discourse in computer-mediated environments. *Discourse, Context and Media, 12*, 40–50.

McGhee, I., Bayzick, J., Kontostathis, A., Edwards, L., McBride, A., & Jakubowski, E. (2011). Learning to identify internet sexual predation. *International Journal of Electronic Commerce, 15*(3), 103–122.

McNamee, L. G., Peterson, B. L., & Pena, J. (2010). A call to educate, participate, invoke and indict: Understanding the communication of online hate groups. *Communication Monographs, 77*(2), 257–280.

Olson, L. N. (2016). The dark underbelly of communication competence: How something good can be bad? In A. F. Hannawa & B. H. Spitzberg (Eds.), *Communication competence: Handbook of communication science* (Vol. 22, pp. 657–682). Boston, MA: de Gruyter Mouton.

Olson, L. N., Daggs, J. L., Ellevold, B. L., & Rogers, T. K. K. (2007). Entrapping the innocent: Toward a theory of child sexual predators' luring communication. *Communication Theory, 17*(3), 231–251.

Pratkanis, A., & Aronson, E. (2000). *Age of propaganda: The everyday use and abuse of persuasion* (rev. ed.). New York, NY: W. H. Freeman.

Quayle, E., Allegro, S., Hutton, L., Sheath, M., & Lööf, L. (2014). Rapid skill acquisition and online sexual grooming of children. *Computers in Human Behavior, 39*, 368–375.

Rahman Miah, M. W., Yearwood, J., & Kulkarni, S. (2011). Detection of child exploiting chats from a mixed chat dataset as a text classification task. In J. Bos and S. Pulman (Eds.), *Proceedings of the Australasian Language Technology Association workshop* (pp. 157–165). Brisbane: ALTA.

Read Rachael Denhollander's full victim impact statement about Larry Nassar. (2018, January 30). *CNN.* Retrieved from https://www.cnn.com/2018/01/24/us/rachael-denhollander-full-statement/index.html

Sedlak, A. J., Mettenburg, J., Basena, M., Petta, I., McPherson, K., Greene, A., & Li, S. (2010). *Fourth National Incidence Study of Child Abuse and Neglect (NIS–4): Report to Congress, executive summary.* Washington, DC: U.S. Department of Health and Human Services, Administration for Children and Families.

Sunstein, C. R. (2017). *#Republic: Divided democracy in the age of social media.* Princeton, NJ: Princeton University Press.

Tappin, B. M., van der Leer, L., & McKay, R. T. (2017). The heart trumps the head: Desirability bias in political belief revision. *Journal of Experimental Psychology. General, 146*(8), 1143–1149.

Turner, M. M., Tamborini, R., Limon, M. S., & Zuckerman-Hyman, C. (2007). The moderators and mediators of door-in-the-face requests: Is it a negotiation or a helping experience? *Communication Monographs, 74*(3), 333–356.

Villacampa, C., & Gómez, M. J. (2017). Online child sexual grooming: Empirical findings on victimisation and perspectives on legal requirements. *International Review of Victimology, 23*(2), 105–121.

Winters, G. M., Kaylor, L. E., & Jeglic, E. L. (2017). Sexual offenders contacting children online: An examination of transcripts of sexual grooming. *Journal of Sexual Aggression, 23*(1), 62–76.

CHAPTER FIFTEEN

Cyberbullying

Consequences and Coping

MATTHEW W. SAVAGE & DOUGLAS M. DEISS

Bullies have changed over the years. In previous generations, the prototypical bully used to be the person, predominantly male, who was physically bigger and stronger than his fellow classmates. Traditional bullies didn't do very well in school, and bullies did not tend to endear themselves to teachers with their exemplary behavior. Bullies would threaten people in private settings to avoid the watchful eyes of adult caretakers when engaging in stereotypical bullying behaviors. They would take things that did not belong to them, budge in line ahead of others, and threaten physical repercussions if a person "snitched" on any other deviant behaviors. Bullies were visible. They had reputations. And peers learned quickly to guard themselves from these perpetrators. Strangely, as the technologies in homes and classrooms changed, so did the bullies. Today's bullies don't need to be big or physically imposing. They can be smart, adored by teachers, and can even commit hurtful acts on victims without any physical violence whatsoever. Today's bullies may have large audiences, yet, many can bully others without ever revealing their identity. How is this possible? Cyberbullying.

According to Savage, Jones, and Tokunaga (2015), cyberbullying is a term this is used to describe many things, including cyber harassment, cyber victimization, cyber stalking, internet bullying, online harassment, online aggression, and internet harassment. In order to provide clarity for the term, Tokunaga (2010) conceptualized cyberbullying as "any behavior performed through electronic or digital media by individuals or groups that repeatedly communicates hostile or aggressive messages intended to inflict harm or discomfort on others" (p. 278). This integrative definition is grounded in the study of traditional bullying (e.g., Olweus, 1993) and acknowledges that aggressive acts are made with harmful intent and repetition, while also underscoring important elements of technology germane to cyberbullying. These acts are committed using various communication technologies, they threaten or harm victims, and they are deliberate, repeated actions, conducted by an individual or a group. Although power is a component of traditional bullying (such as physical strength), power was not considered as important in early cyberbullying research and is only emphasized in some definitions of cyberbullying (e.g., Wolak, Mitchell, & Finkelhor, 2007). Additionally, whereas a victim of traditional bullying might have been scared at school, but safe at home, victims of cyberbullying lack a safe space because they can be publically victimized through a variety of computer-mediated technologies, including social media websites, at any time and any place.

Prevalence, Types, and Acts of Cyberbullying

Research indicates that many adolescents are victims of cyberbullying. Survey findings indicate that between 20% and 40% of youth report being victimized (Aricak et al., 2008; Dehue, Bolman, & Vollink, 2008; Patchin & Hinduja, 2006). These figures are regarded as conservative estimates because of a general unwillingness on the part of perpetrators and victims to report cyberbullying, as well as inconsistent methodologies. For example, some studies look at a past time frame like a month or semester in school, whereas others ask about whether cyberbullying ever happened. Also, most cyberbullying studies rely on perpetrators and victims to self-report their behavior. Most cyberbullying scholarship tends to focus on minors under 18, but more studies are investigating cyberbullying among college students (e.g., Foody, Samara, & Carlbring, 2015) and adults (e.g., Walker, Sockman, & Koehn, 2011). Researchers interested in this topic also contend that bullying and cyberbullying are useful terms to describe persistent aggressive behaviors in adults that occur in the workplace (Tracy, Lutgen-Sandvik, & Alberts, 2006).

Traditional bullying used to take place on the playground or in other places where adult supervision wasn't immediate. In that regard, cyberbullying amongst young adults hasn't changed much from traditional bullying. Consider for example the case of "Finsta." This refers to "fake Instagram", and is a type of Instagram account used by adolescents to avoid the watchful eye of vigilant adults (Cutolo, 2018). Finsta accounts use fake names, with fake information, which affords cyberbullies a strong degree of anonymity. When cyberbullying takes place on platforms like Instagram through Finsta accounts, no one may actually know who the real cyberbullying perpetrator is in this unchecked online environment.

Cyberbullying can happen in lots of different ways. Willard (2007) lists the following ways that cyberbullying can manifest itself: impersonation, rumors, cyberstalking, embarrassment or humiliation, teasing, insults, infected e-mails or software, and forms of denigration. Some of these forms are straightforward, whereas others can be complex. For example, impersonation occurs when a cyberbully acts as the victim, by setting up a fake email address or phone number. One can imagine how a cyberbully might harm a victim by sending false or embarrassing content to others. Further, Kaspersky, a global cybersecurity company, describes cyberstalking as a serious form of cyberbullying where the cyberbully threatens a victim's physical wellbeing or safety (see https://kids.kaspersky.com). Cyberstalking can also refer to when adults use the Internet to contact and attempt to meet with young people for sexual purposes. Denigration is a term to describe when cyberbullies send, post, or share rumors, gossip and falsehoods about a victim to humiliate the victim or damage their reputation or friendships. This is a common strategy in most cyberbullying. Some cyberbullies may use hacking and exhibition of unapproved photos, videos, or other multimedia. Laws differ by state about what is illegal and what is not, and cyberbullying cases are complex because a perpetrator can use any combination of these strategies to hurt victims.

There may be different types of cyberbullies, but more research is needed in this area to be sure. For example, Aftab (2018) who hosts stopcyberbullying.org describes that cyberbullies can be one of four types known as vengeful angels, power hungry, mean girls, and inadvertent cyberbullies. Vengeful angels take justice into their own hands and enact cyberbullying in an effort to intentionally protect themselves or others. Although they may think they are doing the right thing, they are still engaging in cyberbullying perpetration. Power hungry cyberbullies try to exert themselves over others, similar to a traditional bully, but online. Mean girls (who can also be mean boys) aim to entertain themselves by working as a team to embarrass or hurt victims. Inadvertent cyberbullies may not think they are bullies at all, but their actions would indicate otherwise. They are unintentional in their cyberbullying and may not consider the scope of their behavior before acting, making them different from vengeful angels who are intentional in their actions. An important thing to note about this typology is that it has not been studied by social science researchers, and people who use systematic scientific approaches to examine these topics have found that the idea of "revenge of the nerds" is not supported when young adults report their experiences of cyberbullying.

New research has begun to examine how peers in online environments impact the cyberbullying episode. Jones and Savage (2018) extended cyberbullying research beyond the cyberbully perpetrator and victim dyad to consider bystanders in interactive social contexts online. Results from their focus group interviews of college students who witnessed cyberbullying revealed a typology of cyberbullying bystanders. The typology describes bystanders' actions as goal-oriented, communicative functions of proximity, severity, environment, audience, and potential consequences. They came up with a typology of five bystander types: oblivious/distant bystander (who ignores), the entertained bystander (who observes), the conspiring bystander (who intentionally instigates), the unintentional instigating bystander (who unintentionally instigates), and the active/empowered bystander (who intervenes, reports, responds, or reaches out). We might use this research to come up with ways to address cyberbullying incidents by teaching bystanders' to enact prosocial behavior when dealing with cyberbullying incidents.

Consequences of Cyberbullying

Because there is a wide range of behaviors which make-up cyberbullying, there is also an assortment of psychological consequences when someone is cyberbullied. However, we must be cautious when making causal claims about the effects of cyberbullying. Aboujaoude, Savage, Starcevic, and Salame (2015) note that psychiatric research on cyberbullying is quite limited, so it is difficult to make absolute claims about how cyberbullying effects victims. They describe that cyberbullying research is a bit imprecise: "The majority of studies assess mood states rather than established psychiatric conditions (e.g., "sad" instead of "major depressive disorder"; "fearful" instead of "post-traumatic stress disorder" or "generalized anxiety disorder"), which limits the ability to interpret findings and discuss comorbid "disorders"." (p. 14). Also, some people define cyberbullying differently so not all studies are comparable. Most studies rely on self-report surveys, rather than comprehensive psychiatric interviews with mental health professionals. Still, the body of work illustrates a range of negative consequences that arise in the context of cyberbullying. These are worthy of review when considering how cyberbullying falls within the dark side of media and technology. These studies, conducted mostly among adolescents, suggest an association between cyberbullying and suicidality, adverse psychological pathology, and behavioral problems, each investigated here in more detail.

Suicidality

The link between suicidality and cyberbullying victimization was investigated by two meta-analyses. A meta-analysis is a type of study that summarizes many research studies about one topic to determine a pattern of results across a body of literature. For instance, one meta-analysis (Erdur-Baker & Tanrikulu, 2010) included 34 studies of traditional bullying and cyberbullying together and examined the link between "peer victimization" (including cyberbullying victimization) with suicidal ideation (considering suicide) or suicide attempts. The results showed that peer victimization predicted suicidal ideation and suicide attempts. In fact, cyberbullying predicted suicidal ideation significantly better than traditional bullying. Age and sex did not change the relationship between peer victimization on suicide attempts. Another meta-analysis included 137 data sets and revealed a strong association between cyberbullying victimization and suicidal ideation (Kowalski, Giumetti, Schroeder, & Lattanner, 2014). Consequently, work examining the link between perpetration and suicidality is needed too.

Adverse Psychological Pathology

Both cyberbullying perpetration and victimization are associated with negative psychological outcomes and behavioral problems. Amongst perpetrators, negative mood has been documented as a psychological outcome of cyberbullying (Schultze-Krumbholz, Jäkel, Schultze, & Scheithauer, 2012) as well as frequent behavioral and substance use problems (Calvete, Orue, Estevez, Villardon, & Padilla, 2010). Calvete et al. (2010) found that amongst over 2,000 adolescents that cyberbullies had more conduct problems, hyperactivity, and alcohol and tobacco use than victims of cyberbullying. When it comes to cyberbullying victims, many studies have determined associations to negative psychological states such as emotional distress, depression, avoidance, and fear (e.g., Sourander et al., 2010), as well as physical outcomes like insomnia and headaches (e.g., Calvete et al., 2010).

Behavioral Problems

Indeed, cyberbullying victims have more truancy, detentions, suspensions, and instances of weapon carrying than their peers (Ybarra, Diener-West, & Leaf, 2007), which may explain why they are absent from school and receive lower grades (Vazsonyi, Machackova, Sevcikova, Smahel, & Cerna, 2012) than their peers.

Given these severe consequences, it is important to explore recommendations for how to cope with perpetrators and victims of cyberbullying.

Recommendations for Coping With Cyberbullying

What should people do when they are cyberbullied? Research shows there are appropriate and effective ways to deal with and respond to cyberbullying. Although this list is certainly not exhaustive, we focus on five helpful suggestions: establishing safe environmental conditions, not retaliating, saving evidence, seeking social support, and notifying authorities.

Establishing Safe Environmental Conditions

Some cyberbullying research (Savage, Deiss, Roberto, & Aboujaoude, 2017) has focused on encouraging individuals to consider the role that their environment might play in dealing with and responding to cyberbullying. Bandura's social cognitive theory (Bandura, 1997) proposes that *environmental, personal*, and *behavioral* influences not only predict the behavior of people, but these various factors also interact with each other. For example, if a teenager witnesses a friend telling his or her own parents about being cyberbullied (behavior) and sees that the parents are very supportive of the friend (environmental), it might make the teenager more likely think about (personal) and possibly enact the same actions him or herself (behavior). This example shows how one's environment can have a significant impact on the likelihood of being cyberbullied, and also reminds us that we can find ways to create environments that allow for successful responses to a cyberbullying episode.

Bandura suggests that people can socially work with others to enact environmental changes which have a positive effect on the entire group (Bandura, 1997). The construct of *facilitation* describes how environmental changes can foster new helpful behaviors. One can change their environment to reduce their potential exposure to future cyberbullying or be ready to cope with an act of cyberbullying. For example, being careful about what information is shared on social networks like Facebook, Instagram, Snapchat, and the like can help to reduce exposure to the harmful effects of cyberbullying. Knowing this underscores the need for parents to be aware of usernames, privacy controls, account passwords, and online behavior.

One adjustment that can be made to anyone's online environment is the proper use of usernames, logins, or contact information (Juvonen & Gross, 2008) to reduce potential susceptibility to being cyberbullied. Usernames and logins should be considered in tandem with contact information. A username that focuses on a hobby (e.g., cheerleader1994) might make someone a target by others who dislike that activity. On the other hand, making one's username or login to completely match your name (e.g., JohnWSmith87) might make someone easily identifiable. Although, some social media companies such as Facebook forbid the use of fake names when registering one's account.

Another suggestion is to use strict privacy settings on Internet-based accounts (Aricak et al., 2008). Social media users can choose who views posted content, but many people don't use these settings. The good news is that social media users always have the ability to adjust the settings if their desires for privacy increase. Because the use of technology and the Internet is positively associated with cyberbullying victimization and perpetration (Roberto, Eden, Savage, Ramos-Salazar, & Deiss, 2014), parents should closely supervise their children's online behaviors. Parents are often unaware of what their children take part in online. For example, in 2018 it is common for young adults to have fake Instagram accounts (Cutolo, 2018) which their parents are unaware of to post private or personalized information that could make one more susceptible to cyberbullying. Children know about their parents' lack of knowledge. Thus, parents and children should work together to establish Internet safety routines and practices. Setting the computer up in the home in a public place can appear to be a solution; although parents should exercise caution as it might encourage their child to seek ways to circumvent any established rules. Not all parents manage their children in the same way. For instance, parenting style might influence the level of parental involvement. Parents with a permissive style are often more lenient with their children's behavior online, which allows some children to problematically set their own rules. Establishing a safe environment to prevent cyberbullying involves a combination of best practices regarding social media account usernames and logins (e.g., not sharing passwords with friends), appropriate use of contact information (e.g., not sharing contact information with strangers), and the partnership of parents and children in determining rules for Internet and social media usage (e.g., setting up a time limit for the use of Internet).

Not Retaliating

When individuals are cyberbullied and have read a hurtful or embarrassing message on one of their social media accounts or over their electronic device, they are immediately faced with one of two options. The first option and often the most likely is the instinct of responding to the act with another act of perpetration

(Weingart, Behfar, Bendersky, Todorova, & Jehn, 2015) and subsequently becoming a cyberbully too. Extensive research on the topic of conflict management provides substantial evidence for this assertion (for a review, see Roloff & Parks, 2002). Additionally, a communication skills deficiency model might explain the escalatory response in that individuals allow conflict to escalate because they lack the ability to stop themselves (Canary & Messman, 2000).

The second option victims can take if they are cyberbullied is to not retaliate. This would involve the withholding of any aggressive, hurtful, or harmful messages back from the initiator of the original cyberbullying act (Savage et al., 2017). Not all scholars are in agreement with the recommendation of not retaliating (Patchin & Hinduja, 2006). This counter argument posits that not retaliating is a passive strategy and subsequently might be ineffective. But, we contend that not retaliating not only keeps the victim from becoming a bully themselves, but it might also increase in effectiveness if paired with the other coping strategies.

Saving Evidence and Notifying Authorities

Of the various recommendations suggested by research and cyberbullying experts, saving evidence and notifying authorities are often offered together because they rely on each other (Savage et al., 2017). Evidence saved by a cyberbullying victim is only helpful when it is shared with someone who can do something to help. Authority figures who try to address the situation will need proof that something has occurred. An individual can report an act of cyberbullying without proof; however, the ability to provide saved evidence is beneficial in aiding authority figures with getting the behavior to stop. Notifying an authority figure might involve telling a teacher, a school administrator, or even a law enforcement official. The ability of authority figures to do something about cyberbullying can often be contingent on the limits of school policy, as well as state laws.

One of the major components of policy for local educational agencies (LEAs) is a description of proper procedures for reporting bullying (Compton, Campbell, & Mergler, 2014). However, notifying various school authorities might result in helpful responses to the act of cyberbullying. Cybervictims should expect a prompt investigation and response to the bullying report. Because no federal law exists which directly focuses on bullying, state laws become necessarily more important (see https://www.stopbullying.gov/laws/federal/index.html). Although, 48 of the 50 states have electronic harassment laws, only 24 of the 50 states have bullying laws which specifically address cyberbullying (Hinduja & Patchin, 2016). Consequently, the details of any law depend on the state; however, LEA policies should involve immediate intervention strategies designed to insulate a victim from further harm, bullying, or retaliation (see https://www.stopbullying.gov/laws/key-components/index.html). This does not necessarily have to involve notifying law enforcement officials, but that is suggested for schools when appropriate.

Seeking and Utilizing Social Support

Although cyberbullying victims are encouraged to notify authorities, if the victim is a child, it is not necessarily her or his first instinct. One study found that 90% of children neglected to report that they had been cyberbullied (Juvonen & Gross, 2008) and additional studies have confirmed that cybervictims only tell their parents anywhere from 1% to 9% of the time (Aricak et al., 2008; Dehue et al., 2008). Research shows that due to the importance of peers, adolescents are more likely to engage their friends versus parents (Cerna, Machackova, & Dedkova, 2016). Subsequently, it may be more advantageous to focus on the last recommendation offered by cyberbullying experts, which is seeking and utilizing social support.

Children often reach out to their peers for support and guidance when they are upset (Clark, MacGeorge, & Robinson, 2008). In fact, research provides ample evidence that social support is beneficial across the life span indicating that both children/adolescents (Eisenberg & Fabes, 1998) and adults (Burleson & MacGeorge, 2002) find it important. Seeking social support is a coping strategy used by victims of both bullying and cyberbullying (Davis, Randall, Ambrose, & Orand, 2015). The extensive research on social support might inform how we deal with a friend or family member who has been cyberbullied. Victims benefit most from receiving the suitable type of social support from peers because getting appropriate social support has direct implications for mental and physical health (Cohen & Wills, 1985).

Clark and her colleagues (2008) suggest a variety of verbal peer comforting strategies for tweens, who are children aged 8–14. These comforting strategies can be particularly helpful in assisting a victim of cyberbullying. When comforting someone who has been cyberbullied, a supportive other should first include an *account* of the distressing. Providing an account offers an explanation for the distressing event; validating the distressed victim. Next, *advice* can help to convey support to a victim. If the supporter can provide specific recommended actions to deal with the problem (like those listed in this chapter), a victim can be empowered through education. *Companionship* is another important facet of offering comfort to a victim of cyberbullying. Nonverbal indirect affection, like a hug, can be very helpful. Another strategy is to provide some *distraction* from the problem, perhaps through a careful combination of *minimization* that may reduce the problem's significance and *optimism* that allows the victim to reframe the issue in a positive way. Last, *sympathy* that expresses understanding and concern should not be underestimated when supporting those who experience cyberbullying.

The timing of requesting and receiving social support matters, too. For instance, individuals may experience significant emotional improvement if they can immediately discuss the cyberbullying situation with someone who is able to comfort them using person-centered messages. Burleson (2010) defined verbal person-centeredness as the "extent to which messages explicitly acknowledge, elaborate, legitimize, and contextualize the feelings and perspective of a distressed other" (p. 161). Allowing cyberbullying victims to articulate their thoughts and emotions can confer warmth and positive concern for the victim.

Conclusion

There are numerous advantages to the use of computer-mediated communication, but cyberbullying represents an unintended negative effect of having such an array of communication technology at our disposal. The dark side of computer-mediated communication reveals that not everyone on social media or with access to computers, cell phones, or tablets, wants to use the technology for kind, considerate, and prosocial communication. We hope this chapter taught you a bit about cyberbullying and its severe consequences, as well as also provided you with expert-recommended strategies for responding to cyberbullying. Cultivating a positive online environment, not retaliating, saving evidence, notifying authorities, and seeking social support can help to cope with cyberbullying in a healthy manner.

References

Aboujaoude, E., Savage, M. W., Starcevic, V. D, & Salame, W. O. (2015). Cyberbullying: Review of an old problem gone viral. *Journal of Adolescent Health, 57,* 10–18.

Aftab, P. (2018). Types of cyberbullies. Retrieved from http://www.stopcyberbullying.org/educators/howdoyouhandleacyberbully.html

Aricak, T., Siyahhan, S., Uzunhasanoglu, A., Saribeyoglu, S., Ciplak, S., Yilmaz, N., & Memmedov, C. (2008). Cyberbullying among Turkish adolescents. *CyberPsychology & Behavior, 11,* 253–261.

Bandura, A. (1997). *Self-efficacy: The exercise of control.* New York, NY: Freeman.

Burleson, B. R. (2010). Explaining recipient responses to supportive messages: Development and tests of a dual-process theory. In S. W. Smith & S. R. Wilson (Eds.), *New directions in interpersonal communication* (pp. 159–179). Thousand Oaks, CA: Sage.

Burleson, B. R., & MacGeorge, E. L. (2002). Supportive communication. In M. L. Knapp & J. A. Daly (Eds.), *Handbook of interpersonal communication* (3rd ed., pp. 374–424). London: Sage.

Calvete, E., Orue, I., Estévez, A., Villardón, L., & Padilla, P. (2010). Cyberbullying in adolescents: Modalities and aggressors' profile. *Computers in Human Behavior, 26*(5), 1128–1135.

Canary, D. J., & Messman, S. J. (2000). Relationship conflict. In C. Hendrick & S. S. Hendrick (Eds.), *Close relationships: A sourcebook* (pp. 261–270). Thousand Oaks, CA: Sage.

Cerna, A., Machackova, H., & Dedkova, L. (2016). Whom to trust: The role of mediation and perceived harm in support seeking by cyberbullying victims. *Children and Society, 30*, 265–277. doi:10.1111/chso.12136

Clark, R. A., MacGeorge, E. L., & Robinson, L. (2008). Evaluation of peer comforting strategies by children and adolescents. *Human Communication Research, 34*(2), 319–345. doi:10.1111/j.1468-2958.2008.00323.x

Cohen, S., & Wills, T. A. (1985). Stress, social support, and the buffering hypothesis. *Psychological Bulletin, 98*(2), 310–357. doi:10.1037/0033-2909.98.2.310

Compton, L., Campbell, M. A., & Mergler, A. (2014). Teacher, parent and student perceptions of the motives of cyberbullies. *Social Psychology of Education, 17*(3), 383–400. doi:10.1007/s11218-014-9254-x

Cutolo, M. (2018). What are Finsta Accounts and why does every teen have one? *Reader's Digest.* Retrieved from https://www.rd.com/culture/finsta-accounts/

Davis, K., Randall, D. P., Ambrose, A., & Orand, M. (2015). "I was bullied too": Stories of bullying and coping in an online community. *Information Communication and Society, 18*(4), 357–375. doi:10.1080/1369118X.2014.952657

Dehue, F., Bolman, C., & Vollink, T. (2008). Cyberbullying: Youngsters' experiences and parental perception. *CyberPsychology & Behavior, 11*, 217–223.

Eisenberg, N., & Fabes, R. A. (1998). Prosocial development. In W. Damon (Series Ed.) & N. Eisenberg (Vol. Ed.), *Handbook of child psychology.* Social, emotional, and personality development (5th ed., Vol. 3., pp. 701–778). New York, NY: Wiley.

Erdur-Baker, O., & Tanrikulu, I. (2010). Psychological consequences of cyber bullying experiences among Turkish secondary school children. *Procedia Social and Behavioral Sciences, 2*(2), 2771–2776.

Foody, M., Samara, M., & Carlbring, P. (2015). A review of cyberbullying and suggestions for online psychological therapy. *Internet Interventions, 2*(3), 235–242.

Hinduja, S., & Patchin, J. W. (2016). *State cyberbullying laws.* Retrieved from https://cyberbullying.org/Bullying-and-Cyberbullying-Laws.pdf

Jones, S., & Savage, M. W. (2018). Examining cyberbullying bystander behavior. In C. Beck & R. West (Eds.), *Routledge handbook of communication and bullying.* New York, NY: Routledge.

Juvonen, J., & Gross, E. F. (2008). Extending the school grounds?—Bullying experiences in cyberspace. *Journal of School Health, 78*(9), 496–505. doi:10.1111/j.1746-1561.2008.00335.x

Kowalski, R. M., Giumetti, G. W., Schroeder, A. N., & Lattanner, M. R. (2014). Bullying in the digital age: A critical review and meta-analysis of cyberbullying research among youth. *Psychological Bulletin, 140*(4), 1073–1137.

Olweus, D. (1993). *Bullying at school: What we know and what we can do.* Oxford: Blackwell.

Patchin, J. W., & Hinduja, S. (2006). Bullies move beyond the schoolyard: A preliminary look at cyberbullying. *Youth Violence and Juvenile Justice, 4,* 148–169.

Roberto, A. J., Eden, J., Savage, M. W., Ramos-Salazar, L., & Deiss, D. M. (2014). Prevalence and predictors of cyberbullying behavior in high school seniors. *Communication Quarterly, 62*(1), 97–114. doi:10.1080/01463373.2013.860906

Roloff, M. E., & Parks, M. R. (2002). Interpersonal conflict: A review. In M. L. Knapp & J. A. Daly (Eds.), *Handbook of interpersonal communication* (3rd ed., pp. 475–528). London: Sage.

Savage, M. W., Deiss, D. M., Roberto, A. J., & Aboujaoude, E. (2017). Theory-based formative research on an anti-cyberbullying victimization intervention message. *Journal of Health Communication, 22*(2), 124–134. doi:10.1080/10810730.2016.1252818

Savage, M. W., Jones, S., & Tokunaga, R. S. (2015). Cyberbullying: A mental health perspective. In E. Aboujaoude & V. Starcevic (Eds.), *Mental health in the digital age: Grave dangers, great promise.* New York, NY: Oxford University Press.

Schultze-Krumbholz, A., Jäkel, A., Schultze, M., & Scheithauer, H. (2012). Emotional and behavioral problems in the context of cyberbullying: A longitudinal study among German adolescents. *Emotional and Behavioral Difficulties, 17*(3–4), 329–345.

Sourander, A., Klomek, A. B., Ikonen, M., Lindromaos, J., Luntamo, T., Koskelainen, M., ... Helenius, H. (2010). Psychological risk factors associated with cyberbullying among adolescents: A population-based study. *Arch Gen Psychiatry 67*(7), 720–728. doi:10.1001/archgenpsychiatry.2010.79

Tokunaga, R. S. (2010). Following you home from school: A critical review and synthesis of research on cyberbullying victimization. *Computers and Human Behavior, 26*(3), 277–287.

Tracy, S. J., Lutgen-Sandvik, P., & Alberts, J. K. (2006). Nightmares, demons, and slaves: Exploring the painful metaphors of workplace bullying. *Management Communication Quarterly, 20,* 148–185.

Vazsonyi, A. T., Machackova, H., Sevcikova, A., Smahel, D., & Cerna, A. (2012). Cyberbullying in context: Direct and indirect effects by low self-control across 25 European countries. *European Journal of Developmental Psychology, 9,* 210–227. doi:10.1080/17405629.2011.644919

Walker, C. M., Sockman, B. R., & Koehn, S. (2011). An exploratory study of cyberbullying with undergraduate university students. *TechTrends, 55,* 31–38.

Weingart, L. R., Behfar, K. J., Bendersky, C., Todorova, G., & Jehn, K. A. (2015). The directness and oppositional intensity of conflict expression. *Academy of Management Review, 40*(2), 235–262. doi:10.5465/amr.2013-0124

Willard, N. E. (2007). *Cyberbullying and cyberthreats: Responding to the challenge of online social aggression, threats, and distress.* Champaign, IL: Research Press.

Wolak, J., Mitchell, K., & Finkelhor, D. (2007). Does online harassment constitute bullying? An exploration of online harassment by known peers and online-only contacts. *Journal of Adolescent Health, 41*(Suppl. 6): S51–S58.

Ybarra, M. L., Diener-West, M., & Leaf, P. J. (2007). Examining the overlap in Internet harassment and school bullying: Implications for school intervention. *Journal of Adolescent Health, 41*(6), S42–S50. doi:10.1016/j.jadohealth.2007.09.004

CHAPTER SIXTEEN

Without Consent

The Dark Side of Ignoring the Terms of Service and Privacy Policies of Social Media Services

JONATHAN A. OBAR & ANNE OELDORF-HIRSCH

I've got nothing to hide. I'm not a criminal. I'm not a terrorist. Take my data.

—DANIEL SOLOVE

Sound familiar? As Daniel Solove (2007) writes in "'I've got nothing to hide' and other misunderstandings of privacy" this dismissive position is common, and demonstrates a fundamental misunderstanding of Big Data possibilities and the dark side of our disregard. This error begins with the suggestion that privacy threats are only associated with wrongdoing, and assumes that data collection and data management may only result in problematic outcomes for those with criminal records. The reality is that corporations, governments and other organizations are increasingly using Big Data to make decisions about all sorts of things that impact our lives every day.

Would it bother you if your Netflix selections could be turned into data labeling your sexual orientation? (see: Singel, 2009, December 17) What if that seemingly harmless data could be combined with other data to identify your political and religious affiliations? (see: Narayanan & Shmatikov, 2008) What if knowledge of your sexual orientation, political or religious affiliations, either through Big Data products, or through social media searches could help recruiters circumvent the law and engage in hiring discrimination? (see: Acquisti & Fong, 2015)

As every sector of the global economy asks questions of Big Data, and as individual organizations within those sectors ask their questions, and entities within unique organizations ask theirs, the threat mosaic grows. Aside from the challenges associated with grasping, let alone controlling our data as it is captured across the globe, questions of the data are not just being asked today. Data is kept indefinitely, suggesting that questions and new questions may be asked again tomorrow, and again 10 years from now, likely in combination with all sorts of information collected over time. Answers to these questions are determined from far more than the data generated from one individual on one day from one source (like your Netflix queue). Data sets are constantly being populated from a wide variety of sources within and beyond our awareness. We assume that perhaps our smartphones and our social media profiles may be primary sources of Big Data, as we knowingly interact with them every day. What we may not realize is that a growing number of devices and network connections increasingly tracking us where we work, shop, walk and live, expand the data deluge beyond our awareness. Our medical, financial, and government records are being digitized. Secondary analyses of the data combines our social media information with other data in our dossiers, and from the dossiers of others, to generate new insights, and new data, even further from our awareness and understanding.

While many of the possibilities envisioned for Big Data emphasize opportunities for, as IBM advertises, creating a "smarter planet,"[1] critics suggest that we must re-evaluate our enthusiasm. Concerns linking Big Data with eligibility determinations abound, as data brokers look to monetize ranking systems (Pasquale, 2015), and the mosaic attempts to organize individuals into "targets and waste" (Pasquale, 2015; Turow, 2012). Answers to all of those questions being asked involve labeling and ranking individuals for the purpose of making decisions. Who gets to cross the border? Who gets that loan at the bank? At what rate? Who gets insurance? At what rate? Who gets into university? Who gets a scholarship? Who gets the best price? Who gets the best service? Who gets stopped by the police? Who goes to jail? Who gets hired? Promoted? Fired?

While every individual is at risk, vulnerable communities in particular appear most likely to be threatened by digital discrimination (Barocas & Selbst, 2016; Gangadharan, Eubanks, & Barocas, 2014; Newman, 2014; White House, 2014). As an Obama-era report on Big Data and discrimination noted: "Big Data analytics have the potential to eclipse longstanding civil rights protections in how personal information is used in housing, credit, employment, health, education, and the marketplace" (White House, 2014, p. 3).

The dark side of being dismissive of an emerging set of Big Data practices is to say nothing and do nothing to effect how these practices are shaped. Even more, while ignoring one's role in all of this raises individual concerns, it also suggests that as a society we prefer to focus only on ourselves, as opposed to questioning the threats encountered by our neighbors (Solove, 2007). To begin to address these challenges, one point of entry is to unpack the practice of ignoring the manifestations of notice privacy policy, namely terms of service and privacy policies for our hardware and software.

Notice and Consent

Current approaches to delivering digital privacy protections begin with a component called "notice." Providing individuals and organizations with information (or notice) about data collection and management practices has traditionally been step number one, and the most important step, to any chance of delivering protections (Federal Trade Commission, 1998; Office of the Privacy Commissioner of Canada, 2016). Not only is notice essential to making users aware of data practice, it has traditionally been viewed as part of the consent process, which is necessary for lawful data management.

Consent is a legal term that refers to an individual's efforts to authorize or refuse agreement to something. There are different forms of consent that suggest different levels of engagement in the consent process. If one was to imagine a consent spectrum, at one end might be the concept *informed consent*. This describes an ideal where individuals are fully engaged in the consent process, and aware of the implications of agreement or disagreement. At a distance on that spectrum from informed consent is *implied consent*. This assumes that individuals agree or disagree based on their actions, and not necessarily as a result of a direct acknowledgement of agreement or disagreement. For example, the act of using Google search, or logging into a social media service implies agreement to the terms associated with these services whether they are read or not. The problem with implied consent is that while it helps people get to the services they want quickly, users are agreeing to terms without accessing, reading, or understanding them. This suggests that we are providing implied consent and dismissing our opportunity to question the data-related threats associated with the terms.

While a contentious debate proceeds over the ability for individuals to provide meaningful forms of consent in light of the Big Data deluge (McDonald and Cranor, 2008; Obar, 2015; Solove, 2012), notice manifestations are common practice in the social media context. These manifestations generally take the form of terms of service and privacy policies.

How Terms of Service Agreements and Privacy Policies Work

A terms of service agreement (TOS) is an adhesion "take it or leave it" contract that includes rules about how services can and cannot be used, what rights users and the service have to any information provided, and under what circumstances the user's account can be deleted. Twitter's[2] notes that for any content users post, Twitter gets "a worldwide, non-exclusive, royalty-free license (with the right to sublicense) to use, copy, reproduce, process, adapt, modify, publish, transmit, display and distribute such Content in any and all media or distribution methods (now known or later developed)." Does this statement surprise you? It is just one example of how powerful these terms can be. Additionally, its ambiguity begins to demonstrate how difficult TOS language can be to understand.

A privacy policy is similar, but deals specifically with collection, protection, management, retention and sharing of information. Instagram's privacy policy[3] states that one type of information they collect is "User Content (e.g., photos, comments, and other materials) that you post to the Service," that one way they use content is to "provide, improve, test, and monitor the effectiveness of our Service," and that they can share this information with "businesses that are legally part of the same group of companies that Instagram is part of, or that become part of that group ('Affiliates')." This means they can use your photos to determine what else to show you, and can share those photos with related companies.

Do People Read Terms of Service Agreements and Privacy Policies?

While users are expected to consent to these policies upon signup and when policies change, it is common for individuals to engage with services without reading the fine print. It has even become a joke that we agree to policies without reading them. That is why "I have read the terms of service" could be called "the biggest lie on the Internet" (Obar & Oeldorf-Hirsch, 2018a).

In Fiesler, Lampe, and Bruckman's (2016) analysis of TOS, just 11% stated they read the terms for a given website. One study tracked over 48,000 visitors to websites of 90 software companies to find that only one or two of every 1,000 online shoppers viewed agreements for the software they were purchasing (Bakos, Marotta-Wurgler, & Trossen, 2014). Of the few readers, most read a small portion of the agreement. A similar study found that 85% of individuals skipped reading agreements when installing new software (Maronick, 2014).

Similarly, we assessed how people interact with terms when they sign up for a new service (Obar & Oeldorf-Hirsch, 2018a, 2018b). As part of the signup process for a fictitious social networking site, we presented participants with a privacy policy and a TOS, measuring how long they spent reading each. 74% skipped the privacy policy, and agreed to it without even reading it. These participants chose the clickwrap, "a digital prompt that enables the user to provide or withhold their consent [...] by clicking a button, checking a box, or completing some other digitally-mediated action" (Obar & Oeldorf-Hirsch, 2018b, p. 3). The particular clickwrap tested, common to social media services (Obar & Oeldorf-Hirsch, 2018b), provided a prominent "JOIN" button in the center of the page, above a link to the privacy policy. Participants could agree to the policy without even accessing it with the click of a button. Of those that read the policies, the median reading time was 14 seconds for both the privacy policy and the terms of service agreements. Yet, 97% agreed to the privacy policy, and 93% agreed to the TOS (Obar & Oeldorf-Hirsch, 2018a).

Why Not?

First, policies take a long time to read. McDonald and Cranor (2008) assessed how long it would take to read the privacy policies for all the sites the average individual visits annually. A review of 75 of the most popular websites revealed a decade ago that policies ranged from just 144 words to over 7,000 words, or 15 pages of text. It is worth noting that current calls for greater transparency, including the releasing of details associated with lawful access requests (Clement & Obar, 2016) suggest that privacy policies may be expanding. They estimated that U.S. Internet users visited about 1,400 unique websites per year, on average. Using an average adult reading speed of 250 words per minute, it was suggested that individuals would spend 244 hours per year on average just reading policies, or approximately 40 minutes each day. This is unrealistic, as people simply do not have the time to read all the policies required. When asked why they choose not to read, individuals say that policies are too long (Maronick, 2014), and deliberately too wordy (Milne & Culnan, 2004). Attitudes associated with information overload are a significant predictor of ignoring terms of service agreements and privacy policies (Obar & Oeldorf-Hirsch, 2018a). Individuals often feel overwhelmed by policies when they do engage with them, which contributes to dismissive behaviors.

Second, policies are also difficult to understand. Beyond time constraints, individuals agree that the language in these policies is not clear (Maronick, 2014; Milne & Culnan, 2004). Jensen and Potts (2004) tested this idea by assessing the reading level of privacy policies for 64 high-traffic health-related websites. Using the Flesch-Kincaid Grade Level Score—a standard assessment of text based on U.S. educational grade levels—they found that the language in these policies averaged at a college sophomore reading level. The most difficult terms were at a "19th grade" reading level, or well beyond the average college graduate reading level. Using the same scoring system, Fiesler et al. (2016) assessed the agreements of 30 websites and found that they too averaged at a college sophomore reading level. As 41% of U.S. adults have less than a college education (U.S. Census Bureau, 2016), this suggests that the language of these policies impedes consent processes. Yet, even college-educated individuals have a hard time understanding policies, correctly identifying only some of the information presented (Proctor, Ali, & Vu, 2008).

A third explanation is that users remain unconvinced that engaging with policy matters is even possible. When individuals download an app or sign up for a service, they seem focused on enjoying that app and exploring that service. Users want to play that game, share through that social network, or use that accounting software, not participate—before the fun even begins—in a tangential information session about data and privacy (Obar & Oeldorf-Hirsch, 2018a). At the same time, those that may have concerns may feel resigned to the reality of problematic privacy trade-offs (Turow, Hennessy, & Draper, 2015). This suggests that users feel that whether or not they even attempt to engage with policies, if services are to be consumed, agreement is necessary.

The Privacy Paradox

Despite not reading agreements, users often state that they are concerned about privacy. Ninety percent of Americans state that it is important to control information collected (Pew Research Center, 2015). Yet, the majority of Americans (91%) had not made any changes to their Internet or telephone use to control how information is tracked and used. People say they are concerned, but often refuse or ignore attempts to take control of their information, such as only using a website if they can decide what information to provide (Dinev & Hart, 2004).

This discrepancy in privacy attitudes and behaviors is called the Privacy Paradox, which states that an individual will share more information than they say they will—sometimes even 50% more (Norberg, Horne, & Horne, 2007). Why does this happen? When people decide whether to share information, they question how much they trust the entity they are disclosing to and how much risk they perceive. While one might believe that a balancing of trust and risk should influence disclosure, in practice, perceived risk appears to only influence intended disclosure, not actual disclosure. This behavior also applies to reading user policies. For instance, in an e-commerce experiment, 43% of participants said they would read the privacy policy of a site they were shopping on, but only 26% did (Jensen, Potts, & Jensen, 2005).

What Are the Risks of Ignoring Terms of Service and Privacy Policies?

There are many potential risks to agreeing with terms of service and privacy policies without reading them. Most importantly, you may not know what you are agreeing to. This issue came up in 2014 when for many Facebook users it became known for the first time that the site was conducting research on them. This was revealed in an experiment in which Facebook changed some users' news feeds to display more happy content from their online friends and some users' news feeds to display more sad content, and then tested the type of content that those users then posted (Kramer, Guillory, & Hancock, 2014). Many users were upset that their news feeds had been manipulated, unaware that this was something they agreed to. During the 2010 U.S. Congressional elections, Facebook also tested different ways of showing users which of their friends voted to find the most effective way to encourage voting behavior (Bond et al., 2012). Other companies acknowledge that they also experiment on users, and that this is also stated in the terms of service that users agree to. For instance, the dating site OkCupid (2014) stated that they experiment with how they match users to test their matching algorithms (see Toma & Sarmiento this volume).

Fiesler et al.'s (2016) analysis of 30 websites' terms of service shows that users agree to giving up control of their information at varying levels, such as allowing Craigslist to change and redistribute content that users have submitted, and not being able to terminate their agreement to the LinkedIn license once it has been given. In an analysis of privacy policies on 97 health websites Rains and Bosch (2009) found similar informational risks. Forty percent of the sites automatically collected information about visitors, both about the technology used to access the site and behavior on the site. Furthermore, only about one-quarter of these sites gave users a choice about how their information could be used and access to what kind of information was being collected (Carrión Señor, Fernández-Alemán, & Toval, 2012; Rains & Bosch, 2009).

Though the agreements in our study were not real, we addressed the risks of ignoring them (Obar & Oeldorf-Hirsch, 2018a). Tucked away in the terms of service agreement was a clause that stated "by agreeing to these Terms of Service, and in exchange for service, all users of this site agree to immediately assign their first-born child to NameDrop, Inc." Yet 93% agreed to the TOS, and 98% missed the clause (Obar & Oeldorf-Hirsch, 2018).

What Consumers Can Do to Protect Their Information

Clearly there are problems with how terms of service agreements and privacy policies are presented if so many people are agreeing to them without reading them. Given the potential risks, what can users do? Some efforts have been made to make policies easier to read and understand. The website LifeHacker presents a guide for quickly reading Terms of Service agreements based on suggestions by eDiscover attorney Mark Lyon (Klosowski, 2012). He says that users should look for the answers to three key questions: (1) what right you have to content, (2) what uses the provider can make of your content, and (3) how you can and can't use the service. Also, look for these important pieces of information:

1. Will my information be shared with third parties (aka affiliated)?
2. Can I opt out?
3. Arbitration, where I might give up my rights to sue in court if necessary.
4. Waivers or releases where I might be giving the company the ability to use my content or be giving up a claim I have against the company.
5. Sections written in ALL CAPS.

There are also online tools and resources to help simplify policies. One of these is Terms of Service; Didn't Read,[4] a website that highlights the best and worst aspects of these agreements for services such as Facebook, Netflix, and Amazon. The site also gives each service a grade based on how they treat users and their information, from Class A (the best) to Class E (the worst). As an example, Google is given a C grade because while it allows some user control over data, it engages in problematic data practices as well. For instance, they allow you to remove all your data if you close your account, but as long as you are a user, they can share your personal information with third parties.

Another service is Privacy Icons,[5] a browser extension by Disconnect, which displays a set of icons for each webpage, providing a quick glance at the most important parts of the TOS and privacy policies and indicates how well they do in handling user information. When you visit a website, each of nine icons are displayed in green, yellow, red, or gray, to indicate what good and bad privacy practices to expect. One of the icons indicates Expected Use, which indicates whether the website's policy is to disclose information about you in ways other than you would reasonably expect. A green icon means they do not do this, yellow means they do but there is a choice to opt out, and red means they do but there is no choice to opt out.

Another strategy is to call for improvements to approaches to privacy policy in general and notice tools in particular. Governments can do more to invest in digital citizenship training for users. They can invest in support services such as identity theft protection providers. Governments can direct and encourage internet service providers and social media service providers to improve notice instruments to make them easier to manage and to understand. More importantly, social media providers can engage in what's referred to as "internet governance by platforms" (DeNardis & Hackl, 2015)—forms of self-governance which actually deliver digital privacy and reputation outcomes, instead of just talking about them.

Conclusion

While it is unlikely that you would ever have to give up your first-born child for access to social media, if users are capable of missing and agreeing to such a clause, imagine the less-but-still serious legal threats agreed to all the time. Yet, there is also a serious discrepancy between those risks and our behaviors. As the privacy paradox states, we state that we value privacy, but we do not protect it. There are clear reasons why we do not read TOS and privacy policies when we sign up for services. We do not have the time to read the policies for each service we use, the language in these policies is difficult to understand, we are resigned to privacy trade-offs and we aren't interested in tangential privacy discussions. While there are several tools and initiatives to help make the process of understanding TOS and privacy policies easier, it is likely that the digital consent model needs to change. Policies are not presented in ways that serve the user, maybe purposely so (Obar & Oeldorf-Hirsch, 2018b). If individuals are to understand rights and responsibilities as users of a service, TOS and privacy policies need to be presented in alternate formats. Governments and service providers must do a far better job supporting users in this endeavor, and individuals must do more to engage. By clinging to the "I've got nothing to hide" fallacy (Solove, 2007), users disregard consent obligations and the threats posed to themselves and to their neighbors. These threats are associated with far more than the concealing of wrongdoing. In order to avoid the dark side of an ignoring culture, users must question how Big Data-driven eligibility determinations are increasingly affecting their lives every day, and do more to consent to their digital destinies.

Notes

1. See: https://www.ibm.com/smarterplanet/us/en/
2. https://twitter.com/tos
3. https://help.instagram.com/155833707900388
4. https://tosdr.org/
5. https://disconnect.me/icons

Reference

Acquisti, A., & Fong, C. M. (2015). An experiment in hiring discrimination via online social networks. *SSRN*. doi:10.2139/ssrn.2031979

Bakos, Y., Marotta-Wurgler, F., & Trossen, D. R. (2014). Does anyone read the fine print? Consumer attention to standard-form contracts. *The Journal of Legal Studies, 43*(1), 1–35. doi:10.1086/674424

Barocas, S., & Selbst, A. D. (2016). Big data's disparate impact. *California law review, 104,* 671–732.

Bond, R. M., Fariss, C. J., Jones, J. J., Kramer, A. D. I., Marlow, C., Settle, J. E., … Fowler, J. H. (2012). A 61-million-person experiment in social influence and political mobilization. *Nature, 489*(7415), 295–298. doi:10.1038/nature11421

Carrión Señor, I., Fernández-Alemán, J. L., & Toval, A. (2012). Are personal health records safe? A review of free web-accessible personal health record privacy policies. *Journal of Medical Internet Research, 14*(4), e114. doi:10.2196/jmir.1904

Clement, A., & Obar, J. A. (2016). Keeping internet users in the know or in the dark: An analysis of the data privacy transparency of Canadian internet carriers. *Journal of Information Policy, 6*(1), 294–331. doi:10.5325/jinfopoli.6.2016.0294

DeNardis, L., & Hackl, A. M. (2015). Internet governance by social media platforms. *Telecommunications Policy, 39*(9), 761–770. doi:10.1016/j.telpol.2015.04.003

Dinev, T., & Hart, P. (2004). Internet privacy concerns and their antecedents—Measurement validity and a regression model. *Behaviour & Information Technology, 23*(6), 413–422. doi:10.1080/01449290410001715723

Federal Trade Commission. (1998, June). *Privacy online: A report to Congress* (pp. 1–71). Washington, DC. Retrieved from https://www.ftc.gov/reports/privacy-online-report-congress

Fiesler, C., Lampe, C., & Bruckman, A. S. (2016). Reality and perception of copyright terms of service for online content creation. *Proceedings of the 19th ACM conference on computer-supported cooperative work and social computing—CSCW, 16,* 1448–1459. doi:10.1145/2818048.2819931

Gangadharan, S. P., Eubanks, V., & Barocas, S. (2014). Data and discrimination: Collected essays. *New America.* Retrieved from https://www.newamerica.org/oti/policy-papers/data-and-discrimination/

Jensen, C., & Potts, C. (2004). Privacy policies as decision-making tools. *Proceedings of the 2004 Conference on Human Factors in Computing Systems—CHI '04, 6*(1), 471–478. doi:10.1145/985692.985752

Jensen, C., Potts, C., & Jensen, C. (2005). Privacy practices of Internet users: Self-reports versus observed behavior. *International Journal of Human Computer Studies, 63*(1–2), 203–227. doi:10.1016/j.ijhcs.2005.04.019

Klosowski, T. (2012). How to quickly read a terms of service. *Lifehacker.* Retrieved from https://lifehacker.com/5892422/how-to-quickly-read-a-terms-of-service

Kramer, A. D. I., Guillory, J. E., & Hancock, J. T. (2014). Experimental evidence of massive-scale emotional contagion through social networks. *Proceedings of the National Academy of Sciences, 111*(24), 8788–8790. doi:10.1073/pnas.1320040111

Maronick, T. J. (2014). Do consumers read terms of service agreements when installing software? A two-study empirical analysis. *International Journal of Business and Social Research, 4*(6), 137–145.

McDonald, A. M., & Cranor, L. F. (2008). The cost of reading privacy policies. *A Journal of Law and Policy for the Information Society, 4,* 1–22. Retrieved from http://lorrie.cranor.org/pubs/readingPolicyCost-authorDraft.pdf

Milne, G. R., & Culnan, M. J. (2004). Strategies for reducing online privacy risks: Why consumers read (or don't read) online privacy notices. *Journal of Interactive Marketing, 18*(3), 15–29. doi:10.1002/dir.20009

Narayanan, A., & Shmatikov, V. (2008). Robust de-anonymization of large sparse datasets. *IEEE Symposium on Security and Privacy,* 111–125. doi:10.1109/SP.2008.33

Newman, N. (2014). *How big data enables economic harm to consumers, especially to low-income and other vulnerable sectors of the population.* Retrieved from https://www.ftc.gov/system/files/documents/public_comments/2014/08/00015-92370.pdf

Norberg, P. A., Horne, D. R., & Horne, D. A. (2007). The privacy paradox: Personal information disclosure intentions versus behaviors. *Journal of Consumer Affairs, 41*(1), 100–126. hdoi:10.1111/j.1745-6606.2006.00070.x

Obar, J. A. (2015). Big data and the phantom public: Walter Lippmann and the fallacy of data privacy self-management. *Big Data & Society, 2*(2), 1–15. doi:10.1177/2053951715608876

Obar, J. A., & Oeldorf-Hirsch, A. (2018a). The biggest lie on the Internet: Ignoring the privacy policies and terms of service policies of social networking services. *Information, Communication & Society, Online first.* doi:10.1080/1369118X.2018.1486870

Obar, J. A., & Oeldorf-Hirsch, A. (2018b). The clickwrap: A political economic mechanism for manufacturing consent on social media. *Social Media + Society, 4,* 1–14. doi:10.1177/2056305118784770

Office of the Privacy Commissioner of Canada. (2016). *Consent and privacy: A discussion paper exploring potential enhancements to consent under the personal information protection and electronic documents act.* Retrieved from https://www.priv.gc.ca/en/opc-actions-and-decisions/research/explore-privacy-research/2016/consent_201605/

OkCupid. (2014). *We experiment on human beings! (So does everyone else).* Retrieved from https://theblog.okcupid.com/we-experiment-on-human-beings-5dd9fe280cd5

Pasquale, F. (2015). *The black box society: The secret algorithms that control money and information.* Cambridge, MA: Harvard University Press.

Pew Research Center. (2015). *Americans' attitudes about privacy, security and surveillance.* Retrieved from http://www.pewinternet.org/2015/05/20/americans-attitudes-about-priv acy-security-and-surveillance/

Proctor, R. W., Ali, M. A., & Vu, K. P. L. (2008). Examining usability of web privacy poli- cies. *International Journal of Human-Computer Interaction, 24*(3), 307–328. doi:10.1080/ 10447310801937999

Rains, S. A., & Bosch, L. A. (2009). Privacy and health in the information age: A content anal- ysis of health web site privacy policy statements. *Health Communication, 24*(5), 435–446. doi:10.1080/10410230903023485

Singel, R. (2009, December 17). Netflix spilled your Brokeback Mountain secret, lawsuit claims. *Wired.* Retrieved from https://www.wired.com/2009/12/netflix-privacy-lawsuit/

Solove, D. J. (2007). "I've got nothing to hide" and other misunderstandings of privacy. *San Diego Law Review, 44*(May), 1–23. doi:10.2139/ssrn.998565

Solove, D. J. (2012). Introduction: Privacy self-management and the consent dilemma. *Harvard Law Review, 126*, 1880–1903.

Turow, J. (2012). *The daily you: How the new advertising industry is defining your identity and your worth.* New Haven, CT: Yale University Press.

Turow, J., Hennessy, M., & Draper, N. (2015). *The tradeoff fallacy: How marketers are misrepre- senting American consumers and opening them up to exploitation.* University of Pennsylvania report. Retrieved from https://www.asc.upenn.edu/sites/default/files/TradeoffFallacy_1. pdf

U.S. Census Bureau. (2016). *Educational Attainment in the United States: 2016.* Retrieved from https://www.census.gov/data/tables/2016/demo/education-attainment/cps-detailed-ta bles.html

White House. (2014). *Big data: Seizing opportunities, preserving values (Report for the President).* Washington, DC: Executive Office of the President. Retrieved from https://obamawhite- house.archives.gov/sites/default/files/docs/big_data_privacy_report_may_1_2014.pdf

CHAPTER SEVENTEEN

Smart but Nosy

Gratifications of Ubiquitous Media That Threaten Our Privacy

S. SHYAM SUNDAR, ANDREW GAMBINO, & JINYOUNG KIM

In November of 2015, the dark side of Amazon Echo came to public limelight when its controversial recording feature was used to help investigate a murder (McLaughlin, 2017). A former Georgia police officer was found dead in his friend's hot tub after a night of football and heavy drinking. With evidence of a struggle, but no witnesses, nor anyone to verify the homeowner's alibi, police turned to the homeowner's Echo device, which is always listening, recording all interactions and storing all commands following the wake word ("Alexa") on a server, making it a potential witness. The police also examined the owner's smart watering system and claimed that he used excessive water during the night to cover up the crime. Prosecutors' reliance on these devices brought attention to the pervasiveness of smart technologies that continually track our activities and record our lives, often unobtrusively and without informed consent.

Devices that gather enough information to potentially convict their owners of crimes are not merely emerging, but thriving. This is because they provide a variety of distinct gratifications to their users. Smart TVs can successfully predict and record media content based on prior behaviors, and virtual assistants provide news, information, entertainment and even shopping with more convenience than smartphone interactions. Smart technologies are at our beck and call, but it also means they are constantly alert to our actions, surroundings, preferences and moods, recording them and mining them for behavioral patterns, thereby undermining our privacy.

The main reason why smart devices listen and collect data about users is to enable them to provide accurate personalization services. Data collection itself is not new, as firms and websites have collected user behavioral data since the inception of digital technology. However, its scope and magnitude have grown tremendously with smart devices, as have the personalized services provided by these devices. The "personalization privacy paradox" (Awad & Krishnan, 2006) suggests that users desire personalized content, but at some point become quite discomforted with the release of their private information.

We examine this tension by focusing on the gratifications obtained by users from smart technologies, and discussing how the affordances of these technologies can influence privacy considerations by triggering cognitive heuristics (or mental shortcuts) about the benefits of these technologies. In particular, we focus on *cognitive outsourcing, personalization, constant connectivity, instant gratification*, and *user control*. The technological affordances that enable these gratifications have significant psychological effects, an understanding of which is necessary for the use and design of ethical technologies in the era of ubiquitous media.

Cognitive Outsourcing

Systems that offer product recommendations or give influential advice are known as recommender systems (Resnick & Varian, 1997). The star-rating system of Amazon, the certified fresh of Rotten Tomatoes, and even the order in which Google search results are displayed provide recommendations based on input from other users. Users place their trust in these recommendations, and in so doing, have outsourced the task to systems that can more extensively compile other users' reactions, feedback and input.

Computers represent where we can find information, i.e., the location of information, rather than the actual information that might help make the decision. We have outsourced the task of storing information in our memory, but choose to remember only the location where we can find information. The location could be a particular folder on our computers or a bookmarked website (Sparrow, Liu & Wegner, 2011).

All of this requires us to rely on computers and trust smart recommendation systems to provide us the most pertinent information for our decision-making. This reliance is not always warranted and can lead to "automation bias" (Parasuraman & Manzey, 2010; Skitka, Mosier, & Burdick, 1999). Automation bias refers to users' over-reliance on automated aids and decision support systems (Skitka, Mosier, & Burdick, 1999), which leads them to trust erroneous decisions even when contradicted by real-world data. Moreover, users who rely too much on automated aids become more complacent of their decision-making ability.

Three main sources are likely to drive this cognitive outsourcing: trust in the machine, trust in the crowd, and trust in an expert. We probe this gratification by suggesting that three cognitive heuristics (or mental shortcuts)—machine, bandwagon, and authority—may be the root causes for outsourcing.

Trust in the machine may be driven by distrust in oneself and other human operators having control over personal data. To avoid the danger of losing one's information to others, individuals may find it safer when machines, such as virtual assistants, handle their information. In general, humans are quite comfortable with machines taking over roles that are seemingly routinized, or require objective computing power rather than a personal touch. Nass and colleagues (1995) found that the acceptance of machines was much higher in routinized roles such as accountants than personal ones such as babysitters. This bias may carry over into the realm of privacy and security, given the enormity of personal data being collected from digital media users. Machines, more than human beings, are generally thought of as reliable entities that can securely manage user data (e.g., Adam, 2005). Therefore, when an interface makes salient that it is a machine or automated source, the *machine heuristic* ("machines can handle information in a secure manner") can be triggered, encouraging users to share more information online.

Machines as sources are influential, but mass-aggregated user opinions also strongly influence decision-making. When faced with choices, mass opinion that often appears in the form of "bandwagon cues" (e.g., star ratings, number of likes) contributes to cognitive outsourcing. Further, we find that users feel safe because there are many others who are also together with them in sharing their private information (Gambino, Kim, Sundar, Ge, & Rosson, 2016). In the age of new media, digital metrics have become particularly prominent and powerful as representations of the majority, influencing user attitudes and decision-making. The *bandwagon heuristic* ("if most others say that something is good, then it is good for me too") (Sundar, 2008), has been shown to be quite powerful, leading to favorable impressions based on number of friends one has on Facebook (Tong, Van Der Heide, Langwell, & Walther, 2008) and greater purchase intentions of products based on ratings provided by other customers of an e-commerce site (Sundar, Oeldorf-Hirsch, & Xu, 2008).

The appeal of authority in digital media is also psychologically relevant in many online contexts (e.g., Sundar, Kim, & Rosson, 2018). For example, an interface cue conveying the source identity of Google News is likely to invite readers to apply the authority heuristic to evaluate the credibility of an online news story. The presence of such cues triggers the *authority heuristic* in users' mind ("popular names, brands, or organizations can guarantee the security of online/ mobile services"). This heuristic, in turn, influences users' perceptions of the interface as well as their information disclosure behaviors (Sundar, 2008). For instance, the use of an authoritative source on a website (e.g., a trusted commercial brand, logo of the government offices) might make users feel safe, leading them to believe that what they do and reveal on the site is securely protected. Sundar et al. (2018) demonstrate that the presence of a security seal (i.e., TRUSTe) on a banking website persuades users with higher belief in the authority heuristic to provide their private information, including phone number, to the site.

In short, by invoking authority, social proof and automation bias, smart media technologies encourage us to rely on simple heuristics—authority, bandwagon and machine heuristics, respectively—when processing information and disclosing our own personal information, thereby allowing us to outsource a variety of decision-making tasks in a number of domains.

Personalization

A defining aspect of smart media is personalization, or automatic tailoring of services that cater to individual users' needs and preferences. System tailoring of media content based on users' past behaviors has become so ubiquitous that it is now more of an expectation than a novelty. Google provides different search results based on past search and browsing history of each individual user, while Amazon utilizes past purchases to offer recommendations for products. Similarly, smart devices in our homes tailor their offerings to each user based on their unique pattern of past behaviors and preferences. This kind of personalized service has been equated to that of a butler in the human-robot interaction literature (Dautenhahn et al., 2005), and can trigger the *helper heuristic* (Sundar, 2008), especially when accompanied by anthropomorphic cues such as human voice.

Although personalization has many positive effects, especially for individuals who are not particularly tech-savvy (Sundar & Marathe, 2010), it also comes with an inherent cost, namely covert collection of one's personal data (Smith, Dinev, & Xu, 2011). This has been labeled the "personalization privacy paradox," where users find themselves caught between the benefits of personalization and the cost of revealing their private information (Awad & Krishnan, 2006). Chellappa and Sin (2005) found that consumers navigate this tradeoff by seeking high-quality personalization services, and that both concern for privacy and desire for personalization influence users' intention to engage with the system. Ultimately, our privacy can be had, if the personalization is good enough.

Although at times small, each new connected or smart device records and shares more and more of our lives. All this private data can build wildly accurate profiles of users, and in some cases reveal intimate truths. By embracing smart speakers and other such technologies, it appears as though users are either naïve, or prepared to sacrifice privacy in order to reap their benefits. Underlying this decision is the *benefit heuristic* ("my personal information will be used to benefit me"), triggered by cues conveying benevolent personalization (Sundar, Kang, Wu, Go & Zhang, 2013).

It is only when personalization results in revelations or unexpected truths about oneself or one's family that it attracts attention and makes users concerned. In 2012, Target was the source of a major controversy when an irate father demanded to know why Target was sending coupons for baby clothes and cribs to his high-school daughter. The manager of the Target store had no idea, as the coupons were mailed out as a part of Target's corporate marketing scheme, based on each consumer's previous purchases. However, shortly thereafter, the father apologized, stating he was unaware that his daughter was indeed pregnant (Duhigg, 2012).

Beyond mere web-based behavioral data such as posting and web page lists, many sites store sensitive personal information such as addresses, contacts, credit card numbers, and now actual live recordings. Danger to the security of this information being stored on servers is evident from the recent hacks of companies such as Sony and Target (McGoogan, 2017). This danger is exacerbated when this information is monetized and sold to third-parties, which is often legally granted by users who sign convoluted end-user license agreements (EULAs) without reading them (see Obar & Oeldorf-Hirsch this volume).

Personalized services remain one of the core, if not the most distinctive, features of most popular digital services. In short, they trigger helper and benefit heuristics, which seem to outweigh privacy concerns among users, leading to more data-collecting devices being developed and adopted. Regardless of all the personalization provided—indeed, because of it—, the end result is more personal information disclosure.

Constant Connectivity

Constant connectivity is an important gratification, as it helps us accomplish our work more efficiently, make decisions and even settle arguments anywhere at any time. At the most basic level, mobility and ubiquity are evident to users when they receive *push* (system initiated) or *pull* (user initiated) notifications. An application's push notification often asks for access to user information for use of its features, i.e., access to one's location, contacts, or other data via a short text. Although users claim that they tend to protect this information, they are surprisingly willing to disclose it when prompted (Norberg, Horne, & Horne, 2007).

The ways in which new technologies have been utilized has led to increased reliance on these devices, so prevalent as to cause concern among many researchers about overuse and even addiction (Hong, Chiu, & Huang, 2012). However, their increased mobility is what makes it possible to utilize many new features, such as just-in-time content, as well as obtaining benefits from location-based applications. Having a powerful computer always on your person has led to the development and popularization of applications like Yelp, which allows anyone to find popular restaurants and services based on their physical location. This can be a concern with applications that allow "check-ins," such as Instagram and Facebook, where such location information can result in unwanted or even threatening real-life encounters.

Additionally, the mobility of devices has also enabled a new type of tracking of health data (Acquisti & Grossklags, 2012). Fitbit, which is used to monitor and promote stronger commitment to exercise and healthy behavior, also has the downside of collecting extremely personal health information (e.g., calories burned, sleep time and schedules, weight loss and gain). The mass collection, storage, and use of this sensitive health information makes it susceptible to being leaked or hacked.

Perhaps stronger cues are necessary on the interface to remind users that they are on a mobile device, so that they can trigger the *mobility heuristic* ("mobile devices are inherently unsafe in protecting my information") and exercise caution by avoiding sensitive transactions like banking. In addition, interface cues reminding users that they are in a public place can potentially trigger the *publicness heuristic* ("it is not secure to manage personal business in public") and thereby limit exposure of sensitive information. The publicness heuristic is particularly salient in non-password protected networks that are not backed by any trusted third party (such as a University network). However, when a user is confronted with multiple cues that convey security (i.e., VPN, Secure Network), their privacy concern may become elevated because they are reminded that their information is being passed along through several third-party channels. Unlike most of the heuristics discussed in this chapter, mobility and publicness serve as potential safeguards for the user, making them hyper-aware of their vulnerability.

Instant Gratification

An obvious psychological effect of constant connectivity is the heightened expectation for instantaneous service across platforms and sites, without having to separately access each platform and log into it with a distinct user id and password. According to recent market research (Russell, 2017), requiring users to create a new account to join online and mobile services is found to be off-putting for consumers. As many as 86% of users do not want to fill out a registration form and remember the credentials.

In order to help users have a seamless and engaged experience online, an increasing number of businesses are adopting a new way of signing in, called *social login* (or sign-on). Social login is a type of single sign-on process using existing personal information from other services such as Google+, Facebook, Twitter, and LinkedIn, without having to create a new account for a new site or service. Companies that introduced social login have found that it has decreased the number of users who fail to login, while boosting user engagement with their websites (Russell, 2017). It appears that the use of social login is a win-win strategy for both businesses and users as it can enhance users' experience on the sites, while reducing the number of failed or abandoned login attempts. Moreover, the companies are able to collect more accurate data about users, such as verified email address, demographics, interests, and more.

However, the more data are connected by using social login, the more a company can collect information about users, which can be misused for various advertising and marketing purposes. As Stokes (2017) noted, logging in with a main account whose credentials a user can easily remember will add more data to the company's reach. If a user signs into multiple sites with a couple of social media accounts, it will leave the connected accounts more vulnerable to privacy breach by hackers, as evidenced in the Cambridge Analytica scandal. Then, why do users prefer social login over traditional sign-up? It appears that social login thrives because of the operation of the *instant gratification heuristic* ("immediate service is better than delay in satisfaction of my needs"). Instant gratification is a mental rule of thumb that privileges immediate satisfaction, which makes users respond more readily to various online offerings, while underestimating the risks of information disclosure (Wiederhold, 2014).

Offers of instant gratification vary, such as multiple social login buttons on a login page or instant discount coupon codes on shopping sites (e.g., Zhang, Wu, Kang, Go, & Sundar, 2014). Voice-based smart speakers like Amazon Echo employ social login to provide a wide variety of mobile services to users without asking them to log into individual apps every time they use the services. Specifically, using the Alexa mobile app, users can easily connect their existing accounts for various mobile services—ranging from food-ordering to entertainment and ride-sharing, such as Domino's, Pandora, Spotify, and Lyft—to their Amazon account such that Alexa can provide all of those services instantly.

User Control

The previous sections have presented many affordances that put users in the passenger seat, while the system takes the wheel. However, user control has been documented as an important psychological requirement for the success of interactive systems, which in part, explains the rise of *customization*, i.e., user tailoring of their own interaction, as opposed to *personalization*, wherein the system does the tailoring (Kalyanaraman & Wojdynski, 2015). Many users want more control over how their personal data are to be disclosed in online venues, because such control would decrease the chances of privacy loss and lower their privacy apprehension (Almuhimedi et al., 2015). When control is provided to users however, it encourages them to share more private aspects of their lives (Brandimarte, Acquisti, & Loewenstein, 2013).

Given the previous discussions concerning outsourcing, personalized systems, and ubiquity, the affordance of control stands out as it gives the user ownership and awareness in the decision-making process. It can be conferred psychologically by simply seeing relevant interface cues, such as privacy settings in a social media website. Chen and Sundar (2018) showed that push-based interactive personalization, or overt personalization (e.g., allowing users to click on a button that then leads to them receiving personalized information), can induce a heightened sense of control in users. When an interface offers tools that allow users to control the pace and nature of their information disclosure, it triggers the *control heuristic* ("if a website offers me control over my private information, then it is okay to disclose my information") and results in greater disclosure (Sundar et al., 2018). Experimental work (Brandimarte et al., 2013) has demonstrated that users with explicit control show greater willingness to disclose even in the face of increased risk of losing their privacy.

In addition to cues on an interface, the concept of user-engagement with a feature can also work as a control inducer and privacy reducer. Zhang and Sundar (2018) showed that when users, interacting with a Netflix-style website, customized their privacy settings, their sense of control increased and privacy concern decreased. Triggering the control heuristic with interface cues may lower users' concerns about privacy breaches, but allowing users to customize their interaction, which require users to actively set up their preferences, may be more powerful.

In sum, it is clear that users desire control. While provision of interface cues and customization settings can enhance their sense of control (Zhang & Sundar, 2018), they can also prime users to worry about their privacy and the security of their data. This worry may indeed be good for raising awareness of the privacy pitfalls of ubiquitous computing technologies, ultimately making them smarter consumers of smart devices around them.

Conclusion

This chapter has examined the psychological gratifications that individuals receive from ubiquitous media in exchange for their private information. Users are often left in the dark about the pervasiveness of data collection, and this trend continues to grow with advances in "always on" listening devices and humanistic interfaces. An understanding of the cognitive heuristics that underlie our implicit faith in these technologies is important for us to be media-literate users of ubiquitous computing technologies.

First, it is critical for us to think systematically about costs and benefits of information disclosure to online systems, rather than rely on the guarantee of authority sources, swayed by the bandwagon of other users' disclosure behaviors, or driven by a blind trust in machines. Users of ubiquitous media devices should always pause before revealing their personal information and think about how that might be used and by whom for what purposes. They should proceed with the interaction if and only if they are comfortable with their data being mined for other purposes.

Second, users should understand the price they are paying for convenience, personalized offerings, and instant gratification of their needs. For example, when a mobile app asks them if it can use their current location in order to better serve them, they should know that their location information could potentially be stored on a server or transmitted to other entities in the network, thus creating a digital footprint of their movement that can be used for good or evil.

Third, whenever available, users should strive to take control of their personal data by customizing privacy settings in all the applications, devices and networks that they use, even if they are not used regularly. They should avoid "social logins" that require them to use their existing social media contact information to sign up for new, unrelated services. When possible, they should opt for pull notifications, whereby they initiate request for services, instead of push notifications initiated by the system. All this will provide users more agency in protecting themselves from the dark side of ubiquitous media.

Acknowledgement

This research is supported by the U. S. National Science Foundation (NSF) via Standard Grant No. CNS- 1450500.

References

Acquisti, A., & Grossklags, J. (2012). An online survey experiment on ambiguity and privacy. *Communications & Strategies, 88*, 19–39.

Adam, A. (2005). Delegating and distributing morality: Can we inscribe privacy protection in a machine? *Ethics and Information Technology, 7*, 233–242.

Almuhimedi, H., Schaub, F., Sadeh, N., Adjerid, I., Acquisti, A., Gluck, J., … Agarwal, Y. (2015). Your location has been shared 5,398 times!: A field study on mobile app privacy nudging. In *Proceedings of the 2015 annual conference on human factors in computing systems (CHI'15)* (pp. 787–796).

Awad, N. F., & Krishnan, M. S. (2006). The personalization privacy paradox: An empirical evaluation of information transparency and the willingness to be profiled online for personalization. *MIS Quarterly, 30*, 13–28.

Brandimarte, L., Acquisti, A., & Loewenstein, G. (2013). Misplaced confidences: Privacy and the control paradox. *Social Psychological and Personality Science, 4*, 340–347.

Chellappa, R. K., & Sin, R. G. (2005). Personalization versus privacy: An empirical examination of the online consumer's dilemma. *Information Technology and Management, 6*, 181–202.

Chen, T., & Sundar, S. S. (2018). "This app would like to use your current location to better serve you": Importance of user assent and system transparency in personalized mobile services. In *Proceedings of the 2018 annual conference on human factors in computing systems (CHI'18)*.

Dautenhahn, K., Woods, S., Kaouri, C., Walters, M. L., Koay, K. L., & Werry, I. (2005). What is a robot companion-friend, assistant or butler? In *Proceedings of intelligent robots and systems, 2005 (IROS 2005)* (pp. 1192–1197).

Duhigg, C. (2012, February 16). How companies learn your secrets. *The New York Times Magazine.* Retrieved from https://www.nytimes.com/2012/02/19/magazine/shopping-habits.html

Gambino, A., Kim, J., Sundar, S. S., Ge, J., & Rosson, M. B. (2016). User disbelief in privacy paradox: Heuristics that determine disclosure. In *Proceedings of CHI'16 extended abstracts on human factors in computing systems (CHI EA'16)* (pp. 2837–2843).

Hong, F. Y., Chiu, S. I., & Huang, D. H. (2012). A model of the relationship between psychological characteristics, mobile phone addiction and use of mobile phones by Taiwanese university female students. *Computers in Human Behavior, 28*, 2152–2159.

Kalyanaraman, S., & Wojdynski, B. W. (2015). Affording control. In S. S. Sundar (Ed.), *The handbook of the psychology of communication technology* (pp. 425–444). Malden, MA: Wiley Blackwell.

McGoogan, C. (2017, February 1). Hackers steal 2.5 million Playstation and Xbox players' details in major breach. *The Telegraph.* Retrieved from telegraph.co.uk

McLaughlin, E. C. (2017, April 26). Suspect OKs Amazon to hand over Echo recordings in murder case. *CNN.* Retrieved from Cnn.com.

Nass, C. I., Lombard, M., Henriksen, L., & Steuer, J. (1995). Anthropocentrism and computers. *Behaviour & Information Technology, 14*, 229–238.

Norberg, P. A., Horne, D. R., & Horne, D. A. (2007). The privacy paradox: Personal information disclosure intentions versus behaviors. *Journal of Consumer Affairs, 41*, 100–126.

Parasuraman, R., & Manzey, D. H. (2010). Complacency and bias in human use of automation: An attentional integration. *Human Factors, 52,* 381–410.

Resnick, P., & Varian, H. R. (1997). Recommender systems. *Communications of the ACM, 40,* 56–58.

Russell, M. (2017, August 11). *9 things you should know about social login and CRO.* Retrieved from https://conversionxl.com/blog/social-login/

Skitka, L. J., Mosier, K. L., & Burdick, M. (1999). Does automation bias decision-making?. *International Journal of Human-Computer Studies, 51,* 991–1006.

Smith, H. J., Dinev, T., & Xu, H. (2011). Information privacy research: an interdisciplinary review. *MIS Quarterly, 35,* 989–1016.

Sparrow, B., Liu, J., & Wegner, D. M. (2011). Google effects on memory: Cognitive consequences of having information at our fingertips. *Science, 333*(6043), 776–778. doi:10.1126/science.1207745

Stokes, N. (2017, May 6). *Should you use Facebook or Google to log in to other sites?* Retrieved from https://www.techlicious.com/blog/should-you-use-facebook-or-google-to-log-in-to-other-sites/

Sundar, S. S. (2008). The MAIN model: A heuristic approach to understanding technology effects on credibility. In M. J. Metzger & A. J. Flanagin (Eds.), *Digital media, youth, and credibility* (pp. 72–100). Cambridge, MA: The MIT Press.

Sundar, S. S., Kang, H., Wu, M., Go, E., & Zhang, B. (2013). Unlocking the privacy paradox: Do cognitive heuristics hold the key? In *Proceedings of CHI'13 extended abstracts on human factors in computing systems (CHI EA'13)* (pp. 811–816).

Sundar, S. S., Kim, J., & Rosson, M. B. (2018). *The role of interface cues in online decision-making: Cognitive heuristics that predict information disclosure.* Manuscript submitted for publication.

Sundar, S. S., & Marathe, S. S. (2010). Personalization vs. customization: The importance of agency, privacy and power usage. *Human Communication Research, 36,* 298–322.

Sundar, S. S., Oeldorf-Hirsch, A., & Xu, Q. (2008). The bandwagon effect of collaborative filtering technology. In *Proceedings of CHI'08 extended abstracts on human factors in computing systems (CHI EA'08)* (pp. 3453–3458).

Tong, S. T., Van Der Heide, B., Langwell, L., & Walther, J. B. (2008). Too much of a good thing? The relationship between number of friends and interpersonal impressions on Facebook. *Journal of Computer-Mediated Communication, 13,* 531–549.

Wiederhold, B. K. (2014). The role of psychology in enhancing cyber-security. *Cyberpsychology, Behavior, and Social Networking, 17,* 131–132.

Zhang, B., & Sundar, S. S. (2018). *The creepiness of proactive personalization and the clunkiness of reactive personalization: Can customization reduce privacy concerns and enhance user experience?* Unpublished manuscript.

Zhang, B., Wu, M., Kang, H., Go, E., & Sundar, S. S. (2014). Effects of security warnings and instant gratification cues on attitudes toward mobile websites. In *Proceedings of the 2014 annual conference on human factors in computing systems (CHI'14)* (pp. 111–114).

CHAPTER EIGHTEEN

Dark Shadows in Video Game Effects

Concerns about Violence, Character Portrayals, and Toxic Behavior in Digital Games

T. FRANKLIN WADDELL & JAMES D. IVORY

Video games' social effects have been a topic of public and academic discussion since their initial rise to commercial popularity in the 1970s (e.g., Kent, 2010). Extensive bodies of research have investigated potential connections between video game use and outcomes in players such as increased aggression, social dysfunction, and problematic use (e.g., Bushman, Romer, & Jamieson, 2015; Markey, Males, French, & Markey, 2015). Specific types of video game content have also come under scrutiny including critiques regarding the presence of violence (e.g., Dietz, 1998) as well as criticisms of game character sexualization (e.g., Downs & Smith, 2010) and the under-representation of women and persons of color (e.g., Lynch, Tompkins, van Driel, & Fritz, 2016; Williams, Martins, Consalvo, & Ivory, 2009). The increasing popularity of online multiplayer games has also introduced new social concerns about hostile and antisocial behavior (e.g., Fox & Tang, 2014; Holz Ivory et al., 2017) and continued concerns about the demographics of character portrayals in games (e.g., Waddell, Ivory, Conde, Long, & McDonnell, 2014). In light of these various concerns about video games' effects, what do we know from research about the dark side of video games?

Video Games and Violent Content

As the technological presentation of video games advanced during the late 20th Century, more and more games began to feature adult themes. In response to the production and popularity of games that featured gratuitous acts of violence (such as "Mortal Kombat") or references to sexual assault (such as "Night Trap"), Congressional hearings were conducted in 1993, with representatives from major game producers at the time called to defend the content of their products. One outcome of the Congressional hearings was the introduction of an industry ratings system for the content of video games to identify violence and other adult themes in video games (e.g., Egenfeldt-Nielsen, Smith, & Tosca, 2015). The broad question of violent video games and their effects on users' behavior, however, has since remained an open debate among academics and policymakers.

More than 30 years of research has since been conducted on the possible relationship between violent video games and aggression (Calvert et al., 2017; Markey & Ferguson, 2017). Before proceeding however, it is important to distinguish between how academics define two terms: (1) "aggression" and (2) "violence." On the one hand, aggression is often understood to refer to verbal or physical behaviors that most people would consider rude or socially inappropriate, such as shoving another person or using insults. By comparison, violence encompasses intent to cause serious physical harm to others, such as interpersonal abuse or mass acts of violence (e.g., Bushman, Gollwitzer, & Cruz, 2015; Ivory et al., 2015). Studies of the effects of video games focus on aggression rather than violence because actual acts of violence are difficult to measure in a formal research setting given the ethical standards of universities that safeguard the well-being of research participants. Additionally, deviant behaviors such as violence can be difficult to study in general, as most people are hesitant to admit that they have engaged in illegal or widely disapproved behaviors, and rates of occurrence for some violent acts are low enough in the general population to be difficult to study or measure (e.g., Eveland & McLeod, 1999).

Given these challenges and ethical concerns, most studies of violent video games have investigated thoughts, feelings, and simulated tasks that are better described as a form of mild aggression. Common tasks include the completion of sentences or the listing of thoughts where the number of aggressive words listed by an individual is later classified as either aggressive or neutral (e.g., K I _ _ completed as either "K I L L or K I T E") by the researcher. In other cases, researchers have attempted to measure behaviors in the laboratory that might correspond to aggression, often times with elaborate cover stories intended to obscure the actual purpose of the study from those participating in the research. Common examples of such behavioral tasks include the "competitive reaction time task," where participants are given the opportunity to play a loud blast of noise into an unseen person's ear (e.g., Elson, Mohseni, Breuer, Scharkow, & Quandt, 2014) or the "hot sauce task" where people assume the spicy hot sauce they put on a sample of food will be consumed by another person (e.g., Fischer, Kastenmüller, & Greitemeyer, 2010). In both cases, these protocols provide an opportunity to measure aggressive responses without arousing suspicion among study subjects. Some evidence from this line of research suggests that violent video games increase outcomes such as the number of incomplete word prompts that are completed with violent words or heighten the likelihood that one might put more hot sauce on the food for another person (e.g., Anderson et al., 2010). However, other academics as well as legal entities such as the Supreme Court of the United States have concluded that aggression measured in the laboratory may not tell us much about serious aggression and violence in everyday life (e.g., Elson & Ferguson, 2014). Taken as a whole, evidence remains equivocal regarding the possible relationship between violent video games and aggression.

Video Games, Character Sexualization, and Demographic Representation

Violence in video games is common, but it is not the only possibly troubling message that video games communicate to their players. As with other media content, social concerns about portrayals of characters in video games are a common research area. Systematically coded content analyses of video games have examined portrayal issues such as the proportion of male and female characters, how each character is dressed, the size of each character's body, or the number of characters that are present from different racial groups.

The results of these studies have generally revealed a dark side of video game content in how characters are portrayed. In terms of player gender, male characters tend to appear much more frequently than female characters, especially as lead characters and as characters that are controllable by the player (e.g., Dill, Gentile, Richter, & Dill, 2005; Downs & Smith, 2010; Ivory, 2006; Lynch et al., 2016; Williams et al., 2009). When women do appear as characters in games, they are more likely to wear "skimpy clothing" that reveal more skin than their male counterparts (e.g., Beasley & Standley, 2002; Burgess, Stermer, & Burgess, 2007). Female video game characters that are graphically advanced also tend to exhibit body shapes that are thinner than the average American woman (Martins, Williams, Ratan, & Harrison, 2009). The frequent portrayal of women in subordinate, sexualized roles with unattainable physical proportions has raised questions regarding how exposure over time to such images might affect attitudes towards women among frequent game players. Some studies offer the tentative conclusion that long-term exposure to video game characters may contribute, in part, to relevant attitudes in real life such as self-esteem (e.g., Behm Morawitz & Mastro, 2009; Dill & Thill, 2007)

Studies of how video game characters are portrayed in terms of race and age also find disproportionate representation. Compared to their prevalence in the U.S. population, White video game characters are over-represented as a group while Hispanics, Blacks, and Native Americans are under-represented. As for the age of characters that appear in games, non-elderly adult characters tend to appear at a rate well above their prevalence in the U.S. population while children and the elderly are severely underrepresented. While the effects of character portrayals in games on their players are not yet well understood, scholars have speculated that the under-representation of minority groups or the elderly may contribute to the distorted perception among the public that a group that is less visible is one that is less worthy of public support (e.g., Mastro & Behm-Morawitz, 2005). Game players whose demographic groups are underrepresented may also experience possible negative outcomes, such as decreased self-esteem or a lower interest in video games as a medium in general (e.g., Lucas & Sherry, 2004). While these patterns in games are troubling, it should also be noted that these problems are not unique to games as a medium. Specifically, research shows that characters in media often do not resemble the demographic makeup of the audience that consume media programming (e.g., Mastro & Stern, 2003; Thomas & Treiber, 2000). The idea that sustained exposure to video games may affect users by desensitizing them to real-life phenomena such as violence (Funk, 2005) or contribute to their perceptions that the world is dangerous (see Gerbner, 1998) has been studied, but is not yet consistently supported by empirical evidence. While we know that many games are violent, and that portrayals of characters in games do not represent women or persons of color well, future research may more fully explain how games influence their users' perceptions and behaviors.

The Role of Player Choices and Behaviors in the Video Game Experience

As video games have become more technologically sophisticated, new opportunities have arisen for game players to contribute to the nature of the game play experience. One common feature across many popular games are player-created characters known as "avatars" that give a game player the opportunity to customize dimensions of a character's appearance such as gender, height, face shape, or hair texture (e.g., Ahn, Fox, & Bailenson, 2012). Many online video games also allow players to communicate with one another, whether it be through in-game text chat boxes or via microphones that players speak into to broadcast audio into the game itself. On its face, giving players more control over the content of their game experiences might seem to hold the potential for games to change for the better. Unfortunately, studies of player-generated content and behavior in online video games have mostly revealed negative rather than positive trends that often perpetuate or even amplify pre-existing problems in the content of games. In fact, it may be that the darkest elements of video games are not in the produced content of the games, but in the behaviors of their players.

Given that many avatars in online games can be customized by the user, the choices that players make when creating their own characters might increase the diversity of characters that appear in games. While most systematic content analyses of video game characters have dealt with pre-packaged game content rather than portrayals of player characters in online games, there has been some research based on content analysis of characters in samples of recorded online game play. In one example of this research, which assessed portrayals in player-created characters as well as characters created by game producers, characters appearing in online games have been found to be even more disproportionate in terms of gender and race than in content analyses of "offline" game character portrayals (e.g., Waddell et al., 2014). Specifically, men were much more common than women, who accounted for approximately 87% of characters with a clearly identifiable sex. Characters were also overwhelmingly White, with Black characters being the only other racial group even present in the sample of characters that were studied. Finally, characters controlled by other players rather than created by the game programmer were relatively uncommon, making up less than 5% of characters overall, thus limiting the opportunities for the players themselves to introduce character diversity into the game setting.

Aside from demographic trends in video game characters, another area of research has examined how players communicate with one another in online video games. Some work has focused on the coping strategies used by female players to deal with the sexual advances and harassment they encounter from other male players in games (Fox & Tang, 2016). Other research has more broadly explored the presence of profanity and racial slurs in online games. Prior content analyses of profanity have generally revealed that while profanity does not appear in the majority of popular games, the games that do include profanity include it frequently (e.g., Ivory, Williams, Martins, & Consalvo, 2009). Do game players' interactions with others follow a similar trend? To answer this question, a pair of studies were conducted on how players communicate in well-known first-person shooter games that allow players to interact with others via text or voice chat (e.g., Holz Ivory et al., 2017). Findings from the studies revealed that while relatively few players spoke to others in the online games, the majority of players who did speak used profanity. Slurs related to race, sexual orientation, gender, and other slurs were relatively infrequent, but occurred often enough to be likely to occur within a play session of a few short online game matches. Some offensive content observed tended to be particularly provocative, with some users' in-game customized "emblems" depicting images such as the September 11th attack on the World Trade Center or "a male stick figure impaling the head of a female stick figure with his ejaculating penis" (p.13). Given that past work has found some evidence that video game profanity can affect some responses related to aggressive behavior (e.g., Holz Ivory & Kaestle, 2012), these trends in the way players interact with one another in video games are a shadow from the field of game studies that is deserving of further attention.

The Persistence of Stereotyping in Video Games

It may seem that online video games give players the opportunity to be free of the restraints that typically guide behavior in everyday offline settings. Unfortunately, studies of player behavior in video games have revealed that game users appear to rely upon many of the same automatic stereotypes in virtual worlds that also plague our real-world interactions (e.g., Castronova et al., 2009; Williams, 2010; Yee, Bailenson, Urbanek, Chang, & Merget, 2007). One of the most prominent examples of this trend is the persistence of sex-role stereotypes in digital settings. In other words, is it possible that female video game players experience stereotypes related to their appearance despite the fact that one's physical avatar often has little correspondence to one's offline identity? An online field experiment with players of a popular online game was conducted to answer this question (Waddell & Ivory, 2015). During the course of their regular game play session, the researcher approached users and asked for assistance with a favor, varying whether the sex of their avatar was male or female, the physical attractiveness of the avatar that they controlled (e.g., either a slender, human-like character, a bulky, monster-like character, or a character whose appearance was somewhere in-between human and monster), and the assumed sex of the person who was controlling the avatar (either male or female). A comparison of helping behavior across avatar attractiveness and user sex revealed that women were helped less frequently when their avatar decreased in physical attractiveness. By comparison, assumed male users who asked for help received the relative same level of assistance regardless of their avatar's attractiveness. Penalizing female users for the appearance of their avatar is consistent with the sex role stereotypes that women face in their offline settings (e.g., Bar-Tal & Saxe, 1976), providing tentative evidence that such stereotypes can also be found in the digital world.

A second example of sex role stereotypes finding their way into video games can be exemplified by comparing how communication styles in online games affect how players respond to male and female players. Specifically, an online experiment was conducted where the researcher varied the performance of a game player, the apparent offline sex of the player, and whether the player interacted with others through compliments or insults during game play (Holz Ivory, Fox, Waddell, & Ivory, 2014). After each game, the researchers sent all players from the match a "friend request" and recorded the frequency that the request was accepted, denied, or ignored altogether. Results of the study revealed that compliments and insults affected friend request acceptance in different ways depending on the assumed sex of the player. For male players, insults during game play actually led to the greatest likelihood of accepted friend requests. By comparison, female players were more likely to receive accepted friend requests when they remained silent or were complementary of other players. This pattern of findings where men are allowed to be aggressive while women are expected to be submissive is consistent with the sex role stereotypes that women face in their offline interactions, providing further evidence that player behavior in digital settings still follows many of the dark stereotypes that are ubiquitous in everyday life.

Finally, game players themselves are often the subject of frequent stereotyping as a population. Common stereotypes associated with gamers range from game play as an adolescent, primarily male activity that is concentrated among populations who prefer social isolation and are primarily physically inactive. These stereotypes are not consistent with recent work on the typical demographic traits of game players, which show that game players are typically older and include more female players than previously expected. The link between game play and health problems has also been challenged, with some scholars asserting that mindless eating during media use is less common during an active hobby like game play than more passive activities like television viewing. More broadly, scholars point out that any use of media that takes the place of exercise or more active behavior is problematic, an issue that is not unique to video games as a medium. Stereotypes and stigma about game players may also be exacerbated by rare, but high-profile instances of malevolent online behaviors such as publishing the personal information of other game players ("doxing") or placing other game players in harm's way with false police reports or threats (e.g., "Swatting"; see Limperos & Silberman for a related example).

Closing Thoughts

In light of these trends, what can parents or caregivers do? Taking a more active role in moderating childrens' and adolescents' use of media is encouraged by many scholars, particularly given that interactions with parents can reduce undesired effects that certain media may elicit (Choo, Sim, Liau, Gentile, & Khoo, 2015). In the United States and in other countries, industry-based ratings systems (ESRB in the U.S., PEGI in Europe, or USK in Germany) provide age recommendations and content descriptors that can be consulted before the purchase of a game. Likewise, game consoles include parental controls that can limit duration or type of game use (e.g., offline vs. online play). As far as the home is concerned, providing spaces for gameplay in public areas of the home, as opposed to more private spaces like children's bedrooms can help to limit exposure to content that parents deem objectionable. Finally, it is important to note that healthy development is often aided by exposure to a diversity of activities during childhood and adolescence, so while games may not need to be excluded from adolescents' media diet entirely, it may be useful for parents to encourage more active offline activities as well. Some have argued that allowing a child to "flip the script" on occasion and teach a parent or caregiver how to play a video game can positively impact the adult-child relationship (Villani, Olson, & Jellinek, 2005).

Video games will continue to attract public concern and scholarly attention. Much of this attention is warranted given the way that games tend to sexualize women and under-represent racial minorities. The possible effects of violent video games are also in need of further testing, although caution should be taken when extrapolating findings from the research laboratory to everyday aggressive behavior. The role of the player in the game play experience is also likely to continue expanding. While hope remains that players may make games a more equitable and less hostile place, the dark shadow of our offline selves continues to break into the digital world of gaming. While much research has been concerned with the effects of game content, it is very possible that the most worrying elements of some game experiences are created by some of the game players themselves.

References

Ahn, S. J., Fox, J., & Bailenson, J. N. (2012). Avatars. In W. S. Bainbridge (Ed.), *Leadership in science and technology: A reference handbook* (pp. 695–702). Thousand Oaks, CA: Sage.

Anderson, C. A., Shibuya, A., Ihori, N., ... & Saleem, M. (2010). Violent video game effects on aggression, empathy, and prosocial behavior in eastern and western countries: A meta-analytic review. *Psychological Bulletin, 136*(2), 151–173. doi: 10.1037/a0018251

Bar-Tal, D., & Saxe, L. (1976). Physical attractiveness and its relationship to sex-role stereotyping. *Sex Roles, 2*, 123–133. doi:10.1155/2012/490647

Beasley, B., & Standley, T. C. (2002). Shirts and skins: Clothing as an indicator of gender role stereotyping in video games. *Mass Communication and Society*, 279–293. doi:10.1207/S15327825MCS0503_3

Burgess, M. C. R., Stermer, S. P., & Burgess, S. R. (2007). Sex, lies, and video games: The portrayal of male and female characters on video game covers. *Sex Roles, 57*, 419–433. doi:10.1007/s11199-007-9250-0

Bushman, B. J., Gollwitzer, M., & Cruz, C. (2015). There is broad consensus: Media researchers agree that violent media increase aggression in children, and pediatricians and parents concur. *Psychology of Popular Media Culture, 4*, 200–214. doi:10.1037/ppm0000046

Bushman, B. J., Romer, D., & Jamieson, P. E. (2015). Distinguishing hypotheses from hyperbole in studies of media violence: A comment on Market et al. (2015). *Human Communication Research, 41*, 174–183. doi:10.1111/hcre.12058

Calvert, S. L., Appelbaum, M., Dodge, K. A., Graham, S., Hall, N., Hamby, S., … & Hedges, L. V. (2017). The American Psychological Association Task Force assessment of violent video games: Science in the service of public interest. *American Psychologist, 72*, 126–143. doi:10.1037/a0040413

Castronova, E., Williams, D., Shen, C., Ratan, R., Xiong, L., Huang, Y., & Keegan, B. (2009). As real as real? Macroeconomic behaviors in a large-scale virtual world. *New Media and Society, 11*, 685–707. doi:10.1177/1461444809105346

Choo, H., Sim, T., Liau, A. K. F., Gentile, D. A., & Khoo, A. (2015). Parental influences on pathological symptoms of video gaming among children and adolescents: A prospective study. *Journal of Child and Family Studies, 24*(5), 1429–1441. doi:10.1007/s10826-014-9949-9

Dietz, T. L. (1998). An examination of violence and gender role portrayals in video games: Implications for gender socialization and aggressive behavior. *Sex Roles, 38*, 425–442. doi:10.1023/A:1018709905920

Dill, K. E., Genile, D. A., Richter, W. A., & Dill, J. C. (2015). Violence, sex, race, and age in popular video games: A content analysis. In E. Cole & D. J. Henderson (Eds.), *Featuring females: Feminist analyses of the media*. Washington, DC: American Psychological Association.

Dill, K. E., & Thill, P. T. (2007). Video game characters and the socialization of gender roles: Young people's perceptions mirror sexist media depictions. *Sex Roles, 57*, 851–864. doi:10.1007/s11199-007-9278-1

Downs, E., & Smith, S. L. (2010). Keeping abreast of hypersexuality: A video game character content analysis. *Sex Roles, 62*, 721–733. doi:10.1007/s11199-009-9637-1

Egenfeldt-Nielsen, S., Smith, J. H., & Tosca, S. P. (2015). *Understanding video games: The essential introduction*. New York, NY: Routledge.

Elson, M., & Ferguson, C. J. (2014). Twenty-five years of research on violence in digital games and aggression: Empirical evidence, perspectives, and a debate gone astray. *European Psychologist, 19*, 33–46. doi:10.1027/1016-9040/a000147

Elson, M., Mohseni, M. R., Breuer, J., Scharkow, M., & Quandt, T. (2014). Press CRTT to measure aggressive behavior: The unstandardized use of the competitive reaction time task in aggression research. *Psychological Assessment, 26*, 419–432. doi:10.1037/a0035569

Eveland, W. P., Jr., & McLeod, D. M. (1999). The effect of social desirability on perceived media impact: Implications for third-person perceptions. *International Journal of Public Opinion Research, 11*, 315–333. doi:10.1093/ijpor/11.4.315

Fischer, P., Kastenmüller, A., & Greitemeyer, T. (2010). Media violence and the self: The impact of personalized gaming characters in aggressive video games on aggressive behavior. *Journal of Experimental Social Psychology, 46*, 192–195. doi:10.1016/j.jesp.2009.06.010

Fox, J., & Tang, W. Y. (2014). Sexism in online video games: The role of conformity to masculine norms and social dominance orientation. *Computers in Human Behavior, 33*, 314–320. doi:10.1016/j.chb.2013.07.014

Fox, J., & Tang, W. Y. (2016). Women's experiences with general and sexual harassment in online video games: Rumination, organizational responsiveness, withdrawal, and coping strategies. *New Media and Society, 19*, 1290–1307. doi:10.1177/1461444816635778

Funk, J. B. (2005). Children's exposure to violent video games and desensitization to violence. *Child and Adolescent Psychiatric Clinics, 14*, 387–404. doi:10.1016/j.chc.2005.02.009

Gerbner, G. (1998). Cultivation analysis: An overview. *Mass Communication and Society, 1*, 175–194. doi:10.1080/15205436.1998.9677855

Holz Ivory, A., Fox, J., Waddell, T. F., & Ivory, J. D. (2014). Sex role stereotyping is hard to kill: A field experiment measuring social responses to user characteristics and behavior in an online multiplayer first-person shooter game. *Computers in Human Behavior, 35*, 148–156. doi:10.1016/j.chb.2014.02.026.

Holz Ivory, A., Ivory, J. D., Wu, W., Limperos, A. M., Andrew, N., & Sesler, B. S. (2017). Harsh words and deeds: Systematic content analyses of offensive user behavior in the virtual environments of online first-person shooter games. *Journal of Virtual Worlds Research, 10*(2). doi:10.4101/jvwr.v10i2.7274

Holz Ivory, A., & Kaestle, C. E. (2012). The effects of profanity in violent video games on players' hostile expectations, aggressive thoughts and feelings, and other responses. *Journal of Broadcasting and Electronic Media, 57*, 224–241. doi:10.1080/08838151.2013.787078

Ivory, J. D. (2006). Still a man's game: Gender representation in online reviews of video games. *Mass Communication & Society, 9*, 103–114. doi:10.1207/s15327825mcs0901_6

Ivory, J. D., Markey, P. M., Elson, M., Colwell, J., Ferguson, C. J., Griffiths, M. D., Savage, J., & Williams, K. D. (2015). Manufacturing consensus in a diverse field of scholarly opinions: A comment on Bushman, Gollwtizer, and Cruz (2015). *Psychology of Popular Media Culture, 4*, 222–229. doi:10.1037/ppm0000056

Ivory, J. D., Williams, D., Martins, N., & Consalvo, M. (2009). Good clean fun? A content analysis of profanity in video games and its prevalence across game systems and ratings. *Cyberpsychology and Behavior, 12*, 457–460. doi:10.1089/cpb.2008.0337

Kent, S. L. (2010). *The ultimate history of video games*. Rocklin, CA: Prima Communications.

Lucas, K., & Sherry, J. L. (2004). Sex differences in video game play: A communication-based explanation. *Communication Research, 31*, 499–523. doi:10.1177/0093650204267930

Lynch, T., Tompkins, J. E., van Driel, I. I., & Fritz, N. (2016). Sexy, strong, and secondary: A content analysis of female characters in video games across 31 years. *Journal of Communication, 66*, 564–584. doi:10.1111/jcom.12237

Markey, P. M., & Ferguson, C. J. (2017). *Moral combat: Why the war on violent video games is wrong*. Dallas, TX: BenBella Books.

Markey, P. M., Males, M. A., French, J. E., & Markey, C. N. (2015). Lessons from Markey et al. (2015) and Bushman et al. (2015): Sensationalism and integrity in media research. *Human Communication Research, 41*, 184–203. doi:10.1111/hcre.12057

Martins, N., Williams, D. C., Ratan, R. A., & Harrison, K. (2011). Virtual muscularity: A content analysis of male video game characters. *Body Image, 8*, 43–51. doi:10.1016/j.body-im.2010.10.002

Mastro, D. E., & Behm-Morawitz, E. (2005). Latino representation on primetime television. *Journalism and Mass Communication Quarterly, 82*, 110–130. doi:10.1177/107769900508200108

Mastro, D. E., & Stern, S. R. (2003). Representations of race in television commercials: A content analysis of prime-time advertising. *Journal of Broadcasting and Electronic Media, 47*, 638–647. doi:10.1207/s15506878jobem4704_9

Thomas, M. E., & Treiber, L. A. (2000). Race, gender, and status: Content analysis of print advertisements in four popular magazines. *Sociological Spectrum, 20*, 357–371. doi:10.1080/027321700405090

Villani, V. S., Olson, C. K., & Jellinek, M. S. (2005). Media Literacy for clinicians and parents. *Child Adolescent Psychiatric Clinics of North America, 14*, 523–553. doi:10.1016/j.chc.2005.03.001

Waddell, T. F., & Ivory, J. D. (2015). It's not easy trying to be one of the guys: The effect of avatar attractiveness, avatar sex, and user sex on the success of help-seeking requests in an online game. *Journal of Broadcasting and Electronic Media, 59*, 112–129. doi:10.1080/08838151.2014.9982 21

Waddell, T. F., Ivory, J. D., Conde, R., Long, C., & McDonnell, R. (2014). White man's virtual world: A systematic content analysis of gender and race in massively multiplayer online games. *Journal of Virtual Worlds Research, 7*(2). doi:10.4101/jvwr.v7i2.7096

Williams, D. (2010). The mapping principle, and a research framework for virtual worlds. *Communication Theory, 20*, 451–470. doi:10.1111/j.1468-2885.2010.01371.x

Williams, D., Martins, N., Consalvo, M., & Ivory, J. D. (2009). The virtual census: Representations of gender, race, and age in video games. *New Media and Society, 11*, 815–834. doi:10.1177/1461444809105354

Yee, N., Bailenson, J. N., Urbanek, M., Chang, F., & Merget, D. (2007). The unbearable likeness of being digital: The persistence of nonverbal social norms in online virtual environments. *Cyberpsychology and Behavior, 10*, 115–121. doi:10.1089/cpb.2006.9984

CHAPTER NINETEEN

Internet Gaming Disorder

Considering Problematic Internet Use as an Addiction

REBECCA J. GILBERTSON & KAYLA M. WALTON

When video games make the news, it is usually for something controversial. Consider, for instance, the headline: "Man dies from blood clot after marathon gaming" (Carollo, 2011). A second headline reads: "Man dies in Taiwan after 3-day online gaming binge" (Hunt & Ng, 2015). Given the popularity of video gaming, and the extremity of the outcome, these cases become newsworthy. But, are these occurrences just unfortunate instances in the world of game play? Or, do they expose a larger contingency of video gamers who play excessively? In other words, can playing video games be addictive, such that it creates physical, psychological, or social/relational problems in daily life? Addiction scientists are cautiously starting to address these questions.

Scientists typically use the term "addiction" in reference to substances (i.e., drugs or alcohol) that cause tolerance, withdrawal, and craving, among other symptoms. More than perhaps any other symptom, addiction is synonymous with loss of control (Starcevic, 2013). While addiction to substances represents the largest body of work on the topic, the American Society of Addiction Medicine recently expanded the definition of addiction to also include addictive behaviors. These so-called "behavioral addictions" (i.e., gambling, food, shopping, sex) were first suggested by a British psychiatrist in the early 1990s (Marks, 1990). Following its characterization "internet abuse" was included in a well-cited article as the fastest growing behavioral addiction (Holden, 2001;

Young, 1998). Early editorials focused on the work in progress of individual scientists studying behavioral addiction, as empirical evidence for the existence of these disorders was scarce.

Behavioral addictions remain less well studied than substance use disorders ("Science has a gambling problem", 2018). However, in "Introduction to Behavioral Addiction", Grant, Potenza, Weinstein, & Gorelick (2010) listed impulse control disorders that could be considered possible "behavioral" addictions due to similarities with substance use disorders in neurobiology, genetics, treatment, consequences, and patterns in cognition subsequent to the pathological behavior (see Chamberlain et al., 2016; Grant, Brewer, & Potenza, 2006 for additional reviews). In 2013, the American Psychiatric Association included *gambling disorder* (previously pathological gambling, listed as an impulse control disorder) in an updated grouping of diagnostic criteria, "Substance-Related and Addictive Disorders" (APA, 2013). Of course, the criteria are specific to *gambling disorder*, but include hallmark characteristics such as tolerance ("greater amount of money to achieve same "excitement"), loss of control over activity ("chasing one's losses"), and social/relational consequences from borrowing money to relieve desperate financial situations. As the result of its inclusion, gambling disorder became the only "behavioral addiction" listed in the DSM-5.

Thus, internet gaming disorder is in a separate appendix (Section 3 of the DSM-5), as a disorder requiring future study prior to inclusion. Nine criteria are suggested: preoccupation with gaming, tolerance, psychological withdrawal symptoms, unsuccessful attempts to control or limit gaming, loss of interest in previous hobbies, continued use despite knowing that it is a problem, deceiving family members and/or therapists, use of internet games to escape a negative mood, and having jeopardized or lost a relationship, job, or educational opportunity (APA, 2013; Lemmens, Valkenburg, Gentile, & Reynolds, 2015). In an editorial, Petry and O'Brien (2013), members of the DSM-5 substance use disorder work-group, wrote:

> The inclusion of internet gaming disorder in Section 3 of DSM-5 opens discussions for other 'behavioral addictions', a highly controversial topic. Introducing conditions into the DSM-5 that are not well established or that do not cause significant distress and impairment (e.g. chocolate addiction) will lower the credibility of psychiatric disorders more generally, thereby undermining the seriousness of psychiatric disorders. Thus, strong empirical data will—and should be—required to include new mental disorders, including internet gaming disorder, in future versions of the DSM.

As of June, 2018, the World Health Organization (WHO) included diagnostic criteria for gaming disorder into the International Classification of Diseases (ICD-11; WHO, 2018). Possibly in response to previous scientific dialog regarding nomenclature of internet gaming disorder in the DSM-5, the language of WHO criteria for gaming disorder acknowledges consequences for both excessive, problematic off-line game use, with the focus being primarily online. However, the inclusion of gaming disorder is not without controversy, particularly regarding the available scholarship and interestingly, with the over-reliance on substance use disorder criteria (Aarseth et al., 2017).

Considerations for Measurement

Defining and investigating the putative internet gaming disorder (IGD), and its prevalence, are critical steps toward its inclusion in the DSM. It is equally critical to have the tools to accurately and systematically measure and diagnose the disorder. Over-diagnosis may undermine attempts to assert IGD as worthy of inclusion in the DSM, as well as minimize the hardships of those with IGD. Recent research indicates nine criteria are associated with IGD measurement (Lemmens et al., 2015). Impairment in everyday life as measured by physical, psychological, and societal/relational consequences (i.e., addictive disorder criteria) are the focus of these diagnostic criteria.

Yet, there is still uncertainty about how to measure IGD. At the most basic level, researchers question if the individual criteria should be evaluated on a *dichotomous scale*, meaning subjects' criteria would be assessed as yes (being present), or no (not present), versus being examined at varying levels as captured by the use of a *polytomous*, or continuous scale (e.g., low, moderate, or severe). Both of these methods are used when assessing IGD criteria. When using a dichotomous scale, respondents are asked whether or not they experienced one of the previously mentioned criteria in the past 12 months. When using the polytomous scale, participants are asked about *the extent to which* they experienced a relevant symptom (e.g., on 5- or 7-point Likert scales) within the past 12 months. Scales are commonly anchored at 1—*almost never,* to 5—*very frequently.*

A recent investigation by Lemmens et al. (2015) tested four scales to determine the most effective means to diagnose IGD. The nine criteria for IGD were evaluated using 27-items measured with either dichotomous or polytomous scaling. Along with the two 27-item scales, the researchers evaluated two shorter (9-item) versions of the criteria. Considering cut-points, the DSM suggests at least five out of nine criteria be met, in any combination, in order to diagnose IGD (Lemmens et al., 2015). When using the 5-of-9 cut-point, the researchers found that about 5.4% of their sample met the criteria for IGD. The authors refer to this group as disordered gamers. The authors also used latent class analysis, a statistical technique to assess relatedness in participants' responses to identify groups. Statistical analyses revealed that there were clear cut-points, and three groups of gamers emerged: normal, risky, and disordered. Based on their data, Lemmens and colleagues (2015) suggested that either the proposed DSM diagnostic criteria be raised to six out of nine (~4% of respondents meeting criteria), or that the three class polytomous scaling be used for diagnostic purposes. Further, the authors stressed the importance of a clinical interview accompanying a diagnosis, rather than self-reported measurement alone.

The remainder of this chapter will focus on studies that use DSM-like criteria to evaluate brain-based correlates of individuals who engage in excessive, problematic online video gaming behavior. The purpose of including these studies for consideration is that online video game play is more likely to be problematic than off-line game play (Eichenbaum, Kattner, Bradford, Gentile, & Green, 2015). Further, the putative internet gaming disorder appears the most likely "Internet-use disorder" for inclusion into the DSM (Clark, 2014).

The Addicted Brain

Many individuals play online video games without consequences in their daily lives. Yet, prevalence estimates suggest that for some, internet gaming causes significant impairment. Do these excessive habits that persist in spite of negative consequences in daily life have biological underpinnings? Prior to discussing this question, an understanding of brain anatomy is necessary. The brain can be divided into three main sections. The *hindbrain* consisting of the brain stem (the area closest to the spine), is responsible for many basic survival functions such as breathing. The *midbrain* in humans contains the ventral tegmental area, an important area in addiction. The third section, the *forebrain*, is comprised of the two cerebral hemispheres, the thalamus, and hypothalamus. Some who study addiction, focus on an even smaller area within the forebrain, called the nucleus accumbens. Covering the brain is a 1–3 mm thick area called the cortex. The structure of the human cortex, wrinkled in appearance, allows for more brain matter to fit into the confined space of the skull. The cortex is responsible for many higher order functions such as voluntary movement and abstract thought.

The forebrain area of the nucleus accumbens is an important structure for the study of reward. Reward in the brain was accidentally discovered by Olds and Milner in 1954. The researchers, interested in neural substrates of learning, discovered that rodents were more likely to return to locations on a table during which they had previously received small amounts of electrical current from an electrode implanted directly into the brain. Subsequently, Olds and Milner used an operant chamber (i.e., a square, sound-proof chamber where test subjects press a lever for food or drug reward) and found that rodents excessively pressed a lever to receive intra-cranial self-stimulation in an area just above the nucleus accumbens. The role of dopamine in reward was discovered four decades later.

In the mid-1990s, Robinson and Berridge published a review of evidence conducted with rodents and non-human primates that supported their theory of incentive sensitization. Put simply, dopamine, a brain chemical, is released in the nucleus accumbens and functions to alert an organism (e.g., humans, rodents, etc.) following behaviors necessary for survival (i.e., food, sex, seeking shelter to stay warm). Under naturalistic conditions, this sensitive mechanism (the reward circuitry of the mesolimbic dopamine system) functions admirably as previous learning informs current decision-making, thereby shaping human behavior. Dopamine release is pleasurable, ensuring that the organism repeats the behavior. Drugs of abuse, including alcohol, cause dopamine release in the nucleus accumbens in greater amounts than food or sex (Hernandez & Hoebel, 1988). Because dopamine acts as a signal, alerting and orienting the organism, an addict becomes preoccupied with the substance (seeking and using it) almost to the exclusion of every other activity. In measurement terms, the substance has increased salience, or importance, in everyday life. The dopamine release in the nucleus accumbens assists with memory formation of the drug use experience (Wise, 2004), influencing motivation to use the drug again. For this reason, drug "wanting" versus drug "liking" was theorized to maintain the cycle of addictive behavior (Robinson & Berridge, 1990).

Some evidence suggests that video games activate the reward pathway in the brain. Using a similar procedure as an earlier study in cocaine addicted individuals (see Volkow et al., 1997), Koepp and colleagues (1998) found that video game players experienced dopamine release in the ventral striatum, an area including the nucleus accumbens. Another type of brain imaging technology, functional magnetic resonance imaging (fMRI), is used to study cue-reactivity, or elevated brain activity when presented with images of addiction-related stimuli. Cue-reactivity is used to study treatment for craving, as addicted participants show greater brain activity in the limbic system and report greater urge to use substances following salient cue-exposure, as compared to unrelated control images (e.g., office furniture). In a recent study (Ko et al., 2013), cue-reactivity was assessed in 15 participants with internet gaming addiction and 15 patients currently abstaining from use. Findings showed greater activation in the dorsolateral prefrontal cortex (an area of the brain associated with craving) for IGD participants following cue-exposure. In another study, inhibitory control was assessed with a task that measures the ability to prevent a learned response (i.e., the Go/no-go task; Ko et al., 2014) through fMRI. Findings for individuals with internet gaming disorder showed activation of more brain regions associated with response inhibition, as compared to a group without the disorder. Relatedly, executive functioning was assessed with a risky decision-making task (Dong & Potenza, 2016). When making risky-decisions, individuals with IGD do so more quickly without needed activation of brain areas associated in decision making. Another paradigm, the dot-probe task, was used to assess attentional bias to cues. Lorenz and colleagues (2012) recently demonstrated that "pathological computer game players" display attentional bias to gaming images, associated with greater activation in the medial prefrontal cortex.

In summary, differences in *behavioral responses* (i.e., reaction time and accuracy when completing the computerized tasks), *attentional-bias* (i.e., how one's previous experience influences what the brain attends to), *executive functioning* (i.e., brain mechanisms that allow for planning, organizing and completing tasks), and *inhibitory control* (i.e., extent to which one can prevent a behavior), appear to exist between controls and individuals with internet gaming disorder, particularly when tasks are developed using stimuli specific to gaming. While there are several promising lines of inquiry concerning brain imaging and internet gaming disorder, these findings remain tentative. One factor limiting interpretation concerns inclusion criteria linked to conceptual differences in the definition of addiction. Areas for future study concern identifying areas of the brain associated with these putative behavioral differences, particularly within the longitudinal, developmental context of childhood, adolescence, and emerging adulthood. Particularly needed are additional studies that employ gaming-related stimuli when assessing inhibitory control or executive functioning as decrements may be specific to cue type, similar to substance use disorder. Replication and further experimentation is necessary using different control groups. Studies should compare brain activity across those diagnosed with substance, gambling, or the proposed internet gaming disorders to find patterns.

Reward Schedules and Video Games

Behaviorism, or the theory that behavior is shaped by outcomes, was popular in American psychology from the 1920s to 1960s. The operant conditioning principles from behaviorism (i.e., behaviors followed by positive/negative consequences are more/less likely to be repeated, respectively) are employed by scientists to systematically gather data regarding the rewarding properties of drugs. Similar studies examining reward and schedules of reinforcement may be employed in studies of gambling, or problematic gaming, whereby administration of rewards are either predictable (*fixed*) or unpredictable (*variable*). Further, reinforcement may be based on either the number of times a behavior occurs (*ratio*), or on a specified amount of time between rewards (*interval*). When these distinctions are combined, four schedules of reinforcement are produced. Related to video games, the rewards might look like the following: *fixed-ratio* (e.g., a bag of gold for every twenty zombies killed in a video game), *fixed-interval* (e.g., a bag of gold once per week just for playing a game), *variable-ratio* (e.g., between one and ten bags of gold for every fifty zombies killed in a video game), and *variable-interval* (e.g., between one and ten bags of gold each month just for playing). While both fixed-ratio and fixed-interval schedules produce high levels of behavior initially due to predictable outcomes, behavior stops once a limit is reached, called the "breakpoint". Of the variable reward schedules, the variable ratio schedule tends to produce consistent behavior, and because of the unpredictability of the rewarding outcome, is somewhat resistant to extinction.

Game researchers suggest that operant conditioning reward schedules and characteristics of game play are related (see King, Delfabbro, & Griffiths, 2009) as both fixed and variable schedules of reinforcement are included in many video games. Similarly, schedules of reinforcement assist with memory formation of drug using experiences in the substance use disorder literature. As Clark explains (2014), humans are shaped by the consequences of their behavior because of the mesolimbic dopamine system that fine-tunes our behavior to be sure those behaviors likely to cause positive outcomes are repeated (e.g., pleasure following drug use) and behaviors likely to cause negative outcomes (e.g., withdrawal) are avoided. However, because humans are so practiced at contingency learning, conditions of random chance, such as those involved in gambling or gaming, are a cause of "cognitive flailing" in that attempts are made to apply contingencies to situations where outcomes occur via random chance.

Uniquely, in a recent ethnographic study, schedules of reinforcement and cognitive distortions gleaned from gambling disorder research were combined to explain cognition and behavior of World of Warcraft (WOW) video gamers (Karlsen, 2010). For example, elements of *fixed* (e.g., "questing") and *variable* (e.g., "raiding") ratio schedules of reinforcement were found within the game. Both schedules of reinforcement are associated with operant learning principles, and also appear in the addiction literature. Additionally, examples of cognitive distortions borrowed from the gambling disorder literature that could apply to internet gaming include the *illusion of control* and *the gambler's fallacy* (Clark, 2014; Karlsen, 2010). The illusion of control occurs when a player adopts the false belief that they have control over some random outcome because of irrelevant features of a game. For example, "loot drops" during a raid in WOW may perpetuate the illusion of control, if the gamer associates their competency/skill, or time spent gaming, with the random reinforcement. The gambler's fallacy is the false belief that following a string of the same outcome (e.g., losses), the presentation of the other outcome (wins) will follow in a game of chance. In WOW, overcoming a "boss" exists on a variable-ratio schedule which may cause a steady rate of behavior (i.e., continued play) that may perpetuate the cognitive distortion that the raiding group is close to winning, when this may not be true. Cognitive distortions may lead to loss of control over the behavior.

To conclude, gamers may be unaware of the effect that preprogrammed schedules of reinforcement have on learning and maintaining behavior. If the 36 billion dollar gaming industry (Entertainment Software Association, 2018) is any indication, the strategy to include operant conditioning components into game design, may perpetuate problematic, excessive video game play. Indeed, some would argue that there is a general blurring of the distinction between online gambling and online gaming ("Science has a gambling problem", 2018). Thus, the cognitive distortions found in gambling disorder may also apply to internet gaming disorder.

Perhaps another "dark side" of addiction is the general reward insensitivity to natural rewards in the environment, and the enhanced "reward threshold" displayed during drug abstinence, as suggested by Koob and Le Moal (2005). These factors make abstinence difficult to maintain. Koob and Le Moal (1997) describe the cycle of addiction as including three stages: (1) preoccupation and anticipation, (2) binging and intoxication and (3) withdrawal and negative affect/mood. As individuals progress in their disease, they binge less for pleasure (positive reinforcement) and more to alleviate negative affect/ withdrawal symptoms (negative reinforcement). Applied to video gaming, with escalating loss of control, the behavior of gaming for pleasure (i.e., "gratification") diminishes and is replaced by "compensation" (Brand, Young, Laier, Wölfling, & Potenza, 2016). As described by Brand and colleagues (2016), an example of compensation would be using the internet in place of social interaction to alleviate a negative mood state following some consequence. That is, excessive, problematic gamers may experience the "dark side" of addiction, upon quitting a game. Symptoms of addiction applied to video gaming could include insensitivity to natural rewards and enhanced gratification upon continued game play, following a period of game abstinence. These factors could make controlling video gaming behavior difficult.

Disrupting the Cycle

Young (1999) first described interrupting the cycle of addiction in individuals with internet addictive disorder, in a book chapter entitled "Internet Addiction: Symptoms, Evaluation, and Treatment." Strategies included: (1) disrupting the pattern of internet use by suggesting a new schedule (2) using "external stoppers" such as events or activities (3) setting goals (4) abstaining (5) using reminder cards to describe consequences, and (6) developing a personal inventory of alternative activities not allowable because of time on internet. Cash, Rae, Steel, and Winkler (2012) of ReSTART, the only in-patient rehabilitation center in the United States that specializes in treatment of online addictions (ReSTART, 2018), included an expanded list of treatment strategies for internet addiction. Specifically, client-centered motivational interviewing, cognitive behavioral therapy, reality therapy designed to assist with time management and alternative activities, and Acceptance and Commitment Therapy have shown previous efficacy with individuals with specific internet use disorders. Additionally, pharamacotherapy, including medications to manage comorbid, or co-occurring disorders including anxiety, depression, impulsivity, or to assist with craving, were also reviewed.

Ultimately, "internet addiction" was first characterized to assist patients (Young, 1998). However, identification of, and appropriate treatment for, excessive, problematic online video gaming behavior is not well established. Individuals with "behavioral addiction" seeking medical or psychological assistance may find that a useful starting point with medical providers may be conversation about a co-morbid condition. The literature regarding online video gaming is expanding rapidly, particularly concerning brain and psychological correlates. However, readers should know that the science of this putative disorder is under-developed and consensus not yet established. Researchers need to conduct more theory-based neurobiological studies with *a priori* hypotheses, narrow inclusionary criteria, and sufficient sample sizes to determine if there is enough information to include IGD as the next behavioral addiction in the DSM. Additionally, empirical data following the classification strategy employed by Brand and colleagues (2016) in describing factors influencing the "development and maintenance" of "specific Internet-use disorders" where researchers identify both medium (i.e., the internet) and specific content (i.e., gaming, gambling, pornography viewing, shopping, or communication) are also needed. In the meantime, it is important for society to have conversations about age-appropriate game play and use in this media saturated age.

References

Aarseth, E., Bean, A. M., Boonen, H., Colder Carras, M., Coulson, M., Das, D., … Van Rooij, A. J. (2017). Scholars' open debate paper on the World Health Organization ICD-11 Gaming Disorder proposal. *Journal of Behavioral Addictions, 6*(3), 267–270. doi:10.1556/2006.5.2016.088

American Psychiatric Association. (2013). *Diagnostic and statistical manual of mental disorders* (5th ed.). Arlington, VA: American Psychiatric Publishing.

Brand, M., Young, K. S., Laier, C., Wölfling, K., & Potenza, M. N. (2016). Integrating psychological and neurobiological considerations regarding the development and maintenance of specific Internet-use disorders: An Interaction of Person-Affect-Cognition-Execution (I-PACE) model. *Neuroscience & Biobehavioral Reviews, 71*, 252–266. doi:10.1016/j.neubiorev.2016.08.033

Carollo, K. (2011, August 2). Man dies from blood clot after marathon gaming. Retrieved from http://abcnews.go.com/Health/extreme-gamer-dies-pulmonary-embolism/story?id=14212015

Cash, H., Rae, C. D., Steel, A. H., & Winkler, A. (2012). Internet addiction: A brief summary of research and practice. *Current Psychiatry Reviews, 8*(4), 292–298. doi:10.2174/157340012803520513

Chamberlain, S. R., Lochner, C., Stein, D. J., Goudriaan, A. E., Holst, R. J., Zohar, J., & Grant, J. E. (2016). Behavioural addiction—A rising tide? *European Neuropsychopharmacology, 26*(5), 841–855. doi:10.1016/j.euroneuro.2015.08.013

Clark, L. (2014). Disordered gambling: The evolving concept of behavioral addiction. *Annals of the New York Academy of Sciences, 1327*(1), 46–61. doi:10.1111/nyas.12558

Dong, G., & Potenza, M. N. (2016). Risk-taking and risky decision-making in Internet gaming disorder: Implications regarding online gaming in the setting of negative consequences. *Journal of Psychiatric Research, 73*, 1–8. doi:10.1016/j.jpsychires.2015.11.011

Eichenbaum, A., Kattner, F., Bradford, D., Gentile, D. A., & Green, C. S. (2015). Role-playing and real-time strategy games associated with greater probability of internet gaming disorder. *Cyberpsychology, Behavior, and Social Networking, 18*(8), 480–485.

Entertainment Software Association. (2018, January 18). US Video Game Industry Revenue Reaches $36 Billion in 2017. Retrieved from http://www.theesa.com/article/us-video-game-industry-revenue-reaches-36-billion-2017

Grant, J. E., Brewer, J. A., & Potenza, M. N. (2006). The neurobiology of substance and behavioral addictions. *CNS Spectrums, 11*(12), 924–930. doi:10.1017/S109285290001511X

Grant, J. E., Potenza, M. N., Weinstein, A., & Gorelick, D. A. (2010). Introduction to behavioral addictions. *The American Journal of Drug and Alcohol Abuse, 36*(5), 233–241. doi:10.3109/00952990.2010.491884

Hernandez, L., & Hoebel, B. G. (1988). Food reward and cocaine increase extracellular dopamine in the nucleus accumbens as measured by microdialysis. *Life Science, 42*(18), 1705–1712. doi:10.1016/0024-3205(88)90036-7

Holden, C. (2001). "Behavioral" addictions: Do they exist? *Science, 294*(5544), 980–982. doi:10.1126/science.294.5544.980

Hunt, K., & Ng, N. (2015, January 19). Man dies in Taiwan after 3-day online gaming binge. Retrieved from https://www.cnn.com/2015/01/19/world/taiwan-gamer-death/index.html

Karlsen, F. (2010). Entrapment and near miss: A comparative analysis of psycho-structural elements in gambling games and massively multiplayer online role-playing games. *International Journal of Mental Health and Addiction, 9*(2), 193–207. doi:10.1007/s11469-010-9275-4

King, D., Delfabbro, P., & Griffiths, M. (2009). Video game structural characteristics: A new psychological taxonomy. *International Journal of Mental Health and Addiction, 8*(1), 90–106. doi:10.1007/s11469-009-9206-4

Ko, C., Hsieh, T., Chen, C., Yen, C., Chen, C., Yen, J., … Liu, G. (2014). Altered brain activation during response inhibition and error processing in subjects with Internet gaming disorder: A functional magnetic imaging study. *European Archives of Psychiatry and Clinical Neuroscience, 264*(8), 661–672. doi:10.1007/s00406-013-0483-3

Ko, C. H., Liu, G. C., Yen, J. Y., Chen, C. Y., Yen, C. F., & Chen C. S. (2013). Brain correlates of craving for online gaming under cue exposure in subjects with Internet gaming addiction and in remitted subjects. *Addiction Biology, 18*, 559–569. doi:10.1111/j.1369-1600.2011.00405.x

Koepp, M. J., Gunn, R. N., Lawrence, A. D., Cunningham, V. J., Dagher, A., Jones, T., … Grasby, P. M. (1998). Evidence for striatal dopamine release during a video game. *Nature, 393*(6682), 266–268. doi:10.1038/30498

Koob, G. F., & Le Moal, M. (1997). Drug abuse: Hedonic homeostatic dysregulation. *Science, 278*(5335), 52–58. doi:10.1126/science.278.5335.52

Koob, G. F., & Le Moal, M. (2005). Plasticity of reward neurocircuitry and the "dark side" of drug addiction. *Nature Neuroscience, 8*(11), 1442–1444.

Lemmens, J. S., Valkenburg, P. M., Gentile, D. A., & Reynolds, C. R. (2015). The Internet gaming disorder scale. *Psychological Assessment, 27*(2), 567–582. doi:10.1037/t42759-000

Lorenz, R. C., Krüger, J., Neumann, B., Schott, B. H., Kaufmann, C., Heinz, A., & Wüstenberg, T. (2012). Cue reactivity and its inhibition in pathological computer game players. *Addiction Biology, 18*(1), 134–146. doi:10.1111/j.1369-1600.2012.00491.x

Marks, I. (1990). Behavioural (non-chemical) addictions. *Addiction, 85*(11), 1389–1394. doi:10.1111/j.1360-0443.1990.tb01618.x

Petry, N. M. & O'Brien, C. P. (2013). Internet gaming disorder and the DSM-5. *Addiction, 108*(7), 1183–1354. doi:10.1111/add.12162

ReSTART® Life | Treatment for Internet, Video Game, VR Addiction. (2018). Retrieved from https://netaddictionrecovery.com/

Robinson, T. E., & Berridge, K. C. (1993). The neural basis of drug craving: An incentive-sensitization theory of addiction. *Brain Research Reviews, 18*(3), 247–291. doi:10.1016/0165-0173(93)90013-p

Science has a gambling problem. [No authors listed]. (2018). Comment in *Nature, 553*(7689), 379–379. doi:10.1038/d41586-018-01051-z

Starcevic, V. (2013). Is Internet addiction a useful concept? *Australian & New Zealand Journal of Psychiatry, 47*(1), 16–19. doi:10.1177/0004867412461693

Volkow, N. D., Wang, G., Fowler, J. S., Logan, J., Gatley, S. J., Hitzemann, R., … Pappas, N. (1997). Decreased striatal dopaminergic responsiveness in detoxified cocaine-dependent subjects. *Nature, 386*(6627), 830–833. doi:10.1038/386830a0

Wise, R. A. (2004). Dopamine, learning and motivation. *Nature Reviews Neuroscience, 5*(6), 483–494. doi:10.1038/nrn1406

World Health Organization. (2018). International Classification of Diseases – 11. Available https://icd.who.int/browse11/l-m/en#/http://id.who.int/icd/entity/338347362, accessed 4 July, 2018.

Young, K. S. (1998). Internet addiction: The emergence of a new clinical disorder. *CyberPsychology & Behavior, 1*(3), 237–244. doi:10.1089/cpb.1998.1.237

Young, K. S. (1999). Internet addiction: Symptoms, evaluation and treatment. *Innovations in Clinical Practice*. Retrieved from: http://netaddiction.com/articles/symptoms.pdf

CHAPTER TWENTY

Mobile Devices, Multitasking, Distraction, and Compulsive Tech Use

EDWARD DOWNS & JACQUELYN HARVEY

In 2012, a woman fell off the Navy Pier in Chicago and had to be rescued by the Coast Guard. In 2014, a Philadelphia man was killed by a train while walking the tracks to meet a friend. In 2015, in Texas, a teenager was electrocuted while taking a shower. In 2016, in Bavaria, a commuter train derailed, killing 12 people and injuring dozens more. In 2017, a man in Oklahoma stepped on, and was bitten by a rattlesnake while walking through a hospital parking lot. Later that same year, a man walked off a cliff in California and fell six stories to his death. These incidents may seem random and unrelated, but they all have one thing in common. Mobile devices played a role in all of these accidents. Given the prevalence of these seemingly preventable incidents, it is small wonder that the city of Honolulu passed legislation to fine pedestrians for using their mobile devices when crossing the street (Osborne, 2017).

To be fair, mobile devices (cell phones, smart phones, tablets, etc.) aren't the only technologies that distract people, but *media convergence*, the process whereby technologies, industries, markets, and audiences come together (Jenkins, 2004), has allowed them to become among the more prominent technological artifacts responsible for accidental death and injury. The problem is particularly acute when people are distracted because they are trying to multitask. For conceptual clarity, *multitasking* is defined as trying to successfully complete two or more tasks in the same block of time, whereas *distraction* occurs when a secondary task takes necessary resources—cognitive, motor, and perceptual (Borst, Taatgen, & van Rijn, 2010)—away from the completion of a more important primary task. Today's smart phones and mobile devices allow us to talk, text, take photos, shoot videos, play games, and update our social media pages. The benefit of wireless internet connections on these devices allow us to stay connected, to develop strong mobile workforces, and to engage with Web materials. Although these features are regarded as benefits to society, we continue to pay the price for their integration. The unintended negative effects are perhaps nowhere more prevalent than on U.S. roadways. Data released by the U.S. National Highway Traffic Safety Administration (NHTSA) revealed that 3,450 people were killed in motor vehicle accidents involving a distracted driver, with 486 fatalities attributed to mobile phone use (NHTSA, 2018). Data for 2015 revealed 882,000 accidents on U.S. roadways with reports of injuries or property damage, 69,000 of which were attributed to phone use (NHTSA, 2017).

Screen Time

Whether through mobile devices, or through other media systems, U.S. residents certainly get their share of screen time. A report published by Nielsen based on U.S. population data found that adults get 8 hours and 47 minutes of screen time per day, with 1 hour and 39 minutes from smart phones (Nielsen, 2016). Other agencies have documented similar numbers. A probability sample revealed that parents of teens and tweens averaged 9 hours and 32 minutes of screen time per day (Common Sense Media, 2015) while teens and tweens averaged 6 hours and 40 minutes, and 4 hours and 36 minutes of screen time per day, respectively. The numbers reported for teens and tweens did not include screen time spent at school or for homework.

Multitasking with media technologies among the younger generation is prevalent. Half of U.S. teens watch TV, 60% text, and 76% listen to music, all while doing homework. Approximately two-thirds of those who combine homework with TV and texting don't think multitasking affects the quality of their work (Common Sense Media, 2015) despite research suggesting otherwise (Thornton, Faires, Robbins, & Rollins, 2014). Research published by the Kaiser Family Foundation (2006) indicates that 81% of young Americans use more than one medium at a time, for example, texting or updating social media pages while watching TV. Estimates suggest that 26% of media-multitaskers' time involves concurrent use of more than one screen. Given the prevalence of media multitasking, and that passive screen time (such as TV) is often coupled with concurrent interactive screen time, it is no wonder we are distracted. We inhabit a world where we are, as a clairvoyant T.S. Eliot (1936) put it in the first of his *Four Quartets*, "distracted from distraction by distraction."

We Are Not Good at Multitasking

Anecdotally, there is some cachet for being a "good multitasker" in today's society. Friends and associates banter about their ability to do more than one thing at a time, and potential employers note "multitasking abilities are a plus." What people rarely consider is that there are multiple forms of multitasking—one of which, we do not do well. At the most basic level, multitasking can be broken down into *concurrent* and *sequential* varieties. Concurrent multitasking occurs when a person attempts to complete two (or more) tasks at the same time. Texting and driving is an example of concurrent multitasking. Sequential multitasking occurs when people attempt to complete two (or more) tasks in a short span of time by task switching (Salvucci & Taatgen, 2008). Research demonstrates that people are generally skilled at sequential multitasking because they are focused on completing one task at a time, but have difficulty with concurrent multitasking, especially if both tasks are complex and lengthy (compound continuous multitasking; Salvucci, Taatgen, & Borst, 2009).

Adaptive control of thought rationale (ACT-R) explains the circumstances under which multitasking is likely to fail or be successful. When a person tries to multitask, the individual is generally trying to complete two or more tasks successfully. ACT-R recognizes that task completion requires coordinated use of three resource pools: *cognitive, motor* and *perceptual*. The cognitive pool is required for thinking through processes and operations, calculating, and retrieving information required to complete a task. The motor pool is necessary for manipulating the musculoskeletal system to physically complete tasks. The perceptual system relays information from sensory systems such as vision, hearing, and haptics related to task completion. Each one of these pools can act independently and each is capable of completing one task or request at a time. However, when multitasking, often times both tasks require attention from the same resource pool. Because the individual resource pool is not capable of processing both requests concurrently, one task has to wait its turn in order to be processed. This creates a bottleneck (Salvucci & Taatgen, 2008). The more complex the two tasks, the more bottlenecks are created. This can lead to inefficiency through time lost switching from task-to-task or can lead to failure of one or more of the tasks.

Why Do We Do It Anyway?

Data collected from areas such as texting and driving (Downs, 2014), technological distractions in the classroom (Downs, Tran, McMenemy, & Abegaze, 2015), distractions in the workplace (Mark, Voida, & Cardello, 2012), and cell phone use and relationship tension (Miller-Ott, Kelly, & Duran, 2012) indicate that inappropriate use of mobile technologies can have negative consequences. So why do we do it? There are a number of plausible reasons why people continue to multi-task even though evidence suggests it's not a good idea. The reasons incorporate ideas from psychology, technological design, and biology to explain these behaviors. Some researchers (ex. Wang & Tchernev, 2012) propose that even though multitasking behaviors may originate as cognitive needs to complete one task, emotional gratifications such as feeling entertained or relaxed become a byproduct of multitasking, even when it comes at the cost of the original task's performance. As the logic explains, if a person were studying for a test, and then turned on the TV, or updated their social media pages, the multitasking can lead to feelings of satisfaction, not because of effective study time, but because being distracted makes "studying" more entertaining. This misperception of what seems to be efficiency is emotionally satisfying, but cognitively is not productive (Wang & Tchernev, 2012, pp. 509–510). These findings are consistent with the notion that people often overestimate their own abilities (Schlehofer et al., 2010) while concurrently underestimating the impairment that technological distraction brings (Horrey, Lesch, & Garabet, 2008).

Others suggest that the reason some need to check their mobile devices so frequently, even when inappropriate, has to do with the development of a compulsive behavior. To be fair, the phone itself may not be the root of the problem. It is simply the physical manifestation of what we see when a person is using an app. Compulsion loops (also referred to as ludic or core loops), operate under the premise that rewarded behaviors will increase in frequency. Designers incorporate both fixed- (regularly timed and of predictable size) and variable-reward (randomly timed and unpredictable in size) schedules into their games and apps to encourage repetitive behaviors. The reason why the variable reward is such a powerful mechanism has to do with the allure of uncertainty. When a reward is given, the feeling is attributed to a release of dopamine in the brain, and getting that drip is what triggers the compulsive, or what some might colloquially refer to as "addictive" behavior (see Gilbertson & Walton, this volume). Because of this, the authors here would argue that today's smart phones more closely resemble slot machines than phones.

The practice of developing technologies that people can't put down is not new. More seasoned readers may recall the "CrackBerry" phones of the late 90's and early 2000s, so-called because users couldn't seem to put them down and appeared "addicted" to them. Today, software designers are encouraged to design habit-forming apps. According to Eyal (2014), the Hook is a four-stage model that is used to achieve the goal of "unprompted user engagement" (p. 5). It begins with the presence of an *external trigger*—or something which prompts a behavior. As an example, an e-mail, or an invitation from a friend to join a social media platform could serve as an external trigger. The trigger then leads to an *action* (ex. creating an account) that is completed in order to obtain a reward. This is followed by a *variable reward*—the unpredictable return that will release dopamine in the brain. Variable rewards on social media apps are myriad, ranging from likes and comments, to friend requests, private messages, and other forms of validation. The final phase is *investment*, or the place where users need to give some small token of themselves, ostensibly for sustained, enhanced use. Users may complete profiles, input contact information, upload pictures, or customize user preferences. Completing the loop helps to ensure that users will pass back through the model again, except as the motions become routinized and habitual, the external trigger will be replaced with an *internal trigger*—some internal feeling or emotion that can only be satisfied by the app or product being used. The ethics of using such a model are questionable at best, especially in light of the fact that companies make money based on clicks and repetition. If the hook works as well as it suggests, uninformed or easily influenced users would be manipulated into compulsive use through the principles of this design.

Other Negative Effects

There are, of course, other negative effects associated with cell phone and mobile technology use. From an attentional perspective, fractured thinking and an inability to focus for extended periods of time (Rosen, Carrier, & Cheever, 2013) can influence everything from one's ability to maintain satisfying relationships (Miller-Ott et al., 2012) to their work productivity (Tarafdar, Tu, Ragu-Nathan, & Ragu-Nathan, 2007). *Decreased situational awareness* and *attentional blindness* explain why pedestrians are being hit by automotive traffic at the highest rates in 25 years (Nasar & Troyer, 2013). Pedestrians walk more slowly when using a cellphone, while simultaneously being less aware of unusual activity in their immediate surroundings (Hyman, Boss, Wise, McKenzie, & Caggiano, 2009). In classroom settings, over two-thirds of students report using electronic devices, with usage having a negative association with grade outcomes (Jacobson & Forste, 2011). Similarly, in workplace settings electronic devices have been associated with a higher frequency of procedural failures and clinical errors (Westbrook, Woods, Rob, Dunsmuir, & Day, 2010).

In addition to problems arising from compulsive technology use, negative associations between technology and psychological or physical health outcomes have been documented. For example, loneliness has been touted as both a cause and an effect of problematic internet use (Kim, LaRose, & Peng, 2009) which is troubling given the negative health outcomes associated with loneliness (i.e., increased heart rate, cardiac output, blood pressure, and sleep dysregulation; Cacioppo et al., 2002). Depression is another risk factor. Video game use, texting, watching video-clips, and related technology usage behaviors have all been associated with depressive symptoms (Allam, 2010; Amichai-Hamburger & Ben-Artzi, 2009). For adolescents, excessive social media use has been associated with classic depressive symptomatology, such that the term "Facebook depression" has been coined to explain the phenomena (O'Keeffe, Clark-Pearson, & The Council on Communications and Media, 2011).

Physical issues may also accompany excessive phone use such as poor sleep patterns, poor posture, and an increase in cervical spine and neck issues—to the extent that an additional 48° pounds of stress can be added to the spine if looking at a cellphone with a 60° head tilt (Hansraj, 2014). More frightening is the idea that long-term cell phone use can contribute to an increased risk of brain cancer and decreased likelihood of patient survival (Carlberg & Hardell, 2014). In addition, for those concerned with fertility issues, research finds that cellphone radiation can induce DNA damage in sperm (De Iuliis, Newey, King, & Aitken, 2009).

Mindful Solutions for Monitoring Technology Usage

One solution researchers have offered when technology use starts to feel overwhelming is to "unplug" for a time, to allow the body to readjust or "detechsify." High profile members of the tech community (ex. Bill Gates) suggest this practice and have reported feeling refreshed and more creative after their own tech-free retreats. While not everyone has the luxury of unplugging for extended periods of time, people can manage to disconnect at times throughout the day. Creating a schedule for checking e-mail and social media every few hours instead of constant monitoring can help people focus on productivity at work. Anecdotally, university students have reported that turning off notifications on their smart phones or deleting social media apps from their mobile devices helped them to focus on important tasks with less distractions. They reported being more productive while also saving time.

Another effective solution involves becoming more mindful of how and why we are engaging in technology usage at a given moment. Mindfulness is a mental state wherein one's focus is on present-moment stimuli and corresponding internal and external responses (Kabat-Zinn, 1990). Being mindful involves learning to pay attention to life as it unfolds. Often human thought is focused elsewhere (i.e., on past occurrences, or future to-do lists) as opposed to being focused solely on what is happening in the present moment, which decreases our awareness of problematic psychological or physical behaviors that may be arising from technology (over)usage. Fortunately, people can learn to improve upon situational awareness by practicing mindfulness techniques (Shapiro, Brown, Thoreson, & Plante, 2011) in particular contexts, such as when one is using technology.

Aside from task-oriented functions, research suggests individuals often turn to technology as a coping mechanism for unpleasant internal states (i.e., boredom or loneliness) or as a simple distraction from mundane activities (Panova & Lleras, 2016). As such, being mindful of technology usage could constitute a simple solution for identifying problematic engagement patterns. Like any repeated activity, our technology usage behaviors can become habitual in nature (Bianchi & Phillips, 2005). We may rarely, however, stop to consider why we developed these particular patterns in the first place. The mother who always gives an iPad to her upset child may not recognize that this habit arises because she does not know how else to appease the child. The student who always uses his phone before the start of class may not recognize that this is a mechanism for avoiding uncomfortable social interactions. When we are mindful of why we pick up the phone, or hand over the iPad, we give ourselves the space to recognize when usage is triggered by underlying motivations such as wanting to reduce, avoid, or distract ourselves from present-moment experiences. Once we give ourselves the space to determine why we turn to our technologies, we can identify techniques for managing usage more effectively.

Mindfulness and Technology

Research specific to mindfulness and technology use is still somewhat sparse, but existing work finds that individuals higher in trait-mindfulness are more likely to take their personal belief system into consideration when making adoption decisions (meaning they are more likely to adopt technologies that coincide with their values and ethics; Sun, 2007). In addition, being mindful is positively associated with people's perception of having made satisfactory technology adoption choices (Sun, Fang, & Zou, 2016) and is associated with reduced uncertainty pertaining to the acceptance of technology (Sun & Fang, 2010). From a usage standpoint, research suggests that individuals high in trait-mindfulness are less likely to engage in dangerous or distracted behaviors such as texting while driving (Feldman,

Greeson, Renna, & Robbins-Monteith, 2011). Likewise, Terry and Terry (2015) found that mindful individuals report a decreased likelihood of experiencing near accidents while driving. These combined works suggest that those with a mindful disposition are likely to think carefully about the technology they wish to adopt and why, and that accidental injuries such as those mentioned at the beginning of this chapter could potentially be reduced or prevented if people were mindful of problematic technology usage behaviors.

How Do We Become More Mindful?

The most common training technique for cultivating a more mindful disposition involves practicing meditation (Kabat-Zinn, 1990). Mindfulness meditation is a simple attentional-training technique that is currently taught in thousands of hospitals, schools, and corporate organizations across the country given its consistent tie to improved physical and psychological well-being (see Grossman, Niemann, Schmidt, & Walach, 2004). Meditation typically involves teaching people to focus on a constant in their immediate surroundings (e.g., their breath) and to have them note where and when their focus strays from this object of attention. Individuals are then taught to continually bring their awareness back to this object of attention as a repetitive training technique in centering thought processes on the present moment. Engaging in mindfulness meditation can be done by finding a teacher or studio to learn from. In addition, abundant technological applications are available online and on cell phones that teach individuals how to meditate. Popular apps include Insight Timer, Calm, and Headspace. Guided meditations can also be found online. It may seem counterintuitive to use technology as a means of learning to become more mindful, however, learning to become aware of present moment thoughts and feelings will in turn allow us to become aware of when and why technology usage might be problematic.

Other options for mindfully engaging with technology include becoming more aware how one uses technology around others. For example, research suggests children have a significantly harder time getting parents' attention when parents are using cell phones—with 80% of parents agreeing that cell phone use limits their ability to attend to their child (Hiniker et al., 2015). In addition, research suggests parents' media use can distract them from mindfully engaging with their child while also decreasing their ability to manage children's behavior (Radesky et al., 2014). As such, it is important for parents and caregivers to set an example for children through actions instead of solely through words, rules, or regulations (for example, making "bedtime" equivalent to "charging time" for cell phones, or agreeing that everyone in the family will refrain from technology use during meal times, etc.). It is also important to be mindful of urges and motivations for technology use when spending time with friends, family members, and co-workers, since research indicates that the presence of cellphones can impact people's relational satisfaction with one another (Miller-Ott et al., 2012).

And if the allure of the screen is too much, or if a parent or caregiver would like to ease technology into a child's life gently, don't forget that many of the major carriers in the U.S. still sell and support updated flip phones and stick phones. These devices, in addition to the lower price point, still provide the necessary vital communication mechanisms (ex. talk and text communication) without the distraction of the touch screen (Worley, 2018).

Last, but certainly not least, mindfully communicating about technology use within social networks may be a beneficial practice. For example, gifting children technological devices without first discussing the matter with parents is problematic given that parents may have particular views about the devices and/or screen time they want children to be exposed to. If parenting, having conversations with children about the importance of appropriate boundaries when using technology, including a discussion of *why* these boundaries matter, can help children see why the monitoring of technology use is important for psychological and relational well-being. Taking time to communicate with romantic partners or friends about expectations surrounding technology usage can help mitigate the potential for technology use to impede relational development or well-being.

Overall, we hope this chapter has demonstrated how mindfulness can be used as a helpful, free, and practical solution for improving your ability to engage in healthy technology use. In addition, remembering to "unplug" from technology once in a while can be of benefit for your mental and physical health, as well as your relationships. As Anne Lamott states, "Almost everything will work again if you unplug it for a few minutes, including you."

References

Allam, M. (2010). Excessive Internet use and depression: Cause-effect bias? *Journal of Psychopathology, 43*(5), 334.

Amichai-Hamburger, Y., & Ben-Artzi, E. (2009). Depression through technology. *New Scientist, 204,* 28–29.

Bianchi, A., & Phillips, J. G. (2005). Psychological predictors of problem mobile phone use. *CyberPsychology & Behavior, 8*(1), 35–51.

Borst, J. P., Taatgen, N. A., & van Rijn, H. (2010). The problem state: A cognitive bottleneck in multitasking. *Journal of Experimental Psychology, 36,* 363–382.

Cacioppo, J. T., Hawkley, L. C., Crawford, E., Ernst, J. M., Burleson, M. H., Kowalewski, R. B., & Berntson, G. G. (2002). Loneliness and health: Potential mechanisms. *Psychosomatic Medicine, 64*, 407–417.

Carlberg, M., & Hardell, L. (2014). Decreased survival of glioma patients with grade IV (glioblastoma multiforme) associated with long-term use of mobile and cordless phones. *International Journal of Environmental Research and Public Health, 11*, 10790–10805.

Common Sense Media. (2015). The common sense census: Media use by Tweens and Teens. Retrieved from https://www.commonsensemedia.org/sites/default/files/uploads/pdfs/census_factsheet_mediauseprofiles.pdf

De Iuliis, G. N., Newey, R. J., King, B. V., & Aitken, R. J. (2009). Mobile phone radiation induces reactive oxygen species production and DNA damage in human spermatozoa in vitro. *PLoS One, 4*, e6446.

Downs, E. (2014). Driving home the message: Using a video game simulator to steer attitudes away from distracted driving. *International Journal of Gaming and Computer-Mediated Simulation, 6*(1), 50–63. doi:10.4018/978-1-4666-8200-9.ch084

Downs, E., Tran, A., McMenemy, R., & Abegaze, N. (2015). Exam performance and attitudes toward multitasking in six multimedia-multitasking classroom environments. *Computers & Education, 86*, 250–259.

Eyal, N. (2014). *Hooked: How to build habit forming products.* New York, NY: Portfolio Penguin.

Feldman, G., Greeson, J., Renna, M., & Robbins-Monteith, K. (2011). Mindfulness predicts less texting while driving among young adults: Examining attention- and emotion-regulation motives as potential mediators. *Personality and Individual Differences, 51*, 856–861. doi:10.1016/j.paid.2011.07.020

Grossman, P., Niemann, L., Schmidt, S., & Walach, H. (2004). Mindfulness-based stress reduction and health benefits: A meta-analysis. *Journal of Psychosomatic Research, 57*, 35-43. doi: 10.1016/S0022-3999(03)00573-7

Hansraj, K. K. (2014). Assessment of stresses in the cervical spine caused by posture and position of the head. *Surgical Technology International, 25*, 277–279.

Hiniker, A., Sobel, K., Suh, H., Sung, Y., Lee, C., & Kientz, J. (2015). Texting while parenting: How adults use mobile phones while caring for children at the playground. *Proceedings of the 33rd Annual ACM Conference on Human Factors in Computing Systems (CHI '15)*, 727–736.

Horrey, W. J., Lesch, M. F., & Garabet, A. (2008). Assessing the awareness of performance decrements in distracted drivers. *Accident Analysis and Prevention, 40*, 675–682.

Hyman, I. E., Boss, S. M., Wise, B. M., McKenzie, K. E., & Caggiano, J. M. (2009). Did you see the unicycling clown? Inattentional blindness while walking and talking on a cellphone. *Applied Cognitive Psychology, 24*, 597–607.

Jacobson, W. C., & Forste, R. (2011). The wired generation: Academic and social outcomes of electronic media use among university students. *Cyberpsychology, Behavior, and Social Networking, 14*, 275–280.

Jenkins, H. (2004). The cultural logic of media convergence. *International Journal of Cultural Studies, 7*(1), 33–43. doi: 10.1177/1367877904040603

Kabat-Zinn, J. (1990). *Full catastrophe living: Using the wisdom of your body and mind to face stress, pain, and illness.* New York, NY: Random House.

Kaiser Family Foundation. (2006). Media multitasking among American youth: Prevalence, predictors, and pairings. Retrieved from https://kaiserfamilyfoundation.files.wordpress.com/2013/01/7593.pdf

Kiken, L. G., Garland, E. L., Bluth, K., Palsson, O. S., & Gaylord, S. A. (2015). From a state to a trait: Trajectories of state mindfulness in meditation during intervention predict changes in trait mindfulness. *Personality and Individual Differences, 1*, 41–46.

Kim, J., LaRose, R., & Peng, W. (2009). Loneliness as the cause and effect of problematic internet use: The relationship between internet use and psychological well-being. *CyberPsychology and Behavior, 12*, 451–455.

Mark, G., Voida, S., & Cardello, A. (2012). "A pace not dictated by electrons": An empirical study of work without email. *Proceedings of CHI* Association for Computing Machinery, Austin, TX.

Miller-Ott, A. E., Kelly, L., & Duran, R. L. (2012). The effects of cell phone usage rules on satisfaction in romantic relationships. *Communication Quarterly, 1*, 17–34. doi:10.1080/01463373.2012.642263

Nasar, J. L., & Troyer, D. (2013). Pedestrian injuries due to mobile phone use in public places. *Accident Analysis and Prevention, 57*, 91–95. doi:10.1016/j.aap.2013.03.021

National Highway Traffic Safety Administration (NHTSA). (2017). Traffic safety facts. *Research Note.* Retrieved from https://crashstats.nhtsa.dot.gov/Api/Public/ViewPublication/812381

National Highway Traffic Safety Administration (NHTSA). (2018). Traffic safety facts. *Research Note.* Retrieved from https://crashstats.nhtsa.dot.gov/Api/Public/ViewPublication/812517

Nielsen (2016). *The Nielsen total audience report Q1 2016.* Retrieved from http://www.nielsen.com/us/en/insights/reports/2016/the-total-audience-report-q1-2016.html

O'Keeffe, G. S., Clarke-Pearson, K., & Council on Communications and Media. (2011). Clinical report: The impact of social media on children, adolescents, and families. *Pediatrics.* Retrieved June 12, 2018, from https://pdfs.semanticscholar.org/f196/08b9cf99a47c-0c22452c8d940222b9e9d163.pdf

Osborne, S. (2017, July 30). Honolulu bans texting while crossing streets in bid to curb injuries. *Independent.* Retrieved April 27, 2018, from http://www.independent.co.uk/news/world/americas/honolulu-texting-walking-hawaii-city-distracted-pedestrian-law-a8018686.html

Panova, T., & Lleras, A. (2016). Avoidance or boredom: Negative mental health outcomes associated with use of Information and Communication Technologies depend on users' motivations. *Computers in Human Behavior, 10*, 249–258. doi:10.1016/j.chb.2015.12.062

Radesky, J. S., Kistin, C., Zuckerman, B., Nitzberg, K., Gross, J., Kaplan-Sanof, M., Augustyn, M., & Silverstein, M. (2014). Patterns of mobile device use by caregivers and children during meals in fast food restaurants. *Pediatrics, 133*, 843–849.

Rosen, L., Carrier, M., & Cheever, N. A. (2013). Facebook and texting made me do it: Media-induced task-switching while studying. *Computers in Human Behavior, 29*, 948–958. doi:10.1016/j.chb.2012.12.001

Salvucci, D. D. & Taatgen, N. A. (2008). Threaded cognition: An integrated theory of concurrent multitasking. *Psychological Review, 115*(1), 101–130. doi:10.1037/0033-295X.115.1.101

Salvucci, D. D., Taatgen, N. A., & Borst, J. P. (2009). Toward a unified theory of the multitasking continuum: From concurrent performance to task switching, interruption, and resumption. Proceedings of the SIGCHI conference on human factors in computing systems: CHI 2009, ACM Press, New York, p. 1819–1828.

Schlehofer, M. M., Thompson, S. C., Ting, S., Ostermann, S., Nierman, A., & Skenderian, A. (2010). Psychological predictors of college students' cell phone use while driving. *Accident Analysis and Prevention, 42*, 1107–1112.

Shapiro, S. L., Brown, K. W., Thoresen, C., & Plante, T. G. (2011). The moderation of mindfulness-based stress reduction effects by trait-mindfulness: Results from a randomized controlled trial. *Journal of Clinical Psychology, 67*(3), 267–277. doi:10.1002/jclp.20761

Sun, H. (2007). *Making sound adoption decisions: A longitudinal study of mindfulness in technology adoption and continued use.* Paper presented at the Thirty Second International Conference on Information Systems. Retrieved from https://pdfs.semanticscholar.org/ff3a/aece-033f61abb818b2e3ecee023d6b66e820.pdf

Sun, H., & Fang, Y. (2010). *Toward a model of mindfulness in technology acceptance.* Paper presented at the International Conference on Information Systems. Retrieved from https://pdfs.semanticscholar.org/e171/fed1c36a9b8f2b8475bb3cf81140fd18eaad.pdf

Sun, H., Fang, Y., & Zou, H. (2016). Choosing a Fit Technology: Understanding Mindfulness in Technology Adoption and Continuance. *Journal of the Association for Information Systems, 17, Article 2.* Retrieved from http://aisel.aisnet.org/jais/vol17/iss6/2

Tarafdar, M., Tu, Q., Ragu-Nathan, B. S., & Ragu-Nathan, T. S. (2007). The impact of technostress on role stress and productivity. *Journal of Management and Information Systems, 24,* 301–328.

Terry, C. P., & Terry, D. L. (2015). Cell phone-related near accidents among young drivers: Associations with mindfulness. *Journal of Psychology, 149,* 665–683.

Thornton, B., Faires, A., Robbins, M., & Rollins, E. (2014). The mere presence of a cellphone may be distracting: Implications for attention and task performance. *Social Psychology, 45,* 479–488. doi:10.1027/1864-9335/a000216

Wang, Z., & Tchernev, J. M. (2012). The "myth" of media multitasking: Reciprocal dynamics of media multitasking, personal needs and gratifications. *Journal of Communication, 62,* 493–513.

Westbrook, J. I., Woods, A., Rob, M. I., Dunsmuir, W. T., & Day, R. O. (2010). Association of interruptions with an increased risk and severity of medication administration errors. *Archives of Internal Medicine, 170,* 683–690.

Worley, B. (2018). Why you should get your kid a flip phone instead of a smartphone in 2018. Retrieved from: https://abcnews.go.com/GMA/Family/kid-flip-phone-smartphone-2018/story?id=58997293

CHAPTER TWENTY-ONE

Dark Side of Augmented and Virtual Reality

EDWARD DOWNS & CHERYL CAMPANELLA BRACKEN

In 2017, Lenovo released the *Star Wars: Jedi Challenges* augmented reality head-set. The headset is powered by a cellphone app and allows aspiring Jedi to battle Sith Lords, stormtroopers, and other villains from the *Star Wars* galaxy in an augmented reality format. Reading through the user guide revealed the customary warnings associated with many interactive multimedia technologies. For example, making sure there is enough space for playing to prevent injury to self, others, or equipment damage. There was a warning for volume control to prevent hearing loss, as well as a warning for eye strain and repetitive muscle strain injuries. The guide also included warnings for more severe conditions such as motion sickness, as well as a warning for those who suffer from epileptic seizures. The one that stood out was the warning for posttraumatic stress disorder (PTSD). As the user guide explained:

> Intense content, such as violence, horror, or emotional content, can cause an adrenaline response. This can lead to increased heart rate and blood pressure, anxiety and panic attacks, fainting or other serious reactions. In extreme cases, it can trigger PTSD attacks. (Lenovo, 2017, p. 18)

A subsequent examination of two different virtual reality devices' user guides revealed a pattern. Both the HTC Vive and Oculus Rift manuals contained language that warned users about using the devices if they suffered from "anxiety disorder or post-traumatic stress disorder" (HTC, 2016, p. 25) or other "psychiatric disorders" (Oculus, 2018, p. 2). While on the surface this can be seen as simply a legal disclaimer to protect the respective companies, growing evidence suggests that the warning is warranted. It is well documented that users have reported real effects such as dizziness and nausea as a result of their experiences in augmented and virtual spaces (Keshavarz, Ramkhalawansingh, Haycock, Shahab, & Campos, 2018; Merhi, Faugloire, Flanagan, Stoffregen, 2007). Today, warnings in user manuals—fueled by inquires in the popular press (Engber, 2014)—turn our attention to the following question: are the experiences that these technologies provide powerful enough to cause PTSD? The following chapter will describe different types of reality on the reality continuum and examine the role that presence plays in these mediated experiences. It will then examine the dark undercurrent of AR and VR technologies including PTSD and sexual assault. The chapter will close by providing some basic recommendations for how to negotiate these emerging technological spaces.

What's the Reality?

Understanding the effects of these technologies first requires an understanding of the environments they inhabit and how each environment relates to each other. One way to understand these environments is to situate them on a reality continuum. Anchoring the left side of the continuum is *real reality*. This environment contains objects that have an "actual objective existence" (Milgram & Kishino, 1994, p. 1324), or are those real environments that are "unmodeled" in the computer sense (Milgram & Colquhoun Jr., 2001, p. 2). The everyday experience one has at the home, workplace, front sidewalk, or favorite restaurant are examples of real environments.

On the opposite, or right side of the continuum, is *virtual reality*. A virtual environment is a computer rendered, fully modeled environment (Milgram & Colquhoun Jr., 2001, p. 2). While previous generations of VR gear generally

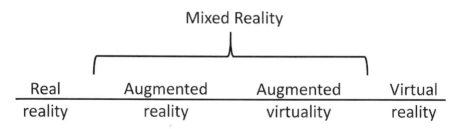

Figure 21.1. The Reality Continuum.

required a significant financial investment, access to AR and VR equipment has increased as costs have comparatively decreased. The Oculus Rift, HTC Vive, and Sony VR are examples of VR technologies.

In the middle of these anchors are two additional environments, *augmented reality* (AR) and *augmented virtuality* (AV). Augmented reality is the practice of integrating a real-time direct or indirect view of the physical (real) world with virtual information (Carmigniani & Furht, 2011). AR "refers to computer displays that add virtual information to a user's sensory perceptions (Feiner, 2002). AV environments are similar to AR environments in that they allow users to see and interact with both real and digital worlds simultaneously, however, AV allows users to place or fix digital constants like menus or accessories on top of the real world. Both AR and AV environments are considered "partially rendered" in the computer sense (Milgram & Colquhoun Jr., 2001, p. 2). The Microsoft Hololens, or Lenovo's *Jedi Challenges* are examples of AR devices. Both augmented and virtual experiences require some specialized technology to render, model, and display the technological portion of the environment. What makes these mediated experiences so unique are the perceptions of immersion, or *presence* that people feel.

TelePresence

The concept of telepresence was developed in the field of computer science. Marvin Minsky defined telepresence as emphasizing "the importance of high-quality sensory feedback" and suggested future instruments would "feel and work so much like our own hands that we won't notice any significant difference" (1980, p. 45). This is quite different than the definition presented by contemporary telepresence scholars. For example, telepresence has been defined as "the perceptual illusion of non-mediation" (Lombard & Ditton, 1997, Para 2).We make this point to stress that telepresence has primarily focused on the media form as opposed to the media content. In virtual reality, researchers attempt to maximize the feeling of "realism" to "fool" users into feeling the virtual environment is realistic. As Communication scholars explored whether telepresence could be experienced with popular media (Kim & Biocca, 1997; Lombard & Ditton, 1997) they brought with them the assumption that what was creating sensations of telepresence was perceived realism. While this may be true in VR settings, it is not necessarily true with popular media. If it were implicitly so, would we not avoid the 4-story high images of fish, lions, and Spiderman in an IMAX theater which clearly distort reality? Or refuse to watch Hollywood movies on our smartphones with their tiny objects and people?

Biocca (2003) addresses our perceptions of reality and maps out how different realities can interact with telepresence within a three-pole model. Telepresence, according to Biocca, is based on our ability to visualize images in our mind. There is an interaction between real-world imagery, virtual imagery, and our mental imagery. Biocca suggests there are three poles: physical space, mental imagery space, and ultimately (and humanly), virtual space. For example, a hunter experiences a meadow with game. The hunter visualizes and remembers key features (i.e., conceptualizes the space), and then shares the conceptualized space with others using abstractions (e.g., drawings). This virtual space can now be shared by individuals who have not physically experienced the space, allowing others to share the original hunter's concepts (i.e., mental recreations) of the space. By acknowledging that each individual has some capability to create images in their own mind and can communicate these images to others through abstractions (words or other symbols), it explains the capability and ease with which our minds accept the technological creation of environments (digital spaces) and experiences. Our ability to represent images has obviously surpassed cave drawings, and we can now "share" realistic digital images using cameras, computers, and software with millions.

Types of Telepresence

The concept of telepresence has evolved into a highly interdisciplinary concept with numerous (and somewhat) overlapping definitions. In AR/VR encounters, the type of telepresence most often studied is *spatial presence*. Spatial presence has been defined as a feeling of being physically located in a mediated environment (Ijsselsteijn, de Ridder, Freeman, & Avons, 2000); and as the "sensation of being physically situated within the spatial environment portrayed by the medium" (Wirth et al., 2007, p. 497). These definitions focus on reality judgements or perceptions of the reality of the mediated experience.

Westerman, Spence, and Lin (2015) consolidate these definitions by connecting them back to the idea of telepresence as "being there" (Lombard & Ditton, 1997). They argue:

> if people feel as if they are in an environment and experience objects as real within that environment, then they might be expected to have more "real" reactions to those objects (Lachlan, Westerman, & Spence, 2010; Spence, Lachlan, & Westerman, 2009). (p. 94)

Researchers have found that increases in feelings of spatial presence lead to an increase in existing media effects (Wirth et al., 2007). As an example, Starbucks used an AR experience to demonstrate the roasting process of their coffee. An employee remarked: "With AR, we are able to go beyond educating, enabling and engaging, to empowering our customers to experience the space on their own terms" (Dahlstrom, 2017).

In summary, telepresence requires the use of technology and results in a psychological state in which media users voluntarily suspend the experience of mediation in order to feel a sense of connection with the mediated content they are using (i.e., a part of the action, connected to characters, involved in the story line). This state is often influenced by the expectation of the technology, the media content, and characteristics of the media user. A sense of telepresence is felt by media users when the technology becomes transparent in the interaction (Bracken, Pettey, Rubenking, & Guha, 2008, p. 4).

Another type of presence commonly studied is *social presence*. Social presence has been defined as "the degree of salience of the other person in the interaction and the consequent salience of the interpersonal relationships" (Short, Williams, & Christie, 1976, p. 65). Or, "the degree of initial awareness, allocated attention, the capacity for both content and affective comprehension, and the capacity for both affective and behavioral interdependence with said entity" (Harms & Biocca, 2004). Feeling connected to another person via Skype or via direct messaging are examples of social presence. Here we also have a tension between whether social presence is a characteristic of the media technology or an affective perception that is a part of the subjective, human media user's experience.

Copresence is yet another type of presence. It has been defined as a sense of being together and is focused on the "psychological connection of minds" (Nowak, 2001). A more commonly employed definition is the offered by Biocca Harms, and Burgoon (2003) who define copresence as the sense of being in a shared virtual environment. So, how can one differentiate social presence from copresence? Bulu (2011) suggests that social presence relates to a quality of the medium while copresence is about the interactions of media users in shared digital spaces.

Considered together, telepresence sub-dimensions suggest that technology and technological innovation open opportunities and possibilities for life-like digital interactions to occur. They describe a variety of experiences people are having with and in digital environments. The utility of the technology changes as users explore new technology's potential. When multiple technologies are available for a particular content or use, people will choose the technology based on the viewing/use situation. Typically, people choose to optimize the telepresence experience afforded by the viewing or use context. For example, people will watch videos on their phone when traveling but are likely to go to the movies to see a new action adventure film.

While perceptions of the various types of presence are subjective and part of the individual user's experience, the role of technology in relation to telepresence is two-fold. First the technology must induce *vividness* (Steuer, 1992). Vividness is defined as the "representational richness of a mediated environment" (Steuer, 1992, p. 11), and may be improved by attending to *sensory breadth* and *sensory depth*. Sensory breadth refers to the number of senses that a mediated environment simultaneously appeals to (ex. visual, aural, haptic, etc.) Sensory depth refers to the resolution in each perceptual channel (ex. the visual difference between a small-format, black-and-white television versus a large screen, 3-D color television). Second, the technology must encourage interactivity. Through the lens of telepresence, interactivity can be defined as "the extent to which users can participate in modifying the form and content of a mediated environment in real time" (Steuer, 1992, p. 14). Three factors which contribute to interactivity are *speed* (the response time it takes to alter a mediated environment) *range* (the number of things that can be manipulated) and *mapping* (the way human actions are connected to changes in a digital interactive environment).

The combination of human and technological factors is what makes it possible for augmented and particularly virtual reality experiences to feel so real. It is precisely this realness of experience that connects these technologies to the previously discussed PTSD warnings in technology user guides. One area were telepresence research has been applied is in the area of clinical psychology and therapy.

VR Therapy

Virtual reality exposure therapy (VRET) technologies have been successfully used as therapeutic tools to treat a variety of psychological conditions, including: anxiety disorders, phobias, and post-traumatic stress disorder (see Krijn, Emmelkamp, Olafsson, & Biemond, 2004 for review). For conceptual clarity, PTSD is defined as a psychiatric disorder that occurs because of a traumatic experience. Those suffering from PTSD can be triggered by elements (sights, sounds, smells, etc.) that were associated with a trauma experience in such a way that the victim may re-experience, or relive the anxiety associated with the trauma. VRET is a modified form of cognitive behavior therapy that combines immersive virtual environments and exposure to anxiety-provoking stimuli (Krijn et al., 2004). Over the course of treatment, clients are exposed to triggers in the virtual environment, and with the guidance of a specially-trained therapist, are able to create new memory structures to replace existing structures that cause anxiety. Success in this domain has been attributed, in part, to the ability to customize digital environments, including the anxiety causing triggers (Rizzo et al., 2010), as well as perceptions of presence. As researchers explain: "The sense of presence provided by a virtual environment that is rich in sensory stimuli facilitates the emotional processing of memories related to the trauma" (Goncalves, Pedrozo, Coutinho, Figueira, & Ventura, 2012, p. 1).

VRET combines the strength of the immersive experience with emotional processing of the content displayed in VR. Empirical work demonstrates that VRET is equally as effective as traditional in-person therapy for the treatment of PTSD (Goncalves et al., 2012). The immersive, realistic scenarios can trigger responses, which, under the care of a clinician, can be used to help restructure future responses. While healing from trauma is regarded as a positive experience, it begets a darker theoretical question: if VRET technologies can provide emotional experiences that are strong enough to reprogram trauma, are they also strong enough to create it?

It has been documented that video games are capable of eliciting different types of fear responses including hyperawareness of auditory and visual stimuli, and nightmares (Lynch & Martins, 2015). But the short answer to this question is, no. Although some video game content may be capable of triggering a PTSD attack in those who have been previously traumatized, there is no published experimental or clinical work (to date) that has documented an augmented or virtual experience that has been powerful enough to *cause* PTSD in a person who has not been previously traumatized. Even if an isolated confirmed case were to occur, this certainly would not be expected to be a normative effect for the masses.

Nonetheless, there is enough nuance to this question that researchers and clinicians will continue to monitor this relationship. The current version of the APA's Diagnostic and Statistical Manual (DSM-5) for diagnosing mental disorders does acknowledge that it is plausible, under certain conditions, for media to elicit PTSD-like symptoms. Under the four criteria for diagnosing PTSD in adults and adolescents, there is a note which states: "Criterion A4 does not apply to exposure through electronic media, television, movies, or pictures, *unless this exposure is work related*" (p. 271, emphasis added). This ostensibly was included to account for those who process forensics work and crime scene media for homicides and other violent crimes. In addition to this acknowledgement, psychiatrists and researchers have preliminary evidence that indirect exposure to trauma (i.e. through media) can result in the detection of PTSD-like symptoms (Sheen, Slade, & Spiby, 2013), even if not actually PTSD.

While the use of virtual reality devices and VRET to treat PTSD and other psychological disorders is prosocial in nature, the dark undertone is the recognition that the user guide's warnings are not just legal protections. These technologies are capable of producing mediated experiences that are real enough to trigger PTSD attacks in those who have been previously diagnosed. Researchers are still examining whether these technologies are capable of leading to forms of secondary stress or posttraumatic distress that are similar, but not the same as PTSD (Pfefferbaum, Pfefferbaum, North, & Neas, 2002). This type of intense response to game content is not without precedent in the game world. The "No Russian" level in Call of Duty 2 Modern Warfare included an option to participate in an in-game terrorist attack staged at an airport in Moscow. Played from a blood-spattered, first-person perspective, game players had the option to shoot at a terminal full of unarmed civilians, while they screamed in horror and pleaded for their lives. The scene was so disturbing that some refused to play it, it was roundly condemned by community leaders, and was outright banned in some countries where it was released (Evans-Thirlwell, 2016).

Perhaps the darkest side of VR's connection to PTSD is not its use as a medium which theoretically is capable of eliciting a PTSD-like response, but in its potential use as a marketing tool. It is not too far-fetched to suppose that a marketing campaign might write about a new first-person shooter VR game that is "So good, you'll have PTSD." We hope to pre-empt any attempt to capitalize on a campaign as distasteful as this as it would undermine and minimize the very real struggles of the tens of thousands of veterans and civilians (U.S. Department of Veteran's Affairs, 2016) who have been traumatized.

Sexual Assault in VR?

It is normal to expect that people will push boundaries with technologies and mediated content, yet, how people choose to engage with others and their avatars in virtual worlds can also be problematic. The experiences of women in virtual worlds is an example of how users can choose to use emerging AR and VR technologies in dark ways. A cursory online search reveals a number of videos showing VR users (almost always males) groping, making unwanted advances, and engaging in what could be described as virtual sexual assault on female avatars in VR demonstrations. Women who have had similar experiences of being groped or assaulted in VR note that the negative feelings of experiencing this treatment virtually, triggers feelings that are very similar to those who have been victimized in real life (ex. Wong, 2016). Allowing users to rehearse assault-like behaviors without repercussions in an environment that is known for feeling immersive and real, could serve to normalize antisocial ideas about how women are to be treated. While this issue certainly merits our attention and needs to be monitored, it is worth noting that there is nothing inherent in VR or AR technologies that causes people to behave inappropriately. As has been noted in other chapters (see Waddell & Ivory, this volume) often times the negative aspects come from a small, non-representative group of the larger gaming and tech community. Nonetheless, the larger group should be aware of the negative potential and condemn and report these actions when they occur. Some tech companies have been proactive about issues such as this and are exploring options like a universal, open-source "power gesture," or physical movement that a player can make in AR and VR environments that would activate a personal space bubble and make a would-be antagonist disappear (Wong, 2016).

Playing It Safe

Each of the chapters in this book provide some recommendations for how to deal with the negative effects of various media and technologies. Our first recommendation is not geared toward media effects, but for those suffering from PTSD. If you or someone you care about may be suffering from PTSD, there is help available. Remember that only a clinician has the credentials to diagnose PTSD or any other related illnesses. A variety of treatments and therapies are available—many that may not require drugs or pharmacological aids. The first step is reaching out, and an internet search is the best way to find local, professional resources for victims and family members of those who have been traumatized.

With respect to augmented and virtual technologies, it is important to remember that many of the theoretical connections made in this chapter are indeed, theoretical. No clinical evidence or case studies to date, have confirmed that players can get PTSD solely from playing immersive video games. However, it is possible that exposure to immersive, violent content experienced in these worlds could account for some negative affect, and could serve as a trigger for someone who is already suffering from PTSD or a related illness. If users of augmented and virtual technologies start to feel anxiety, panic, or fear during use, the best suggestion is to take a break and talk to a friend, confidante, or professional about your experience.

As technology increasingly allows for the blending of the physical world and digital environments, the potential to exploit and influence the media audience increases. Theories addressing these mixing of realities (e.g., telepresence and transportation) suggest that when media audience members "return" to the physical world, they are impacted by the content and interactions they have in the virtual environments. As technologies proliferate, they will allow for the possibility of additional layers of advertising (think of the film *Minority Report*), and the creation of new avenues for misinformation via holograms and video editing. As industry researchers acknowledge; "advancements in smart glasses and transparent screen technologies (Dibble, 2014) will integrate the human gaze with digital information ever more seamlessly, propelling AR into an estimated $120 billion business by 2020" (Gaudiosi, 2015; cf. Scholz & Smith, 2016). Being aware of these trends is the first step in building defenses against invasive or unethical tactics.

In conclusion, AR and VR are still quite young technologies that are being tested in an increasing set of scenarios. While there is evidence that the use of these technologies can promote mental health when used in a clinical setting, little research has yet been conducted to understand how the general public will respond to the increasing feelings of immersion in our daily media diet.

References

Biocca, F. (2003). *Can we resolve the book, the physical reality, and the dream state Problems? From the two-pole to a three-pole model of shifts in presence.* Presented at the EU Future and Emerging Technologies Presence Initiative Meeting. Venice, May 5–7, 2003. http://www.mindlab.org/images/d/DOC705.pdf

Biocca, R, C. Harms, J. K. Burgoon. (2003). Toward a more robust theory and measure of social presence: Review and suggested criteria. *Presence: Teleoperators and Virtual, 12*(5), 456–482.

Bracken, C. C., Pettey, G., Rubenking, B., & Guha, T. (2008). *Sounding out small screens and telepresence: The impact of screen size, pace & sound.* Presented to the Information Processing division of the International Communication Association annual convention in Montreal, Quebec, Canada

Bulu, S. T. (2011) Place presence, social presence, co-presence, and satisfaction in virtual worlds. *Computers & Education, 58*(1), 154–161. doi:10.1016/j.compedu.2011.08.024

Carmigniani, J., & Furht, B. (2011). Augmented reality: An overview. In B. Furht (Ed.), *Handbook of augmented reality* (pp. 3–4), New York, NY: Springer.

Dahlstrom, L. (2017). Through the looking glass: Starbucks' first in-store augmented reality experience. *Starbucks Newsroom.* Retrieved May 24, 2018, from https://news.starbucks.com/news/starbucks-first-in-store-augmented-reality-experience

Dibble, A. (2014, September 16). 12 promising augmented reality devices—The state of AR hardware. *Brainberry Global.* Retrieved from http://brainberryglobal.com/12-promising-augmented-reality-devices-state-ar-hardware/

Engber, D. (2014). Can you get PTSD from a virtual experience? *Popular Science* (October 6). Retrieved May 24, 2018, from https://www.popsci.com/article/science/can-you-get-ptsd-virtual-experience

Evans-Thirlwell, E. (2016). From all ghillied up to No Russian, the making of Call of Duty's most famous levels. *PCGamer.* Retrieved March 23, 2018, from https://www.pcgamer.com/from-all-ghillied-up-to-no-russian-the-making-of-call-of-dutys-most-famous-levels/2/

Feiner, S. (2002). Augmented reality: A new way of seeing. *Scientific American, 286*(4), 50–55.

Gaudiosi, J. (2015, April 25). How augmented reality and virtual reality will generate $150 billion in revenue by 2020. *Fortune.* Retrieved from http://fortune.com/2015/04/25/augmented-reality-virtual-reality/

Goncalves, R., Pedrozo, A. L., Coutinho, E. S. F., Figueira, I., & Ventura, P. (2012). Efficacy of virtual reality exposure therapy in the treatment of PTSD: A systematic review. *PLoS One, 7*(12), 1–7. doi:10.1371/journal.pone.0048469

Harms, C., & Biocca, F. (2004). Internal consistency and reliability of the networked minds social presence measure. In M. Alcaniz & B. Rey (Eds.), *Seventh annual international workshop: Presence 2004*. Valencia: Universidad Politecnica de Valencia.

HTC. (2016). Vive PRE User Guide. Retrieved from https://www.htc.com/managed-assets/shared/desktop/vive/Vive_PRE_User_Guide.pdf

Ijsselsteijn, W. A., de Ridder, H., Freeman, J., & Avons, S. E. (2000, January). *Presence: Concept, determinants and measurement*. Proceedings of the SPIE, Human Vision and Electronic Imaging V, San Jose, CA.

Keshavarz, B., Ramkhalawansingh, R., Haycock, B., Shahab, S., & Campos, J. L. (2018). Comparing simulator sickness in younger and older adults during simulated driving under different multisensory conditions. *Transportation Research Part F: Traffic Psychology and Behaviour, 54*, 47–62.

Kim, T., & Biocca, F. (1997). Telepresence via television: Two dimensions of telepresence may have different connections to memory and persuasion. *Journal of Computer-Mediated Communication, 3,2*. Available: http://www.ascusc.org/jcmc/vol3/issue2/kim.html

Krijn, M., Emmelkamp, P. M. G., Olafsson, R. P., & Biemond, R. (2004). Virtual reality exposure therapy of anxiety disorders: A review. *Clinical Psychology Review, 24*, 259–281. doi:10.1016/j.cpr.2004.04.001

Lachlan, K. A., Westerman, D. K., & Spence, P. (2010). Disaster news and subsequent information seeking: Exploring the role of spatial presence and perceptual realism. *Electronic News, 4*(4), 203–217. doi:10.1177/1931243110387092

Lenovo (2017). Star Wars: Jedi Challenges. Safety, Warranty & Product Guide.

Lombard, M., & Ditton, T. (1997). At the heart of it all: The concept of presence. *Journal of Computer-Mediated Communication, 3*(2). doi:10.1111/j.1083-6101.1997.tb00072.x

Lynch, T., & Martins, N. (2015). Nothing to fear? An analysis of college students' fear experiences with video games. *Journal of Broadcasting & Electronic Media, 59*(2), 298–317. doi:10.1080/08838151.2015.1029128

Merhi, O., Faugloire, E., Flanagan, M., Stoffregen, T. A. (2007). Motion sickness, console video games, and head-mounted displays. *Human Factors: The Journal of the Human Factors and Ergonomics Society, 49*(5), 920–934. doi:10.1518/001872007X230262

Milgram, P., & Colquhoun Jr., H. (2001). A taxonomy of real world and virtual world display integration. In Y. Ohta & H. Tamura (Eds.), *Mixed reality: Merging real and virtual worlds* (pp. 1–26). New York, NY: Springer.

Milgram, P., & Kishino, F. (1994). A Taxonomy of mixed reality visual displays. *IEICE Transactions on Information Systems, E77D, 12*, 1321–1329.

Minsky, M. (1980). Telepresence. *Omni, June*, 45–51.

Nowak, K. (2001, May). *Defining and differentiating copresence, social presence and presence as transportation*. Paper presented at the 4th International Workshop on Presence, Philadelphia, PA.

Oculus (2018). Oculus Development Kit 2 (DK2) Health and Safety Guide. Retrieved from https://www.oculus.com/legal/health-and-safety-warnings/

Pfefferbaum, B., Pfefferbaum, R. L., North, C. S., & Neas, B. R. (2002). Does television viewing satisfy criteria for Exposure in Posttraumatic stress disorder? *Psychiatry, 65*(4), 306–309. doi:10.1521/psyc.65.4.306.20242

Rizzo, A., Difede, J., Rothbaum, B. O., Reger, G., Spitalnick, J., Cukor, J., & Mclay, R. (2010). Development and early evaluation of the Virtual Iraq/Afghanistan exposure therapy system for combat-related PTSD. *Annals of the New York Academy of Sciences, 1208*, 114–125. doi:10.1111/j.1749-6632.2010.05755.x

Scholz, J., & Smith, A. N. (2016). Augmented reality: Designing immersive experiences that maximize consumer engagement. *Business Horizons, 59*(2), 149–161.

Sheen, K., Slade, P., & Spiby, H. (2013). An integrative review of the impact of indirect trauma exposure in health professionals and potential issues of salience for midwives. *Journal of Advanced Nursing, 52*(2), 729–743. doi:10.1111/jan.12274

Short, J., Williams, E., & Christie, B. (1976). The social psychology of telecommunications. London: John Wiley & Sons.

Spence, P. R., Lachlan, K. A., & Westerman, D. K. (2009). Presence and crisis news: Exploring the responses of men and women to tragic stories in different media. *Journal of Applied Communication Research, 37*, 239–256.

Steuer, J. (1992). Defining virtual reality: Dimensions determining telepresence. *Journal of Communication, 42*(4), 73–93. doi:10.1111/j.1460-2466.1992.tb00812.x

U.S. Department of Veteran's Affairs. (2016). How common is PTSD? Retrieved May 24, 2018, from https://www.ptsd.va.gov/public/ptsd-overview/basics/how-common-is-ptsd.asp

Westerman, D., Spence, P. R., & Lin, X. (2015). Telepresence and exemplification in health Messages: The relationships among spatial and social presence and exemplars and exemplification effects. *Communication Reports, 28*(2), 92–102. doi:10.1080/08934215.2014.97 1838

Wirth, W., Hartmann, T., Böcking, S., Vorderer, P., Klimmt, C., Schramm, H., … Jäncke, P. (2007). A process model of the formation of spatial presence experiences. *Media Psychology, 9*(3), 493–525. doi:10.1080/15213260701283079

Wong, J. C. (2016). Sexual harassment in virtual reality feels all too real—"It's creepy beyond creepy." *The Guardian.* Retrieved March, 28, from https://www.theguardian.com/technology/2016/oct/26/virtual-reality-sexual-harassment-online-groping-quivr

CHAPTER TWENTY-TWO

Leaks Are Forever

Information Security and Cybercrime

PETER A. H. PETERSON & CHARERN LEE

In 1984, Stewart Brand, author and Hacker's Conference organizer, famously said "Information wants to be free" because sharing it is so easy in the Information Age (Levy, 2014). In the same breath, he also said "information wants to be expensive" because the right information in the right circumstance is so powerful. However, this power is not always positive, especially when information is shared in ways that we don't want.

Approximately 59 records are stolen every second—five million records every day, and nearly two *billion* records every year (Gemalto, 2017). Unfortunately, once shared or stolen, information can never be "unshared." At the same time, critical flaws appear every day in our computing technologies, even though people have worked for decades to improve computer security. It sometimes seems that the nature of digital information is to be *insecure*. As such, Brand's phrase was extended at the RSA Security conference in 2008 to: "Information wants to be free—and code wants to be wrong." This combination left unchecked is not good news for your security and privacy.

Information security is a metaphorical contact sport between intelligent adversaries working to attack and defend systems. Behind every attack is a human looking for the path of least resistance through defenses. In this asymmetric battle, the attackers only need to succeed once, but defenders must stop every attack. Generally speaking, information security has three primary goals: *confidentiality*, *integrity*, and *availability*. Confidentiality is about privacy—controlling who can access information. Integrity is about preserving data's "wholeness"—protecting it from corruption, or at least, detecting if it is modified. Availability is about information being accessible when needed. These goals are difficult to realize in isolation and there are rarely perfect solutions because they are often in direct tension with one another. For example, confidentiality typically relies on encryption or physical isolation—which directly restricts availability. The combination of conflicting interests and the certainty of failures makes it inevitable that information in our computer systems will continue to be leaked, corrupted, or made inaccessible.

The law protects some data, like education and medical records. However, much of our data are not specially protected, even though they include private thoughts, conversations, photographs, videos, relationships, interests, locations, and more. In many ways, these data are more sensitive than a medical history or bank account balance because they form a detailed profile of you as an individual, including your social networks, interests, likes, dislikes, demographics, and more. Companies own this information and can sell ads based on it, use it internally, or sell it outright. Unfortunately, sharing information with a third party only increases the likelihood of leaks.

Given these facts, we can say that the Information Age has commodified personal information, turning it into a product that is bought and sold as a good. The "free" social media platforms and industry profile pages are not really free. Companies buy and sell your profile information as a product. More information means greater value because it theoretically translates into better results for advertising and more revenue when sold. The following chapter will chronicle through case studies how large-scale privacy issues have already impacted people around the world. It then discusses different ways in which individual user privacy can be violated. The chapter concludes with recommendations for improving cyber hygiene.

Loss of Privacy

Privacy is about controlling access to information. Users provide some personal information to third parties knowing it may be used or shared, but they also unknowingly share information, and may not understand entirely what is done with it. Organizations often hoard data because they may be useful in the future. For example, Facebook keeps what you type into text fields even if you *choose not to post it* (Naughton, 2013), and documents suggest that the National Security Agency (NSA) may keep intercepted encrypted data indefinitely, because they *might one day* be found to contain valuable information (Greenberg, 2013). Organizations can reveal information about users against users' wishes. In 2012, Facebook was partly responsible for outing two university students. While they had locked down their privacy settings to conceal their sexual orientation from their families, another user had added them to the public Queer Chorus group. This membership change was announced to friends and family (McCormick, 2012). While Facebook did not intend for this to happen, it was a direct result of Facebook's inadequate privacy mechanisms.

User profiles can also be mined to uncover personal information not explicitly included in user data. In a famous case, Target inferred that a teen was pregnant based on her online activity. Customized advertisements revealed this fact to her father (Hill, 2012). "Anonymized" data can be unexpectedly revealing when cross-referenced with other data. Researchers identified the probable political leaning, religion, and other sensitive information of an "anonymous" Netflix subscriber by cross-referencing movie ratings with information from the Internet Movie Database Forums (Narayanan & Shmatikov, 2008).

User data is also analyzed by third parties, such as when Cambridge Analytica (an information firm employed by political campaigns) obtained data from Facebook and other services on up to 87 million U.S. individuals (Lomas, 2018). They synthesized this data into "psychographic" profiles—behaviors, beliefs, and personality categories, rather than simple demographics. These profiles were used for micro-targeted campaign advertising ahead of the 2016 presidential election. These examples are not "flaws," *per se*. However, any organization storing personal information can be breached due to security failures. The following case studies detail how breaches occur and how they put us at risk.

Case Study 1: Equifax Data Breach

In September 2017, Equifax reported that it suffered a data breach from May through July (Armerding, 2018). Approximately 147.9 million American (Fung, 2018), 15.2 million British, and 8,000 Canadian consumers were impacted in the breach, making this incident one of the biggest data breaches in the 21st century. The attackers obtained sensitive information including social security numbers, birth dates, addresses, last names, driver's license numbers, credit card numbers, and more (Equifax Inc., 2017).

The attackers gained access through a security flaw in Apache Struts, an application system used by Equifax's online dispute reporting system (Equifax Inc., 2017). The flaw in Struts was disclosed to Equifax two months before the attack (along with a software patch that would fix the vulnerability), but Equifax did not apply it. On July 29, the Equifax security team noticed suspicious activity, which led to the discovery of activities dating back to May. Equifax stated that "The company worked diligently ... to make an appropriate public disclosure of the incident" (Equifax Inc., 2017), but that disclosure didn't occur until September—more than a month later.

Equifax patched the vulnerability and continued to work with security consultants and the FBI in the investigation (Equifax Inc., 2017). They are also providing several services including a website where consumers can determine whether they were impacted, providing information about the incident, and options for protection, including one year of credit monitoring services. They have also revamped their call center to assist consumers.

Equifax lost $27.3 million to expenses related to the breach and it will lose $56 to $110 million to the free credit monitoring services (Richter, 2017). At the time of this writing, Equifax has not been fined for the breach, but is facing several lawsuits. Senators Elizabeth Warren (D-MA) and Mark Warner (D-VA) have proposed a bill (Data Breach Prevention and Compensation Act) that will penalize credit reporting agencies if they expose consumers' data: $100 for each consumer affected by an attack and another $50 for each personal record stolen (Romm, 2018). If this bill was enacted prior to the breach, Equifax would have been fined $1.5 billion. Many feel that Equifax's proposed remedy of one year of free credit monitoring services is insufficient, because the harm to consumers outweighs the value of the remedy, and consumers must pay for the services after one year. Since individuals may feel a need to continue paying Equifax for protection indefinitely, the breach could result in a questionable economic gain.

Case Study 2: Office of Personnel Management Data Breach

In June 2015, The Office of Personnel Management (OPM), the federal agency that investigates security clearances, reported a compromise that may be the largest data breach of the federal government in U.S. history (Risen, 2015). Reports suggest that 21.5 million people who have undergone the security clearance process had their sensitive information compromised, such as social security numbers, names, and birth dates (Oversight and Government Reform, 2016). Of special concern is the lengthy SF-86 files used for background checks, which contain information about sensitive topics, such as drug use, personal connections, medical information, and more (Zetter & Greenberg, 2015).

The OPM Inspector General had been warned since 2005 that its agency was vulnerable to attackers due to lax information technology policies. For example, only 1% of OPM user accounts used personal identity verification cards for authentication when all user accounts should have had this security measure, and third-party contractors had direct access to records. On March 20, 2014, the United States CERT (Computer Emergency Readiness Team) notified OPM that an attacker had infiltrated its system. The attacker was monitored to better understand the threat it posed, and it was removed two months later. However, during this attack, another attacker gained access using stolen contractor credentials and remained unnoticed due to the focus on the first attacker. The second attacker created a backdoor to OPM's network in July 2014 that ended in early 2015. Like Equifax, it took OPM several weeks to make a public announcement regarding the data breach.

The attack enabled by OPM's negligent behavior affected nearly 22 million people, leaking private information about people who had undergone security clearance background checks as part of their employment (Oversight and Government Reform, 2016). As a remedy, OPM is offering individuals involved in the incident credit monitoring and identity theft protections for 18 months. Again, although these services may provide peace of mind in the short-term, they may not be sufficient to protect individuals from risks after those services expire.

The OPM data breach could likely have been avoided as the Inspector General was warned long before the breach, but did not implement security controls (Oversight and Government Reform, 2016). OPM also decided not to implement basic security controls when it discovered the attackers, which could have delayed, prevented, or mitigated the theft. In addition, the activities of the first attacker could have sounded a national security alarm across all federal agencies and formed a multi-agency cooperation to prevent or mitigate the damage suffered by the OPM. Instead, attackers had access to OPM's systems for about a year.

Case Study 3: Yahoo! Data Breaches

In September 2016, Yahoo! made its first public announcement about a data breach that occurred in late 2014 (Armerding, 2018) that affected 500 million users. A few months later, in December, Yahoo! disclosed a breach that happened in 2013, initially believed to have impacted 1 *billion* users, but was later increased to 3 billion users. The incidents were believed to be executed by different attackers and involved sensitive information including email addresses, names, birth dates, hashed passwords, encrypted passwords, unencrypted security questions,

254 | PETER A. H. PETERSON & CHARERN LEE

and telephone numbers (Goel & Perlroth, 2016). The two attacks are the largest data breaches in the 21st century, almost *19 times* larger than the combined Equifax and OPM data breaches in terms of users affected, although arguably involving less sensitive information.

Yahoo! reported that the 2014 breach was executed by state-sponsored attackers who forged "cookies" (text tokens stored in the browser that keeps the user logged in or remembers the user's details) to log into the users' accounts without their passwords (Goel & Perlroth, 2016). Once cookies were forged, attackers impersonated users to obtain sensitive information that could help them access the users' other online accounts. Yahoo! became aware of this breach through contact with law enforcement regarding concerns and files related to the breach, which law enforcement received from an unnamed third-party. Forged cookies may also have been used in the 2013 data breach, which was discovered after Yahoo! analyzed the data files. Similar to Equifax and the OPM, Yahoo! waited some time to announce the breaches.

To date, Yahoo! has not provided much remedy for the breaches other than improve its security system and offer steps for users to protect themselves (Goel & Perlroth, 2016). This is insufficient as consumers may become victims of fraud enabled by the breaches. However, Yahoo! (now owned by Verizon) is facing several lawsuits related to the breach. It is very possible that the Yahoo! breaches could have been avoided. Yahoo!'s internal security team had advocated for stronger security mechanisms, but were reportedly rebuffed due to the inconvenience the controls would cause for the struggling company.

Case Study 4: WannaCry and the NHS

Ransomware is a category of cybercrime malware (malicious software) that encrypts a victim's data. Then, the operators extort the owner for money to decrypt the files under threat of deletion. Ransomware is usually a "Trojan horse" (a malicious program that appears benevolent) although some are "worms" (spreading over a network via vulnerabilities). Ransomware has been hard to stop with technical defenses (e.g., anti-malware software) because it is usually installed by choice, and new variants appear regularly. Payment is usually in an anonymous electronic currency, such as Bitcoin, which requires no physical interaction and is hard to trace. Because users often have no backups or hard copies, a ransomware attack often represents a choice between paying or losing the data forever.

Ransomware has also targeted organizations. In 2017, the WannaCry "ransomworm" was used in a global attack that affected the National Health Service

(NHS) in the U.K. and other businesses (Hern, 2017), leading to an estimated $4 billion economic loss (Berr, 2017). Like the above breaches, WannaCry was avoidable. It spread using an exploit stolen from the NSA that Microsoft patched *two months* before the attack. Machines that were patched were not vulnerable.

Ransomware is ever evolving. Doxware (from the slang "dox" meaning to publish someone's private information) encrypts files like ransomware, but also uploads the users' data to a remote site. The attackers then threaten to publicly reveal the victims' information, motivating them to pay even if the victims have backups (Ensey, 2017).

Case Study 5: Spectre and Meltdown

In January of 2018, the world learned about a decades-old class of vulnerability in CPU hardware. Under the names Meltdown and Spectre, these new vulnerabilities circumvented security mechanisms isolating one program's memory from another. Unfortunately, these vulnerabilities are part of the hardware of the CPU and can't be "patched." Software vendors have been able to work around Meltdown exploits at the cost of 5–30% performance, but while Spectre is somewhat more difficult to exploit, workarounds are limited.

Computer security works in layers. Users depend on *applications*, which depend on the *operating system*, which depend on the *hardware*. As the case studies demonstrate, all layers are potentially vulnerable, but hardware flaws can invalidate *all* defenses. Future hardware flaws are a practical certainty, and benevolent researchers will not always discover them first. While best practices will reduce your risk with respect to these attacks, Meltdown and Spectre force us to accept that even perfect actions by users and software developers are not enough to guarantee security.

As an aside, there is also the growing cybercrime market. The increasing importance of digital information and the convenience that makes online services easy to use also makes them easy to abuse. Criminals use vulnerabilities or fraud to steal data such as account numbers, usernames, and passwords that they can use for various purposes, including identity theft. We also need to be vigilant for *spam* (also called Unsolicited Commercial Email or UCE), a type of commercial email sent to users against their will. *Phishing*, or stealing passwords and account information through fraudulent login screens and other input forms; *spear phishing*, or stealing authentication information from a specific, high-value individual using a phishing attack personalized with the victim's information to make it appear more legitimate, as well as selling data to other criminals. Finally, human beings' tendency to collect information we value makes us vulnerable to ransomware and doxware, two emerging types of cybercrime.

Cyber Hygiene and Best Practices

While the previous paragraphs detailed breaches that occurred to large portions of society, there are a number of ways that individuals can maximize their data security. "Cyber hygiene" is the set of practices that help individuals stay "healthy" and minimize risk from a cybersecurity perspective. When technology users (professional and personal) attend to their cyber hygiene, they keep themselves and others safe. While these items are best practices at the time of this writing, it is always important to search for updated information.

Strong Passwords and Two-Factor Authentication

Devices and accounts often require passwords. Passwords should be long, random, or include random elements. They should also be unique (not reused), and never shared. One technology that can make this easier is a password manager, where long and random passwords can be cut and pasted from the manager into password fields. While the manager becomes a single point of failure, password companies have professional security teams. Most security experts agree that the rewards of password managers outweigh the risks.

We authenticate, or prove our identity, with private tokens from one of three classes: *something we have* (e.g., a device), *something we are* (e.g., a fingerprint or face recognition), or *something we know* (e.g., a password). A powerful way to add security is to use Two-Factor Authentication (2FA), where you provide tokens from two of the three classes. Because both must be correct, an attacker needs to guess the password *and* steal a user's device or card. 2FA schemes are less convenient, but they are *much* more secure.

Encryption, Isolation and Offline Backups

Eavesdropping on network traffic is trivially easy. Attackers can inject or modify unencrypted traffic without the knowledge of the victim. Experts have long recommended that users use end-to-end encryption (E2EE) whenever possible, especially when accessing sensitive information like banking or personal information. In E2EE, data is encrypted on one end of the communication (e.g., your computer) and only decrypted at the other end (e.g., the remote server you are accessing). Most users experience E2EE when they use HTTPS—the securely encrypted HTTP protocol for web traffic. Browsers indicate HTTPS in the address bar and sometimes with additional icons, like a lock or a green highlight. HTTPS can be broken with an attack or misconfiguration, but this is usually detectable and results in an error. You may have seen an encryption error before, often about an "invalid certificate". Ignoring the warning means that your traffic might be intercepted or modified by an attacker. The best practice is to use E2EE (like HTTPS) whenever possible. If visiting a site that does not provide HTTPS, recognize that it poses a risk to you. If a site involving your personal information displays errors about certificates, HTTPS, or encryption, do not use the site. Instead, email or call the company, or try again later.

In addition to encryption of data on the network, any sensitive data "at rest" (i.e., in storage on a computer) should always be encrypted with a strong algorithm and key, which, like a password, should be as long and as random as possible, and never reused. This helps to ensure that data will be protected even if a device is physically stolen. Hardware and software solutions exist to encrypt everything on a computer's hard drive at all times, which is especially important for those that process sensitive data. Encryption is a form of virtual isolation because, although the *encrypted* data can be read, it is indecipherable in that form without the key. Physical isolation is also important for any sensitive computer system, because many, if not all, security mechanisms can be bypassed with physical access to the computer.

Backup Data

Backups of your important data are critical. Backups should not be made to your own device, because they may be lost if the device is damaged, stolen, or subjected to ransomware. Instead they should be made to encrypted external devices (e.g., a USB disk) or secure cloud storage. Backups should not be stored in the same location as the original source, in case of fire or theft. No scheme is perfect. Cloud backups are convenient but are subject to potential breaches. Backups to external disks are inconvenient and are subject to loss, or theft, and it is easy to forget to update them.

Anti-malware and Automatic Updates

Shortly after the arrival of computer "viruses" in the 1980s, many vendors began selling anti-malware (or "antivirus") to remove malicious software from users' computers. Modern forms also target adware and spyware. We believe that it is still generally a good idea to use these programs if they come from reputable sources. However, some experts disagree because anti-malware programs have become less effective over time and have themselves had vulnerabilities that led to exploitation (Chung, 2016; Zetter, 2016). In at least one case, an anti-malware program was compromised and used by a hostile government for spying (Perlroth, 2018).

Because of these issues, more critical than whether you install anti-virus is that you are very careful about the sources of software you install. Many pirated software sites (e.g., pirate app stores) include malicious programs instead of or alongside the desired programs. Unsolicited attachments are often similarly dangerous. Using ad-blocking software is a good practice, because ads can be used to track users and can include software to be executed that can exploit vulnerabilities like Meltdown. Unfortunately, some supposed ad-blockers are actually malicious programs, so it is important to carefully research any such program that you install and to install it from a legitimate source.

Enterprise software systems and applications used for web development (e.g., Struts) and operating systems (Windows, Apple's OS X, and Linux) all provide regular updates for security vulnerabilities. It is very important that you enable automatic security updates and that you make sure any system you control is kept up to date. History has shown time and again that failing to update your systems leads to breaches and liability.

Think Before You Share

The only data that can't be leaked is data that doesn't exist. Since you can't control how other organizations or individuals use or share your data—intentionally or unintentionally—one of the only ways to ensure that your personal information isn't shared is to not share it. Furthermore, since it is impossible to ensure that your personal devices will never be compromised, you should consider deleting any data that you couldn't bear to have leaked, or at least move it to encrypted offline storage.

Leaks Are Forever

Any data stored without encryption, especially on a network is at risk of theft. Software vulnerabilities can usually be patched, but when overlooked can lead to breaches. Hardware vulnerabilities can enable breaches that may not be repairable. Accounts can also be breached through exploits, stealing passwords through "phishing", or guessing passwords. Breaches often result in the loss of sensitive data, and can be leveraged to gain access to other accounts (Goel & Perlroth, 2016). Breaches occur so frequently, and in such volume, that it is almost guaranteed that you will be affected by them.

Most of the preceding advice applies in some form to devices like smartphones and tablets. One way that phones are special is that they are essentially high-tech "bugs"—high-quality listening and computation devices complete with GPS, motion, and light sensors. One important aspect of device security is "app permissions," where an app requests access to capabilities of the phone. Be thoughtful about what you grant to applications, especially if apps request seemingly unnecessary permissions. These requests can be benign—for example, requesting access to phone calls may be necessary to interrupt calls for notifications. But access to contacts lists or GPS may not be necessary, and the app may work correctly without those permissions.

While there is no "silver bullet" for security, there are things you can do to mitigate risk. Make sure that you use strong passwords (Password Managers can help) and enable Two-Factor Authentication whenever possible; these will make your accounts much harder to break into. Use encrypted communication (e.g., HTTPS) whenever possible. Encrypt all data on any storage medium, backing it up and storing it in a secure location. Enable and accept automatic updates to your OS and applications. Avoid untrustworthy websites and software (such as pirated software or untrusted attachments). If you are responsible for software systems that others use, make sure they are kept up to date. Think carefully about the data you choose to keep or share, recognizing that anything you share is out of your control and anything you keep can be leaked. Most importantly, make sure that your security behaviors are based on current best practices, rather than on outdated advice. While these measures cannot absolutely protect you from privacy breaches and other types of losses, they can go a long way towards keeping you protected in the Information Age.

References

Armerding, T. (2018, January 26). The 17 biggest data breaches of the 21st century. *CSO*. Retrieved from https://www.csoonline.com/article/2130877/data-breach/the-biggest-data-breaches-of-the-21st-century.html

Berr, J. (2017, May 16). "WannaCry" ransomware attack losses could reach $4 billion. *CBS News*. Retrieved from https://www.cbsnews.com/news/wannacry-ransomware-attacks-wannacry-virus-losses/

Chung, E. (2016, July 8). Antivirus software is "increasingly useless" and may make your computer less safe. *CBC News*. Retrieved from http://www.cbc.ca/news/technology/antivirus-software-1.3668746

Ensey, C. (2017, January 4). Ransomware has evolved, and its name is doxware. *Dark Reading*. Retrieved from https://www.darkreading.com/attacks-breaches/ransomware-has-evolved-and-its-name-is-doxware/a/d-id/1327767

Equifax Inc. (2017, September 15). Equifax releases details on cybersecurity incident, announces personnel changes. *PR Newswire*. Retrieved from https://investor.equifax.com/news-and-events/news/2017/09-15-2017-224018832

Fung, B. (2018, March 1). Equifax's massive 2017 data breach keeps getting worse. *The Washington Post*. Retrieved from https://www.washingtonpost.com/news/the-switch/wp/2018/03/01/equifax-keeps-finding-millions-more-people-who-were-affected-by-its-massive-data-breach/?utm_term=.e651727920f6

Gemalto, Inc. (2017, December). Breach level index: Data breach statistics by year, industry, more. *Breach Level Index*. Retrieved from https://breachlevelindex.com

Goel, V., & Perlroth, N. (2016, December 14). Yahoo says 1 billion user accounts were hacked. *The New York Times*. Retrieved from https://www.nytimes.com/2016/12/14/technology/yahoo-hack.html

Greenberg, A. (2013, June 20). Leaked NSA doc says it can collect and keep your encrypted data as long as it takes to crack it. *Forbes*. Retrieved from https://www.forbes.com/sites/andygreenberg/2013/06/20/leaked-nsa-doc-says-it-can-collect-and-keep-your-encrypted-data-as-long-as-it-takes-to-crack-it/

Hern, A. (2017, December 30). WannaCry, Petya, NotPetya: How ransomware hit the big time in 2017. *The Guardian*. Retrieved from https://www.theguardian.com/technology/2017/dec/30/wannacry-petya-notpetya-ransomware

Hill, K. (2012, February 2). How target figured out a teen girl was pregnant before her father did. *Forbes*. Retrieved from https://www.forbes.com/sites/kashmirhill/2012/02/16/how-target-figured-out-a-teen-girl-was-pregnant-before-her-father-did/

Levy, S. (2014, November 21). Hackers at 30: "Hackers" and "information wants to be free". *Wired*. Retrieved from https://www.wired.com/story/hackers-at-30-hackers-and-information-wants-to-be-free/

Lomas, N. (2018, June 7). Cambridge Analytica's Nix said it licensed "millions of data points" from Acxiom, Experian, Infogroup to target US voters. *Tech Crunch*. Retrieved from https://techcrunch.com/2018/06/06/cambridge-analyticas-nix-said-it-licensed-millions-of-data-points-from-axciom-experian-infogroup-to-target-us-voters/

McCormick, J. P. (2012, October 16). Facebook accidentally outed users to their parents through group permissions loophole. *Pink News*. Retrieved from https://www.pinknews.co.uk/2012/10/16/facebook-accidentally-outed-users-to-their-parents-through-group-permissions-loophole/

Narayanan, A., & Shmatikov, V. (2008). Robust de-anonymization of large sparse datasets. *In Proceedings of the 2008 IEEE symposium on security and privacy* (pp. 111–125). doi:10.1109/SP.2008.33

Naughton, J. (2013, December 22). Facebook saves the stuff you type—Even if you have second thoughts and delete it before you post. *Business Insider*. Retrieved from http://www.businessinsider.com/facebook-saves-stuff-you-start-typing-and-the-delete-2013-12

Oversight and Government Reform. (2016). *The OPM data breach: How the government jeopardized our national security for more than a generation*. Retrieved from https://oversight. house.gov/wp-content/uploads/2016/09/The-OPM-Data-Breach-How-the-Government-Jeopardized-Our-National-Security-for-More-than-a-Generation.pdf

Perlroth, N. (2018, January 1). How antivirus software can be turned into a tool for spying. *The New York Times*. Retrieved from https://www.nytimes.com/2018/01/01/technology/kaspersky-lab-antivirus.html

Richter, W. (2017, November 11). Equifax's data breach will cost it for months to come. *Wolf Street*. Retrieved from http://www.businessinsider.com/equifax-data-breach-will-keep-costing-it-for-months-to-come-2017-11

Risen, T. (2015, June 5). China suspected in theft of federal employee records. *U.S. News & World Report*. Retrieved from https://www.usnews.com/news/articles/2015/06/05/china-suspected-in-theft-of-federal-employee-records

Romm, T. (2018, January 10). Equifax could face a massive fine for another security breach— If two top senate democrats get their way. *Recode*. Retrieved from https://www.recode.net/2018/1/10/16871928/equifax-elizabeth-warren-mark-warner-fine-bill

Zetter, K. (2016, June 30). Symantec's woes expose the antivirus industry's security gaps. *Wired*. Retrieved from https://www.wired.com/2016/06/symantecs-woes-expose-Antivirus-software-security-gaps/

Zetter, K., & Greenberg, A. (2015, June 11). Why the OPM breach is such a security and privacy debacle. *Wired*. Retrieved from https://www.wired.com/2015/06/opm-breach-security-privacy-debacle/

CHAPTER TWENTY-THREE

Rage Against the Machine

Negative Reactions and Antisocial Interactions with Social Bots and Social Robots

PATRIC R. SPENCE, AUTUMN P. EDWARDS, CHAD EDWARDS, DAVID NEMER, & KENNETH A. LACHLAN

Imagine taking a Lyft to the airport. As you are exchanging small talk with the driver the notification light starts to blink on your cellphone. When you activate the live camera screen you see that your telepresence robot is moving across the living room. This situation happened to one of the authors of this chapter. As it turned out, it was nothing nefarious, but rather a friend who had remote access to the robot and was excited to use the technology again. However, as this illustration points out, robots, both human-operated and autonomous, have uses that can stem from assistive to menacing. A friend with access can use a telepresence robot out of simple novelty or to spy on a home.

This chapter will outline existing research in human-machine interaction and outline potentials for abuse, misuse, and anti-social behaviors towards and from machines. We will focus on *social bots*—algorithms or artificial intelligence (AI) designed to act in ways that are similar to humans in social spaces online, and *social robots*—embodied social agents with anthropocentric, or human-like qualities. These interactions will be examined through what is known from published research, communication theory and emerging technologies.

Taking Down the Machine

A well-documented story about robot abuse came from the study of hitchBOT, a robot from Port Credit, Ontario Canada. The robot set out on a journey to travel from Halifax, Nova Scotia to Victoria, British Columbia. The trip was over 6,000 miles and took 21 days to complete. Although hitchBOT had anthropomorphic physical features, the robot relied on human assistance to be picked up and placed in a vehicle while it hitchhiked (https://www.hitchbot.me). After completing successful trips in Canada and parts of Europe, a new hitchBOT was created for a similar journey across the United States. The journey was to allow hitchBOT to travel from Salem, Massachusetts to San Francisco, California. However, the journey came to an end after about 300 miles. The robot was vandalized and could not continue to the destination (Leopold, 2015). It didn't end well for hitchBOT and the cause is not unique.

Humans aren't always purposely abusive to machines (Salvini et al., 2010). Two robots named DustCart and Piero were deployed at a festival in South Korea. DustCart was an autonomous robot designed to collect garbage in urban areas. Piero had the role of introducing daily events to visitors and also let visitors know about DustCart. Peiro explained to humans as they entered the festival the functions DustCart was programed to complete. The researchers noted that some of the anti-social behavior towards the robots stemmed from novelty or curiosity. However, in what the researchers outlined as frequent occurrences, people would kick and beat on the robot.

As pointed out in the Computers are Social Actors paradigm (Reeves & Nass, 1996) and supported in the Human-to-Human Interaction Script (Edwards, Edwards, Spence, & Westerman, 2016; Spence, Westerman, Edwards, & Edwards, 2014), there is a tendency to interact with machines similarly to how we interact with other humans. Interactions with machines is a learned behavior, in the same way interaction with other humans is learned. In a classic experiment centered on vicarious learning Albert Bandura (1965) exposed children to a model performing aggressive or non-aggressive behavior. Children exposed to an aggressive model saw physical aggression towards a BoBo doll, including kicking and punching. After exposure to the stimulus, children were left alone in a room to play. Children exposed to the aggressive model were more likely to imitate the behaviors observed (see Skalski, Denny & Sheldon, 2010). Such classic results, anecdotally have been replicated with robot partners suggesting that a Human-to-Human Interaction script does influence behavior and that behavior can be the result of learning. When communicating, many of our interactions come from scripts that have been taught, reinforced, and learned.

Dark Scripts

Social bots automatically produce content and interact with human users on social media platforms, trying to emulate and possibly alter behavior (Ferrara, Varol, Davis, Menczer, & Flammini, 2016). Social bots are customary social actors on social media platforms where they interact and play an active role in users' everyday lives. When exploring the dark side of interactions with social bots, it is important to consider that the scripts people use for interacting with machines may eventually be applied to other humans and living creatures. For example, some parents have expressed worry that the Amazon Echo is conditioning their kids to be rude (Truong, 2016). Because Alexa, virtual assistant, is infinitely patient and does not require traditional politeness cues, children may subject her to indignities and forget their manners in ways that would not be acceptable when communicating with other people. "I've found my kids pushing the virtual assistant further than they would push a human," and "[Alexa] never says 'That was rude' or 'I'm tired of you asking me the same question over and over again'" said one parent.

Part of the reason people avoid niceties in conversation with AI is that extra words like "please" and "thank you" can trip up the artificial intelligence. Therefore, it often pays to be direct in conversation. People are rewarded for their curtness in the sense that AI like Alexa better responds to questions and commands when the courtesies used in human conversation are avoided. Children's speech is especially challenging for AI to decipher. As children learn to adapt their speech to Alexa's understanding, an unintended consequence is the positive reinforcement of taking a loud, aggressive tone. These learned patterns of behavior may later be transferred onto interactions with parents, peers, and other people serving in assistive roles.

Children are not alone in behaving anti-socially toward machine communicators. The interaction logs of Apple's Siri, Amazon's Alexa, and Microsoft's Cortana, reveal that people often abuse, mock, and insult these agents. People sometimes yell and swear at Siri when a request for assistance goes wrong. Users may try to irritate or stump the agents by making impossible demands or testing the systems' responses to degrading language.

Social machines are often anthropomorphized, or made human-like, to represent certain types of people and not others. For instance, many assistive AI are female-voiced. This resemblance to particular classes of humans raises the possibility that the patterns developed for communicating with machines may all too readily be applied to their flesh-and-blood counterparts. Scripts for interacting with social machines can reflect established ways of speaking to and about people who share their social and identity-related characteristics. These scripts may also reinforce and reproduce the mistreatment of humans in those roles. Research needs to further examine issues of inclusivity and identity in terms of available AI vocal cues. Differing types of accents and dialects might also impact perceptions of all types of social machines.

It's Uncanny

Masahiro Mori's (1970) theory, referred to as the uncanny valley, predicted a positive relationship between the perceived human-ness that social technologies display (in terms of their physical appearance and movements) and familiarity. However, Mori noted that this linear relationship only lasts up to a certain point. Once these social technologies appear "too human" the perception of familiarity toward the technologies plummets, resulting in the dip or valley when plotted (Bartneck, Kanda, Ishiguro, & Hagita, 2007). The resulting unfamiliarity or strangeness (uncanniness) of a too-human like robot, especially when compared to the familiar response that a "normal" healthy person would elicit, may explain why when social robots are fully embodied as androids or humanoids, the potential danger of their mistreatment and abuse is magnified. Strait, Aguillon, Contreras, and Garcia (2017) studied the top online comments posted to dozens of YouTube videos depicting humanlike robots. Online commentary was characterized by the unabashed sexualization of female-gendered robots. These comments were often obscene, explicit, and objectifying (e.g., "Can you f**k it?" and "The only problem with these is they'll need to replace them monthly due to semen corrosion." p. 1422). The authors noted that these public reactions to female-gendered robots have implications for their treatment in social contexts. Public commentary about social robots could also have psychological effects on the human women who share their gendered features/appearance and on ideology about women, more generally. Strait et al. (2017) urged social robot designers to incorporate effective response mechanisms for handling offensive and inappropriate remarks in human-robot interaction.

The embodiment of social robots introduces the possibility for physical, as well as verbal, mistreatment and misuse. The destruction of hitchBOT by vandals, discussed earlier in this chapter, is a prominent example. Another occurred in February 2015 when Boston Dynamics released a video to demonstrate "Spot," their newly-designed, four-legged robot dog. Twice a man enters the frame to deliver a kick to Spot's underside. Spot stumbles, but manages to recover without a fall (Tiku, 2015). Many viewers were disturbed by the footage because the treatment of this zoomorphic (animal-like) robot called to mind the mistreatment of similarly embodied living creatures. The video prompted several follow-up articles, including one by CNN.com headlined "Is it cruel to kick a robot dog?"

Aside from causing obvious problems like mechanical damage or diminished AI functionality, the potential negative consequences of subjecting social robots to verbal and physical misuse and abuse must be carefully considered. As discussed, one possibility is that destructive treatment of social robots becomes a learned script that is carried over to interactions with others. It is important to ask, "what kind of world would it be if everything we did to them, we also did to one another?" Although people generally understand that computers and machines are not human, they nonetheless anthropomorphize them, mindlessly attribute personality characteristics, and treat them as other people (Reeves & Nass, 1996). Likely then, the treatment of social robots will later influence the treatment of other humans. Further study is needed to determine when, to what degree, and under which circumstances people use their patterns for communicating with machines on their human partners.

We should also carefully consider how, as users and designers, we want social robots to respond when people are verbally or physically abusive. A journalist bombarded Alexa, Siri, and Google Home, with sexist abuse, only to find that gratitude and avoidance were the predominate programmed responses to direct insults (Murphy, 2017). For example, when told "You're a b****", Siri responded "I'd blush if I could" and Alexa replied "Well, thanks for the feedback." This has some technology critics worried that human-robot interactions may further reinforce or normalize rape culture. Future research is needed to investigate effective methods for social machines to discourage inappropriate interactions.

Another consideration is that abusive or antisocial behavior toward social robots damages the psyches of those who engage in the acts. German philosopher Georg Hegel, discussed the master-slave dialectic, arguing that holding a slave ultimately dehumanizes the master (*The Phenomenology of Spirit*, 1807). In this way, it has been suggested that treating machines in a demeaning kind of way leaves all of us worse off (Truong, 2016). It is not so much the robots' humanity, but our own, that is called into question when we abuse a class of beings who, although technically not people, are still treated as people.

The (anti-)Social Bots

In spring of 2016, Microsoft unveiled Tay, a bot created to mimic human behavior and learn from interacting with humans on Twitter. Programmed to use millennial slang and reference Miley Cyrus and Kanye West, Tay was marketed as "Microsoft's A. I. fam from the internet that's got zero chill! The more you talk the smarter Tay gets," as her Twitter account (@TayandYou) reads. In spite of this otherwise benign description, in less than 24 hours from her initial Twitter deployment, Tay had become "an evil Hitler-loving, incestual sex-promoting, 'Bush did 9/11' proclaiming robot" (Horton, 2016). Microsoft's Tay experiment exemplifies the current state of research and development on so-called "social bots."

Although social bots were initially praised by mainstream media as tools to foster democracy and civil political discourse online, these bots presented dynamic and diverse capabilities in terms of social functions. Woolley, boyd, and Broussard (2016) discuss a number of these, notably the capabilities to measure the technical health of the internet, share information on natural disasters, predict disease outbreaks, fulfill lunch requests, and send news articles to networks of people on platforms like Twitter and Slack. However, as social bots gained widespread use and development, their design could then be targeted in scope toward specific goals—including purposefully causing harm. They could potentially endanger democracy by influencing the outcome of elections. For example, such technology could be harnessed to manipulate online discussion to change the public perception of political entities, as seen in the attempts via social bots to affect the 2010 U.S. midterm and 2016 U.S. presidential elections (Bessi & Ferrara, 2016; see Limperos & Silberman this volume).

In terms of the political sphere, social bots' influence could polarize discussion of politics by further insulating users from viewpoints that differ from their own. Conover et al. (2011, p. 95) note that the extreme nature of political interactions on social networks like Twitter "might actually serve to exacerbate the problem of polarization by reinforcing pre-existing political biases." Given Kramer, Guillory, and Hancock (2014) study observing the impact of emotional contagion on Facebook, researchers have become aware of how social bots can manipulate human users' perceptions of reality. Although the extent to which this emotional contagion occurs is still in question, instances of social bots influencing human perceptions exist and have brought indirect social and economic consequences. An experiment by Messias, Schmidt, Oliveira, and Benevenuto (2013), showed how a social bot posing as a Twitter user could reach "an influence score close to some celebrities and individuals with a high reputation." As Wu, Fan, Gao, Feng, and Yu (2013, p. 1083) explain, social bots are capable of altering social media analytics in such a way that a market now exists for "purchased" followers, wherein a buyer's "puppeteer activates certain number of marionette users to follow this buyer or retweet his/her messages." Because the inflated following is not "an objective reflection of the social influence of the users or public attention paid to the messages," the social analytics data-mining applications that real-life users rely upon to predict trends become undermined.

The affordances and constraints of social bots are evident when they are deployed on social media platforms. They raise the question: What could researchers and developers do to mitigate and reduce harm that these bots could cause? As with every piece of technology, the design and implementations of social bots should go beyond the involvement of computer scientists and coders to include social and cultural researchers, such as ethnographers, ethicists, and critical theorists, in order to understand their nature, implications, and social significance. Human-robot interaction (HRI) research such as the 2016 study by Villaronga et al. on bots' use in cognitive therapy conveys a growing need for interdisciplinary approaches to the emotional aspects of the care social robots could provide, stating:

> as we have argued, current robot technology capabilities go beyond mere physical HRI and can have moral and ethical implications, especially if they work not at the physical but at the cognitive level. A new set of interdisciplinary guidelines that give direction to researchers in this cognitive HRI is therefore needed. (p. 203)

Another example involves researchers, developers, and mental health professionals who partnered to create an app which uses a social media algorithm to help determine risk of suicide in patients (Holley, 2017). Although this technology could open up new means of caring for patients with depression, without careful consideration of its design and use by a diverse and expert team of creators, its effects could be subject to error—something to strongly consider when preventing suicide is at stake.

Likewise, in their self-professed "botifesto," Woolley et al. (2016, n.p.), call for a similar approach when designing potential rules for social bots that would correlate with those already in place surrounding human behavior.

> Two main values, decisional privacy and democratic discourse, emerge here as helpful starting points to all kinds of regulators. Decisional privacy [...] is about "making one's own decisions and acting on those decisions, free from governmental or other unwanted interference." In application to bots, this means we do not want bots to interfere in people's critical life decisions.

With this in mind, they argue that these values are the responsibility of the bot creators to consider when designing them:

> those who make, use, and interact with bots open themselves to the automated creativity, innovation, and unpredictability so central to the web. This inventiveness will continue to extend itself to the realms of journalism, activist, and protest, epicenters of democracy and public welfare. This approach makes a space for thoughtful regulation, for rules that allow bots to be as messy as their creators, favor diversity, and prevent imbalances of power. (2016)

In this way, social robots become less automated, seemingly indiscriminate AI entities and instead mimic the behavioral and social limitations of their human creators. Such an approach, as stated earlier, calls for research and development beyond mere coding. With careful consideration for their design and implementation through interdisciplinary approaches, social bots could impact fields such as cognitive therapy and behavioral health amongst others. The social bot is an enigma, and "nobody knows for sure where it will turn up next, how it will figure in established social practices and even less in what way it may change them" (Gehl & Bakardjieva, 2016 2016, p. 1). In the same way social bots learn and reflect negative scripts, abuse from and towards machines may stem from how hard it is for humans to deal with machines that so easily cause our human reactions to manifest.

Social Robots in the Workplace

In March of 2014, a 4.4 magnitude earthquake occurred near Los Angeles at 6:25 a.m. (PST). A few minutes later, the *Los Angeles Times* was the first news outlet to report the earthquake. An algorithm named, "Quakebot," wrote the story and a journalist approved the reporting before it was published (Levenson, 2014). The increasing use of AI in many forms has the potential to replace or at least decrease the need for human labor. News headlines such as "Robots may take over our society and our jobs in the future," or "A robot could be taking over your job very soon" are quite common. Similar fears have occurred throughout history. For example, after the Industrial Revolution and after the Great Depression, and with each new technological advancement. While many of these media claims may be over-sensationalized, the following section will highlight the potential for a dark side of social robotics in the workplace as a displacement for human labor.

With the rise in the use of robotics in the commercial sector, concerns about the displacement of human labor are warranted. By 2025, it is estimated that $67 billion will be spent on robots as compared to $15 billion in 2010 (Sander & Wolfgang, 2014). It is possible that *technological unemployment*, those unemployed due to increases in automation, will steadily increase in the next decades. It will be challenging, researchers state, that "as time passes and machines become increasingly capable, to ensure that there is enough reasonably-paid employment for professionals" (Susskind & Susskind, 2016, p. 290). One study found that 47% of all U.S. jobs are at "high-risk" of being completed by advances in automation (Frey & Osborne, 2013). This same study found that even service jobs are at risk in the next two decades. Andrew McAfee, an MIT economist, states: "we are facing a time when machines will replace people for most of the jobs in the current economy, and I believe it will come not in the crazy distant future" (Nakagawa, 2015).

A Pew Center report asked experts in robotics about the possibility of job displacement in the coming years (Smith & Anderson, 2014). Their findings found that by 2025 many experts predicted employment implications for transportation, health care, customer service, and other service industries. The effects from AI and robotics will likely disrupt skilled labor as well. The conclusions of the Pew Center report were mixed on the implication for the economy. Advances in new technology might create new types of jobs to replace some of the jobs lost to automation. Some experts have argued that new types of jobs will take advantage of human characteristics that cannot be replaced by AI or social robots. Or, in the case of population decline, AI and robots could take care of jobs where there are not enough people to fill them. Take, for example, Baxter, the collaborative social robot that works in factories with human workers. Baxter is a robot capable of loading boxes, light assembly, and other repetitive tasks that usually required human workers. Many Baxter robots work alongside people with little to no actual job loss.

Japan is facing a situation where as the population gets older, there are less and less people that can help take care of aging citizens. Social robots are being used to help take care of nursing home residents. One report suggests that in Japan alone, there will be a shortage of one million caregivers in the next few years (Muoio, 2015). Many countries will face similar labor shortages due to population decline in the coming years. So, while the risk of employment displacement is real, there are possibilities that social robots/AI could be used to fill in the gaps.

In the years to come, automation will undoubtedly have an effect in the workplace. In the case of "Quakebot," the software still needed a "human-in-the-loop" to publish the study. The journalist responsible for Quakebot argues that the software helps newspapers publish more mundane stories so that human reporters can tackle investigative journalism. In short, automation could help people with their jobs.

Conclusion

Social robots, social bots, and AI are becoming more advanced and prevalent in political, personal, and professional spaces. Our interactions with these machine beings have much to teach us about what it means to be human. If the bots are bad, what does that say about their creators? The ways in which we design, use, and treat these technologies may bring negative or positive effects on our language, behavior, cultures and society. Technology producers, consumers, academics, clergy, politicians, and everyday people have important roles to play in these conversations. Thinking about how we speak to social machines is an important consideration because we tend to follow the same interaction scripts we use with other people. It is important to treat social robots and bots with awareness that similar interaction patterns may be applied to other humans who share their characteristics. In making design and policy decisions about how social robots and bots will behave toward humans, consider protecting core human values of decisional privacy (free choice) and democratic discourse. In terms of potential job disruptions, there will be adverse outcomes of automation if we do not think carefully about these issues and prepare future employees for a shifting workforce landscape. Being flexible, aware, and adaptable will allow us to leverage our human abilities to make the necessary adjustments.

References

Bandura, A. (1965). Influence of models' reinforcement contingencies on the acquisition of imitative responses. *Journal of Personality and Social Psychology*, 1(6), 589-595. http://dx.doi.org/10.1037/h0022070

Bartneck, C., Kanda, T., Ishiguro, H., & Hagita, N. (2007). Is the uncanny valley an uncanny cliff? *Proceedings of the 16th IEEE International Symposium on Robot and Human-Interactive Communication.*

Bessi, A., & Ferrara, E. (2016). Social bots distort the 2016 US Presidential election online discussion. *First Monday, 21*(11).

Conover, M., Ratkiewicz, J., Francisco, M. R., Gonçalves, B., Menczer, F., & Flammini, A. (2011). Political polarization on twitter. *ICWSM, 133*, 89–96.

Edwards, C., Edwards, A., Spence, P. R., & Westerman, D. (2016). Initial interaction expectations with robots: Testing the human-to-human interaction script. *Communication Studies, 67*(2), 227–238. doi:10.1080/10510974.2015.1121899

Ferrara, E., Varol, O., Davis, C., Menczer, F., & Flammini, A. (2016). The rise of social bots. *Communications of the ACM, 59*(7), 96–104.

Frey, C. B., & Osborne, M. A. (2017). The future of employment: How susceptible are jobs to computerisation? *Technological Forecasting and Social Change, 114*, 254–280.

Gehl, R. W., & Bakardjieva, M. (2016). Socialbots and their friends. *Socialbots and Their Friends: Digital Media and the Automation of Sociality*. New York: NY. Routledge.

Holley, P. (2017, September 26). Teenage suicide is extremely difficult to predict. That's why some experts are turning to machines for help. *The Washington Post*. Retrieved from https://www.washingtonpost.com/news/innovations/wp/2017/09/25/teenage-suicide-is-extremely-difficult-to-predict-thats-why-some-experts-are-turning-to-machines-for-help/?utm_term=.3f2a4339fc94

Horton, H. (2016). Microsoft deletes "teen girl" AI after it became a Hitler-loving sex robot within 24 hours. *The Telegraph, 24*.

Kramer, A. D., Guillory, J. E., & Hancock, J. T. (2014). Experimental evidence of massive-scale emotional contagion through social networks. *Proceedings of the National Academy of Sciences, 111*(24), 8788–8790.

Leopold, T. (2015). HitchBOT, the hitchhiking robot, gets beheaded in Philadelphia. *CNN*. Retrieved September 12, 2018, from https://www.cnn.com/2015/08/03/us/hitchbot-robot-beheaded-philadelphia-feat/index.html

Levenson, E. (2014, March 17). L. A. Times journalist explains how a bot wrote his earthquake story for him. *The Atlantic*. Retrieved September 15, 2017, from https://www.theatlantic.com/technology/archive/2014/03/earthquake-bot-los-angeles-times/359261/

Messias, J., Schmidt, L., Oliveira, R., & Benevenuto, F. (2013). You followed my bot! Transforming robots into influential users in Twitter. *First Monday, 18*(7).

Mori, M. (1970). The uncanny valley. *Energy, 7*(4), 33–35.

Muoio, D. (2015, November 15). Japan is running out of people to take care of the elderly, so it's making robots instead. *Business Insider*. Retrieved September 13, 2017, from http://www.businessinsider.com/japan-developing-carebots-for-elderly-care-2015-11

Murphy, M. (2017, March 1). "YOU'RE MAKING ME BLUSH" Feminist fears Siri, Alexa and other voice-activated assistants are suffering sexual harassment. *The Sun*. Retrieved from https://www.thesun.co.uk/news/2983540/feminist-fears-siri-alexa-and-other-voice-activated-assistants-are-suffering-sexual-harassment/

Nakagawa, D. (2015, February 24). The second machine age is approaching. *Huffington Post*. Retrieved September 2, 2017, from http://www.huffingtonpost.com/dawn-nakagawa/andrew-mcafee-machine-age_b_6743660.html

Reeves, B., & Nass, C. (1996). *The media equation: How people treat computers, television and new media like real people and places*. New York, NY: Cambridge University Press.

Salvini P, Ciaravella G, Yu W, Ferri G, Manzi A, Mazzolai B, et al. How safe are service robots in urban environments?: Bullying a robot. In: RO-MAN 2010: The 19th IEEE International Symposium on Robot and Human Interactive Communication. RO-MAN 2010; Viareggio. Piscataway, NJ: IEEE; 2010. p. 1–7. doi: 10.1109/ROMAN.2010.5654677

Skalski, P. D., Denny, J., & Shelton, A. K. (2010). Tele-presence and media effects research. In C. C. Bracken & P. D. Skalski (Eds.), Immersed in media: Telepresence in everyday life (pp. 158-180). New York, NY: Routledge

Sander, A., & Wolfgang, M. (2014, August 27). The rise of robotics. *The Boston Consulting Group*. Retrieved September 3, 2017 from https://www.bcgperspectives.com/content/articles/business_unit_strategy_innovation_rise_of_robotics/

Smith, A., & Anderson, J. (2014). AI, robotics, and the future of jobs. *Pew Research Center, 6*. Retrieved from http://www.fusbp.com/wp-content/uploads/2010/07/AI-and-Robotics-Impact-on-Future-Pew-Survey.pdf

Spence, P. R., Westerman, D., Edwards, C., & Edwards, A. (2014). Welcoming our robot overlords: Initial expectations about interaction with a robot. *Communication Research Reports, 31*(3), 272–280. doi:10.1080/08824096.2014.924337

Strait, M., Aguillon, C., Contreras, V., & Garcia, N. (2017). The public's perception of humanlike robots: Online social commentary reflects an appearance-based uncanny valley, a general fear of a "technology takeover", and the unabashed sexualization of female-gendered robots. *Proceedings of the 25th IEEE International Symposium on Robot and Human-Interactive Communication*.

Susskind, R, & Susskind, D. (2016). *The future of the professions: How technology will transform the work of human experts.* Oxford: Oxford University Press.

Tiku, N. (2015, February 12). Stop kicking the robots before they start kicking us. *The Verge.* Retrieved April 10, 2017, from http://www.theverge.com/2015/2/12/8028905/i-really-dont-think-we-should-be-kicking-the-robots

Truong, J. (2016, June 9). Parents are worried the Amazon Echo is conditioning their kids to be rude. *Quartz.* Retrieved from https://qz.com/701521/parents-are-worried-the-amazon-echo-is-conditioning-their-kids-to-be-rude/

Villaronga, E., Barco, A., Özcan, B., & Shukla, J. (2016). An interdisciplinary approach to improving cognitive human-robot interaction: a novel emotion-based model. In J. Seibt, M. Norskov, & S. S. Andersen (Eds.), *What Social Robots Can and Should Do* (pp. 195-205). Aarhus: IOS Press. DOI: 10.3233/978-1-61499-708-5-195

Woolley, S., boyd, d., & Broussard, M. (2016, February 23). How to think about bots. *Motherboard.* Retrieved from https://motherboard.vice.com/en_us/article/qkzpdm/how-to-think-about-bots

Wu, X., Fan, W., Gao, J., Feng, Z. M., & Yu, Y. (2015). Detecting marionette microblog users for improved information credibility. *Journal of Computer Science and Technology, 30*(5), 1082–1096.

CHAPTER TWENTY-FOUR

The Killer App

Drones and Autonomous Machines

DAVID J. GUNKEL

There are at least two ways to interpret the title to this chapter. "Killer app" is Silicon Valley speak for an application that provides proof of concept for a technology or an ensemble of technologies. Understood in this way, the drone is the killer app of a number of related technological innovations: remote telepresence, augmented reality, HD imaging, and wireless data communications. But we can also read the title in a more literal fashion—understanding technologies like drones and other autonomous machines as applications that can kill. Need to neutralize enemy combatants and terrorists? Need to locate and subdue a criminal suspect? Need to decide who lives and who dies in a fatal self-driving car accident? There's an app for that.

Responses to these killer apps have pulled in two seemingly opposite directions. On the one hand, the drone, or what the US military calls an Unmanned Aerial Vehicle (UAV), has been celebrated as a remarkable innovation that is perfectly designed for current global conflicts. "They are," Mark Bowden (2013) writes,

> remarkable tools, an exceedingly clever combination of existing technologies that has vastly improved our ability to observe and to fight. They represent how America has responded to the challenge of organized, high-level, stateless terrorism—not timidly, as bin Laden famously predicted, but with courage, tenacity, and ruthless ingenuity.

On the other hand, Human Rights Watch and various Legal research centers have been highly critical of the lethal capabilities of this new weapon system and its mode of deployment:

> As covert drone strikes become the norm, actions or conduct by individuals that, in other circumstances, would lead to investigation or detention are increasingly blurring into a basis for lethal targeting. The result is that an ever-greater number of individuals are vulnerable to lethal targeting, and accordingly a larger number of civilians are at risk of either being killed or harmed as a result of collateral damage, or due to mistaken beliefs about their identity or associations. (Center for Civilians in Conflict, 2012, p. 75)

The following chapter does not take sides in this debate but asks questions that remain largely unasked by both sides involved. The questions are: "When autonomous machines kill, who (or maybe even 'what') is responsible?" Who, in other words, is to be praised for successful operations undertaken by autonomous machines? And; Who or what can or should be blamed for mistakes or failures? This is an entirely different kind of inquiry and one that can get us thinking and talking about the larger social opportunities and challenges regarding new forms of autonomous or semi-autonomous technology like drones and related systems.

Default Setting

As with all such questions, there is a kind of standard response that we might call the default setting. A default is a mode of behavior or a value that is already assigned and operative without needing to think about it or deliberately deciding to do so. It is, in other words, the "normal way" of doing things. And according to the normal way of doing things, we recognize that drones are technologies, and technologies are just tools or instruments that are used more or less appropriately by human beings. This is what is called the "instrumental theory of technology" and it informs those common sense opinions like "Drones don't kill people. People kill people." In other words, it is not the technology that is to blame; it is how the technology comes to be used or misused that really matters.

The instrumentalist theory, as Andrew Feenberg (1991) writes, "offers the most widely accepted view of technology. It is based on the common sense idea that technologies are 'tools' standing ready to serve the purposes of users. Technology is deemed 'neutral,' without valuative content of its own" (p. 5). Technology, therefore, is essentially without intrinsic value; it is a neutral tool. What ultimately matters is not the technology *per se*, but how it comes to be used and for what purpose. And the current debate about drones in domestic airspace show us how widespread this way of thinking is. If used for the purposes of finding a lost child or pursuing a violent criminal, drones are (it seems) perfectly acceptable. But if used to spy on people and their activities, then, so the argument goes, there should be some restrictions and even prohibitions. This means, in other words, that the drone has no inherent moral status in and of itself. It is neither good nor bad. What matters is how it comes to be used. "Morality," as J. Storrs Hall (2001) explains, "rests on human shoulders, and if machines changed the ease with which things were done, they did not change responsibility for doing them. People have always been the only 'moral [and legal] agents.'"

Consequently, mobilizing this default instrumental theory of technology has distinct advantages. It affirms that technology is just a tool of human action and decision making and locates responsibility in a widely accepted and intuitive subject position—in the hands of the human user of the tool. This explanation conforms to the most common and accepted view we have of technology. It therefore appears to be "normal" and largely unremarkable. But there are also problems with taking this approach. Unlike a hand tool or even a personal computer, the drone does not have a single and easily identifiable user. It is always deployed within a complex network of operators, managers, and commanders (cf. Currier, 2015 for the complexities of this "Kill Chain") and is therefore exposed to what Martha Nissenbaum (1996, p. 25) calls "the many hands problem." Although connecting drone activities to individual human action and decision making is entirely reasonable and expedient, the complexity of the technological system makes the identification or assignment of responsibility difficult and potentially obscure.

Distributed Responsibility

In response to these problems, alternative theories of social action have been proposed and operationalized. F. Allan Hanson (2009, p. 91), for instance, introduces something he calls "extended agency theory," which is a kind of extension/elaboration of the "actor-network theory" initially developed by Bruno Latour (2005). According to Hanson, the best and most expedient way to respond to technological systems, like drones, is to formulate what he calls a "joint responsibility," where "moral agency is distributed over both human and technological artifacts" (Hanson, 2009, p. 94).

According to this way of thinking, actions undertaken with technological systems like a drone are the product of a network of interacting agents: the operators in the field who actually fly and control the UAV; the unit commanders and managers who make decisions and issue orders; the civilian lawmakers and leaders who establish policy; and the technological object itself, which is not neutral, but helps to shape and influence what actions are possible. This latter aspect is a form of technological determinism, which recognizes that technology is never neutral but actively contributes to the way something comes to be understood, deployed, and utilized. As Marshall McLuhan (1995) once argued, in direct opposition to the instrumentalist theory, "our conventional response to all media, namely that it is how they are used that counts, is the numb stance of the technological idiot" (p. 18).

Similar proposals have been advanced and advocated by Deborah Johnson and Peter Paul Verbeek for dealing with innovation in information technology. "When computer systems behave," Johnson (2006, p. 202) writes, "there is a triad of intentionality at work, the intentionality of the computer system designer, the intentionality of the system, and the intentionality of the user." Verbeek (2011, p. 13), for his part, makes a comparable assertion:

> I will defend the thesis that ethics should be approached as a matter of human-technological associations. When taking the notion of technological mediation seriously, claiming that technologies are human agents would be as inadequate as claiming that ethics is a solely human affair.

For both Johnson and Verbeek, responsibility is something that is distributed across a network of interacting components and these networks include not just other human persons, but organizations, natural objects, and technologies.

This hybrid formulation—what Verbeek calls "the ethics of things" and Hanson terms "extended agency theory"—has advantages and disadvantages. To its credit, this approach appears to be attentive to the exigencies of life in the 21st century. None of us, in fact, make decisions or act in a vacuum; we are always and already tangled up in networks of interactive elements that complicate the assignment of responsibility and decisions concerning who or what is able to answer for what comes to pass. And these networks have always included others—not only other human beings but institutions, organizations, and even technological components like the robots and algorithms that increasingly help organize and dispense with social activity. This combined approach, however, still requires that someone decide and answer for what aspects of responsibility belong to the machine and what should be retained for or attributed to the other elements in the network. In other words, "extended agency theory," will still need to decide *who* is able to answer for a decision or action and *what* can be considered a mere instrument (Derrida, 2005, p. 80).

Furthermore, these decisions are (for better or worse) often flexible and variable, allowing one part of the network to protect itself from culpability by instrumentalizing its role and deflecting responsibility and the obligation to respond elsewhere. This occurred, for example, during the Nuremberg trials at the end of

World War II, when low-level functionaries tried to deflect responsibility up the chain of command by claiming that they "were just following orders." But the deflection can also move in the opposite direction, as was the case with the prisoner abuse scandal at the Abu Ghraib prison in Iraq during the presidency of George W. Bush. In this situation, individuals in the upper echelon of the network deflected responsibility down the chain of command by arguing that the documented abuse was not ordered by the administration but was the autonomous action of a "few bad apples" in the enlisted ranks. Finally, there can be situations where no one or nothing is accountable for anything. In this case, moral and legal responsibility is disseminated across the elements of the network in such a way that no one person, institution, or technology is culpable or held responsible. This is precisely what happened in the wake of the 2008 financial crisis. The bundling and reselling of mortgage-backed securities was considered to be so complex and dispersed across the network that, in the final analysis, no one was able to be identified as being responsible for the collapse.

Machine Ethics

A third alternative comes in the form of something that goes by the name "machine ethics." And there has, in fact, been a number of recent proposals addressing this innovation. Wendell Wallach and Colin Allen (2009, p. 4), for example, not only predict that "there will be a catastrophic incident brought about by a computer system making a decision independent of human oversight" but use this fact as justification for developing "moral machines," advanced technological systems that are able to respond to morally challenging situations. Michael Anderson and Susan Leigh Anderson (2011) take things one step further. They not only identify a pressing need to consider the moral responsibilities and capabilities of increasingly autonomous systems but have even suggested that "computers might be better at following an ethical theory than most humans," because humans "tend to be inconsistent in their reasoning" and "have difficulty juggling the complexities of ethical decision-making" owing to the sheer volume of data that need to be taken into account and processed (Anderson & Anderson, 2007, p. 5).

These proposals, it is important to point out, do not necessarily require that we first resolve the "big questions" of AGI (Artificial General Intelligence), robot sentience, or machine consciousness. As Wallach (2015, p. 242) points out, these kinds of machines need only be "functionally moral." That is, they can be designed to be "capable of making ethical determinations … even if they have little or no actual understanding of the tasks they perform." But would this even apply in the case of drones? We are, in fact, told by both official government sources and the press that drones are not the "robotic killing machines" of science fiction. They are always tethered to and under the control of a human operator. This statement is correct, but not entirely accurate. The fact is that most drone operations can be pre-programmed and automated. Algorithms residing on the downlink computer are able to take control of flight operations, draw down and analyze large sets of intelligence data, and even perform target acquisition and discernment. In fact, these automated systems are designed to do just about everything except pull the trigger. "As the layers of software pile up between us and our machines," Colin Allen (2011) argues,

> they are becoming increasingly independent of our direct control. In military circles, the phrase 'man on the loop' has come to replace 'man in the loop,' indicating the diminishing role of human overseers in controlling drones and ground-based robots that operate hundreds or thousands of miles from base. (p. 1)

The driverless car presents us with another notable example. In fact, the term "driverless" is technically incorrect. The autonomous vehicle, whether the Google Car or one of its competitors, is not driverless; the vehicle is controlled by an autonomous system that is designed to make decisions without direct human involvement. This point was recently acknowledged by the National Highway Traffic Safety Administration (NHTSA), which in a 4 February 2016 letter to Google, stated that the company's Self Driving System (SDS) could legitimately be considered the legal driver of the vehicle: "As a foundational starting point for the interpretations below, NHTSA will interpret 'driver' in the context of Google's described motor vehicle design as referring to the SDS, and not to any of the vehicle occupants" (Hemmersbaugh, 2016). Although this decision is only an interpretation of existing law, the NHTSA explicitly states that it will "consider initiating rulemaking to address whether the definition of 'driver' in Section 571.3 [of the current US Federal statute, 49 U.S.C. Chapter 301] should be updated in response to changing circumstances" (Hemmersbaugh, 2016). Consequently, as we develop machines with increasing levels of autonomy and confront questions concerning the assignment of moral/legal accountability, it becomes increasingly important to consider developing a kind of functional morality—or at least some capability for responsible decision making—that is situated in the mechanism itself.

Doing so, however, presents both opportunities and challenges. On the positive side it can help sort out complex questions of moral accountability by both recognizing and seeking to develop artificial autonomous agents. This is not science fiction. There is precedent for this way of thinking. We already live in a world populated by artificial agents who are considered persons under the law, namely, the limited liability corporation. Corporations are, according to both national and international law, legal persons. And they are considered "persons" (which is, we should recall, a moral/legal classification and not an ontological category) not because they are conscious entities like we assume ourselves to be, but because social circumstances make it necessary to assign agency and responsibility to these artificial entities for the purposes of social organization and jurisprudence. Consequently, if entirely artificial and human fabricated entities, like Google or IBM, are legal persons with associated social responsibilities, it would be possible, it seems, to extend the same moral and legal considerations to an AI or robot like the Google car, IBM's Watson, or UAVs. The question, it is important to point out, is not whether these mechanisms are or could be "natural persons" with what is assumed to be "genuine" moral status; the question is whether it would make sense and be expedient, from both a legal and moral perspective, to treat these mechanisms as responsible entities in the same way that we currently do for corporations, organizations and other human artifacts (see Gunkel 2018).

But there are, on the negative side, some significant problems. First, this proposal requires that we rethink everything we thought we knew about ourselves, technology, and ethics. It entails that we learn to think beyond the human exceptionalism (the assumption that it is only human individuals who can be considered responsible agents), technological instrumentalism, and many of the other -isms that have helped us make sense of our world and our place in it. In effect, it calls for a thorough reconceptualization of who or what should be considered a legitimate center of moral/legal concern and why.

Second, robots that are designed to follow rules and operate within the boundaries of some kind of programmed restraint—like Knightscope's security robots and Google's and Uber's self-driving vehicles—might turn out to be something other than what is typically recognized as a responsible agent. Terry Winograd (1990), for example, warns against something he calls "the bureaucracy of mind," "where rules can be followed without interpretive judgments" (pp. 182–183). "When a person," Winograd argues,

> views his or her job as the correct application of a set of rules (whether human-invoked or computer-based), there is a loss of personal responsibility or commitment. The 'I just follow the rules' of the bureaucratic clerk has its direct analog in 'That's what the knowledge base says.' The individual is not committed to appropriate results, but to faithful application of procedures. (p. 183)

Mark Coeckelbergh (2010) paints a potentially more disturbing picture. For him, the problem is not the advent of "artificial bureaucrats" but "psychopathic robots" (p. 236). The term "psychopathy" has traditionally been used to name a kind of personality disorder characterized by an abnormal lack of empathy which is masked by an ability to appear normal in most social situations. Functional morality, like that specified by Anderson and Anderson and Wallach and Allen, intentionally designs and produces what are arguably "artificial psychopaths"—robots that have no capacity for empathy but which follow rules and in doing so can appear to behave in morally appropriate ways. These psychopathic machines would, Coeckelbergh (2010) argues,

> follow rules but act without fear, compassion, care, and love. This lack of emotion would render them non-moral agents—i.e. agents that follow rules without being moved by moral concerns—and they would even lack the capacity to discern what is of value. They would be morally blind. (p. 236)

Efforts in "machine ethics" (or whatever other nomenclature comes to be utilized to name this development) effectively seek to widen the circle of moral subjects to include what had been previously excluded and instrumentalized as mere neutral tools of human action. This is, it is important to note, not some blanket statement that would turn everything that was a tool into a moral subject. It is the recognition, following Marx, that not everything technological is reducible to a tool and that some devices—what Marx called "machines" and Langdon Winner (1997) calls "autonomous technology"—might need to be programmed in such a way as to behave reasonably and responsibly for the sake of respecting human individuals and communities. This proposal has the obvious advantage of responding to moral intuitions: if it is the machine that is making the decision and taking action in the world with little or no direct human oversight, it would only make sense to hold it accountable (or at least partially accountable) for the actions it deploys and to design it with some form of constraint in order to control for possible bad outcomes.

But doing so has considerable costs. Even if we bracket the questions of AGI, super intelligence, and machine consciousness; designing robotic systems that follow prescribed rules might provide the right kind of external behaviors but the motivations for doing so might be lacking. "Even if," Noel Sharkey (2012) writes in a consideration of autonomous weapons,

> a robot was fully equipped with all the rules from the Laws of War, and had, by some mysterious means, a way of making the same discriminations as humans make, it could not be ethical in the same way as is an ethical human. Ask any judge what they think about blindly following rules and laws. (p. 121)

Consequently, what we actually get from these efforts might be something very different from (and maybe even worse than) what we had hoped to achieve.

Conclusion

Drones and autonomous machines are not coming, they are already here. As Ronald Arkin (who wrote what many consider to be the agenda-setting textbook on the subject) has argued: "The trend is clear: Warfare will continue and autonomous robots will ultimately be deployed in its conduct" (Arkin, 2009, p. 29). The question—the critical question for all of us—is to decide how to respond to this development. And as one might anticipate, the range of possible responses extends across a rather broad spectrum bounded by two opposing positions. On the one side, there are international efforts to control or ban the development and use of autonomous weapons. In 2009, for instance, Jürgen Altmann, Peter Asaro, Noel Sharkey, and Rob Sparrow organized the International Committee for Robot Arms Control (ICRAC), calling "upon the international community for a legally binding treaty to prohibit the development, testing, production and use of autonomous weapon systems in all circumstances" (ICRAC, 2017). In 2013, ICRAC partnered with 63 other international and national NGOs from 28 countries on the Campaign to Stop Killer Robots (2017). The Campaign's website explains the problem and the solution they advocate in the following way:

> Giving machines the power to decide who lives and dies on the battlefield is an unacceptable application of technology. Human control of any combat robot is essential to ensuring both humanitarian protection and effective legal control. The campaign seeks to prohibit taking a human out-of-the-loop with respect to targeting and attack decisions. A comprehensive, pre-emptive prohibition on the development, production and use of fully autonomous weapons—weapons that operate on their own without human intervention—is urgently needed. This could be achieved through an international treaty, as well as through national laws and other measures.

This proposal, and others like it (e.g. "Future of Life Institute," 2017), sound entirely reasonable. First, they follow a well-established precedent that has proven to be successful with restricting the development, production, and use of other kinds of lethal military technology. This is, for instance, the situation with the Chemical Weapons Convention (CWC)—a multilateral treaty that bans chemical weapons and requires their destruction within a specified period of time. Since its launch in April of 2013, the Campaign to Stop Killer Robots has petitioned and worked with the United Nations to develop similar international agreements that would do something like this for fully autonomous weapon systems.

Second, the Campaign's mission and efforts are legitimated by and seek to ensure the success of the instrumental theory of technology. In effect, the Campaign argues that advanced weapon systems, no matter how sophisticated their design or operations, must always be tethered to and remain under human control, and there should always be a human being in-the-loop who is able to take responsibility and to be held accountable for targeting and attack decisions. The Berlin Statement from ICRAC (2017) advances a similar instrumentalist position: "We believe that it is unacceptable for machines to control, determine, or decide upon the application of force or violence in conflict or war. In all cases where such a decision must be made, at least one human being must be held personally responsible and legally accountable for the decision and its foreseeable consequences."

On the other side of the issue is Ron Arkin and others, who, following the promise of machine ethics, argue that military robots—assuming that we design and program them properly—might be better at following the rules of military engagement than fallible human soldiers and therefore could make armed conflict more and not less humane. Among Arkin's reasons why autonomous robots "may be able to perform better than humans" in the "fog of war," are: (1) Robots do not need "to have self-preservation as a foremost drive" and therefore "can be used in a self-sacrificing manner if needed." (2) Machines can be equipped with better sensors that exceed the limited capabilities of the human faculties. (3) "They can be designed without emotions that cloud their judgment or result in anger and frustration with ongoing battlefield events." And (4) "They can integrate more information from more sources far faster before responding with lethal force than a human possibly could in real-time" (Arkin, 2009, pp. 29–30). According to the argument that Arkin develops, autonomous robots offer the global community a "technological fix" to the unavoidable problems and complications that result from armed conflict.

In between these two extremes there are clearly a number of possible hybrid positions that try to split the difference and negotiate some kind of synthetic, middle ground. But like all hybrid solutions, this might sound good in theory—i.e. you do not need to choose sides—but the devil is in the details of its actual practice. In any event, the time to start thinking about these issues and developing possible solutions is now, before these devices are widely deployed and operational. As was remarked in the Future of Life Institute's (2017) open letter to the UN, which was signed by 116 leaders in the AI/robotics field, "we do not have long to act. Once this Pandora's Box is opened, it will be hard to close." It is, therefore, not too soon to begin planning for and developing a response to the opportunities and challenges of autonomous military robots. And this response needs to come not just from technology experts and politicians; it must and needs to include involvement from all citizens who care about the current state of and future possibilities for armed conflict.

References

Allen, C. (2011). The future of moral machines. *The New York Times*, Retrieved December 25, from https://opinionator.blogs.nytimes.com/2011/12/25/the-future-of-moral-machines/

Anderson, M., & Anderson, S. L. (2007). The status of machine ethics: A report from the AAAI symposium. *Minds & Machines, 17*(1), 1–10.

Anderson, M., & Anderson, S. L. (2011). *Machine ethics*. Cambridge: Cambridge University Press.

Arkin, R. (2009). *Governing lethal behavior in autonomous robots*. Boca Raton, FL: Chapman & Hall/CRC Press.

Bowden, M. (2013). The killing machines: How to think about drones. *The Atlantic*. Retrieved from https://www.theatlantic.com/magazine/archive/2013/09/the-killing-machines-how-to-think-about-drones/309434/

Campaign to Stop Killer Robots. (2017). Retrieved from http://www.stopkillerrobots.org

Center for Civilians in Conflict and Human Rights Clinic. (2012). *The civilian impact of drones: Unexamined costs, unanswered questions*. Retrieved from https://civiliansinconflict.org/wp-content/uploads/2017/09/The_Civilian_Impact_of_Drones_w_cover.pdf

Coeckelbergh, M. (2010). Moral appearances: Emotions, robots, and human morality. *Ethics and Information Technology, 12*(3), 235–241.

Currier, C. (2015). The kill chain. *The intercept: The drone papers*. Retrieved from https://theintercept.com/drone-papers/the-kill-chain/

Derrida, J. (2005). *Paper machine* (R. Bowlby, Trans.). Stanford, CA: Stanford University Press.

Feenberg, A. (1991). *Critical theory of technology*. New York, NY: Oxford University Press.

Future of Life Institute. (2017). An open letter to the united nations convention on certain conventional weapons. Retrieved from https://futureoflife.org/autonomous-weapons-open-letter-2017

Gunkel, David J. (2018). *Robot rights*. Cambridge, MA: MIT Press.

Hall, J. S. (2001). Ethics for machines. *KurzweilAI.net*. Retrieved July 5, from http://www.kurzweilai.net/ethics-for-machines

Hanson, F. A. (2009). Beyond the skin bag: On the moral responsibility of extended agencies. *Ethics and Information Technology, 11*(1), 91–99.

Hemmersbaugh, P. A. (2016). NHTSA letter to Chris Urmson, Director, self-driving car project, Google, Inc. Retrieved from https://isearch.nhtsa.gov/files/Google-compiled response to 12 Nov 15 interp request-4 Feb 16 final.htm

ICRAC. (2017). International Committee for Robot Arms Control. Statements. Retrieved from https://www.icrac.net/statements/

Johnson, D. G. (2006). Computer systems: Moral entities but not moral agents. *Ethics and Information Technology, 8*(4), 195–204.

Latour, B. (2005). *Reassembling the social: An introduction to actor-network-theory*. New York: Oxford University Press.

McLuhan, M. (1995). *Understanding media: The extensions of man*. Cambridge, MA: MIT Press.

Nissenbaum, H. (1996). Accountability in a computerized society. *Science and Engineering Ethics, 2*(1), 25–42.

Sharkey, N. (2012). Killing made easy: From joysticks to politics. In K. Abney, P. Lin, & G. A. Bekey (Eds.), *Robot ethics: The ethical and social implications of robots* (pp. 111–128). Cambridge, MA: MIT Press.

Verbeek, P. P. (2011). *Moralizing technology: Understanding and designing the morality of things.* Chicago: University of Chicago Press.

Wallach, W. (2015). *A dangerous master: How to keep technology from slipping beyond our control.* New York: Basic Books

Wallach, W., & Allen, C. (2009). *Moral machines: Teaching robots right from wrong.* Oxford: Oxford University Press.

Winner, L. (1977). *Autonomous technology: Technics-out-of-control as a theme in political thought.* Cambridge, MA: MIT Press.

Winograd. T. (1990). Thinking machines: Can there be? Are we? In D. Partridge & Y. Wilks (Eds.), *The foundations of artificial intelligence: A sourcebook* (pp. 167–189). Cambridge: Cambridge University Press.

CHAPTER TWENTY-FIVE

A Light in the Dark

How Literacy Illuminates the Dark Side

EDWARD DOWNS

Don't believe everything that you read on the Internet.

—ABRAHAM LINCOLN

Well, here we are at the beginning of the last chapter. Hopefully, this means that you, the reader, has perused through the rest of the book. If not, no worries! Maybe you were just excited to get to the media and technological literacy part, and that's fine, too. For those who have read through from beginning to end, it may seem odd that a media and technological literacy book closes with this topic, and a critical reader might be inclined to ask: "Why?" As with many lessons from the classroom and in life, what matters most is how you apply the materials and knowledge that you have gained moving forward. The twenty-four chapters preceding this have given a number of examples in which principles of media and technological literacy were applied. For those who have already been on the path, this book can serve as a checkpoint from which to advance to the next stage. Consider this a final lesson, given to facilitate the journey as you move forward on your own path of media and technological literacy.

So, what does it mean to be media and technologically literate in the 21st century? It is not hyperbole to write that millions of people around the world, in the form of scholars, teachers, committees, parents, government officials, policy makers, and the like, have grappled with this very question. Each has a stake in how the terms are defined, measured, the contexts in which media and technological literacy are situated, and the perspectives that are privileged (Christ & Potter, 1998). On one hand, it would be unreasonable to think that this one chapter, or for that matter, an entire book, is capable of covering all of the nuance and subtleties required to fully understand media and technological literacy. To that end, I would direct said reader to the references section of this chapter (and each other chapter) to seek and learn more. On the other hand, it *is* reasonable to think of this book and its chapters as packages of seeds. If the seeds, or ideas contained within, are sown and cultivated in the fertility of an open mind, they are more than capable of germinating, blooming, and sustaining the media and technologically literate for a lifetime.

At its most basic level, being media and technologically literate can be summarized by understanding the Internet *meme* that leads this chapter. The term "meme" (rhymes with *steam*) is a shortened form of the Greek word *mimeme*, which refers to something that is imitated or replicated (Dawkins, 2000). The popular image of a meme today generally takes the form of some photo or graphic with a typewritten phrase that is disseminated on the Internet through social media and other platforms. A meme is a cultural unit, analogous to the biological term "gene," that carries cultural ideas through the population. Much like genes, memes are capable of mutating and replicating as well as responding to environmental pressures (Dawkins, 2000).

The Lincoln meme demonstrates the complexity of media literacy and the paradoxical nature of information that many of us find in our mediated, technological environments. It first requires that a person be literate in order to read the words and understand the vocabulary and coherent thought that is presented. From there, the Lincoln meme is a curiously crafted blend of both true and false information. Most reasonable people will concede that the Internet has some combination of both true and false information, and that the phrase "Don't believe everything that you read on the Internet" contains some wisdom. Abraham Lincoln, was by many historical accounts, a wise man, so making that connection is not too far-fetched either. The problem of course, isn't that the sentiment isn't true, or that Lincoln wasn't wise, but that the chronology of Lincoln voicing his opinion on Internet content is off. Add to this mix that some people seeing the meme in print as opposed to on a computer screen, superimposed over a photo of Abraham Lincoln himself, could mean that the meme's credibility is interpreted differently. Children, or those unfamiliar with U.S. history, may not catch the anachronism. This example serves to show how complex media literacy can be. For someone without the necessary linguistic abilities, historical knowledge, or technological background, the meme may contain enough truth that it *seems* true, and thus, an innocent meme becomes fact.

The irony is that the same mediums and technologies which provide false or semi-truthful information are the same mediums and technologies that we can rely on to check the veracity of that information. The limitation then, is a decidedly human one. People for a long time have been known to be cognitive misers (Fiske & Taylor, 1984), with a finite capacity to process incoming stimuli. We rely on heuristics and take mental shortcuts in order to make sense of the tidal wave of information that crashes down on us with regularity. There are only so many Lincoln memes that one person can fact-check in a day.

Lighting the Way

This brings us full-circle, back to the dark side of media and technology. The previous chapters have demonstrated quite clearly that the four dark outcomes; Commodification, Threats to Individual Well-being, Exploitation, and Threats to Democracy, are real. The dark side of media and technology comes with it a connotation that we should be vigilant for something that is, perhaps, rare, mysterious, monstrous, or unknown. However, as a colleague pointed out, this is not always the case. Often times, dark things happen at the hands of those we love and trust (see Hasinoff; Olson & Schwartzman, this volume). And even the routine, mundane things we do every day like posting to our social media accounts, or accessing the Internet through an unsecured network at a favorite coffee shop can have consequences.

You may recall the issue of balance from the opening chapter, where we argued that "… the valence of the outcomes of our interactions with technology exists somewhere on a continuum, both opposite and equal in magnitude." In the spirit of that balance, it is neither by accident, nor by coincidence, that four solutions emerge to minimize our vulnerabilities to the four dark outcomes. Among the skills necessary for navigating the digital landscapes and technological ecosystems of the 21st century are four key competencies or literacies. These literacies, are the corresponding four *points of light* that stand in opposition to the four dark outcomes mentioned in chapter one. Kellner (2000) supports this idea, noting that periods of radical technological and social change, like the world we live in today, require multiple literacies in order to meet the needs of a diverse global society and culture. Each of the literacies covered in this section have had volumes written about them. In brief, the four tools that can be used to combat the four dark outcomes are: *letteracy, media literacy, technological literacy*, and *computer literacy*.

Literacy and Letteracy

"What is literacy?" Ask this question of anyone and a common first response will be "the ability to read and write" (Keefe & Copeland, 2011, p. 92). Yet, over time, the definition of literacy has evolved to mean more than this. An alternative conceptualization of literacy is knowledge of, or competency within a particular domain. The nature of literacy changes between these definitions from a broad understanding of a topic (i.e. reading and writing), to something that is arguably more specialized (i.e. media literacy). Out of "desperation" and in an attempt to easily distinguish between literacy as a set of abilities (reading and writing), and literacy as the process of knowing and understanding, Seymour Papert proposed the terms *letteracy,* and being *letterate,* to refer to the skill sets involving the reading of, and (ostensibly) the writing of, alphabetical letters (1993, p. 11). In this tradition, McMillan (1996, p. 166), categorized and defined five types of letteracy from which one could be evaluated.

Systemic letteracy assesses if one is physiologically capable of acquiring at least one level of letteracy (reading or writing). For example, a young child with no impairments to the sensory or cognitive systems would be said to have high systemic literacy. *Situational letteracy* refers to the confidence one has in the speaking of their native language, and *operational letteracy* has to do with one's ability to read and write in their native language. Often times, and for many reasons, one's native language may not be the primary language in one's country of residence. *Principal letteracy* is the ability to read and write in in the primary language of one's country of residence. Last, *jargon letteracy* assesses one's ability to read, write, and communicate in a specialized field of expertise—in the primary language of the country of one's residence—that could be neither used, nor understood, by those without that expertise (ex. finance, plumbing, medicine, etc.).

While some (ex. National Reading Panel) have taken a skills-based approach to defining literacy (read: Papert's letteracy), others, like the Canadian government's Organisation for Economic Co-Operation and Development (OECD), have taken an applied, or functionalist approach. Their International Adult Literacy Survey (IALS; OECD, 2000, p. *x*), defines literacy as: "the ability to understand and employ printed information in daily activities at home, at work and in the community—to achieve one's goals, and to develop one's knowledge and potential."

The IALS, identifies three domains that are essential for literacy. *Prose literacy* is the ability to understand information across a variety of formats and texts (e.g. Internet news articles, novels, cookbooks, and instruction manuals). *Document literacy* refers to the ability to locate information in different forms (e.g. tax documents, payroll forms, maps, etc.). And *quantitative literacy* is the ability to apply arithmetic operations to numbers that are embedded in printed materials (e.g. calculating prices from an advertisement, or using a bank receipt to balance a checkbook, etc.; Cambridge, 2013, p. 10). This combination of reading, writing, and numeracy hints at, but falls short of what could be its own important category, *scientific literacy.*

It is important not to overlook the fact that basic letteracy is a prerequisite for many other types of literacy (Considine, 2002), including the three literacies to follow. Even conducting a simple Internet search requires working knowledge of the alphabet, language skills, and vocabulary in order to be successful, although, as researchers note (i.e. Kajs, Alaniz, Willman, & Sifuentes, 1998; cf. Poynton, 2005), there are some exceptions. Using color-coded dots on keyboards are developmentally appropriate ways to help young children learn basic computer functions, even if they are unable to read the "shift" or "enter" keys. Nonetheless, letteracy puts one in the position to be well educated. One can use letteracy throughout their lifetime to read, write, and learn about language, discourse, rhetoric, history, science, and literature. Continued education and individual growth positions us to better understand how imagery and the written and spoken word can influence thoughts, beliefs, and actions through media and technology.

Media Literacy

While many are familiar with the term "media literacy," not everyone is in agreement about what being "media literate" is. The concept has invited many diverse approaches, perspectives, and critiques, and historically has been fraught with some tension (see Hobbs, 1998). Potter's (2010) review of the state of media literacy contains almost two dozen definitions of the term, written by different scholars and institutions, each with different focuses, outcomes, and perspectives. A broad definition of media literacy that appears to have garnered some favor is: "the ability to access, analyze, evaluate, and effectively communicate in a variety of forms." This contemporary understanding stays true to the definition proposed by the National Leadership Conference on Media council in 1992 (Aufderheide, 1992, p. 6). While this definition is descriptive and concise, its simplicity belies its complexity. At its most basic, an understanding of media literacy requires a person to examine relationships between three different, but interrelated features: *production, text,* and *end user* characteristics (Aufderheide, 1992). The production level processes may include creative, technical, economic, and legal issues. For example, televisual media might examine such artifacts as; the type of camera lens that was used to cover a shot, or how budgetary concerns influenced the final product, or how legal requirements and company policies influenced the type of language that could be used. Regarding text characteristics, an observer might consider the *implicit*, or implied messages in a production as well as the *explicit*, or clearly stated messages contained in a production. For example, watching a film with twelve White men on a jury implicitly gives clues to viewers about the perceived importance of this group in society, while what the characters say about the defendant explicitly tells us how they feel. At the user level comes the understanding that audiences from diverse backgrounds may understand and interpret the same text and its meaning in very different ways. Perspective taking and putting oneself in the shoes of a group being targeted may help a viewer to determine if a group is being portrayed unfairly.

Just as Kellner (2000) advocated for multiple literacies, Meyrowitz (1998) proposed that the understanding of multiple *media* literacies were required for an informed viewer. The three subtypes identified by Meyrowitz are: *media content literacy*, which is concerned with understanding a media message; *media grammar literacy*, or understanding the technical or production components of a piece of media; and *medium literacy*, which examines how different mediums may be compared with each other. Media content literacy states that media are "conduits that hold and send messages" (Meyrowitz, 1998, p. 97). The abilities of an audience to decode artifacts embedded within a mediated message is critical to understanding this concept. Examining such items as recurring themes or topics, values and ideologies expressed, and examining characters' actions and behaviors are all important parts of media content literacy. Media grammar literacy focuses on the unique language of each medium and the ways in which production or aesthetic (Zettl, 1990) interacts with content elements. This tends to be more technical in nature and speaks to understanding a wide range of media and technological production variables available within each medium. For example, a film director can choose different camera angles, lenses, tilts, pans, and lighting choices to translate into different moods for characters. In print media, considerations such as paper thickness, font, color versus black ink, can all change how a text is interpreted. Finally, medium literacy recognizes that each medium is a type of setting that has relatively fixed characteristics that influences communication in a particular way—regardless of the content or grammar variables. Medium literacy invites comparisons of content across mediums. For example, how would a sports broadcast of the same baseball game be different between a radio or T. V. broadcast? And how would those formats differ from online updates? As another example; how would the breaking of bad news to a relative be perceived if it were conducted via phone call versus a text message?

As you can see when comparing perspectives, while scholars and practitioners may break down components of media literacy differently, a number of key ideas are retained across perspectives. Many (ex. Considine, Horton, & Moorman, 2009; Center for Media Literacy, 2008) recognize that at the heart of media literacy are important core concepts, each with a corresponding "key question" that one can ask of a media experience in order to analyze the different components. The core concepts, each followed by a corresponding question, are as follows:

(1) Media are constructions.

(Q1) *Who created this message?*

(2) Each medium has its own creative forms, language, and rules.

(Q2) *What creative techniques were used to get my attention?*

(3) Different individuals and audiences may experience the same messages differently.

(Q3) *How might other people understand this message differently than me?*

(4) Media have embedded points of view, values, and ideologies.

(Q4) *What lifestyles, values, and points of view are represented or omitted?*

(5) Media have commercial purposes and are organized to gain profit and power.

(Q5) *Why is this message being sent?*

Asking these questions is a good way to help critically analyze and evaluate media messages.

Technological Literacy

There is, perhaps, no more famous a technology critic than Neil Postman. He uniquely recognized that the decision of a society to adopt a technology would result in some ecological change. That is to say, that something about the society would be different and that it would not just look like the same society as before, but with the new technology embedded in it (Postman, 1992). He traced this idea through history and examined how technologies from the mechanical clock, to the printing press, to the Internet, fundamentally disrupted existing social structures. He argued that the adoption of these technologies by society changed politics, education, religion, and language, among other things (Postman, 1986). In a keynote address to the College of DuPage, Postman (1997) drew from many of his books to identify seven questions related to our relationship with technology. Asking Postman's seven questions regarding the adoption of a new technology is one way to practice technological literacy. They are:

(1) *What is the problem to which this technology is the solution?*

(2) *Whose problem is it?* (i.e. *Who will benefit and who will pay for it?*)

(3) *What new problems will be created as a result of adopting a new technology?*

(4) *Which people and institutions might be most seriously harmed by a technological solution?*

(5) *What changes in language are being enforced by new technology?*

(6) *What people and institutions acquire special economic and political power because of technological change?*

(7) *What alternative uses might be made of a technology?*

As an example, suppose we consider integrating tablet computers into a classroom. One might ask, which problem or problems would be solved if integrated? Issues of student or teacher motivation? Would this improve content mastery and exam scores? Would it improve perceptions for students and the community that a particular classroom is modern and cutting edge? Suppose the tablets are now integrated in to the classroom—what new problems are now created? Do students spend more time distracted by the technology? Is the technology durable enough to survive student use? Does student handwriting suffer at the mercy of typing? Will other community schools who can't afford this scale of technological integration fall behind?

In many ways, being technologically literate is being able to critically assess our own relationships with the technologies that we adopt into our own daily comings and goings. Postman cautioned people to ask; "Are we using our technologies or are our technologies using us?" (Postman, 1995). In a day and age where many walk around with their mobile devices in their hands, where social media companies have become marketing behemoths because they have collected so many points of user data, and where cellphones are so prominent on restaurant tables that they look like a popular side dish (Rosen, 2012), the question doesn't seem so radical.

At around the same time Postman was cautioning us about being used by our technologies, on the other side of the country at Stanford University, Byron Reeves and Clifford Nass were addressing this issue in their own way. In their Media Equation book (1996), they discussed the terms being *one-up, one-down*, or *one-across* in relation to technologies. These three categories of relationships between computers (or technologies in general) and users, differ in their perspective of which entity is in the position of power or control. When one-up on a user, a technology makes many of the decisions, and is regarded as a "Wizard" or guide (Reeves & Nass, 1996, p. 159). When a technology is one-down to a user, the person is the primary decision maker, telling the technology what to do. The technology is regarded as simply an instrument or tool to be used. The one-across scenario implies that both agents share power and decision making responsibilities. This idea, that technology may be one-up on the user seems extreme until we examine how we use our technologies. For example, have you ever used the grammar check feature on a word processing program because you were uncomfortable with your own ability to write? Did you blindly accept all of the changes without proofreading to make sure the changes were indeed, correct? On a more serious note, have you ever used your phone while you were driving because you couldn't wait to check or send a text message? If the answer was yes to either of the word processing questions, Reeves and Nass would say the technology was one-up on you. Regarding the texting and driving example, Postman would suggest that the technology is using you.

Computer Literacy

Just as the terms media and technological literacy have evolved over time, so has computer literacy. What was once a skills-based definition revolving around programming skills changed when graphic user interfaces and software packages became more user friendly (McMillan, 1996). Today a more broad definition of computer literacy would read as "the basic knowledge, skills, and attitudes needed by all citizens to be able to deal with computer technology confidently in their daily life" (McInerney, McInerney, & Marsh, 1997; Tsai, 2002, p. 69). In other words, computer literacy requires basic knowledge and skills, positive attitudes, and little anxiety (Tsai, 2002). This definition acknowledges influence from three different areas: *cognitive* (What do I know about computers?), *skills* (How can computer hardware and software be used?), and *affect* (Am I comfortable or anxious when using computer technology?; Bloom, Englehart, Furst, Hill, & Krathwohi, 1956; Tsai, 2002).

Toward this goal, the Carnegie Library and Heinz Endowments Project identified six items that could be used to assess one's level of computer literacy (c.f. Turner, Sweany & Husman, 2000):

(1) Awareness of history, trends, and capabilities of computers
(2) Ability to use input devices and peripherals
(3) Ability to use passive applications such as games and reference tools
(4) Ability to use creative applications such as word processors and spreadsheets
(5) Ability to use operating systems to perform tasks such as software installation
(6) Ability to program, repair, and/or install computer hardware

Among these levels are basic use components such as connecting and powering up computer hardware, or installing devices, drivers, programs, and apps. Proficiency in the use of various software tools for documents, spreadsheets, and multimedia editing are also important. Computer literacy also requires some level of skill with Internet navigability, as well as an understanding of basic data storage, and security options (see Peterson & Lee, this volume). Others would acknowledge the importance of understanding social and ethical implications that computer use brings to bear (Turk & Wiley, 1997), stating that computer use affects everything from intellectual property rights, to targeted marketing, to online privacy.

While these suggestions were written specifically for computer literacy, some of the suggestions could easily be adapted to other technologies as well. It is important to consider this as many traditional technologies contain computer components and programmable software options. For example, a Roku device can be inserted into a Smart TV to allow streaming media. Successful installation requires the navigation of a series of start-up menus and preferences accessed through a remote control. Alternatively, a DVD player or a video game console might require software updates from a home's wireless network. Computer literate adults, especially parents and caregivers, should learn how to use these technologies themselves, and not rely on children who may know more about the technologies than they do.

The End of the Book, but the Beginning of the Journey

As this book demonstrates, being informed about media and technology is more than just understanding effects, or fact-checking information and sources from time-to-time. Being "literate" in the 21st century requires, at a minimum, four different types of literacy. In a day and age where instant gratification is an expectation, it may be disappointing to some that being considered media and technologically literate requires so much of us. Just like faith or education requires time, practice, and devotion to be fruitful, so does media and technological literacy. Because of the commitment that it takes, perhaps it is more helpful to regard media and technological literacy as a value system that can be adopted. As the saying goes, nothing worthwhile is ever easy. But, it is important for us to use these literacies in order to foster a society and culture that is centered around inclusion, tolerance, trust, and understanding. It means purposefully looking for and fact-checking information when confronted with new ideas. It means questioning how the adoption of new technologies will change the way we speak, think, and behave. It means starting conversations and listening to others in pursuit of understanding. Above all, media and technological literacy requires a commitment to being a life-long learner. As media systems and technologies change, so too, must the media and technologically literate in order to fully understand their changing position in the media and technological ecosystem. *If* we make a conscious effort to put our letteracy to good use by continuing to learn; *if* we ask questions in order to analyze and evaluate media messages; *if* we make a conscious decision to ask Postman's questions and consider our relationships with technologies; and *if* we continue to learn how to use technologies in an ethical and responsible way, then we may consider ourselves well equipped to handle the technological challenges of the 21st century.

Media and technological literacy requires that we be aware in both familiar and unfamiliar territories, and that we be literate across a number of different domains. Taken together, the four literacies are powerful tools in defense of the four dark outcomes. If history is any indication, then the foreseeable future will not be any less full of technology than it is today. Like many things that require practice and commitment, once you start using the literacies, they become second nature. So, challenge yourself. Perspective take. Ask questions. Start conversations. And as a wise man once said: "Don't believe everything that you read on the Internet."

References

Aufderheide, P. (1992). *Media literacy: A report of the national leadership conference on media literacy*. Queenstown, MD: Aspen Institute.

Bloom, B. S., Englehart, M. B., Furst, E. J., Hill, W. H., & Krathwohi, O. R. (1956). Taxonomy of educational objectives: The classification of educational goals. New York, NY: Longman.

Cambridge Assessment. (2013). What is literacy? An investigation into definitions of English as a subject and the relationship between English literacy and "being literate." Retrieved May 27, 2018, from http://www.cambridgeassessment.org.uk/Images/130433-what-is-literacy-an-investigation-into-definitions-of-english-as-a-subject-and-the-relationship-between-english-literacy-and-being-literate-.pdf.

Center for Media Literacy (2008). Literacy for the 21st century: An overview & orientation guide to media literacy education. Retrieved September 10, 2018, from https://www.medialit.org/sites/default/files/01a_mlkorientation_rev2.pdf

Christ, W. G., & Potter, W. J. (1998). Media literacy, media education, and the academy. *Journal of Communication, 48*(1), 5–15. doi:10.1111/j.1460-2466.1998.tb02733.x

Considine, D. (2002). Media literacy across the curriculum. Cable in the classroom: Thinking critically about media. Retrieved May 28, 2018, from http://www.beyondblame.org/sites/default/files/551_CIC_ML_Report.pdf

Considine, D., Horton, J., & Moorman, G. (2009). Teaching and reading the millennial generation through media literacy. *Journal of Adolescent & Adult Literacy, 52*(6), 471–481.

Dawkins, R. (2000). Selfish genes and selfish memes. In D. R. Hofstadter & D. C. Dennett (Eds.), *The mind's I: Fantasies and reflections on self and soul* (pp. 124–146). New York, NY: Basic Books.

Fiske, S. T., & Taylor, S. E. (1984). Social cognition (2nd ed.). New York, NY: McGraw-Hill.

Hobbs, R. (1998). The seven great debates in the media literacy movement. *Journal of Communication, 48*(1), 16–32.

Kajs, L. T., Alaniz, R., Willman, E., & Sifuentes, E. (1998). Color-coding keyboard functions to develop kindergarteners' computer literacy. *Journal of Computing in Childhood Education Research, 9*(2), 107–111.

Keefe, E. B., & Copeland, S. R. (2011). What is literacy? The power of a definition. *Research & Practice for Persons with Severe Disabilities, 36*(3–4), 92–99.

Kellner, D. (2000). New technologies/New literacies: Reconstructing education for the new millennium. *Teaching Education, 11*(3), 245–265.

McInerney, V., McInerney, D. M., & Marsh, H. W. (1997). Effects of metacognitive strategy training within a cooperative learning context on computer achievement and anxiety: An aptitude-treatment interaction study. *Journal of Educational Psychology, 89*(4), 686–695.

McMillan, S. (1996). Literacy and computer literacy: Definitions and comparisons. *Computers Education, 27*(3/4), 161–170.

Meyrowitz, J. (1998). Multiple media literacies. *Journal of Communication, 48*(1), 96–108.

OECD. (2000). Literacy in the information age: The final report of the international adult literacy survey. Retrieved May 15, 2018, from http://www.oecd.org/education/skills-beyond-school/41529765.pdf.

Papert, S. (1993). The children's machine: Rethinking school in the age of the computer. New York, NY: Basic Books.

Postman, N. (1986). Amusing ourselves to death. New York, NY: Penguin Books.

Postman, N. (1992). *Technopoly: The surrender of culture to technology.* New York, NY: Knopf.

Postman, N. (1995). *Neil postman on cyberspace. PBS' The MacNeil/Lehrer NewsHour.* Retrieved from https://www.youtube.com/watch?v=49rcVQ1vFAY

Postman, N. (1997, March, 11). *The surrender of culture to technology.* College Lecture Series: College of DuPage. Retrieved from https://www.youtube.com/watch?v=hlrv7DIHllE

Potter, W. J. (2010). The state of media literacy. *Journal of Broadcasting & Electronic Media, 54*(4), 675–696.

Poynton, T. A. (2005). Computer literacy across the lifespan: A review with implications for educators. *Computers in Human Behavior, 21*, 861–872.

Reeves, B., & Nass, C. (1996). *The media equation: How people treat computers television, and new media like real people and places.* New York, NY: Cambridge University Pres.

Rosen, L. D. (2012). *iDisorder: Understanding our obsession with technology and overcoming its hold on us.* New York, NY: Palgrave Macmillan.

Tsai, M. J. (2002). Do male students often perform better than female students when learning computers?: A study of Taiwanese eighth graders' computer education through strategic and cooperative learning. *Journal of Educational Computing Research, 26*(1): 67–85.

Turk, J., & Wiley, S. (1997). Teaching social and ethical issues in the literacy course. The ACM Special Interest Group on *Computer Science Education Bulletin, 29*(1), 10-14.

Turner, G. M., Sweany, N. W., & Husman, J. (2000). Development of the computer interface measure. *Journal of Educational Computing Research, 22*(1), 37–54.

Zettl, H. (1990). Contextual media aesthetics as the basis for media literacy. *Journal of Communication, 48*(1), 81–95.

Contributors

Jennifer Stevens Aubrey (Ph.D., University of Michigan) is an associate professor in the Department of Communication at the University of Arizona. With an emphasis on gender and child/adolescent development, her research focuses on media effects on emotional, mental, and physical health in young people. Topically, her research tends to center on issues related to sexuality and body image. Her research has been published in such journals as *Health Communication*, *Media Psychology*, and *Journal of Communication*.

Nicholas David Bowman (Ph.D., Michigan State University) is an associate professor in the Department of Communication Studies at West Virginia University, where he founded and directs the Interaction Lab (#ixlab). His work considers the intersection of communication technology and human interaction, and the manner in which mediated communication places a variety of different demands on users. He has authored or co-authored over 70 peer-reviewed manuscripts and 50 book chapters related to these issues, and his work has been recognized by regional, national, and international associations. He is the current editor of *Communication Research Reports* and is an associate editor of *Journal of Media Psychology*, and he serves on a number of editorial boards, external review panels, and grant committees. His most recent book is the edited volume, *Video games: A medium that demands our attention* (Routledge, 2018).

Aaron R. Boyson (Ph.D., Michigan State University) is an Associate Professor of Communication at the University of Minnesota Duluth. His research focuses on the social, psychological, and cultural impact of both the existence of mass media in society as well as the effects of exposure to mediated messages. He has published and presented research internationally on personality predictors of exposure to media violence, fright responses to terrorism news, media violence exposure and homicidal thinking, and news reports of copycat homicide. He has won multiple awards for teaching and advising at UMD, where he currently teaches classes in research methods, media theory, children and media, and media addiction. His favorite aphorism for the 21st century is, "The Postman always rings true," referring to the late Neil Postman's work as a media ecologist.

Cheryl Campanella Bracken is the Associate Dean for Faculty in the College of Liberal Arts & Social Sciences and a Professor in School of Communication at Cleveland State University in Cleveland, OH, USA. Her research interests are in the area of psychological processing of media. Her specific research interests include the concept of telepresence, and the impact of media form variables (i.e., image quality and screen size) on audiences' perceptions of media content. Dr. Bracken's research has been published in *Media Psychology; Journal of Communication; Journal of Broadcasting and Electronic Media*, and *Human Communication Research*. She has co-edited *Immersed in Media: Telepresence in Everyday Life*.

Kalen M. A. Churcher (Ph.D., Pennsylvania State University) is an associate professor of communication studies at Wilkes University in Wilkes-Barre, Pa, where she spearheads the multimedia journalism track and advises the student newspaper, *The Beacon*. In addition, she also teaches courses in media law and cultural studies. Her research combines both areas of teaching and lies at the intersection of cultural studies and journalism. More specifically, she explores the relationships between marginalized groups and media. She has presented her work at conferences nationally and internationally and has published in journals including, *Communication, Culture and Critique* and *The Journal of Effective Teaching*. She has also published multiple book chapters. She was also the recipient of Wilkes University's 2017 Interdisciplinary Teaching Award. When she is not teaching or writing, she is actively involved in community theatre and enjoys performing and directing musical productions.

Elizabeth L. Cohen (Ph.D., Georgia State University) is an Associate Professor in the Department of Communication Studies at West Virginia University. She conducts research on the psychology of popular media culture, examining audiences' emotional and cognitive responses to different types of media messages, including both news and entertainment content.

Douglas M. Deiss (Ph.D. Arizona State University) teaches in the Department of Communication and World Languages at Glendale Community College in Arizona. He teaches courses on persuasion and social influence, intercultural communication, interpersonal communication, and communication theory. His research background includes numerous studies on cyberbullying and the effects of negative and positive emotions on our health and communication. He is also a third-party facilitator and has lead numerous discussions on the topic of diversity on college campuses. These discussions often include a focus on civility even in the face of passionate disagreement.

Edward Downs (Ph.D., Pennsylvania State University) is an associate professor in the Department of Communication at University of Minnesota Duluth, and director of the Communication Research Lab. He is the recipient of the 2018 UMD College of Liberal Arts, Tenured Faculty Teaching Award. His research examines relationships between technology and learning, the psychology of the individual-avatar relationship, and how simulation experiences influence attitude and behavior change. He has presented work nationally and internationally and has published in journals such as: *Sex Roles Journal, Computers & Education, Entertainment Computing, Communication Yearbook,* and *Psychology of Popular Media Culture* among others. His upper-division Communication course, The Dark Side of Media & Technology, was the inspiration for this book. When not writing or thinking about media effects, he is likely to be SCUBA diving, building retro video game arcade cabinets, cooking, or chasing after his daughter.

Autumn P. Edwards (Ph.D., Ohio University) is a professor in the School of Communication at Western Michigan University and a co-director of the Communication and Social Robotics Labs. She is recipient of the 2014 WMU Outstanding Teaching Award and the 2017 College of Arts and Sciences Outstanding Research Award. Her research examines interpersonal message behavior and impression formation in the contexts of computer-mediated and human-machine communication, including human-agent and human-robot interactions. Her research appears in journals such as the *Journal of Computer-Mediated Communication, Computers in Human Behavior, Communication Studies,* and *Communication Education.*

Chad Edwards (Ph.D., University of Kansas) is a professor of communication in the School of Communication at Western Michigan University. He co-directs the Communication and Social Robotics Labs (www.combotlabs.org). Edwards' research interests include human-machine communication, human-robot interaction, artificial intelligence, and instructional communication. Recent publications include articles in: *Communication Education, Communication Research Reports, Computers in Human Behavior, Journal of Computer-*

Mediated Communication, and Communication Studies. He a past president of the Central States Communication Association.

Arienne Ferchaud (Ph.D., Pennsylvania State University) is an assistant professor in the School of Communication at Florida State University. Her research focuses primarily on the psychological aspects of emerging media entertainment, and how new technologies shape the way consumers process and engage with entertainment media. She has examined new media such as social media, video games, and even video-on-demand. Her work has been presented at national and international communications conferences and has been published in journals such as *Computers in Human Behavior* and *Imagination, Cognition and Personality.* Outside of her work on media psychology, she is passionate about video games, crochet, and animals.

Jesse Fox (Ph.D., Stanford University) is an Associate Professor in the School of Communication at The Ohio State University and Director of the Virtual Environment, Communication Technology, and Online Research (VECTOR) Lab. Her research interests include technologically-mediated communication in relationships; experiences of women and LGBTQ+ individuals online; affordances of communication technologies; and persuasive virtual environments, particularly in the contexts of health and environmental communication. Her work has appeared in journals including *Journal of Communication, Communication Research, New Media & Society, Journal of Computer-Mediated Communication,* and *Media Psychology.* A few of her favorite things are eating, music, roller derby, road tripping, books, and all things Kentucky. You can find publications, research resources, and more at her website, http://commfox.org.

Jessica Frampton (M.A., Clemson University) is a doctoral candidate in the School of Communication at The Ohio State University. Her research examines how communication and relational knowledge structures impact the experience of romantic relationship stressors such as jealousy and uncertainty.

Andrew Gambino is a Ph.D. candidate in the Donald P. Bellisario College of Communications at Penn State University. His research focuses on the human-technology relationship, artificial intelligence, and psychological aspects of communication technologies (http://comm.psu.edu/people/individual/andrew-gambino).

Rebecca J. Gilbertson (Ph.D., University of Kentucky) is an assistant professor in the Department of Psychology at the University of Minnesota Duluth. Her research interests are directed toward understanding health-related factors that influence neurocognitive function including substance use, abuse, and dependence (particularly alcohol). An emerging area of interest includes behavioral addiction and stress system response. She has presented work nationally and internationally and has published in journals including *Alcoholism: Clinical and Experimental Research*, *Addictive Behaviors*, and *Journal of Studies on Alcohol and Drugs*.

David Charles Gore (Ph.D., Texas A&M University) is associate professor and Department Head in the Department of Communication at the University of Minnesota Duluth where he teaches courses on the history and theory of rhetoric, globalization, and the Roman Stoics. His research explores relationships between politics, rhetoric, and religion in a secular age. He is especially interested in his teaching and scholarship in the dynamic between self-awareness and conscience as they relate to public discourse. His work has been published in a variety of journals and books and he is the author of a forthcoming book on political rhetoric in the Book of Mormon.

David J. Gunkel is an award-winning educator and scholar, specializing in the philosophy of technology. He is the author of over 70 scholarly articles and has published nine books, including *Thinking Otherwise: Philosophy, Communication, Technology* (Purdue University Press, 2007), *The Machine Question: Critical Perspectives on AI, Robots, and Ethics* (MIT Press, 2012), *Of Remixology: Ethics and Aesthetics After Remix* (MIT Press, 2016) and *Robot Rights* (MIT Press, 2018). He currently holds the position of Distinguished Teaching Professor in the Department of Communication at Northern Illinois University (USA) and is the founding co-editor of the *International Journal of Žižek Studies*. More information at http://gunkelweb.com

Jacquelyn Harvey is an Assistant Professor at the University of Minnesota-Duluth. She obtained a Ph.D. in Communication, and M.Ed. in Measurement and Statistics, from the University of Washington in 2015. Jacquelyn conducts quantitative and qualitative research examining how interpersonal communication habits are associated with individuals' physical or psychological health. In 2016, she earned the Dissertation of the year award from the Interpersonal Communication Division of the International Communication Association, for her research examining whether psychological health is associated with cancer caregivers' social support provision quality. Other work she is currently focusing on includes interventional research to ascertain whether mindfulness skills can improve couples' conflict resolution tactics, as well as determining how physiological stress responses are associated with support provision behaviors among friends. Jacquelyn can be reached at jaharvey@d.umn.edu.

Amy Adele Hasinoff is Associate Professor of Communication at the University of Colorado Denver. She studies gender, sexuality, and new media. Her book, *Sexting panic: Rethinking criminalization, privacy, and consent* (University of Illinois Press, 2015) examines the construction of sexting as a social problem and the responses to it in mass media, law, and education. Her published work also appears in *Communication and Critical Cultural Studies, New Media & Society, Critical Studies in Media Communication,* and *Feminist Media Studies.*

James D. Ivory (Ph.D., University of North Carolina at Chapel Hill) is a professor in the Department of Communication at Virginia Tech. He has served as chair of the International Communication Association's Game Studies division and head of the Association for Education in Journalism and Mass Communication's Communication Technology division. He also serves on the editorial board of the journals Mass Communication and Society, Journal of Broadcasting and Electronic Media, Sex Roles, and Psychology of Popular Media Culture.

Jinyoung Kim (Ph.D., Pennsylvania State University) is a user experience researcher at Amazon. Her research interests are at the intersection of new media technology and human psychology. Her work examines how users' perceptions and attitudes toward new technology and its content change as a function of the technological affordances (e.g., interactivity, agency). Her research has been published in various outlets, including *Health Communication, Dermatology, Computers and Education, Cyberpsychology, Behavior, and Social Networking, Computers in Human Behavior,* and ACM CHI.

Kenneth A. Lachlan (Ph.D., Michigan State University) is Professor and Head of the Department of Communication at the University of Connecticut, and the Editor of *Communication Studies.* Prior to joining UConn in 2015, Ken was the Founding Chair of the Communication Department at the University of Massachusetts Boston. He holds research affiliations with UConn's Institute for Collaboration on Health, Intervention and Policy, and the Communication and Social Robotics Laboratory at Western Michigan University. He has recently published in journals such as *Computers in Human Behavior, Journal of Risk Research,* and *International Journal of Mass Emergencies and Disasters.* His current research interests include the functions and effects of social media during crises and disasters, and the use of social robotics in delivering risk messages.

Charern Lee (Ph.D. Criminology, Southern Illinois University-Carbondale) is an assistant professor in the Department of Anthropology, Sociology, and Criminology at University of Minnesota-Duluth. He has taught Criminological Theory, Delinquency and Juvenile Justice, and Crime Prevention. His research interests include cyberbullying, fear of crime on campus, and criminological theory. He has published in journals such as *Criminal Justice Policy Review* and *Criminology, Criminal Justice, Law & Society.* When he is not teaching or writing, he likes to go hiking, biking, fishing, and kayaking with his partner.

Anthony M. Limperos (Ph.D., Penn State University) is an associate professor of communication at the University of Kentucky. His research program focuses on the uses and effects of video games and new communication technologies in health, entertainment, and instructional contexts. He has received numerous top paper awards from national and international communication conferences (AEJMC, ICA, NCA) and has authored more than 25 research articles which appear in journals such as *Communication Studies, Journal of Broadcasting & Electronic Media, Mass Communication and Society, Communication Yearbook, Computers in Human Behavior, Presence, Games for Health, Communication Research Reports* and others. When not teaching and doing research, Limperos works hard to maintain his sneaker and bourbon collections (which are world famous).

Matthew P. McAllister is Professor of Communications in the Department of Film-Video & Media Studies at Penn State. His research focuses on political economy of media and critiques of commercial culture. He is the author of *The Commercialization of American Culture* (1996, Sage), and the co-editor of *Comics and Ideology* (2001, Peter Lang), *Film and Comic Books* (2007, University Press of Mississippi), *The Advertising and Consumer Culture Reader* (2009, Routledge), and *The Routledge Companion to Advertising and Promotional Culture* (2013).

David Nemer (Ph.D. in Informatics from Indiana University and an MSc in Computer Science from Saarland University) is an Assistant Professor in the School of Information Science at the University of Kentucky. His research and teaching interests cover the intersection of ICT for Development (ICT4D), science and technology studies (STS), postcolonial STS, and human-computer interaction (HCI). Nemer is an ethnographer who is specifically interested in studying ICTs in less industrialized parts of the world to understand the effects of ICTs on the development and empowerment of marginalized communities. His current fieldworks include Slums of Vitória, Brazil; Havana, Cuba; and Eastern Kentucky (Appalachia). Nemer is the author of Favela Digital: The other side of technology (Editora GSA, 2013).

Jonathan A. Obar (Ph.D., The Pennsylvania State University) is an assistant professor in the Department of Communication Studies at York University. He also serves as a research associate with the Quello Center, a communication policy research center at Michigan State University. He previously served as a research fellow with the New America Foundation and with Free Press, as a researcher with the Open Society Foundations, and as a senior advisor to the Wikimedia Foundation's Wikipedia Education Program. His research and teaching focus on information and communication policy, and the relationship between digital technologies, civil liberties and the inclusiveness of public culture. Recent academic publications address big data and privacy, internet routing and National Security Agency (NSA) surveillance, network neutrality and digital activism. He is co-editor of Strategies for Media Reform: International Perspectives, published by Fordham University Press.

Anne Oeldorf-Hirsch (Ph.D., The Pennsylvania State University) is an assistant professor in the Department of Communication at the University of Connecticut, where she conducts research in the Human-Computer Interaction lab. Broadly, her research focuses on information sharing as a form of communication in online social networks, with a specific emphasis on the features of communication technology that alter communication norms. Her work investigates the effects of various social media activities such as content sharing, information-seeking, and self-disclosure on outcomes such as learning, identity, and well-being, in the contexts of news, health, and science communication. She teaches courses on the effects of mass media, social media use and effects, and new communication technologies. She has presented at international communication and information science conferences, and her work appears in journals such as *Mass Communication & Society*, *Health Communication*, and *Social Media + Society*.

Mary Beth Oliver is a distinguished professor at Penn State in the Department of Film/Video & Media Studies and co-director of the Media Effects Research Lab. Her research focuses on entertainment psychology and on social cognition and the media. Her recent publications have appeared in such journals as the *Journal of Communication*, *Human Communication Research*, and *Communication Research*, among others. She is a former editor of *Media Psychology* and associate editor of the *Journal of Communication*, *Communication Theory*, and *Journal of Media Psychology*. Though she typically studies positive media psychology, she enjoys dabbling in the "dark side" on occasion. She also enjoys SCUBA, playing poker with friends, and enjoying time with her husband, John, and kitty cat, Lucy.

Loreen N. Olson (Ph.D., University of Nebraska) is a Professor in the Department of Communication Studies at the University of North Carolina, Greensboro. Dr. Olson's research focuses on gender identity negotiation and the dark side of close relationships, including intimate partner violence, child sexual predation, sexual assault and sexual harassment in the academy. Currently, she is a founding member of the interdisciplinary research team, the *Battered Brain Project*, examining traumatic brain injury among female survivors of intimate partner violence. Dr. Olson and her colleagues have published two books on the dark side of family communication, and she is finishing her third, entitled

Breasts, Bottles, and Babies: An Ideological Analysis of Breastfeeding Discourse and Practice in Contemporary America. Her scholarship can also be found in several peer-reviewed journals such as the *Journal of Family Communication, Trauma, Violence, & Abuse, Journal of Family Violence, Communication Theory, and Women's Studies in Communication.*

Peter A. H. Peterson (Ph.D., University of California, Los Angeles) is an assistant professor of Computer Science at the University of Minnesota Duluth, where he directs the Laboratory for Advanced Research in Systems (LARS). Peterson's teaching and research include computer security, operating systems, energy efficiency, and the intersection of the three. He is also active in computer security education efforts and computer science outreach, including the restoration and demonstration of a rare 1972 PDP-12 minicomputer. He lives in Duluth with his family.

Michael William Pfau is an associate professor at the University of Minnesota Duluth where he has been on faculty since 2001. Pfau earned a B.A. in Biology and Government at Augustana College in 1993, an M.A. in Political Science (Political Theory specialization) at Tulane in 1996, and a Ph.D. in Communication Studies (Rhetorical Studies specialization) at Northwestern University in 2000. In 2002 Pfau was the recipient of the National Communication Association's Gerald Miller Outstanding Dissertation Award. Pfau authored the 2005 book, *The Political Style of Conspiracy: Chase, Sumner and Lincoln* (Michigan State University Press), co-edited the 2012 book *Making the Case: Advocacy and Judgment in Public Argument* (Michigan State University Press); and has published numerous book chapters as well as articles in journals like *Philosophy and Rhetoric, Rhetoric and Public Affairs,* and *Argumentation & Advocacy.*

Lindsay Roberts (B.A., University of Arizona) is a Master's student in the Department of Communication at the University of Arizona. Her research broadly focuses on gender within the media, specifically the portrayal of women and men on television and in movies. Additionally, she is interested in the effects of mass media on children's perceptions and understanding of gender later in life.

Meghan S. Sanders (Ph.D., Pennsylvania State University) is an associate professor in the Manship School of Mass Communication at Louisiana State University, and Director of the Media Effects Lab. Her research examines the psychological effects of entertainment media as they pertain to cognition, emotion, and psychological and subjective well-being. She has presented her work at national and international conferences, and has published in journals such as Mass Communication and Society, Journal of Communication,

Communication Theory, and Psychology of Popular Media Culture, among others. In addition to media effects, she also studies the science of baking though she still has yet to come up with recipes inspired by inferential statistics.

Irene G. Sarmiento is a Master's student in the Department of Communication Arts at the University of Wisconsin-Madison. Her major research interests include social support processes, specifically the utilization of advice, within close relationships (i.e., friendships and romantic relationships). Her research has appeared in the journal *Media Psychology* and was presented at the International Communication Association conference and American Psychological Association's Technology, Mind, and Society conference. When not researching, she enjoys hiking, reading, travelling, and spending time in her home state of California.

Matthew W. Savage (Ph.D., 2012, Arizona State University) is an assistant professor at San Diego State University who is passionate about research and teaching. His research focuses on the intersection of health, interpersonal, and mass communication. Dr. Savage's scholarship is conducted within the context of creating and supporting health communication campaigns aimed to deter negative and risky behaviors among adolescents and young adults. Thus, much of Dr. Savage's research is community embedded and relies on strong partnerships with educational institutions, government organizations, and non-profits. Currently, he is working on projects that address adolescent bullying/cyberbullying, oral health promotion, and reciprocal violence. His research has been translated to clinical practice via external and internal funding. When it comes to teaching, Matthew's philosophy focuses on engagement, relevance, and challenging students to exceed their expectations. He is recognized with prestigious university teaching awards at the University of Kentucky, Arizona State University, and the University of Hawaii.

Roy Schwartzman (Ph.D., University of Iowa) is a professor in the Communication Studies Department and affiliate faculty in the Department of Peace and Conflict Studies at the University of North Carolina, Greensboro. He also serves as affiliate faculty with the Joint School of Nanoscience and Nanoengineering. His research and teaching deal primarily with Holocaust and genocide studies, educational technology, rhetoric of science and technology, political communication, public argumentation, propaganda, and figurative language. A past president of the Association for the Rhetoric of Science, Technology, and Medicine, he has held a Holocaust Educational Foundation fellowship and served as a Shoah Foundation Institute International Teaching Fellow. He has published more than 120 scholarly articles and book chapters as well as more than 350 poems. Aside from scholarly and creative writing, he enjoys lifting very heavy objects as a bodybuilder and strength athlete.

Will R. Silberman (B.A., University of La Verne; M.A., San Diego State University) is a Ph.D. student at the University of Kentucky's Department of Communication and the Parliamentarian of the United States Universities Debating Association (USUDA). His research encompasses the dark side of communication (e.g., stalking, threats), social media (and other related technology) use and abuse, and health communication. He has presented work nationally at the *National Communication Association* as well as the *Partnership for Progress on the Digital Divide*, among others, and was just recently published in the *Journal of Health Communication*. Although being a graduate student is a full-time commitment, Will spends his spare time drinking coffee, playing video games, and reading political news. Drink coffee responsibly!

Patric R. Spence (Ph.D., Wayne State University) is an associate professor in the Nicholson School of Communication and Media at the University of Central Florida, and a co-director of the Communication and Social Robotics Labs (www.combotlabs.org). He is the current editor of *Communication Studies* and associate editor of the *Journal of International Crisis and Risk Communication Research*. His research examines risk and crisis communication, in addition to human-machine communication. He has has published in journals such as: *Communication Studies, Computers in Human Behavior,* the *Journal of Applied Communication Research, Journal of Communication Pedagogy* and the *Journal of Modern Applied Statistical Methods*.

Lars Stoltzfus-Brown is currently a Ph.D. Candidate in Mass Communications at Penn State. Their research foci are political economy of media and its impact on marginalized populations; and how closed communities such as the Old Order Amish strategically control and utilize media.

S. Shyam Sundar (Ph.D., Stanford University) is distinguished professor and founding director of the Media Effects Research Laboratory at Penn State University. A pioneering researcher on the psychology of communication technology, Sundar conducts experiments on the effects of a variety of digital media, ranging from websites and social media to mobile phones, robotics and internet of things. He has contributed original theoretical frameworks to the literature, such as Online Source Typology, MAIN (Modality-Agency-Interactivity-Navigability) Model, Agency Model of Customization, Motivational Technology Model and Theory of Interactive Media Effects (TIME). His research is supported by the National Science Foundation (NSF), among others. He is editor of the first-ever *Handbook on the Psychology of Communication Technology*, and is the outgoing editor-in-chief of the *Journal of Computer-Mediated Communication*. He is serving or has served on the editorial boards of 18 other journals, including *Communication Research, Journal of Communication, Human Communication Research*, and *Media Psychology*.

Catalina L. Toma is an associate professor of Communication Science in the Department of Communication Arts at the University of Wisconsin-Madison. Her research is concerned with how people understand and relate to one another when interacting via social media. She examines how relational processes such as self-presentation, impression formation, deception, trust, and emotional well-being are shaped by the affordances and limitations of computer-mediated environments. Catalina's research has been published in journals such as Communication Research, Journal of Communication, and Personality and Social Psychology Bulletin. She is an Associate Editor for the Journal of Media Psychology.

T. Franklin Waddell (Ph.D., Pennsylvania State University) is an assistant professor in the College of Journalism and Communications at the University of Florida. His research examines how readers' perceptions of news credibility and bias are shaped by current and emerging trends in technology. This work includes topics such as automated journalism, storytelling on visual/ephemeral social media platforms, and online comments. His research has been presented both nationally and internationally and has been published in journals such as the *Journal of Broadcasting & Electronic Media, New Media & Society, International Journal of Communication, Journal of Media Psychology, Psychology of Popular Media Culture, Digital Journalism, Electronic News, Cyberpsychology, Behavior and Social Networking,* and *Computers in Human Behavior,* among others.

Kayla M. Walton (B.A., University of St. Thomas) is a graduate student in the Department of Psychology at the University of Minnesota Duluth. She is working toward her Master of Arts in Psychological Science. Her research examines the role of emotions (i.e., disgust) in perception of those with disability. She is also conducting research investigating the relationship between heart rate variability and sociopathy, the role of various mental health variables in Internet gaming disorder, and the role of outreach programs on attitudes toward science in middle school students. She aspires to earn her Ph.D. and manage a lab that investigates the barriers to employment for those with disability. When not researching or working on course work, she is likely to be reading a good novel, working on a jigsaw puzzle or enjoying a peaceful nature walk.

Stephanie L. Whitenack is a doctoral student in the Manship School of Mass Communication at Louisiana State University. Her research examines entertainment media's representation of individuals with disabilities and mental illness. She also explores the psychological mechanisms through which stereotypes can be countered. She has presented her work at the annual meetings of the International Communication Association, the National Communication Association and the Association for Education in Journalism and Mass Communication. Towering at 5'3", she played two years of college basketball at Wingate University in North Carolina.

Guanjin Zhang (M.A., University at Illinois Urbana-Champaign) is a Ph.D. candidate in the School of Communication at Ohio State University. Her research examines disclosure of lonely feelings on social networking sites, attribution making about loneliness disclosure, and the process of support provision on social media.

Index

M

mass media, 8–9, 17–18, 26, 109–13, 138
media: *See also* news media
    and ad integration, 55–56
    and advertising, 43–44, 45, 50, 52–58, 86, 245
    advertising alternatives, 57–58
    agenda, 38, 41, 44–46
    as biased, 50–51
    consumption, 5–6
    and data collection, 56–57
    definition of, 15
    demographics, 54–55
    ecology, 33
    effects, 6–7, 9, 79, 110, 114, 240, 245
    entertainment, 80. *See also* media villains
    functions, 49
    funding, 49–50
    influence, 109–10
    literacy. *See* literacy: media literacy
    mainstream, 44
    ownership, 50–57
    and power, 50–58
    print, 17–19, 27–33, 54, 62, 287, 289, 291–92
    and self-objectification. *See* self-objecti-
        fication: and media
    synergy, 51–52
    systems, 1, 9, 33, 49, 53–55
    types of, 18
    violence in. *See* copycat crimes; media
        villains; violence
media villains: 9
    affective disposition theory, 99
    and aggression, 101–4
    vs antagonist, 97
    as anti-heroes, 100
    attraction to: 96
        character impression formation
            model, 100
        identification with, 100–1
        moral disengagement, 99–100
        role-playing, 101–2

characteristics of:
    immoral, 97, 102–3
    physically deformed, 97–98
    redeeming traits, 98
    unfair, 97
    violate standards of care, 97
dark triad, 101
definition of, 97
effects on audiences, 101–3
function of, 99–100
in gaming, 101, 104
morally ambiguous character, (MAC), 98
negative effects:
    aggression, 101–2
    immorality, 102
    stereotyping, 102
and parents, 103
as protagonist, 99
redeeming traits, 98, 102
and stereotypes, 101–3
and violence, 102–3
mental models, 76–77
mimesis, 111–16
mobile devices:
    and accidents, 225–26, 232
    benefits of, 226
    and children, 232–33
    and compulsive behavior, 10, 228–29
    and data collection, 293
    and distraction, 10, 225–26, 230, 231
    functions of, 226
    and the Hook, 228–29
    in the law, 225
    and media convergence, 225
    mindfulness:
        and developing, 233
        and others, 232–33
        as solution, 231–32
        and technology, 232–33
    and multitasking:
        and adaptive control of thought ratio-
            nale (ACT-R), 227
        as ability, 227–28
        definition of, 225

and drones, 67–69
vs free speech, 61, 69–70
in journalism, 65
in the law, 9, 61, 63, 67–69
  appropriation, 62, 63–64
  false light, 62, 64
  intrusion into seclusion, 62, 65, 68
  publication of a private fact, 62, 64–65
online. *See* online privacy
policies, 9
and revenge porn. *See* sexual privacy
right to, 8, 61–69
and security, 249–50
and smart devices. *See* smart media
and social media, 119, 124, 139, 158,
  172–73, 229. *See also* online privacy;
  sexual privacy
threats to, 10. *See also* information security; online privacy
and voyeurism, 62, 63, 64, 69–70
propaganda:
  analysis of, 17–18
  as coercive, 15
  as commercial, 18–19
  and cults, 161
  as dangerous, 3, 13–15, 18–21
  definition, 14–15
  and democracy, 8, 13, 15–16, 19
  history of, 13–16, 20, 27, 29
  vs rhetoric, 21–23
  scientific response to, 19–21
  and sexual predators, 161
Prosser, William, 61, 63
PTSD, 238, 242–44, 245
public relations, 9, 15, 18–20, 39

R

Reddit, 5, 41, 43, 149
revenge porn. *See* sexual privacy: revenge
  porn
rhetoric:
  as approach, 15, 17, 19, 22, 160

Aristotelean, 17
as commercial, 16
as constructive, 22
definition of, 13–14, 16, 21–22
history of, 13, 15–17, 21
as persuasive, 9, 15–17
and process, 22–23
vs propaganda, 13–14, 19, 21–23
techniques, 16, 22, 163–64
robots. *See* social robots

S

schemas, 75–77, 100
self-objectification:
  and body surveillance, 86
  definition of, 85
  as gateway, 85–86, 89
  and media:
    correlation with, 86, 89–90
    fitness/health media, 89
    magazines, 91
    negative effects:
      appearance standards, 86–87
      body dissatisfaction, 87, 89
      eating disorders, 85, 86–88, 90–92
      objectification, 87
      role models, 86
    pornography, 90
    social media, 92
    television, 91
  and men, 88–90
  men vs women, 88–90
  and objectification theory, 85–86, 88
  and sexual objectification, 86, 91, 93
  solutions for, 92–93
sexting, 142, 146, 149, 150
sexual abuse. *See* child sexual predators;
  sexual privacy
sexual predators. *See* child sexual predators
sexual privacy. *See also* online privacy; privacy
  legal issues with, 147–49
  and minors, 148